Numbskull in the Theatre of Inquiry

For Al + Judith
With Love,
Bill

Numbskull in the Theatre of Inquiry

Transforming Self, Friends, Organizations, and Social Science

William R. Torbert

Waterside Productions

Cover bronze sculpture “Standing on Head”
by Peter DeCamp Haines

Printed in the United States of America

First Printing, 2021

ISBN-13: 978-1-951805-41-8 print edition
ISBN-13: 978-1-951805-42-5 ebook edition

Waterside Productions

2055 Oxford Ave
Cardiff, CA 92007
www.waterside.com

The building up of true political freedom …
the most perfect of all works of art.
Friedrich Schiller
The Aesthetic Education of Man

To create community (liberty, equality, fraternity) is to
make friendship the form of all personal relations.
This is a religious task which can only be performed
through the transformation of the motives of our behavior.
John MacMurray
Persons in Relation

There's a war between the rich and poor …
There's a war between the man and the woman …
There's a war between the ones who say there
is a war and those who say there's none …
Leonard Cohen
Why don't you come on back to the war?
Women's chorus

Should we not attempt to turn most of our time from
dead time (inattentive, obsessed, etc.) to live time?
Dame Iris Murdoch
Metaphysics as a Guide to Morals

The path you can follow is not the real path.
Lao-Tsu
Tao Te Ching
(trans. Ursula Le Guin)

Table of Contents

Foreword

by Charles J. Palus
Senior Fellow, Center for Creative Leadership

In a moment of inquiry and leadership gone awry, the young William R. (Bill) Torbert dives headfirst into a shallow creek and splits his head on a rock, becoming the titular Numbskull of this memoir and eventually a man of knowledge. Such early attempts at artful tripping—and there are a variety here, including a two-year stint as Director of The Theatre of Inquiry – developed into a life of intentional action inquiry and an enormously powerful and far-ranging scientific theory about the possibility and the difficulties of practicing transforming inquiry, power, and love. In a world that needs it, this bubbling memoir is a guide for those who might similarly choose a life increasingly based on assumption-busting practices at work and at play, discovering mutually-transforming inquiry, power, and love.... All this requiring the development and continual exercise of an unfamiliar kind of attention. This book invites you, not just to read it, but also to ask again and again how you are transforming in your own life.

I am deeply grateful for Bill's life, for his theory, and for his friendship. I have known Bill Torbert since his service at Boston College as Graduate Dean of the School of Management in the 1980s. Since the mid-1990's Bill has provided essential guidance to our research at the Center for Creative Leadership, on our central themes of *relational leadership* and *leadership culture*. Bill's methods for human transformation based in interwoven first-, second-, and third-person inquiry (in the midst of work and leisure) are closely aligned with the beliefs and practices of CCL and have greatly enhanced our work. He taught us his unique brand of action inquiry in 2005, resulting in the founding of the CCL Organizational Leadership practice which continues to thrive as a hotbed of vertical leadership theory and practice.[1] In recognition of his contributions to the profession (including us), Bill was awarded CCL's 2013 Walter F. Ulmer, Jr. Applied Leadership Research Award.

He continues to inform and inspire. He and his business partner, Elaine Herdman-Barker, have shaped the design of our joint Transformations™ card deck, which models his Seven Transformations of Leadership framework. Our shared goal is to reach practically everyone on the planet in this artful, affirmative, developmental way.

His memoir has developed a wonderful voice, intimate, vulnerable, and lively. It has rhythm and it rocks. Artistically, he may well be playing with his own life in the perpetually-evolving Theatre of Inquiry that he co-founded in 1977 and in which he claims, both humorously and seriously, we are all actors whether we yet know it or not. He leads the reader through doorways and more hidden openings. Bill often writes as if at a close distance, confiding his secrets and special places. I am a bit more awake as I read it.

What kind of a theory are we talking about here? It is a theory about what it is to be and to grow as humans, individually and collectively. It says that people evolve in particular patterns in the ways we make meaning in moments and over long periods of time. It is a theory of conscious, intentional social alchemy – of how consciousness and culture and science can transform again and again. Above all it is a theory for practice, of practice, and to be practiced.

It's a theory about how we can work together to solve complex problems and weave together *action* and *inquiry* in timely ways. It is a theory which is tested less on other people and more by trying to put it into practice oneself. Formally, it's called *Collaborative*

1 McGuire, J. B., Palus, C. J., & Torbert, W. R. (2007). Toward interdependent organizing and researching. In Shani, A.B Mohrman, S.A., Pasmore, W.A., Stymne, B. & Adler, N. (Eds.), *Handbook of Collaborative Management Research* (pp. 123–142). SAGE Publications.

Developmental Action Inquiry – **action inquiry** for short. It is the best theory I am aware of for dilemma-describing and problem-solving contexts, including our most difficult ones.

This memoir made the theory come alive for me in a certain way that it never had before. This is the story of the theory and its origins as told from the inside-out rearview mirror while riding up the highway, as if with the author at the time. Here Torbert shows us many of his own stumbles as he practiced and practiced, following many remarkable teachers, but none more than himself.

There are "certain bones" buried here and it was a pleasure to find some of them (you may find different ones)... and all of a sudden to wake up as a man of 62 years, much of my digging now done, but the idea of hidden bones and a practical theory of knowledge still appealing. I had shocks of recognition as I read Bill's review (1977) of E.F Schumacher's book *Guide for the Perplexed* (in Appendix C). There (right there, reading that book by Schumacher) is where I started a key part of my own journey when I was a 23-year-old reading a lot and trying to perceive beyond the obvious façades of people and things. We were asking, "What are the sources and varieties of consciousness and how can that knowledge serve higher ends?"

The 60's and 70's were a period of seeking and sometimes finding more adequate forms and methods of knowledge and wisdom. This memoir conjures, redefines and transforms many of the best spirits of that era and makes them timely now, "in," as Bill likes to say, "the spirit of inquiry."

Charles J. Palus — Philadelphia, August 22, 2020

Introduction

by Members of the Action Inquiry Community

When in 1947, Bill Torbert – the three year old son of an American diplomat stationed in Madrid – yelled down the front steps at the Spanish children on the sidewalk (in English, of course), "You dummies, why don't you speak right?", it did not occur to him that he was practicing "action inquiry," as we all do each time we speak, or otherwise act, whether we know it or not. Without realizing it, and in a Numbskull-ian kind of way, the three-year-old Torbert was testing his assumption that everyone speaks and understands the same language.

Turns out we don't! Well, that's not entirely true either. Sometimes we do. Finding out which is the case in the moment turns out to be most useful.

What makes the book that follows so interesting is that Bill, in a long and interesting life, began to notice not only how many different languages we speak, but also how many different assumption-sets and perspectives we hold, even in cases when we appear to be speaking the same language and trying to deal with the same outer reality.

Gradually, a new kind of inquiry emerged for him: How can we develop deeper personal awareness of our inner incongruities and edge toward increasing integrity (through first-person action inquiry)? What alternative ways of holding conversations, of becoming friends, and of organizing institutions can generate more collaborative inquiry, more mutual power, and more trustworthy intimacy (through second-person action inquiry)? How can we design and conduct sustainability-enhancing, quantitative research on societal and climatological scales, with feedback to the participants, including the formal researchers (through third-person action inquiry)? And how can we interleave these three types of action inquiry, *in the midst of action*, to illuminate our own and one another's assumptions and perspectives, as well as to act in an increasingly effective, transforming, and mutually-timely manner *now*?

Bill's academic career spanned Yale, Southern Methodist University, Harvard, and Boston College. Despite the dominant logic of academia and despite his scholarly productivity, he managed always to be primarily practice-engaged – in his teaching, in his consulting/research, as a board member, or in his organizational leadership roles. Nevertheless, he also made foundational theoretical, empirical, and methodological contributions to the fields now known as adult development, leadership development, and organizational transformation in his long career of scholarly publication (a dozen books, some ninety journal articles and book chapters, and various research awards).

During this time he moved *from* a primarily reflective, intellectual inquiry *toward* a primarily experiential, heartfelt, action-focused inquiry. To use a phrase he coined later in life, Torbert's work advocates for entering into a *living inquiry* if we wish to learn how to work well, how to lead well, how to love well, and how to earn enough money – in short, how to practice a good life that leads toward a more just society. And, to top it off, as he is prone to say: "H'ain't no truth without no humor."

Many of Torbert's ideas originate from his adventures, misadventures, and awakenings as a young adult. Although he had yet to provide these names for his experiences, during the year after his graduation from Yale in 1965 he was lucky enough: 1) to find a type of meditation-in-action (the Gurdjieff Work) to ground his first-person research/practice; 2) to find several types of group self-study (Tavistock, Esalen, and Bethel) to support his second-person research/practice; and 3) to find a unique PhD program, in 'Individual and Organizational Behavior' at Yale for his third-person research/practice.

The year after that, he co-created a rough crucible for engaging in all three types of action inquiry at once – the Yale Upward Bound, War on Poverty program, where he (and the program as a whole) experienced the moral equivalent of war. In the ten years that followed, he continued to explore the action inquiry integration of research and practice, generating a new kind of leadership and a new kind of social science – first at the Southern Methodist University Business School, then at the Harvard Graduate School of Education, and finally at his own entrepreneurial non-profit, The Theatre of Inquiry.

The book ends as he is appointed Graduate Dean at the Boston College School of Management in 1978, with but a single, summary chapter on how he spent the final thirty years of his academic career. Since his retirement from academia in 2008, he has continued to develop the leadership psychometric (now named the Global Leadership Profile [GLP]) used in third-person research on adult, organizational, and scientific development. In the arena of work, he has also co-guided Action Inquiry & GLP workshops with his friends at Global Leadership Associates and Amara Collaboration. In the spirit of play, he brought together 3-day Alchemical Workparties two or three times a year for a decade or so, has co-created the Transformations™ card deck with GLA and CCL, and authored *Eros/Power: Love in the Spirit of Inquiry* with Hilary Bradbury.

The First-Person Purpose in Writing this Book

Bill started to write these memoirs in 1978 at the age of 34. Initially, it was to be a 'scientific' journal that would include only his 'direct' memories, with no elision of unflattering memories. He was writing primarily for himself as a form of first-person research on his life experiences. Although at 34 he was already working with the developmental action-logic theory in his academic research, he was not focused on using it to analyze his early memories. Thus, it was decades before he subtitled the first section of this book "Born Again and Again and Again" in reference to retrospectively recognizing his own gradual transformations through the different developmental action-logics, as discussed in the chapter Endnotes.

It was even longer before he titled the book as a whole **Numbskull**, borrowing a name his three sons playfully gave him when they were wising around and gleefully rubbing the dent on his forehead that they call the Grand Canyon – a souvenir from a Boy Scout incident in his youth. He enjoyed the humor of the name from the start, but then, to his surprise, began to find more and more instances of this numb-skull-ian quality in the physical, emotional, intellectual, organizational, and spiritual stories he tells in this book. Gradually, he accepted this archetypal metaphor as a chief characteristic of his – perhaps, you may say, more like a chief fault than a chief virtue, given his aim of exercising attention for timely (inter)action. Nevertheless, this was one of the long-patterns he gradually discovered in his life (the truth isn't always flattering). He provokes a daunting question for each of us, simply by taking it on himself: How long will it take us to re-search, to 'see,' and to name our chief stumbling blocks and our chief building blocks in life? Light and shadow are deeply intertwined in our lives. The exploration of this entanglement is one of the qualities that makes this book important. How much better for humanity, we may imagine, if everyone came to recognize the shadowy pattern of their Chief Faults, thereby taming them rather than projecting them on others?

The Second-Person Purpose for Writing this Book

Torbert's notes show that as he edited the book, he increasingly concentrated on his second-person purpose for writing. For you, his individual readers, he wished to display the practice of a theory of transformative learning. Can a primarily first-person book – this book – convey something about the struggles that accompany the unique path he opened, in a way that encourages each of us to bush-whack our own very different path in life?

Recognizing that his privileged WASP, male, Boomer-generation angle on life may be relatively difficult for the world's majority to empathize with nowadays and to treat as any sort of model, he has included, as a Postscript, several remarkable developmental stories by Aftab Erfan, a Millenial, Middle Eastern woman of color, currently Director of Equity for the City of Vancouver. You are welcome to transform the Postscript into a 'Prescript,' if you wish, and read her stories first.

Indeed, if you don't already feel free to do such a thing, please, as of now, feel free to dip around in the book at random initially. Once you take on the book from front to back, please read it SLOWLY, to let thoughts and feelings emerge about how it compares and contrasts with your own life at that age. In short, approach this book as an action inquiry of your own — not as a subordinate, passively following the book's lead, but as a peer, actively seeking to discover what you resonate with and what you differentiate yourself from.

In this peer-like spirit, another thing you can do is invite two or three friends to spend an evening together every two or three weeks to discuss two or three chapters at a time, while sharing your own experiences of development with one another.

The Third-Person Purpose for Writing this Book

Torbert's third-person purpose for writing this book is to illustrate how its different theoretical, empirical, and experiential action inquiry contributions interweave with one another to create a new paradigm of social action and social science. This theory and practice highlights parallels among personal, organizational, and social scientific development. The new social scientific paradigm that the book illustrates (and explicitly discusses in Appendix A) transcends and includes Empirical Positivism and Post-Modern Interpretivism. Named Collaborative Developmental Action Inquiry (CDAI), this new paradigm integrates first-, second-, and third-person action inquiry, as well as quantitative, qualitative, and action research.

This Introduction, as well as the Endnotes and Appendices, are written in the third-person voice by colleagues in the action inquiry community of which Bill is a member. Together, these sections do much of the work of explicating the more abstract aspects of CDAI, while the main body of the first-person text illustrate the experiential qualities of CDAI. Readers may turn at any time to Appendix A, which offers brief outlines of Torbert's entire theoretical structure and how it brings together Eastern and Western thought, as well as psychological and political action.

CDAI raises and responds to the fundamental question "*What constitutes timely (inter)action now and for the future for me and for us?*" Timely action requires more than knowledge about the past pattern of whatever variables interest us. It also requires immediate inquiry in the midst of action in the never-before-experienced challenges of each new present moment and setting, as well as research on possible futures we wish to generate, alone and together. Our best chance at timely action, Torbert suggests, arises from triangulating among these three very different, but intimately interrelated, types of inquiry in action.

This book articulates the next big step forward – the coming paradigm shift – in the still unfolding history of science. And while that in itself is obviously a really big deal, it's not even the whole of it: Because, almost unbelievably, the next step for science, is, simultaneously, the next step for the world of human organization and productivity, as well as the next step for religion, spirituality, and friendship. All three steps simultaneously. Because they are all the same step.

Physicists and biologists have moved from categorical theories of matter and life to deeper, dynamic, evolutionary theories that seek to explain how the categories (e.g. the species) transform. With the advent of adult, organizational, and scientific developmental theory, along with action inquiry practice, we now have an evolutionary theory of human activity: a theory of patterns of consciousness, character and organizing that we can continue to articulate, test, and display in our action with others.

Both in the natural sciences and in the human sciences, this evolutionary perspective leads ultimately to the realization that the scientist's or leader's own consciousness and action-logic affects the outcomes intended and observed and must, therefore, be included in the study-and-action project. Torbert invites us to join him and help correct the massive error that the founders of modernist science made as they took the mantle from Big Religion. Both Big Religion and Big

Science have failed to correct a most fundamental mistake: the belief that the most important and most real truths lie outside of us.

Twenty years into the 21st century, the urgency and significance for all of humankind to learn to practice the inside-out, mutually-transforming power of action inquiry in our encounters is becoming increasingly sharply etched. First of all, it, and the loving intimacy it generates, is the only cure for the continuing epidemic of racial alienation, economic inequality, sexual abuse and rape, addiction, and inner loneliness in our own culture and others. Second, in this nuclear and cyber age, there is also a special urgency for a more subtle, more multilateral, and more mutual approach in the realm of international relations, cyber war, and nuclear weapons' proliferation.

Yet a third arena of urgency in learning to exercise action inquiry and mutual power concerns our collective human relationship with our environment, where our short-term, self-centered interests are polluting air and water, killing the world's coral reefs, along with entire animal, fish, and plant species, and perhaps soon ourselves. Today's empirical sciences can begin to tell us what the problems are, but only CDAI can guide us through the inevitably experimental process of dissolving our society-wide enchantment with technologies of distraction and addiction, to creating cultures of mutual attentiveness instead. COVID-19 is nature's latest emissary to us, inviting us to enact — not a culture of dependence, nor a culture of libertarian counter-dependence, nor one of independence, but rather — a culture of inter-independence with nature and with one another.

Perhaps even more insidious than COVID-19, because it initially masqueraded as a purely good thing, we must address the rapid development of artificial intelligence and social media in a new way. Our human species as a whole is particularly poor at reliably generating the mutual power of action inquiry, preferring physical addictions, emotional reactivity, and intellectual habits. The artificial intelligence world is inheriting and magnifying this deficiency. As Greg Brockman, OpenAI's chief technical officer puts it, super-intelligent machines that haven't been taught to "love humanity" represent a potential threat to us (*The New Yorker*, 10/14/19, p.54). Indeed, very few humans know how to love humanity!

We would say, more radically, that unless a great many more of us in the coming decade literally turn our attention toward learning how to exercise mutual power, mutual inquiry, and mutual love with one another, we will have no chance of programming mutuality into our artificially-intelligent robots. By default, the robots will act more and more intelligently to achieve goals through unilateral power, as we humans currently mostly do. Before long, the robots may conclude that humanity is a dispensable or assimilable menace to itself.

Some supposedly smart people can't wait to be uploaded to on-line immortality. But the fact that we are embodied, that we die, and that we cannot be certain about when we will die is what makes us human and what makes any kind of timely action meaningful. With CDAI, science is no longer divorced from meaning. With CDAI's search for timely action, science is no longer estranged from every-day life. If humanity is to survive and flourish with *panache*, the AI of Action Inquiry must be practiced more continually, more comically, more analogically, more profoundly, and more intimately than the AI of Artificial Intelligence. May this book – and your future action inquiry – soon nudge our world in this improbable direction.

Section I – Numbskull: Born Again and Again and Again

Chapter 1

Numbskull's Early Experiences In Madrid, Vienna, and Salzburg, 1944-1955

I – a rather distant relative of the "I" writing now – was born into this particularly-embodied lifetime on February 8, 1944, at Walter Reed Army Hospital in Washington DC, while my father was serving in the Army during World War II.

By virtue of a general anesthetic, my mother's conscious self was absent in the final hours of her difficult 30-hour labor... Which ended with my headfirst emergence into this world.

Upon my advent, I was probably pretty woozy myself, from digesting that same anesthetic Mom had. But I figure I was also probably pretty happy at getting out of that tight place after so long.

Does my mild physical, emotional, and intellectual claustrophobia emanate from my primal birthing experience of difficulty reaching fresh air to breathe? Did my skull first get numbed there, against my mother's pelvic bones, during the long hours of my birthing?

Was that primordial experience perhaps also a causal factor in my strong urge to be born again and again in later life? Have I not wished to learn, again and again, how to slip more and more easily from the 'womb' or 'cave' of my current assumptions about life into an experiencing that is more wakeful in the present, more attuned to the temporal rhythms of personal and social development, and more engaged with the otherness of others? (Endnote 1)

■ ■ ■

My first clear memory is of a spring day in our little backyard in Brookline in 1946 when I had turned two. This early memory came back to me in 1964 when I was twenty and an undergraduate at Yale. I was lying on my back on my bed, relaxing, allowing my memory to sink into the darkness of my early life, seeking new vivid feelings or specific images of a particular locale, or of a person. I had already rediscovered several Spanish memories from when I was three til five, so now I was trying to make contact earlier, when I was two, in Brookline, Massachusetts.

I was doing this memory experiment as one of a dozen or so different ways of seeking self-knowledge at that time with different friends. In this case, I was helping my college roommate, Mac Rogers, conduct psychological experiments on ourselves for one of his courses, about how to welcome back early memories. The memory that then entered my conscious mind came as a full-blown, multi-sensory eternal moment that includes both my mother and father.

> *My mother is leaning out the kitchen door calling, "Applesauce for dessert, boys," to my father and myself. My father is climbing down from a tree. I am in the sandbox. It is a wonderfully warm, late spring day…*
>
> *My mother's call awakens me to the simultaneous presence of the warm sand passing through my hands, my father's relaxation in the tree, the clear air breathing me, and my mother's sweet offer – in short, to my perfect pleasure in the whole situation.*

I can still experience the vividness of this memory from the spring of 1946, and I've repeatedly enjoyed and treasured it. But I have only much later tried to make explicit some of its for-me-archetypal characteristics. In recent years it has occurred to me that this 'sandbox' memory re-presents well my love of my mother's uplifting and convivial spirits, as well as the harmonious trio I felt my father, my mother, and me to be. This memory also exemplifies my very occasional, but distinctively repeated, momentary experiences of time-stopping, synesthetic awareness during childhood – experiences of presence in the present.

To Madrid

In many ways, I was born again when Dad's first Foreign Service posting sent us to Spain in 1947 til 1950. In Madrid, I first went to school – a Spanish school called Estudio – where I was both the only American in the class and the youngest. In Madrid, too, I had my first experience of living in a home with a cook, two maids, and an occasional gardener, all of whom together taught me Spanish the more quickly. Although I knew some English already, my primary language became Spanish during those years.

My two-years-younger brother Jim tells this story:

> *In September of '47, Dad reported in a letter to his mother (Dee): "At least ... he (Bill) has stopped standing at the top of the front steps and shouting down at the Spanish children in the neighborhood, "You dummies, why don't you speak right?*

Brother Bill's foolish and illegitimate bravado (no doubt one version of my archetypal numbskull-ianess) is one of the qualities that's been getting knocked out of me since earliest childhood ... but that nevertheless shows little sign of altogether abating. Indeed, although I have no memory of any such egregious social conduct as my brother and father allege above, my earliest actual Madrid memory portrays a physical action of comparable numbskull-ianness. A small scar at the back of my skull proves that the event of impulsively bashing the back of my head and needing three stitches did occur, and the story was retold once or twice in my childhood. Here is how I now remember it:

One evening in Madrid in our second floor bathroom, at the age of four, I am inspired to realize that the towels to dry my just-scrubbed hands are only apparently out of reach.

I climb onto the laundry hamper to finish the job I have so well begun.

But as I stand triumphantly to pull towel from rack, the very grace and success of my parabolic upward thrust seems to call for a different kind of artful completion than I had at first imagined.

My arms continue upward, my back arches backwards, my eyes glint the sparkle of the white tile floor, the curve feels beautiful and true ...

And I remember no more ... (though blood and towels and the three stitches come into my parents' retellings).

Perhaps the simplest point to be made about this story, in retrospect, is that it represents my first memory of myself in action. You may perhaps be inclined to agree with me that my impulsiveness would have to be questioned and transformed if I was to survive very long ...

The first day of school I remember:

Mom leaving me in the hands of a strange teacher whose language I do not speak. I scream and scream.

Lying on my stomach on a table, lashing out with arms and feet in every direction so that no one can touch me, I scream and scream.

My mother tells me that I kept something-like-this up for the first three days she took me to school, and how hard it was for her to leave me each day.

I made my first friend at Estudio: Javier. Javier seemed stout, reliable and friendly to me, with a special kind of reserve that evidently attracted me... My memory of Javier at school begins like this:

The teacher leaves the classroom, asking all the children to sit quietly with their heads on their arms while she is away. After the door closes, not more than two or three instants of silence occur before my eyes rise slowly from my arms and catch the eyes of other classmates who are also beginning to look up. I also see Javier's head still down, obedient to the teacher's instruction. Within a minute, control gives way, like a lazy long-breaking wave, into a wonderful, carnival pandemonium. Javier alone sits quietly with his head down on his arms. I can see him clearly, as though through the wrong end of a telescope, as something much more powerful draws the rest of us irresistibly to the dance.

The door opens and the teacher returns.

The frenzy freezes.

We sneak back to our seats under her mute cruel eye. Standing completely still, she then calmly visits a terrible judgment upon the class as a whole: we are condemned to sit for an entire hour in her presence, in absolute silence.

Meanwhile, Javier's angelic behavior is praised, and he is invited to visit the next older class.

For many years thereafter, whenever I thought about this event, I would do so with an automatic feeling of admiration for Javier's self-discipline and would flail myself for my weak, influenceable character. Not until I was thirty did it occur to me that different and more positive meaning may be made of this event just as well: NOW, I not only practice a lot of self-restraint as did Javier then, but I also rejoice in the participative side of my character that occasionally chooses the spontaneously-relational as the full flower of the mannered, and that draws me, with others, to the dance. (Endnote 2)

From Spain to Austria

We returned from Spain for home leave in the summer of 1950, spent mostly on Cape Cod, with my brother and I speaking Spanish between ourselves, while also unawaredly (re)learning English. After Cape Cod, our family of five (counting Gito, our dog) returned to Madrid to pack up the furniture and send it ahead by train to my father's next post in Vienna. We followed more slowly by car across France and into Austria. Once in Vienna, at the age of six, I suppose I might claim to have been born yet again. This time I had to learn two new languages – not Spanish and English, which I now somehow knew. Now it was French in the classes at my new school, the Lycee Francaise de Vienne; and German during recesses and with neighborhood friends, Hansi and Ingrid.

When I started at the French Lyçee in Vienna, I found myself once again as in Madrid, in a schoolyard where I knew no one and could understand very little. I did now speak at least some German, as did most of the other students who were Austrian. But almost all the rest of the students and all of the teachers spoke French, which meant nothing to me. Recesses on the rubble-strewn erstwhile-parade-grounds offered few obvious activities other than throwing stones at one another. This process would begin in a somewhat random way, but would predictably evolve, first into the French against the Austrians, and then into everyone against the half dozen Yanks and Brits, who would be making a run for the classrooms, while teachers ineffectively attempted to intervene.

One morning, as we waited in our class lines in the central courtyard for the remaining school buses to arrive, the class line next to mine was composed of 'big kids' some two years older than ourselves. It was dominated by a giant of an Austrian boy, immensely tall and fat, who glowered through his glasses and pushed everybody around with his piping voice, even bumping them bullyishly now and then. On this particular morning, he was picking on a small, French girl in my line. It seemed clear that the beautiful maiden must be protected and the monstrous Goliath opposed. So, heart in mouth, knowing that I would probably get much the worse beating, I punched the giant in his vast stomach region as hard as I could. To my amazement, he immediately doubled over, wheezing and weeping, his glasses shattering on the cobblestones.

Before I could fully taste the fruits of my sudden victory on behalf of justice, I found myself surrounded by peremptory and haughty teachers who seemed to think I was at fault. My mother was called. I was sent home for the day. The next day I was required to render payment for the glasses and an apology to the boy. My mother explained to me, without a sense of blaming me, that the boy not only came from a poor family, but also suffered from a particular glandular disease that made him so fat. This made me realized I ought to render a sincere, official apology. Inwardly, however, I felt cheated of my Goliath and of the proper recognition for my courageous David-like action.

In retrospect, perhaps this episode can be counted as my initiation into twin enigmas that later became central questions in my scholarly research. my professional practice, and my personal life. The first question/enigma is: how to interpret social events correctly across different cultures, classes, and persons' action-logics? The second enigma is: how to intervene in social relations with the desired effects?

We often travelled to the lake called the Wolfgangsee for vacations, so often that I later came to regard it as my spiritual home to which I returned for personal retreats every few years as a grown-up. It was there that I learned the sidestroke was my best 'long' stroke; there that my father urged me up the Schaffberg, the tallest mountain I would ever climb; and there that I had my first experience of feeling like what I called "an extra person." The feeling came over me that I was aware of myself as being in the world, but that I didn't know what to do. Everyone else seemed to play a sort of necessary role in the world, but I was uniquely free (and responsible!) to choose a way of making a distinctive contribution. This was not at all a feeling of satisfied elitism or traditional *noblesse oblige*. Rather it was a feeling of aloneness, alien-ness, and mystery. The feeling did not last long, and I did not think about it in any sort of continuing or obsessive way. But it did leave a residue, and I have felt that same kind of feeling increasingly in my life since – the awareness that I am offered the opportunity to "listen into the dark" now (at any time), beyond my habitual thoughts and actions, for clues about how to act in a unique way that contributes a note in a larger evolving human symphony (*symphony*?). The difference between my feeling at the Wolfgangsee and now is that now I realize we all can potentially find this emptiness and possibility within ourselves.

By the time we got to Salzburg, I was riding my bicycle anywhere and everywhere.

> *Now it is a cloudy, raw November day. I am riding my bicycle through the puddled back ways, returning home from the Army PX store, with the brand new first baseman's glove I have just successfully stolen. My heart is still pounding from the calculated risk I have successfully taken. My eyes are feasting with delight on my treasure. And something within me knows I have done wrong, but I can feel no shame 'cause I got away with it. Suddenly, in the midst of my daydreaming, I am struck in the back by a large rock and sent sprawling from my bike into the mud. As I turn around, I catch a glimpse of a small Austrian boy in the scant, shiny black shorts common among the poor, disappearing behind the house. Anger rises in me, but is suspended as I glimpse the familiar Communist propaganda slogan painted on the cement wall by the path: "Pest Ami Go Home" ("Ami" is short for "American"). I experience my chubbiness, my new jeans, my bicycle, and my stolen glove anew – perhaps as that thin Austrian boy experienced*

the tableau. And now I do feel shame. Momentarily illusionless, I pick myself up and ride the rest of the way home more slowly… Confusedly conscience stricken and reflective, to no immediate end…

I had numerous bi-polar sociological experiences during my childhood years abroad – on the one hand, experiencing myself as a disadvantaged minority in schoolyard rock fights; on the other hand, experiencing myself as a member of an elite, diplomatic, international class, passing to the head of passport lines and owning bicycles and baseball gloves.

When I was eleven, at the beginning of sixth grade at the Army Dependent School in Salzburg, I suggested to our teacher, Mrs. Castagna, that we should rank our whole class in Army style based on our grades, in order to motivate and reward students. Then the 'officers' could sometimes help the non-commissioned ranks with their class exercises. The idea gained acceptance, and at each report period we diligently tried out our mathematical skills by converting our grades into numbers and adding them up. We made a list of the totals for the whole class, then named the three top people General, the next three Colonels, the next three Majors, and so on down the line to the three Privates.

I accepted my rank of General calmly, as though it was my proper due, and, without a trace of self-consciousness, bent over the desk of a tall girl who was having trouble with her addition to help her figure out that she was a Private. Not only was I helpful, I evidently had good taste in friends: two of my three best friends were Colonels and the other was a Major.

As the year went on, however, I became more and more concerned that this was not a true army, for there were as many Privates as Generals. Everyone knows that the proper shape of an army is pyramidal. So obvious was this fact, that no one could resist the implication our system should change to one General, two Colonels, three Majors etc. I helpfully pointed out that most people would be promoted under this scheme and that there would be no privates at all. The proposal passed by some sort of acclamation.

This new system was adopted so late in the year, however, that we were already in the final report period. Only at that period's end, on the last morning of the school year, could we compute our new ranks. I can recall some question as to whether, under the circumstances, this was a task worth bothering with. But my strong sense of duty prevailed and we spent the morning confirming that I was now the sole General.

Perhaps my short and substance-less tenure in this position of supreme command, or perhaps the arbitrariness of my exercise of power in creating the position in the first place, shocked me forever beyond such gestures of infantile despotism. I can't think of anytime since when I've enjoyed the exercise of unilateral power for its own sake.

For a little while in Salzburg I would regularly steal money from my mother's purse (just a dollar or two, which meant a lot of comic books or Butterfingers back then). My most audacious feat in this regard occurred when I took a phone message from Dad that he needed Mom to come by his office with 70 or 80 dollars immediately. I told Mom he needed 80 dollars, ran up to his office from the car and delivered 70, keeping 10 whole dollars for myself, along with two days of worry about whether I'd be caught.

At some later point, a newly-developing conscience began to prick me, and I made a tearful confession to Mom at bedtime one night, along with the solemn promise never to steal again. Nevertheless, my good will weakened, and I stole a dollar or two once more. This time, however, my conscience bit with cubed force, and I in fact never stole again.

While still in Salzburg, another fractal of my life was dedicated to becoming a craftsman, and it was a joyous one to me indeed. When I discovered a house being built across the street, I really wanted to help and to learn the craft of brick laying. I made myself useful to the work gang – some of whose names I can still recall: Heinrich, Louis, Klaus... and Peter, the blond-haired blue-eyed crew boss. I volunteered to mix cement and then later to wheelbarrow it up the bending boards to the spot on the scaffolding where the bricks were currently being laid. I would do this day after day during vacations. Two of the men would even let me hand them the bricks, which they'd slather with wet cement, set solidly in the growing wall, and clean up with a couple of efficient whisks of their trowel.

When Peter called up to see whether any of the masons wanted help, Luis was more and more the one to take me, finally letting me set some bricks myself. My first several were sloppy jobs indeed, but he showed me more slowly how he worked, and quite quickly I could do a finished job myself.

When the highest point of the house was reached and a tree perched on its tip, I was inordinately proud of having bricked about one-third of one room's exterior wall. I was invited to the workers' 'finishing party' at a beer hall downtown. I rode my bike in, wearing my cowboy outfit, and was as happy with my *apfel saft* as were they with their *Zipfer bier*. Later, when I engaged in prolonged research projects and periods of organizational leadership, I would remember and re-identify with my methodical bricklaying, deeply enjoying the sense of gradually building a strong and lasting structure.

■ ■ ■

For many years, into my twenties, I would recall the difficulties of my Spanish and French school years with an amused inner smile and without re-experiencing the pain. It seemed to me that my early failures at diagnosing alien social environments prepared me for later successes in different schools and in work roles, especially in dealing with persons of widely varying racial, political, and religious backgrounds.

I still believe that those early culture shocks deposited in me a taste for coming to appreciate, learn from, and work with the Otherness of others. But I have also come to appreciate how much my later successes derived as well from anxiety, from fear of failure, and from desire to conform and to be liked... Motives with darker shadows, perhaps intensified by those early culture shocks. (Endnote 3)

Chapter 2

Becoming an American Boy, 1956-1961

We returned from Austria for another home leave in 1955, again spent mostly at Cape Cod, with a week at Squam Lake in New Hampshire as well. At Squam I first learned the silent delight of canoeing, whether in mid-lake in sun or in the lakeshore shadows.

This time our home leave was followed by Dad's assignment in Washington DC for the next three years. He attended the National War College for a year and then became Director of Western European Affairs in the State Department. I attended the Quaker school, Sidwell Friends, for 7th, 8th, and 9th grades.

I immediately entered into the American way of life with an avidity and a passivity that shocks me to this day. For the next three years I became an absolute television addict (there had been no tv in Austria), consuming untold numbers of peanut butter and jelly sandwiches as I watched Jackie Gleason or Pat Boone. I also became a sports fanatic, listening to virtually every losing Washington Senators' baseball game for two years. And I became a secret late night in bed rock and roll listener (Elvis: "Love me tender, love me deep").

I also became a torrid reader of child hero books (The Boy Abraham Lincoln, Marco Polo, etc.), as well as historical novels set in the Revolutionary period, detective stories, and baseball books. Most striking was Kenneth Roberts' ***Oliver Wiswell***, which told the story of the Revolution *too persuasively* from the Tory point of view. Was there really a defensible point of view other than OURS? Very infrequently, I would recall the youth who in Europe had somehow actively played outside during most of the time he now spent reading, or in the cellar's darkness watching television.

To my surprise, I was much less motivated by the "big"-boy, Boy Scouts in Washington than I had been by the "little"-boy Cub Scouts in Salzburg. The fact that my new scoutmaster lacked the charismatic army uniform and the easy sense of authority of "Sarge" in Salzburg probably explains a lot, as does the fact that we met in a basement recreation room rather than at an army base where we were taught how to march.

But then a plan was announced for the troop to build a permanent winter encampment in the countryside near Washington. This sounded like a serious adult project to me, and I was eager to participate.

When we arrived at the spot and surveyed the land, it became evident that we needed to bridge the creek and build on the other side where we could see quite a lot of fallen wood. A tree already lying across the creek offered a start. Someone needed to carry one end of a rope to the other side to tie to other fallen logs, so that they could be pulled into place alongside the first one to make a bridge.

I immediately volunteered in order to demonstrate my good balance. Obviously, my aim of demonstrating my balance could best be accomplished by <u>walking</u> across the log, rather than by inching my way on all fours. An even better demonstration would be to keep my hands inside my pockets, rather than holding them out at both sides (as though there was some difficulty about keeping my balance). Following this logic without hesitation, I reached the mid-point of the log without any difficulty, but here my idiosyncratic strategizing took me in an even more unconventional direction.

The apparent likelihood was that I would reach the far bank without mishap. Nevertheless, I realized that my nonchalant posture would make any misstep all the more ignominious, and that the only sure way to avoid mishap was to intentionally dive into the creek. Therefore, once again following my newest calculation without hesitation, I turned 90 degrees and calmly dove into the creek, hands still in pockets.

Naturally, my head was first to hit the rock sticking out of the freezing water, so I was both shivering and bleeding profusely as I emerged from the water to announce, nonchalantly, that I had created the perfect opportunity for the troop to practice making a stretcher. Next, I collapsed into involuntary shivering and shuddering. Soon, though, the troop had me on a newly-constructed stretcher and in the back of a station wagon. A few hours later I had a new set of stitches in the front of my head, as well as something of a dent that's lasted to this day, which my three sons now politely refer to as "the Grand Canyon."

For the most part, however, school was a place for me in those three years where sports and girls were, and where it became important to me to be popular in some sense. This wish was occasionally satiated... by being chosen to be one of the "Three Kings" in the eighth grade Christmas pageant... and later somehow getting elected class president for the ninth grade.

I was mightily attracted to girls, but face to face with any one of them I felt somewhat the same as in the batter's box: scared speechless. Bunny, Judy, Dawn, and Carolyn come immediately to mind, and the Canadian, Jenny, to heart. I danced closely with them during slow dances, almost entirely without speaking, and dreamed all night afterwards that all my friends were still dancing around me. I could not join them, however, because I was confined in bed, embarrassed by being in my pajamas.

In seventh grade I "fell in love" with one particular girl – Marianne. But it was a long distance romance because Marianne was in the other seventh grade section. Late in the year came my first harrowing phone call to her, which I began with my carefully rehearsed, "Of all the girls, you're number one in my book..." Seconds later, I learned that she already had an escort to the upcoming class dance, so I ended the call abruptly and rushed to my mother's lap in tears.

It was not until my third agonizing occasion in the movie theatre with her that, after an hour and-a-half of increasingly intense inner dialogue, I had dared to put my arm around the back of her seat. But by the late fall of our eighth grade year, our relationship had long since matured. That Christmas vacation I was ecstatic when she invited me to her home for lunch.

When I arrived at her home promptly at noon on Tuesday, having taken the bus, I was shocked to find another couple there too. This had not been my vision of the occasion at all; but I had to admit, upon retrospection, that Marianne had actually said nothing whatsoever to suggest that lunch was to be just the two of us. Before I knew quite how to relate to this initial disillusionment, Marianne sent my spirits soaring once again by asking if I would like to take a walk around the block with her alone before lunch. Here was the perfect opportunity, if only I had the courage, to hold her hand in a casual, possessive way and, finally, to kiss her.

As we moved out of sight of her home, she began to speak. At first I barely heard her voice, so attuned was I to the relative posturing of our hands. Then, I could feel myself resisting the import of her words, felt them threatening the bubble of my world and fought to maintain its integrity. But of course, I was already hearing what she was saying and experiencing the implosion of conclusive dis-illusionment. Staying a step or so behind her, I fought to quell my tears as we completed the walk. Then, in abject subordination to the original scenario, I sat through lunch with the other couple, unable to trust myself to speak. Finally I left, keening throughout the bus ride home, the walk up the hill, and the whole evening. I continued to yearn for her from a distance for months.

Mom and Dad

At the end of the summer after my 9th grade year my parents and I parted company for the first time – they toward Rome; I, at thirteen, toward boarding school at Andover, north of Boston. Since we never again lived together year-around, this seems a good place to say more about my experience of Mom and Dad and my father's mother, Dee.

When I was young – and well into my twenties – my feelings toward both my mother and my father were always positive. (Of course, by separating when I went to boarding school, we missed the very years together when parents and children are most likely to experience friction that sometimes seems like pure war.)

Up until my departure for Andover, Mom and Dad were, unsurprisingly, the two central figures of my life. Dad was quiet, mild, prudent, distant, often at work. Without any direct encouragement from him to do so, I treated his Foreign Service work as heroic and wanted to follow in his footsteps by attending Andover and Yale. He was an active outdoors person from whom I learned tennis and canoeing and a love of mountain climbing, but he was not a natural athlete: I was promoted to advanced skiing classes ahead of him in Austria. The only hints he offered of his fine intelligence were his remarkable speed in completing the Sunday New York Times crossword puzzle, which I could never imitate, and his mastery of bridge, which we played often. Only twice during my early teenage years did my father spank me, and both occasions were well-merited!

Mom was a much more active presence in my life, always charming, engaged, funny, and reasonable. She planned and led family picnic trips into the country on weekends, went bicycling with me, had long conversations with me many days after school, and financed my attendance at occasional Washington Senators' baseball games. I can even remember her whistling "Whistle while you work" as she worked in the kitchen in Washington.

Remarkably, throughout my childhood, I never heard or saw my parents have a verbal, let alone a physical, fight. Nor was I aware of any tensions between them. Which tells you in turn just how emotionally oblivious I was, and just how much they taught me about how to handle conflict, other than by avoiding it to begin with.

Dee

Of my four grandparents, Dad's mother Dee is the only one I felt connected to. Dad's father died before I was born, and I have but one clear memory of my mother's father, from just before we left for Madrid when I was three. He died while we were overseas that first time. My mother's mother was confined to a wheelchair, which made our occasional visits rather formal and boring – especially by comparison to Dee, who seemed to me the very spirit of friendly activity.

"Dee" was our family name for her. As a sign of how little story telling there tended to be in our family, I discovered only after her death, when I asked how she had become known as "Dee" to us, that it was I, at age two, who had first summoned this sound "Dee" for her and the name stuck.

Dee was, to put it in a word that never occurred to me as a description of her when she was alive: poor. She would rent out her little cottage in Glen Echo just outside Washington for months at a time in order to take prolonged trips across the country or around Europe, never paying for a hotel, but staying with friends and family instead. She was always welcome because, without being in the least bit boisterous, only alive to the moment, she became the life of the party wherever she was. As I became a teenager and then entered my 20s, her love of poetry, of walking, and of philosophy made her an ideal conversationalist for me, and I loved her in part for that.

I remember returning to Washington from Salzburg when I was eleven, our family driving out to Dee's small country cottage for the first time that I had been there. The trees and vines of her yard created a cool, dark bower on that hot summer day. The screen door was open, but she was nowhere to be found inside. A few minutes later, searching her shadowed yard, my eyes suddenly took in what they were seeing amidst the green: my grandmother sitting cross-legged, eyes closed, and perfectly still. I knew instantly that I was seeing something absolutely new to me, something which I could never have imagined and for which I had no words: a human being wholly devoted, in the moment, to the experience of listening.

In her language, in a poem she dated two years after this episode, but that I did not see until more than a decade later, after her death:

That Moment

"Small change, my Lord," I say,
"This that you ask in pay,
When I would give the livelong incandescent day
And thus my debt defray:
Nay, I'd include the range
Of weeks and months, the change
Of seasons, not one moment only: strange,
To lifetime's bounty You prefer small change.
Why, not to disavow
My debt, I'd servile bow
Beneath thy yoke for eons, take a vow
To serve eternally."
He smiled, "I'll not allow
Such tribute: give one moment only,
But that moment now."

Over the years, I have come to see this elusive sense of the intimacy of eternity – how it curls inside time in the present, how I must be present in the present to 'live' it – as my inheritance from my grandmother, the aspect of her spirit I seek to keep alive in mine. Not only are we humans given the potential to reflect on the past and to imagine possible futures; we also have the potential to experience the surprise of the present as it occurs, at moments of living, conscious inquiry. (Endnote 4)

Boarding School at Andover

My three Washington years had been lived with the distant fore-knowledge that I would be staying in the States at a boarding school when my parents returned overseas again. Otherwise, I might not be exposed to the proper courses to prepare me for admission to a good college. How strong, or strongly felt, an argument this truly was I never tested, for I instantly transformed what might have been an unattractive and intimidating necessity into a romantic adventure – the romance of taking on adult independence and responsibility early by attending the same schools as my father – first Andover and then, hopefully, Yale.

This romantic vision had its dark precipices. Would I be admitted to Andover after three years of 'hacking off' in Washington? Would I survive the demanding, spartan regimen? So concerned was I that I cheated on one of the Andover entrance exams. My demanding but interesting Latin teacher at Sidwell Friends paid me the compliment of trusting me alone in the Latin classroom during the test, and I betrayed her trust by looking something up in one of the available books.

After an occasionally anxious period of waiting to hear from Andover, I was, in fact, admitted. But my concern about surviving at Andover was heightened because, in addition to my secret uncertainty about whether I had "really" passed the Latin exam, I learned that my poor score on the math entrance exam placed me in a remedial math class.

After seeing parents and brother off to Italy at the harbor in New York, that autumn of 1958 at Andover became one of the great ordeals of my life. The courses were hard. There was chapel every morning, **late afternoon classes** after athletics, *classes til noon on Saturdays*, **and** you wore a jacket and tie to all classes and meals.

Virtually every moment not in class, on the athletic fields, or at morning chapel was spent studying. Meals were more or less thrust down at a run, in order to get on to the next activity... and in order to minimize awareness of what you were eating. 'Mystery mounds' were a frequent challenge to one's capacity for deadening one's taste.

Most of my classmates had already come to terms with their talents and roles in this institution, having already attended the previous year. My roommate, Jobe Stevens, was new like me however, and both of us were trying out for the varsity soccer team. A soccer field was the one place where I was confident of my skill from my years in Austria. Few 10th-graders made the varsity team at Andover, yet I had played first string on the Sidwell Friends Varsity in DC the year before, so I imagined myself well positioned. Here was my opportunity to make my mark early, to earn a position of honor, in this new culture.

But soccer at Andover was utterly unlike the game I had played in the winter's mud of Washington DC, essentially uncoached. At Andover, soccer was played in magnificent fall weather, with over a hundred students trying out for the team, many of them better than anything I had seen in Washington. And was there ever a coach!

His name, I eventually learned, was Frank DiClemente. But, in a world where to students every adult was a Mr. or a Mrs., Deke was Deke to everyone. Deke coached soccer in the fall, basketball in the winter, and track in the spring, but soccer was his love and his genius (or at least so it seemed to me). His regimen of laps, windsprints, and exercises showed him just what each player's limits were. The drills were serious and really trained you in new skills. The daily chalk talks taught you the elegance of the game and made you feel part of an elect circle. During the scrimmages, you felt his eye on you almost constantly and frequently heard him addressing you, whether or not you were near the ball. He kept players constantly rotating in and out of the scrimmage, from team to team, and from position to position, so you were constantly being tested in new ways. Throughout, his *sotto voce* comments to the bench kept its members alert to every detail and roaring with laughter.

Both Jobe and I survived the first cut and then the second cut, but I knew that I was disappointing Deke. I was good with the ball and positioned myself well on the field, but I did not drive for the ball or for the goal. I dribbled too often when I should have passed or shot. "Fancy pants," "golden toe" players, who lost the ball while dribbling, earned Deke's greatest contempt.

The following Monday, the final list of the varsity squad, posted in the locker room, included Jobe but not me. *I* had to find my way to my intramural team – the Gauls – to play ragged games on ragged fields against the Greeks, the Romans, and the Saxons for the remainder of the fall. I could show my allegiance to the Varsity only by arriving at the game field first each Wednesday and Saturday afternoon when there was a home game, retrieving balls behind the goal during practice, then running the lines during the game and cheering myself hoarse for the team.

Blackest of All

Certainly, there was little else to cheer about that fall. Blackest of all though, that endless fall, was Thanksgiving. With my parents overseas, I had no home to return to, and I did not yet have the sense to plead with any stranger to take me home with him to his family. Instead, I thought I was being smart by staying at school to catch up on my work. Alone, on an empty campus, I read Wuthering Heights, drowning in Heathcliff's crazed passions and animal inability to speak, as well as in my own sniffling despair. The full agony of loneliness and of homesickness for a home I did not yet even know finally became unavoidable.

When fall semester exams were over, I discovered that I had survived academically. Indeed, I had made the Dean's List (the top quarter of the class). As succeeding semesters brought upward spiraling accomplishment (not just in terms of grades, but also as vice-president of the Asia Society, president of the student government, and member of the varsity soccer team) – a new kind of confidence in my competence grew in me. Fittingly, geometry became my absolutely favorite course when I realized that if I just slowed down, dismissed my anxiety, and concentrated, *there was no way to get the wrong answer* because the reasoning was tightly deductive, based on Euclid's simple axioms.

In any event, by the end of my first year at Andover I had proved to myself that I could develop the discipline to do the academic work. A single incident during my second year at Andover helped me to go beyond the individualistic, craftlike, mental perfectionism of ranking near the top of my year grade-wise. This incident occurred when I received my first grade in Mr. Gierasch's English class. All of us assigned to Mr. Gierasch's class were petrified by his reputation as far and away the hardest grader at the school. On first sight, moreover, he looked mean, even cruel – thin face, hawk nose, with a dry, cynical cackle where a laugh might have sounded. His surprise quizzes commenced with the second class – a question on the reading, two minutes to write. He graded on a 1 to 10 basis, and I feared that I might well receive less than an 8 (80), thereby receiving my worst grade at Andover to date. I reasoned with myself that it would hardly be the end of the world. Nevertheless, my worst fear was that I might just break down and cry.

At the beginning of the following class, Mr. Gierasch passed back the papers one by one, sending them around the circle of students, so that one saw others' grades – a truly callous exposure of anyone with a bad grade, I thought. As I was sitting two persons to his left and the papers were coming around my way, I felt the impact of the "6" that passed before me, and then heard the sob of the boy who received it. I felt badly for him, but it took some of the tension off for me.

Nevertheless, the situation was becoming much worse than I could possibly have imagined. First a "2" and then a "4" next paraded before my horrified eyes! For some reason – largely, I believe, the sob of that other fellow – these numbers suddenly seemed farcical rather than serious. As a result, I felt nothing at all when my "3" arrived, except a kind of detached hilarity.

In one fell swoop, Mr. Gierasch had disentangled my identity from the grading continuum. Appropriately, I cannot remember my grade in the course. Later, when I first recognized this way of understanding Mr. Gierasch's transforming effect on me, I became deeply grateful for the function he had performed. It never occurred to me, though, to approach him again or thank him. Not all "transforming teachers," I thereby began to learn, come in attractive packages…

■ ■ ■

Returning to the story of my soccer career, my second autumn I again tried out for the varsity soccer team. From the first day, Deke's attitude toward me was entirely different. He took me off the front line and put me at fullback, as though that were the most natural thing in the world...And it was. Then he somehow managed to convey to me without words that I was "in," my position on the squad seemingly as assured from the outset as that of the other players who had made the team the year before. The impression was that I had simply needed a different kind of seasoning. And because I had gained "a certain something" through my suffering and my achievements during the intervening year, I have always since been interested each fall in trying to taste how the past year has seasoned me and what new questions I can take on. My new year's resolutions tend to be made in September.

Our team was very good that year, posting something like an 8-3-2 record. But there was a strong sense throughout of building for the following year, when virtually the entire first team would be returning. The fall of my senior year, the team was undefeated over the first two-thirds of its games. As the season progressed, Deke suggested we flow rather fluidly among our positions, staying briefly in whatever position we entered, then continuing the flow, rather than returning to our original positions. This left opponents totally perplexed about whom to guard.

Nevertheless, in spite of our undefeated record, we felt a sense of doom as we approached our next-to-last game of the season against the Harvard freshmen. I wrote to Mom and Dad at the time:

> *I am afraid we do not have much of a chance against Harvard. Every day new and more amazing reports come in about Chris O'Hiri, Harvard's center forward and an Olympian representing Nigeria. He has scored the unbelievable number of 14 goals in his last two games. That is almost half as many goals as our whole team has scored in the whole season! So, I am afraid our undefeated season is about to go down the drain. They are of course undefeated too.*

Deke told our center halfback to stick like glue to O'Hiri at all times, staying between him and the ball, then told all the rest of the backfield to play him as well. Thus it was that the entire backfield held O'Hiri, the unparalleled Nigerian Olympian, after whom the Harvard soccer field was later named, to the two hardest shot goals I've ever been in the proximity of, while we scored three times... But had one called back. Both teams thereby remained undefeated, while we experienced the meaning of a moral victory.

That season's experience began to deposit in me a sensual, preverbal understanding, which I increasingly realize few others share, that human beings can work together to transform their own and others' vision of discipline, commitment, teamwork, and perfection. Furthermore, this "human, transforming perfection" is neither static nor errorless, nor even necessarily graceful in any single simple sense, but is more like a dynamic, emergent symphony in which each player is continuously attuned simultaneously to his own contribution and to the quality of the whole, while facing continual threats of interruption... as well as continual opportunities to make a uniquely timely contribution. (This is challenge enough in a game like soccer with fixed rules and boundaries. It is a challenge of an altogether higher order in one's life as a whole with others...)

I played four disappointing years of soccer at Yale, coached by an old Scott who was a sweet man and may have been a fine player, but was no coach. Never again did I remotely approach on a soccer field the quality of play to which Deke – hectoring and honing, teasing and transforming – had guided us.

Indeed, unlike my first year at Andover, my first year in New Haven at Yale did not feel at all like being born again. It felt a lot like Andover, and in fact 42 of my 1,000 Yale classmates had arrived from Andover with me. But there was definitely more freedom – no hours when you had to be in study hall, or when your lights had to be out, or when you even had to be on campus. There were *choices* about what to eat in the dining hall, ***and***, compared to Andover, the food was good enough to make me feel as though I was eating at a restaurant. Overwhelmed by the munificent offerings of the course catalogue, I took seven courses rather than the usual five, most of them advanced.

(It took me a few weeks to realize that you weren't really expected to read every word of the four or five books assigned each week for the political science course on nuclear deterrence.) Also, Yale brought the world to us, with a steady pace of world-renowned scholars, artists, and politicians visiting the campus.

That first winter at Yale, I became an apprentice journalist at the ***Yale Daily News*** under the tutelage of David Gergen and, a little later, under the chairmanship of Joe Lieberman. Thirty years later, it felt like an intimate occasion when, in the news booth at the Democratic Convention in 1992, David was the Republican analyst and Joe the Democratic one, commenting on two other Yalies who were the Republican and Democratic candidates, George Bush senior and Bill Clinton. (Endnote 5)

Chapter 3

"Bright College Years," 1962-1965

I had first encountered the Yale minister, Reverend William Sloane Coffin Jr., at Andover where he had preached in a booming baritone one Sunday at our otherwise boring weekly church service. He made Christianity seem a joyful possibility, as well as a challenging perspective on human nature and social justice. Coffin was young, handsome, looked like an athlete, was reputed to have been in the CIA, had a great sense of humor, and was the greatest preacher I have ever heard. Although I was already an officially confirmed Episcopalian, I was really a questioning agnostic, totally charmed by Coffin's confident yet humble belief and activism. I wanted what he seemed to have – wanted that rooted, centered, personal value system – wanted his to rub off on me.

One of the first things I did upon arriving at Yale was to find Coffin in his office (only later did I come to realize how unusual and lucky it was for anyone to find him there!). I delightedly accepted his totally unexpected invitation to become a deacon, a role that included the privilege of weekly meetings at his home as well as each Sunday morning at Battell Chapel. Battell was always full when Bill preached, each sermon the most exciting ethical-intellectual engagement of the week. He had a marvelous ability to hone Christian mysteries into Zen koans:

> *It is not because we have value that we are loved, but because we are loved that we have value. Our value is a gift, not an achievement.*

I love the recklessness of faith. First you leap, and then you grow wings.

The woman who most needs liberating is the woman in every man.

Nationalism, at the expense of another nation, is just as wicked as racism at the expense of another race.

There are three kinds of patriots, two bad, one good. The bad ones are the uncritical lovers and the loveless critics. Good patriots carry on a lover's quarrel with their country, a reflection of God's lover's quarrel with all the world.

(All these quotes can be found in Coffin's later book ***Credo***.)

But my enthusiastic engagement in Coffin's activities only highlighted my continuing uncertainty about whether I really believed in God. (I clearly believed in Bill Coffin!)

Given my simultaneous full engagement with Bill Coffin and my uncertain engagement with God, I entered my sophomore year at college with a very definite question about the source of all value, a question I phrased as "Is there God?" Sophomorically, I pledged to myself that I would stop sitting on the fence and discover the answer to this question before the year was out.

With a degree of earnestness that must have seemed from the outside like a caricature (had anyone been watching), I tried to arrange all my courses and other activities that sophomore year to help me answer my basic question. With my friend Mark Foster, I began to conduct interviews with faculty of special repute in order to learn whether and how they connected their scholarly field of inquiry with their life-values. In existential philosophy I pondered Kierkegaard's vision of Christianity as a "leap of faith," as against Nietzsche's vision of the death of God and of man's responsibility for his own values.

I loved Kierkegaard's metaphor for why God would appear to us as the vulnerable Jesus – how the prince who loves a common woman chooses to dress down, leave the castle, and enter the streets as a common man so that his beloved can meet and choose him freely and mutually for love, rather than being influenced by his power, prestige, and authority.

But how many of the billions of human beings throughout history who have believed in a monotheistic God have done so in the spirit of mutual, peer-like love? And, by contrast, how many believers in God have in fact subordinated themselves to religious beliefs that they treat as objectively true, unquestionably authoritative, and worth killing for, rather than as the basis for a mutually-vulnerable, mutually-transforming inquiry in action with one another?

So ... perhaps Nietzsche's darker metaphor of the death of God is more liberating today. Perhaps we must suffer the death of our Father God image before we can develop a mutual relationship with a transclusive God-as-Friend-and-Lover, potentially embodied and to be discovered in each true friendship we make. The story we today need to listen into deeply in support of our own spiritual evolution may be Nietzsche's story of the suffering madman – his own world reeling because he really has felt Father God's death – crying out in the village square that the news of God's death and of man's responsibility for his own values has not yet reached us ...

In addition to my historical-philosophical courses, I signed up for several voluntary, evening, six-week religious study seminars with faculty of special repute: political scientist Karl Deutsch on violence and non-violence; organizational interventionist Chris Argyris on authentic relationships; and political/spiritual activist Bill Coffin (I evidently couldn't get enough of him) on ***The Meaning of the Cross*** (a book by Henry Sloane Coffin, Bill's uncle who had served as President of Union Theological Seminary). All of these were powerful experiences for me, including an impassioned reading over Christmas vacation of Huston Smith's ***The Religions of Man*** which made the non-theistic "religions" of Confucianism, Taoism, and Buddhism seem as plausible, dignified, and inspired as Hinduism, Islam, Judaism, and Christianity in turn... Not to mention less violent on the whole.

Yet none of these readings and experiences generated whatever transformation I needed to permit me to commit without reservation to a single structure of belief and practice. On the contrary, during the winter of that year, I experienced a sophomore slump of epic proportions, becoming so unmotivated that I could often not get out of bed, yet also could not sleep. During this true "slump," I even got bored with food for the only time in my life to date, finding I could not taste what I ate. I wanted to leave wherever I might be as soon as possible and crawl into a cave.

After having been inspired by the conversations in Coffin's seminar about the meaning of the cross, I found myself irritated and incredulous at the advice he had offered us at the end of the seminar. As much as we might like the idea that "You are not loved because you have value; you have value because you are loved," said Coffin, a mere discussion of Christian love could not be the basis for determining whether such love exists. To test the validity of the idea, he said, we would have to pretend to believe the idea and actively try it out in our lives. At the time, this advice seemed self-defeating and undignified to me. How can one *seriously* base one's life on something one is self-consciously *pretending* to believe?

But a few weeks later, in the early spring, I was walking through a courtyard one day... feeling the not-yet-warm-but-promising-freshness of the air... while looking through a budding-but-not-yet-leafed tree at a stone tower, turned to pink-gold by the late afternoon sun... all framed, in turn, by a startlingly blue sky and by a shiver of presencing awareness up my spine...

Suddenly, I felt how it was the *relationships* among these things, including my attention to them, *not the things in themselves*, that caused my feeling of beauty, awareness, and calm, high joy... this sense of personal presence to and attunement with the cosmos.

The quality of this feeling of calm, physical joy and equanimity, associated with this view of leafing-tree/ reflected-sun/

blue-sky, waked memories of several instances in recent weeks when I had experienced, in a variety of circumstances, a similar feeling of aligned-presence-in-a-relational-world.

Then, as I was having this synaesthetic experience, I recalled Bill Coffin's recent peculiar and irritating words about "practicing" love even if you don't yet believe in it. Now, in retrospect, I could see that in one way or another I had indeed experienced what we had intellectually defined as "love" in the seminar on these momentary occasions that waked the profound feeling of direct, free, mutual encounter and calm exchange of liveliness. The idea had come true in my experience in a completely unexpected way!!!

For the first time in my life I felt utterly confident that I had discovered an incontrovertible basis for all my thought, feeling, and behavior. For this "love" was an experience that simultaneously spanned thought, feeling, and behavior. It was not an inapplicable ideal, or an unrationalizable feeling, or an impulsive action. Love interwove dispassionate observation, passionate feeling, and compassionate interaction with the entire environment, including other human embodied-spirits and souls-in-the-making. I desperately felt the lack of such universal alignment in myself most of the time. And I desperately wanted to believe in such alignment and to rediscover it again and again in my practice with others.

Now, suddenly, I could believe... not on the basis of an argument or someone else's ecstatic witness... but on the basis of my own primordial experiencing. I could feel a living relationship with Jesus... who clearly sought and embodied such an awareness, such mutuality... I could turn and speak with Him as a brother (with Thee, dear one)... I felt that I had truly been "born again."

In spite of all this mental attention to love, I realized one day, a year or so after my "born again" experience, that I was still but a babe in this new faith – that I still didn't know how to actively create such experiences of love even though I talked and thought about love a whole lot. I came to realize that genuinely loving moments occurred to me as rarely as ever.

So, I gradually had to admit to myself that my intellectual superstructure, based entirely on the universal primacy of love, was based upon an experience which, while undeniably real in itself, was only hypothetical for me most of the time. Therefore, however valid my system of thought might be in general, it did not describe *me* validly. If anything, this intellectual "grand design" tended to distract me from the disciplined work on myself implicit in my simultaneous capacity to experience love, yet incapacity to love at will. How might I learn to become fully passionate, compassionate, and dispassionate in each present moment? What disciplines might lead to the practice of timely loving action in all the different circumstances of life? With these questions, I was approaching the discipline I eventually called "action inquiry" much more closely than ever before – at least in theory. What about in practice?

Learning Leadership in Somalia

In practice, after my sophomore year in the summer of 1963, off I went to do geological survey work for Sinclair Oil in Somalia, where my father was now serving as Ambassador.

The key event of the summer for me was my first major personal leadership lesson while I was working with the Sinclair geological survey team, seeking oil – the great American business quest, as I then began to learn. Every day, we left our camp in the bush, bouncing along deeply rutted, bulldozed 'lines,' til we reached that day's worksite and began drilling holes, setting charges, and recording the subsurface structures revealed by the dynamite blasts.

I had only been learning the trade for two weeks when first Sandro and then Jami, the two Italian bosses who translated between me and the twelve Somalos when necessary, left camp on other duties, suddenly promoting me to sole leader of the subsurface charting team. I was very nervous about holding so much responsibility conjoined with so little experience and no common language with my subordinates. I was also terribly eager to have Charlie, the genial linebacker-sized Texan chief of the camp, think well of what "my" team accomplished.

One day the "line" we were bulldozing began to cut right through a temporary native village of scattered huts, built out of scraps of cardboard, tin, and canvas. I had been told that the government had given us the right of way in all such cases, but I was both ethically bothered by, and emotionally scared of, disregarding the objections of the natives.

When I described the situation to Charlie upon my return, he said it was OK that I'd stopped for the day, but that I ought to return and go right ahead with the line the next morning. It was important to keep it straight for research purposes, and besides... We would be undercutting both our own authority and the government's if the word got around that we could be influenced by impromptu on-the-ground objections of squatters who had no property rights to the land.

Charlie's relaxed authority made this seem reasonable, natural, all-American, and unobjectionable at the time. But as soon as I got outside his aura, my fears and concerns returned. I ventured forth the next morning with heart in mouth, hoping to get through the scattered huts early, before anyone could rouse themselves to protest. But when we arrived a whole delegation of villagers awaited us and waved to me to come with them to what turned out to be the chief's hut. An extremely old man emerged from the hut. Skeletal, nearly toothless, limping on a stick, and in a thin whining voice, he spoke a few words of English and more in Italian to me, along with rapid fire Swahili to Sido, the Somali truck driver.

Basically, the village elder was gently questioning whether I thought this action was truly just. I felt on very uncertain ground because I was clear that I did not think the action was just. But I felt, just as surely, that I would lose my job if I didn't follow Charlie's gentle orders. Moreover, as the Ambassador's son, whose father's position probably got me the job to begin with, losing it seemed unacceptable and embarrassing. Here was I, the supposed power-possessor, feeling a kind of horrified compassion for this poor, powerless old man, who in turn was acting like a Socratic teacher to me.

I chose not to continue through the village, but rather to pick up the line on the other side. We ultimately got more done that day (cutting 14 km.s of line) than on any other, but I expected the guillotine to fall on my neck upon my return.

I delayed the moment of truth when I got back to camp, by kicking and heading and kneeing my precious soccer ball in a little sand patch amidst the fierce African bush, until an errant foot, knee, or head drove the ball onto a long thorn that actually popped the leather ball. Further deflated, I husbanded my hard-to-locate courage to face Charlie with what I had done. I was dumbfounded to have him dismiss the matter lightly, saying there were thousands of square miles yet to be surveyed.

Now, I was enormously relieved that I had acted according to my conscience. From this, I believe I took the implicit lesson that it is good to listen to and act on our intuitions about what is just, for our fears of negative pragmatic consequences may simply be misplaced. (Of course, our fears are not always misplaced, as I later amply learned, but even then it is rarely wise to be guided by such fears rather than by principle, by as much ongoing research into the situation as possible, and by a hopefully growing sense of what action is simultaneously timely in personal, team, and broader historical terms.)

In the final two weeks of the summer, I was able to meet a Crossroads Africa volunteer from Spellman College several times. We held hands walking on the beach, regretting that neither of us was going to be in Washington for the civil rights march, knowing we would not be able to bridge all the distances between us. Alone, I wrote:

By an Ocean

The dark sand, cool in the shadow of stars
Calmly entertains the tentative white crests
Gently licking and retreating without surcease:
An eternal law of grace forbidding repetition.

Watcher of Waves

Self-forgetting
He is drawn
To communion
With a never-ceasing miracle
Of unconscious grace
More powerful than he.

Self-Finding
He is shown
A gift freely given
In that moment
Of unending quiet
More lasting than he.

Civil Rights

Back at Yale in the fall of 1963, the issue of Civil Rights quickly migrated from the Capitol Mall and Martin Luther King's "I have a dream ..." speech to Bill Coffin's living room. In mid-October, Coffin called me to ask whether I would write an article for the ***Yale Daily News*** about a meeting he was convening at his home with a certain Al Lowenstein who was trying to engage northern white students to come down to Mississippi to help stage a mock election for Governor.

Al showed up on campus and spoke with a group of us (mostly Coffin's deacons, all white, but also three extremely quiet and impressive black Yale Law students, including Marion Wright [later Edelman], who have gone on to become historic figures in civil rights). Loewenstein was talking about going down to Mississippi to help organize a mock election among Negroes (the name then used) to highlight their lack of voting rights.

Like Coffin, Lowenstein was a powerfully charismatic figure. He looked like anything but an effete intellectual – having been a college wrestling champion as well as president of the National Student Association when he was my age ten years earlier. Later, he had smuggled himself into Southwest Africa when it was a UN protectorate of South Africa. He wrote a vivid account of what he found in a book called ***Brutal Mandate*** that played a part in ending South Africa's "protective" role. Now he was a civil rights organizer. In the years ahead, Loewenstein would become a Congressman from New York and would lead the "Dump Johnson" movement that played a role in President Johnson's decision not to run again for President. Then, just as Loewenstein seemed poised for still greater things, he was tragically murdered in his own office by a deranged former associate.

I emerged from that first meeting with Lowenstein at Coffin's home with the clearest sense of urgency and purpose I had ever yet felt in political matters. I was committed, not only to writing an article for the ***Yale Daily News***, but to going down to Mississippi, along with a dozen or so of us who had been at the meeting.

I wrote the op-ed piece calling others to come down to Mississippi, and I felt a moment of great pride because this message drew another 53 students to volunteer to go down to Mississippi. Without yet having coined the phrase "action inquiry," this was definitely the most serious, large-scale, consequential, and indeed transformational organizing process I had ever before participated in. The organizing process in Mississippi drew 80,000 ballots in a mock election for Negro candidate Aaron Henry on the Sunday before election day, attracting the attention of the national media. The official white winner of the election a week later received fewer votes than Henry had. The Kennedy administration began drafting a Voting Rights Act, which President Johnson shepherded through Congress less than two years later as the Voting Rights Act of 1965.

Then, less than a month later, a sorrow and despair inconceivably deeper etched itself into my soul. My diary of that time can't bear to describe the central and forever-memorable, history-changing event of that day:

> *11/22/63: The (Harvard) soccer game lost by me when I let O'Hiri tap in a goal at 3-2. Heard about assassination attempt at half-time: sounded like a bad joke. Then the girls arrive, every thing's called off, and we all go down to the Fosters.*

> *11/23/63: Alternate between the television with tears and games with laughter. Up to New Haven for a wonderful Black Nativity performed in JFK's honor, then over to Pete's for a little singing of our own. "We Shall Overcome ... Someday."*

My terse journal lines are enough reminder to me of my feelings at the time to evoke instant tears now and that same deep sadness that a kind of unnameable intelligence-in-action, who was learning more about himself and about timely action all the time, was stolen from us then, so soon, before any of us had yet caught his full gist.

The *Yale Daily News*

But classes, writing for the Yale Daily News, and life in general did start up again after that weekend. Indeed, it is now amazing to me how many years it was before I recognized just how cataclysmic Kennedy's assassination was, not just for us at the time, but in the history of our country and the world. I now date JFK's assassination as the beginning of the USA's decline.

Two weeks later, our cohort on the ***Yale Daily*** elected our board of officers for the coming year. Various ones of my colleagues had been suggesting that I might win the cohort's vote to become the next Chairman. But another thing had become clear to me that fall, besides the importance of helping the political organizing in Mississippi. I came to realize that I was not in fact primarily committed to a journalistic, observational role in life. So, despite sore initial temptation, I withdrew from candidacy. Once I made the decision, it felt absolutely right. What I next learned was that when we refuse power that is offered, we can sometimes gain a somewhat different kind of power. Suddenly, I was a power broker. My friend Mark Foster and I interviewed both leading candidates, made our choice, shared our view with those who wanted to know, and that man won. Something felt clean and right about this organizational decision-making process. Although I couldn't have named this at the time, I now see that we were exercising power inquiringly, dialogically, and thus collaboratively.

I became Vice-Chairman of the ***YDN***, managing the op ed page and contributing a weekly column, named "Grashing or Frabjous?". "Frabjous" is of course Lewis Carroll's word evoking joy, and "grashing" was my own word, meant to evoke an arbitrary, meaningless world. These two versions of reality were vying for our commitment, I maintained. One of my columns was about a man named G.I.Gurdjieff, whose book ***Meetings with Remarkable Men*** I had found by chance.

I wondered whether any of my fellow students would respond in any way to Gurdjieff's stories about trying to develop a self-questioning attention while in the midst of very worldly dilemmas. To my disappointment, none did. But three weeks later, out of the blue, came a short letter from a Pittsburgh woman I had never heard of (and who did not explain how she had seen my column). She simply asked whether I was really interested in these ideas, but said she would understand if I did not have time to reply. I did reply, and so began a 25-year inner and outer adventure to which we will return in later chapters.

Elihu

Later that spring, I was elected to a senior society named Elihu (for Elihu Yale, the founder of Yale). Its purpose was serious: to bring together for two evenings each week as varied a group of fifteen students as possible, with the intent of becoming lasting friends through meeting and sharing our differences.

My most startling and important learning from participating in Elihu occurred when I tried to get my delegation to work with Professor Chris Argyris. The reader may recall that I had taken a religious study seminar on Authentic Personal Relationships with Chris when I was a sophomore.

My unforgettable lesson occurred when I had tried to get Chris to meet with my Elihu comrades. My idea had been that we proto-adults could have better conversations and become better friends by learning, with Chris' facilitative help, more about how to create trusting, non-manipulative, mutual relationships among ourselves. My new comrades signed up for this plan when I first expressed my enthusiasm the prior spring, and Argyris was willing to meet with us for dinner toward the end of the fall to explore meeting with us regularly during the coming spring semester.

But when the dinner meeting with Argyris occurred, I was shocked to find it exceedingly tense. Some members expressed skepticism and even antagonism about the idea of "talking about relationships." "No agenda?" "Talking about nothing?" "Honesty? You're asking for cruelty."

For a minute or two, the collective glare turned on Argyris as an interloper from a different generation... But he effectively parried the attack by pointing out that he'd been invited and that he was only here this once unless the group as a whole chose to re-invite him. Next, Argyris asked what were the feelings of conflict within the group? Whether we wanted to engage in more of "this" or not, were we willing to make clear our reasons or feelings? Were we willing to be honest with one another about why we were making whichever decision we ended up making?

Although they tried to be indirect and diplomatic about it, it soon began to become clear to me that some members of the group felt that **I** was **forcing** Argyris on them. In urging them to buy into the idea the previous spring, I had said I would probably not join the group if people were not interested in my proposal. Now I could see the manipulative element of what I had originally thought of as simply an honest statement of the depth of my commitment to the idea. I felt exposed, rejected, embarrassed, and defeated. I'd been "caught in the (incongruent) act" of coercing my friends to learn about non-coercive relationships. My action (strong advocacy, little inquiry, leading to no shared vision) was incongruent with my ideal (advocacy of my proposal, balanced by inquiry within the group, leading to a collaboratively determined vision and action). The event was over and I'd been taught my lesson even before I thought it was to begin. My lesson was two-fold: first, that there is a difficult discipline of paying attention to how one is acting *as one acts*; and second, how difficult it is to exercise truly mutual, transforming power.

In the following months, I experimented a great deal with listening more and discovering good questions to ask, and I gradually found out how fascinating everyone is down deep where their passions, their disillusionments, their confusions, and their relationships are based. I also began to feel how much more willing others are to listen to me, if I am genuinely interested in inquiring of them (!!).

Labor, Leisure, and Politics Among Blue Collar Workers in Columbus, Detroit, and Chicago

That summer brought a different kind of baptism into politics, sociology, and organizational behavior. Along with my roommate Mac Rogers, I interviewed blue collar and white collar workers in Chicago, Detroit, and Columbus about their labor, leisure, and politics. In our free time, we slapped mosquitoes while trying to sleep near the Ohio State pig pens and later bailed hay in Wyoming for three weeks. It was the summer of 1964: JFK was dead; Barry Goldwater was running against Lyndon Johnson. We had won one $800 summer research fellowship for the two of us: enough to pay for gas, food, army surplus collapsible cots and winter sleeping bags, but nothing more.

After we completed 209 hour-long interviews and spent the fall and winter coding and analyzing the data, we found out that our hypothesis had been proven as true as any ever is in the social sciences. According to our statistical analyses, the degree of discretion and responsibility a man could exercise in his job accounted for a whopping 81% of the variance in whether his free time was truly leisurely (i.e. active and inquiring rather than passive and reactive).

I emphasize the 81% number because social science variables typically account for no more than 5 to 25% of the variance in a given study. This strong statistical outcome was especially satisfying because, as we had proceeded, professors in the different departments related to our study (economics, political science, psychology, sociology, etc.) repeatedly told us that our topic was too ambitious and our measures too open-ended, warning that we would not attain any statistically significant findings. On the contrary, we created both a new theory and a new methodology for testing it, found results confirming our hypotheses, and the study became Mac's and my first book, ***Being for the Most Part Puppets: Interactions Among Men's Labor, Leisure and Politics***.

The theory of (serious) play that underlay the study, the notion that persons are at their best when they are voluntarily working creatively at what they love and pursuing an active leisure of inquiry and friendship as well, has influenced the whole rest of my life. Put obversely and more dramatically, the main thing I learned – from the whole experience of doing the actual interviews, observing blue collar, robotic work, and smelling the same smells they smelled, day in and day out – was that I hated the conditions under which they worked, where their every move was predetermined.

The Assembly Line

Ten gaunt skeletons treated ten greasy motors to ten shiny covers.

Ten fat carcasses tightened ten heavy bolts with ten cranking strokes.

But nothing was born.

Get a Job"

Back in New Haven in early 1965, I was approaching the moment of responsibility for my own gainful employment by applying for a thousand things with no clarity about what I really wanted to do. In the end, I chose a last minute opportunity to become a "resident tutor" at the

Yale Summer High School (YSHS) and then its Associate Director for the following year. YSHS brought together a rainbow of real worlds, bringing bright boys – black, white, and Native American – from backgrounds of poverty all over the US to Yale for an intensive program during the summer that helped them gain admission and scholarships to good colleges. Its success made it a prototype for the War on Poverty Upward Bound Programs.

I made this choice because this was a more practical role than continuing as a student – a good way to begin learning how to interweave action and inquiry on a regular basis in the famous "real world." The question of how to exercise inquiry, not just in reflection and through analysis of pre-collected data, but also in the midst of present action, to make our collective interaction more timely – seemed to me the most personally meaningful, the most socially significant, and the most scientifically challenging question I could pursue during my professional career. The question felt like a calling.

My fifteen months as Associate Director of YSHS began with my role as a Resident Tutor during the grueling yet also fun and rewarding 16-to-18-hour days of the seven-week residential session itself. The rewards were many – getting to act in Arthur Miller's ***All My Sons*** with a bi-racial cast of faculty and students, alongside Earl Jones, a black student from New Orleans who played my older brother... Getting to sing in the choir and learning how to read music for the first time... Talking late, many an evening, with the mixture of red, white, and black students that made up my tutor group... Or listening in on the class Morris Kaplan taught, a topic I'll say more about in a moment.

During the school year, I hired the next summer's staff, developed curriculum with the teachers, and spent a month alone on Greyhound buses traveling around the country – mainly the Midwest and the South – visiting our students at their schools. Then, during the second summer session, I had virtually full responsibility for the internal workings of the school, while the Director, Joel Fleishman, handled what might be called 'external relations' with the university, the government, the press, and visitors. The whole experience showed me that I could be a very competent administrator, that I loved being on both sides of the teaching-learning process at once, and that my interest for the next years would be in education.

But I also felt sure that radically new forms of education must be devised. The Yale Summer High School was advertised as innovative, but I could see very little that was innovative about it. There was enough money to hire a fine, large staff for the summer, to buy plenty of supplies, to provide provocative speakers and entertainment, and, probably most important, to bring bright, poor, often prickly, under-achieving' students from all parts of the country and all races together for the summer.

The combination of students created tensions which informal conversation and, later, English essays often rendered creative, but the curriculum and the formal organization of the school tended to be conventional. I could not see that they contributed greatly to, or even used, the transformational potential inherent in such a diverse student body and in the constant problems and decisions which living in close quarters provoked. (Endnote 6)

Chapter 4

Coming Closer to Home: From Academic Inquiry to Action Inquiry, 1966

I could imagine a more transformational alternative to the Summer High School because Morris Kaplan, a graduate student in philosophy and a new friend was responsible for the most interesting educational innovation at YSHS – namely, an intensive, college-level, cross-disciplinary seminar, which met four hours daily for 10 returning students.

Initially, Morris' concept was that Greek literature and philosophy were eternally contemporary in their intellectual challenge and emotional immediacy, and that rigorous dialogue and writing rooted in such texts was as good training for high-school students as for college students. Ten bright, but until-then-bored, students blossomed under Morris' nimble, probing, and very demanding teaching during the first summer we both participated in YSHS. The following summer Morris was back again, this time teaching what he called 'The Foundations of American Politics', which somehow managed to encompass, among others, Plato, Shakespeare, Jefferson, the Federalist Papers, various Supreme Court decisions, Freud, and Orwell.

But, during the second summer, Morris was concerned with much more than intellectual pyrotechnics. He had somehow already been aware of and able to use the subtle emotional interplay within a group to help get his and the texts' ideas across, but only recently had he come to recognize the trans-intellectual potential of this interplay for learning.

I recall one memorable occasion when I was present and the class was discussing Kafka's book ***The Trial***, focusing on the scene where a guard at the Gate of the Law tells a petitioner to sit on the bench and await his turn... which never seems to come, even after the petitioner sees others entering with but a glance toward the guard. Several students spoke excitedly about what this meant in terms of our habitual tendency to defer to organizational authority. Meanwhile, another student raised his hand repeatedly, more politely awaiting acknowledgement from Morris, the teacher, the authority. Gradually, the whole class except that student became aware that, like the guard at the Gate of the Law, "the authority" was not about to acknowledge the raised hand on this occasion.

Now the intellectual questions became existential questions: would that student be able to "see through" his own habitual, deferential action-logic and choose a more effective way of initiating on this occasion? Would his classmates join in what could become a kind of practical joke on him, or would any of them act creatively, as a third force, to help the poor student surmount his dilemma? How would the aftermath of his revelation go? Who, if anyone, would check in with him after class?

In fact, the student did experience a moment of public dis-illusionment, when he realized that he was continuing to enact an habitual ritual of obedience to authority after his classmates had already found release into a new freedom and responsibility for the ebb and flow of the class. Then, he and two or three others stayed after the two-hour-long class to continue the discussion of power, powerlessness, and awareness.

Meanwhile my friend, Morris, had gone from being a new friend, to becoming my very first Lifetime Friend (a category I constructed only many years later in an effort to describe this kind of friend). I admired Morris greatly: for his political organizing ability during a Yale student protest the previous spring, for his philosophical mind, for his unbelievably wide reading in both philosophy and literature, for his apparently photographic memory, and for his conversational genius. Although he was only two years older than me, Morris functioned as an elder influence for me in two very different ways. First, he introduced me to the Danforth Graduate Fellowship that he had won, thus leading me to apply and win one too. The Danforth provided me with full financial support for four years from outside my graduate department, giving me a special sense of independence (which, as we shall see, the faculty came to feel I over-exercised). But also and equally important, the emphasis of the Danforth Foundation at the annual Fellows' meetings, on action and on values-oriented interdisciplinary research and teaching, fit with and supported my sense of vocation.

A second way in which Morris influenced me was much more emotional. In the fall of 1966, when I entered Yale's PhD program in Individual and Organizational Behavior, I was feeling torn apart by my forced separation from a woman I loved. I was also no longer buoyed up by holding a grown-up job. I believed I was ethically prohibited from revealing the "Jane situation" to anyone else who knew her and her husband; so I was trying to act 'normal' on the outside. Meanwhile, inside, I was all alone with my bottled-up misery. Finally, however, I swore Morris to secrecy and dissolved into tears telling him my story. He was compassionately attentive and completely discrete. I felt a whole lot more sane thereafter, as well as even more deeply grateful to him than before. (This story is told in greater detail in my 2016 book, ***Eros/Power: Love in the Spirit of Inquiry***, co-authored with Hilary Bradbury.)

Finding the Path You Cannot Follow

At the same time as I was engaged with the Yale Summer High School, I was gradually entering the Gurdjieff Work, by visiting the man in New York recommended by the woman who had seen my ***Yale Daily News*** article a year before. When I reached this man's home the first time, a tall, very thin man in rather worn and undistinguished clothes and a British accent invited me into his study, where we had an interesting conversation which went in no certain direction, with many moments of silence – some awkward, some charged, some profoundly prolonged.

I was catching on, though, that whatever this Work was, it couldn't be bought or stolen or given. It had to be done. It had to be self-initiated. So, at the end of the conversation I asked if I could see him again. I came back several times for short half hour conversations, sandwiched in between the 2-hour drives back and forth from New Haven. When he mentioned, in a sub-clause, that certain study groups met weekly in New York, I asked whether I might join. Thus it was that, in the fall of 1965, I found myself making weekly New Haven-New York trips to the Gurdjieff Foundation brownstone on the upper east side, while spending most Sundays from 9-5 at the countryside acreage where Work days, and occasionally Work weeks, occurred.

At the weekly hour-long meetings in New York, long silences of inner attentional "turning" toward the source occurred – becoming present to one's presence… experiencing one's experience. But how much of this was mere daydreaming, masked by an erect sitting posture? Such silences and daydreaming alternated with alert listening to members' laborious reports of their inner efforts during the week, with either a short or long response from one of our three leaders. Sometimes, I would find the replies incomprehensible, in spite of being spoken in plain English… Then, an attention exercise (e.g. "see yourself seeing") would be offered for us to try during the following week whenever we could remember to do so. (Try it as you continue to read… "see yourself seeing" and see if your experience is anything like mine at first was.)

In the early stages, my principal experiences were how hard it was to make myself sit still for ten minutes in the morning to try the exercise, and how rarely I remembered to try seeing myself seeing in the midst of everyday life. I would frequently go two or three days without a single thought about or gesture toward the attention exercises, even though I intellectually believed this was the most important effort I could possibly be making. Without cultivating a different kind of attention – not passively absorbed in a daydream or any single preoccupation, but rather actively attuning itself to self, others, and to the current circumstances – how can one act with integrity or mutuality, with inquiry or intentional power?

In any event, for myself, I found that the meetings really did intensify a kind of searching beyond words for what it might be appropriate to ask or do... to the point where I could see how I sometimes came to meetings with a beautiful tidbit of experience from the week and a well-rehearsed speech about it. Could I let go of the nugget unspoken? Might it be more instructive to begin speaking without knowing what I was going to say? And what realms of silence and feeling were going unexplored while I preoccupied myself with questions of speaking? (By the way, are you still "seeing your seeing?" See what I mean?)

In addition to these weeknight meetings and, later, the practice of demanding sacred dances, the Sunday "Day of Work" occurred at a large country estate in Armonk, NY, with some 200 or so others. There, an inner exercise would be given at the beginning of the day. Then one would take on an outer task (e.g. helping to build the huge stone fireplace for the new dining hall) and report after lunch how one's experience of seeking to attend simultaneously to an inner and an outer task had gone.

The day usually ended with a twenty-minute reading from one of Gurdjieff's many unpublished talks. By that time, I would frequently find myself doing nothing more significant than trying not to fall asleep. Nevertheless, I was gradually being introduced to the alchemy of a post-cognitive attention that could, at first only at moments, observe oneself and others in the midst of action. Re-awakening to this dimension of being again and again and again was as exciting to imagine as it was hard to exercise in any given now.

But in the car driving home from the Workday, the silent concentration of the day would release itself in spontaneous chanting, a treasured ritual that to this day helps me find my center, my liveliness, and my sense of humility within an awesome creation.

Entering a PhD Program and Directing a War on Poverty Program

Through the Yale PhD Program in Individual and Organizational Behavior, I now hoped to gain a better understanding of how to shape personal leadership actions and organizational structures, so that they became intrinsically and transformationally educational by their very way of being designed and enacted. Chris Argyris, now both Department Chair and my advisor, accepted my proposal to engage in an action research project for my dissertation, during which I would attempt to lead such an intrinsically-educational organization that would invite all its participants to join in research on our own efforts. The dissertation would then not only document our experience, but also help to exemplify and define the new kind of social science that both Argyris and I were interested in doing. As far as I know, mine was to be the first action research dissertation that included the researcher as a subject to be studied.

At the same time, Morris and I had begun to dream about creating an intrinsically-educational organization. Our dream was to create a school in which both classrooms and the community as a whole become arenas for immediate experiential learning about the same issues to be studied in the academic curriculum. The analogy we chose was the development of a community, as studied through our own communal experience at this hypothetical school, on the one hand, and as approached through literature, poetry, the social sciences, and such natural sciences as ethology and ecology on the other. Classes would use intellectual resources (texts, movies, games, etc.), the students' own experiences in the city, the immediate classroom situation, and the general process of living together as analogical inputs into learning.

...Then one evening late in the fall, I suddenly found myself face-to-face with the chance to realize this dream. Joel Fleishman, my former boss at the Yale Summer High School, asked me whether I would like to seek a grant from the Office of Economic Opportunity (part of President Johnson's War on Poverty), to initiate a new summer school—a proposed Yale Upward Bound program for local-area high schoolers.

My proposal won Yale a grant, and, after a fruitless search for a Yale faculty member who would be willing to forego a summer of research for the privilege (?) of entering these unchartered waters, I was asked to take the role of Director rather than Associate Director. What a great opportunity, thought I, to build the school Morris and I had dreamed of, and to study myself in a leadership role for my doctoral dissertation. I wasn't experienced enough to be fazed by the fact that at the tender age of 22, with only one year of work experience in a small organization, I would be younger than the entire faculty, about the same age as the resident tutors, and not many years older than the students.

I began the initial work quickly and easily. Yale officials and New Haven educators were visited. For the first time in months, something important enough was happening in my life to take my mind and some of my heart off the pain of my total separation forever from the woman I loved.

During the winter and early spring of 1967, I was searching for the right first step for Upward Bound. I felt that the initial planning of the program would set the tone and limits for everything that followed. For example, if in our initial planning we *spoke* a great deal about experimenting without ever actually *behaving* experimentally, I doubted whether we would ever reach the point of behaving experimentally during the summer sessions themselves. Instead, the incongruity between our words and our behavior would make the first lesson of our school something like: 'Don't worry about doing what you say; we don't'.

As the number of my 'consultants' increased, so did their concern to get started and their prescriptions for how we ought to start. I, in turn, sensed a one-sidedness in most of their proposals that would miss the central aim of the school, and wished increasingly that they would recognize and help to distill each other's pressures, rather than focusing them all on me. I thought how funny and educational it would be for them suddenly to find themselves all together at a meeting charged with making the decisions each thought so simple from his or her particular perspective. This thought, initially no more than a passing fantasy, fused somehow with a growing recognition on my part that the dilemma of taking a first step was changing from 'How do *I* start this program?' to 'How do *we* start this program?' (Endnote 7)

Section II

Wondering in Action: How to Create Communities of Inquiry?

Chapter 5

First Attempt to Create a Community of Inquiry From Scratch: Yale Upward Bound, 1967

So... in February of 1967, what felt like the right collective first step for Yale Upward Bound became at once obvious and compelling. The first step would simply be to begin meeting together regularly to make the various major decisions that needed to be made. In this way, our first step as a school would adhere to the collaborative form of organization I hoped to realize. Our 'town and gown' advisors would come to weekly meetings, becoming more engaged and directly helpful than advisory boards usually become. At the same time, persons considering joining our staff could come to these meetings and experience the benefits and frustrations of working collaboratively and thus determine whether they were committed to this way of working before deciding to join us. Also, by analyzing tapes of these meetings and pointing out inconsistencies between our intentions and behaviors, I hoped to encourage the process of self-directed learning, first by the staff and me, then by the students. So, Morris and I invited everyone who had seemed concerned to help us to the first of a series of weekly meetings.

The decision to have meetings to begin making decisions about the school did not, of course, do away with the possibility of contradictions between my intention and my behavior. During the first meeting I felt I must concentrate on not becoming an ordinary, externally directive leader. I *did* have to concentrate, because people raised hands to speak, looked to me for recognition and waited expectantly after each speaker said something for my reaction. After describing this pattern to the group and explaining why it posed a problem for me (and us), I sometimes used the tactic of writing notes and neither responding to nor looking at what was going on.

This strategy was temporarily frustrated by Mike, one of the advisors, and David, a potential teacher, who insisted that I share my thinking about the program up to this point. I did so, but without any recommendation about how the group should act now.

Silence... Then, after some initial fumbling, and without my assistance, a conversation sprouted. Thereafter I never had to worry about being the sole initiator in the group.

Responding to success by playing it safe, I didn't say much for the rest of the meeting. After some lively discussions about how our summer school would tie into the New Haven public school and neighborhood structures, the conversation dragged, becoming boring and inconclusive. Still, I stayed in the background.

Afterwards I noted to myself, "I end up with a sense of failure as a participant at not having the courage to express my feeling when the discussion lost its force."

Of course, one might argue that my continued silence tested the group's capacity to reorient the conversation. I attempted to rescue this possible benefit of my behavior by pointing to the group's behavior as one of the dilemmas we faced when I wrote the first of my weekly meeting notes:

UPWARD BOUND MEETING Thursday, March 2, 1967

(I will try each week to write up a brief summary of our meeting for those who missed it, as well as my own analysis of the kinds of dilemmas we have encountered. Bill Torbert)

I opened the meeting by suggesting that: (1) I would try to act more as a researcher of the discussion than as a director; (2)

we might generate an agenda and introduce ourselves to one another at the same time; (3) two agenda items were, (a) should we draw students from a single neighborhood and school in New Haven and, if so, which? (b) should we be co-ed or all male?

After the introductions, which produced no more agenda items, I was asked to review my thinking about the program. Then we moved to a discussion of the single-neighborhood/single-school idea. A number of points were made: it would initially be more difficult to work with students from one area because of their anti-educational group-cohesion; but it would ultimately be easier to work with students from one area because after the program they would reinforce one another's pro-educational norms; we could intensify our influence by working in the Hill area, dovetailing with various other existing and planned programs; but we might find ourselves swamped by, or in conflict with, other organizations, damaging our uniqueness as an anti-school, so perhaps we should work with the Fairhaven area instead.

Questions were raised: is it our aim to help individuals get to college? Or are we primarily responsible for influencing the educational norms of a community? Do we wish by our choice of students and neighborhood to make our work as easy as possible for ourselves, or as difficult as possible? Since we will be inviting more new students to take part in the program next year, should we start with students from two areas and expand in both, or start with one area and continue with that area, or work with one area this year and another next year?

We felt we needed some information (which I will gather through some of you): given 200 students in the freshman class from the Hill, how many meet the financial criteria? How many students in Fairhaven meet the financial criteria? What is the racial constitution of these two areas? Where are the multi-problem families in New Haven?

DILEMMAS: (1) Toward the end of the meeting we found ourselves reiterating the same points, contradicting ourselves, whispering to one another, and, in short, coming close to the atmosphere of a classroom where one is prohibited from exploring the most important comment: this discussion has ceased to be important for me; (2) we were unable to reach a decision, a difficulty we will have to overcome if we truly intend eventually to have even more persons, i.e. our students, share in the decision-making; (3) we were unable to take up our second agenda item, or to project an agenda for next week which would permit us to arrive with some of the kinds of information we found ourselves lacking this week. In sum, as I see it, we found that, deprived of ordinary directive leadership which takes responsibility for how things are done at a business meeting, we could be facile at the level of intellectual principles about our unique organizational intentions, but this facility was not sufficient to induce unique organizational operations.

My tendency to avoid conflict and my inability to name my anger

Only later, with Argyris' help when I debriefed that meeting with him, could I begin to see how deeply my behavior at this first meeting could be interpreted as reflecting my urge to avoid conflict. At the time I could see this pattern in my maintenance of the passive role throughout the meeting. But I did not see that by avoiding looking at people I had also been avoiding a possible open conflict about leadership. Moreover, my use of written notes to discuss my perceptions of the outcome of the meeting afterwards again permitted me to avoid confronting others directly.

Upon reflection, avoidance of conflict seemed a pattern in my earlier life too, modeled by my parents who never had any fights with one another that I was ever aware of. I also remembered the time two years before in my first encounter group, when another participant pronounced me "unbelievably angelic."

On yet another occasion, an acquaintance told me he found me difficult to understand as a person – I seemed terribly intellectual and distant to him. For example, he continued, he had never seen me get angry, really angry. I would become far more human for him, he said, if I could just once express anger at something. I found this comment somewhat awkward since I could not very well prove my ability to express anger on the spot, there being nothing angrifying about our conversation as far as I could see. When I replied that it was true that I rarely expressed anger, but that I believed I could express it when appropriate, he asked, 'Why don't you get angry right now?'

'Well, there is nothing to get angry about,' I replied, somewhat put out by such a nonsensical request.

'What if I goad you into anger?' he asked.

'I don't see what that would prove – it wouldn't be real,' I replied with a growing sense of awkwardness, as I began to suspect that he might actually proceed to do just that.

'Come on, why don't you get angry with me, Bill?' he said in a fake voice.

'Don't be ridiculous,' I replied, somewhat strangled and increasingly uncomfortable and uncertain about how to respond so as to avoid falling into his trap.

'Go ahead, Bill, a little anger won't hurt,' he urged with maddening sweetness.

At this my face grew red (though it was a long moment before I realized it); I clamped my mouth shut and decided not to say a word. I was damned if I would play such a silly game and get angry merely because he asked me to.

After a short silence, he remarked coyly, 'I do believe you are angry *now*.'

'I am not!' burst from me vehemently. And I realized immediately that I *was* angry and that the only way I could have 'avoided his trap' was to feel comfortable in expressing my anger at his game. But I had not even been able to recognize or name my anger until he had exposed it.

■ ■ ■

Speaking of anger and conflict, many of us met often to discuss our responsibilities as graduate students with deferments in the face of the Vietnam War. Most of us saw that war from early on as a horrendous mistake – tactically, strategically, and in term's of America's principles. Tactically, you can't sustainably defend or win territory 10,000 miles from home. Strategically, the government we were claiming to support in the south was less legitimate among the Vietnamese than the one in the north. And, in terms of by now long-forgotten American Constitutional principles, Congress did not declare war on Vietnam.

Back from Somalia and now serving as Assistant Secretary of State for Congressional Relations, my father was regularly trying to justify the war to Senator Fulbright and the Senate Foreign Relations Committee. Most of my friends were against the war, except for one undergraduate named John Kerry, who was inclined to support the war and who eventually entered the Navy. In an attempt to get both my father and my friends engaged in the same serious inquiry, I invited Dad to speak in my rooms at Yale. My father was friendly, the dialogue was strong, and Kerry said afterwards that it was his first exposure to a passionate, principled, and pragmatic argument against the war. (As many readers will recall, Kerry served honorably during the war and then returned to the U.S. to lead an organization of veterans against the war, before he became a Senator, a candidate for president, and, most recently, Secretary of State.)

During the following year, I arranged two weekends at our home in Georgetown, when our entire nuclear family – Dee, as well as Dad and Mom and Jim and I – met to discuss the Vietnam War. Four of us were deeply against the war, and Dad would refuse to reveal any personal position because his job was to defend the war, and if he were to speak against it, it would be his duty to resign. Nevertheless, we pressed him hard and exhaustively on how the administration responded to this or that point. To my ear, way too many of his answers had a tone of "we know things you don't, and I can't tell you for national security reasons." Once, or maybe twice, at moments of peak passion, Dad got up quietly and left the room, but he returned each time.

In retrospect, I have read about the painfully tragic stories of other inter-generational struggles between Vietnam-era "administration fathers" and "anti-war sons." I'm thinking here in particular: of Secretary of State Dean Rusk and his son John; of General Carroll of the Defense Intelligence Agency and his son James, whose award-winning ***American Requiem*** tells their microcosm of the America-in-the-Vietnam-war story; and of CIA Director William Casey and his son Carl who later made a documentary movie about "The Man Nobody Knew."

By comparison, I am oddly awed by our family's cohesiveness even at the height of our disagreements about Americans fighting in Vietnam. Perhaps the worst strain occurred when Dad found himself in the position of being asked to post bond for brother Jim in court in New York on the day he would have been graduating from Columbia had he not been in jail instead, after participating in the occupation of Columbia's administrative offices in the spring of 1968. While Dad defended our right to protest the war, he drew the line, he said, at obstructing our own education. Nevertheless, he bailed Jim out.

Toward the First Week of the Summer Session

As it turned out, during the second meeting of the group of advisors I'd called together to create Yale Upward Bound, we did begin to make decisions as a group, allowing us all to feel easier about our ability to get things done. Nevertheless, with each succeeding meeting my sense of the magnitude of the contradiction between my ideal and our actual behavior increased. I vacillated between feeling I was directing too strongly and not strongly enough. At the same time, I saw how unaware most people were, not only of the actual effects of their behavior, but also of the very possibility of becoming aware and of acting differently. What I was beginning to learn about self-observation-in-action in the Gurdjieff Work and about observing group dynamics unfold in some of my classes and encounter groups was obviously not part of the broader culture's curriculum at that time.

On the other hand, from a purely practical perspective, the process of using staff meetings as a forum for testing personal commitment to the program paid real dividends. Several people who were otherwise highly qualified de-selected themselves because they felt they needed more structure in order to work well. Since the program never lost its hectic, oscillating, ambiguous, emotional quality, they probably would not have worked well during the summer, so it is better that they were not lured to participate on the basis of rhetorically shared ideals. At the same time, a third of the program's staff (eight) was attracted to it directly through these meetings. In addition, our advisors became actively involved and personally helpful rather than mere representatives-on-paper of their various organizations.

By the time our seven-week residential program began, I had hired 24 staff members (six of whom worked voluntarily or part-time) on a budget for 15. Of these, five were to teach 'core' classes of 12 students apiece for two hours each morning on the topic of the week. Another 10 were full-time resident tutors who, along with every other available staff member, would tutor three students in reading and writing in the final hour of each morning and would assume primary responsibility for six students living in the same dormitory entry during the evenings. I and two Associate Directors, Valery Jones and Rob Folbach, took the administrative roles. Morris and five others helped with counseling, drama and sports on a part-time basis during the afternoons. We even had our own doctor, a medical student who probably deserves the prize for the single most constructive intervention of the summer, as you will shortly see...

It was a young staff – only six members were over 30 and ten members were college undergraduates. Ten were women, fourteen men. Eight of the staff members (all full-time) were black. Thirty-six of our students were boys, twenty-four girls. Forty were black, twenty white.

In terms of which students we chose, we reasoned that if the War on Poverty was based on the assumption that our country had not been serving a segment of the population well, then we should work with those least well served. We therefore decided, first of all, that we should take our students after their ninth grade year, rather than after tenth or eleventh grades as most Upward Bound programs did. We did this because many students turn 16 and drop out of school during tenth grade. Given our philosophy of serving those least well served before, we wished to reach students who were not only economically poor, but who were also doing least well in their current schools. So, rather than taking students who got B's and C's at school, as most Upward Bound programs did, we chose 60 students three-fifths of whose grades in the ninth grade were F's. In other words, instead of choosing the students most qualified for success, we chose precisely those who had shown the least likelihood of succeeding in educational terms.

I certainly had myself worked up into a keen sense of historical anxiety about the significance of this new little summer school in New Haven during this time of War in Vietnam and War on Poverty. I was in the last class of entering graduate students who received student deferments from the Vietnam War, but my Andover roommate Dave Hackett had volunteered for the Special Forces. Given the citizen draft (that key to citizen alertness about whether a war is potentially justifiable), others of my generation were dying in Vietnam. Indeed, on Memorial Day at the remembrance ceremony at Andover that I happened to attend I had been completely shocked to hear David's name read out. I felt that my duty on the frontline of the War on Poverty ought to make as significant a contribution to my country as his.

Then too, the stakes were especially high because I was studying my own leadership and the successes and failures of this new kind of school for my dissertation. And the dissertation itself was, in turn, supposed to illustrate a new kind of social science that I was beginning to call "action science."

Creating a Community of Inquiry

At dawn one Sunday morning towards the end of June, unable to sleep, I paced the New Haven streets, jaggedly anxious about whether the program would begin that afternoon as scheduled. In the week before our departure for the camp, the practical complexities of taking 80 inexperienced people to a primitive camp for a week became nerve-rackingly evident. Buses to be scheduled, linen rented, food and utensils for wood-burning stoves to be bought, cabins to be assigned, curricular materials to be prepared and shipped – new details occurred to someone each day, and I was sure two or three necessities had probably been overlooked altogether.

The curriculum for the first week was dedicated to the intellectual and existential topic "New Beginnings: Creating a Community of Inquiry." The design included everything from e.e.cummings poetry ("Pity this poor monster man unkind not…") to our own Constitutional Convention whereby we (students and staff) would design the following six weeks of the program. But would anyone come to this party we were throwing?

To my relief, children and parents, dressed in their Sunday best, laden with suitcases, began to appear half an hour early, in the courtyard of the Yale residential college where we would spend the six weeks after the week at camp. Lemonade and cookies were being served by some resident tutors, some others handed out address lists at the gate, and the rest of us found ourselves in pleasant and animated conversation about our intentions for the summer with parents and other relatives of the students.

After I had made a little speech to the assembled multitude about how we really were going to be a different kind of school, we loaded the buses and all available cars and made off for the camp. Later that night when things quieted down, Morris, Rob, Valery, and I spent a pleasant five minutes congratulating ourselves in hushed tones near the cabins and trading first impressions of various students.

Then we heard the first shrieks from the girls' cabins. The girls were being attacked by the boys. Well, that was only to be expected, vexatious for the staff for a while and fun for the kids. However, the boys' marauding expeditions did not cease. Moreover, it seemed that the girls themselves were inviting the boys in, making assignations through the windows, opening doors for the boys, and slipping out themselves. Since there was no evidence that any of the kids wanted to cooperate at all, nor that they in any way respected or feared the authority of the staff, it appeared utterly impossible to prevent them from doing as they would.

At the same time, however, another kind of interaction was beginning to take place. Fewer staff members were available for 'chasing' duties as the night wore on because increasingly they found themselves calming down one or two students and entering into their first conversations with them. It was during these conversations that several boys first confessed that they were banding together and making a lot of noise because they were afraid of the forest sounds. Such discussions sometimes led to immediate zoology lessons, the tutor identifying each animal sound and describing the characteristics of the animal in question. The following day several lunch-table conversations could be overheard, with one student deriding the others who reported disliking the animal sounds, while self-importantly (but of course casually) relaying his new tidbits of knowledge to them.

Other discussions during the night turned to a comparison of the city and the known fears of the street *versus* the country and the unknown fears of the forest. Participants in these conversations provided some of the initial fuel for class arguments the following morning on the week's curricular theme, 'New Beginnings' or 'Experimenting with the Strange.'

The night-time marauding ended after the second night. We discovered that miraculously, after 48 hours with virtually no sleep, everyone knew everyone else very well indeed, and everyone desperately needed to sleep the third night.

The first cooperative institution that began to work well during the daytime was the early evening International Volleyball Championships. By contrast, the morning meetings to create our school-wide Constitution at first seemed pure and somewhat malicious mayhem. Weren't these like assemblies at high school, where somebody on the stage talks at you while you talk and play among yourselves, occasionally hoot at the stage, and try your best to incite the teachers to throw somebody else out?

During the first and second mornings, while I was trying to ask the students what areas of school life needed organization and who should do it, pandemonium ruled in the hall of the main lodge. Even if I managed to get a student's attention by taking his intended aside seriously, or even when some student made a directly serious contribution, no one else was listening. Or if one side of the room momentarily quieted sufficiently to listen to one of its midst speak, they were soon diverted into screaming imprecations at those on the other side of the room who were not listening.

Our experiment in self-determination threatened once again to collapse, as it did so many times those first days. In retrospect, it is easy to see that it had not yet begun. But at the time I felt as though I was misrepresenting matters when, at the end of the first day's meeting, I announced the five areas of school life that 'we' had decided required structuring. The 'we' amounted to several suggestions shouted from the floor, as well as a couple of things I'd had in mind, which made sense to me. Most persons present hadn't heard them mentioned, forgot them as soon as they heard me summarize them, and probably didn't know why we were there in the first place.

The second day provided a slightly different experience. I had assigned each of the five areas to one of the five class sections to create a plan for the school by Wednesday. Since the teachers raised these issues with their sections Tuesday morning, most students became aware that something was happening and that something had happened at Monday's general meeting. Of course, they didn't really believe they were to have power over such intimate features of their lives as when and for how long classes should occur, when they might wander off campus and about town, and whether there should be any lights-out policy.

So Tuesday's general meeting maintained the same level of pandemonium as Monday's, but this time focused accusatorily on me (this is progress?). If they could do what they wanted, why did they have to have any classes at all? Could boys and girls room together? How about placing only students on the Discipline Committee? Who made the decision that Tim Weston's section would deal with rules about visitors? Why didn't I agree right away with the suggestions that were being made?

I felt exhausted and persecuted after the meetings, especially when several staff members who had doubted the possibility or efficacy of self-structuring all along adopted an I-told-you-so attitude toward me. I was disheartened by the unreasonableness of the students who seemed to totally overlook the need to reach common agreements rather than just establish individual preferences. Not until Morris sat down with me could I begin to see the emotional, developmental logic of students' moving from powerlessness, to self-assertion, and only then – only once one has a sense of personal efficacy – to common organization. So they were practicing self-assertion on me? That was Morris's optimistic theory. Optimistic?

The third morning the attack shifted from me to the student representatives from each section who rose to deliver the preliminary plans devised by their section. It may have been because each representative had a dozen backers to help quiet the others or because each section wanted its plan listened to, but I thought I could detect a slight hiatus in the commotion now and again. Nevertheless, the representatives were annoyed and defensive about their reception. If they tried to argue points with their questioners and detractors, the latter would turn away or the argument would be overwhelmed by the hubbub. I tried to help the speakers by calling for order from time to time, encouraging them to go on, or noting the occasional point that seemed to receive general assent or general dissent.

Afterwards we ran off a two-page summary of the different proposals for the sections to study the following morning. Each section was also to review its own proposal in view of the comments made at the general meeting and check for any inconsistencies with the other proposals. We were to make final decisions the next morning.

Something made the fourth meeting more meeting-like. Perhaps the tangibility of proposals on paper and the votes being taken made the difference. Perhaps community development had been occurring amidst the apparent disorganization of the previous nights and mornings. Perhaps the sections surprised one another into attention by modifying their proposals to take others' opinions into account. In less than an hour, a series of consensual or majority decisions were reached about morning and afternoon schedules, visiting hours, rules and enforcement. All of the decisions seemed to take into account the foremost needs of students, staff and parents.

The decision about enforcement was perhaps the most memorable. It constituted what was to become the most significant and controversial institutional body during the summer – the Discipline Committee. The Committee was to consist of fifteen members, ten students – two from each section – and five staff – two tutors, two teachers and an administrator. Elections were to occur Friday morning.

"He started it when he hit me back"

Thursday afternoon I drove into New Haven and back, picking up some equipment and the staff's paychecks. It was the first afternoon I could imagine leaving the camp and returning without chaos intervening. But on my return to camp, I felt a sinking sensation as I parked outside the dining-hall. At a time of afternoon when everyone was customarily dispersed in the vicinity of the shore, all the students were congregated around the dining-hall, muttering among themselves ominously, without a staff member in sight.

I found the entire staff assembled in the dining-hall, talking angrily around a weeping Regina, one of the tutors. Morris briefed me in a whisper while my other ear and my eyes took in tones and signs of tension, wounded pride and polarized conflict.

There had been a fight at the shore between several students and two tutors, Regina and Tom – all black. Other staff members and students had rushed up to part the combatants, but not before ugly words and hard blows had embittered them. Now Regina and Tom and some other staff members were demanding that the six students be expelled from the school because their kind of violence would otherwise destroy the school and the dignity and authority of all staff members.

Other staff members were arguing vehemently that unilateral expulsion of students by the staff would destroy the school and our credibility, since we as yet had no rules to govern such a situation and were thus governed only by the principle of collaboration with the students. To break this principle was to become untrustworthy and inauthentic.

Time was critical. The longer the conflict continued between these two philosophical factions on the staff, the more divided they would become, and the more divided the staff as a whole would become from the anxious and angry students outside. At the same time, I felt totally uninformed about what had actually happened. Who had 'started' the fight? What had the dispute been about? Why had other measures failed? It appeared the rest of the staff knew the answers to these questions, for they were no longer mentioning such concrete matters.

I did not know what to do. It was clear some kind of leadership was desperately needed, and the way people turned towards me when I entered indicated that they expected the leadership to come from me. Yet in terms of knowledge about what to do, I was the poorest present. And, to find out more would take time we didn't have.

I forestalled decision for one minute by moving around to three staff members who I knew had rapport with the students and asking them to go outside. I didn't tell them what to do. The situation was too far ahead of any of us to merit instructions.

Then for a few moments, the argument around me bordered on the concrete. Each side charged the other with responsibility for the fight, but offered no details. This made me realize that the concrete facts of who had done what to whom had **not** yet been agreed upon. That gave me the courage to do what I had thought there was no time for: I jumped in strongly and insisted that each 'side' tell what events and interpretations made the other side responsible for the fight.

A clear portrait emerged. Several male students were teasing one of the girls, pretending they were going to throw her into the water. As was often true among our black students, the play was noisy and touchy. Boys put their arms around the girl and she screamed.

Many of the staff had great difficulty distinguishing when amusement turned to anger, mutuality to coercion, and control to chaos in such situations because we associated *all* touching-cum-screaming with anger, coercion, and chaos. Herself a middle class black, Regina had decided that anger, coercion, and chaos **were** occurring, so she moved quickly into the group to rescue the girl and put a stop to the harassment.

In so doing, she shoved Jimmy, the smallest but fieriest of the boys. He struck at her. Seeing this, Tom, who was Regina's boyfriend as well as a fellow tutor, dove into the fray, tackling Jimmy. With this, the other guys in the group fell upon Tom.

In short, there was no objective observer of the situation, nor a shared standard of behavior, and this was the cause of the conflict. Neither side could be proven wrong. More than that, like Berkeley's tree in the forest, not falling if unheard and unseen, neither side *was* right or wrong. No common culture or code yet existed among us within which there were rights or wrongs (other than applicable law and the ten commandments). But this condition was itself so unfamiliar that it had remained unperceived. Persons, when deeply threatened, assumed they knew what had happened, what was right, and what they were talking about.

Once we had reviewed the facts, most staff members saw that the primary issue was still to create community among us, rather than to brand one side or the other as responsible for disrupting an imaginary community. The incident highlighted the danger, especially in a cross-cultural situation, of acting on one's own assumptions about what was happening rather than questioning the participants. The incident also spotlighted a form of behavior that seemed to be anathema to all (in spite of how easily it had occurred): physical violence by any member of the community. If we could agree that for us violence would be a primary 'wrong' from here on out, our sense of community could be enhanced.

At this point, decisions were made quickly. We asked the students to join us in the dining-hall. While that was happening, questions arose about who should speak, what line should be taken, what result we would seek. I can't recall exactly how the decisions were reached in that brief minute, but the outcome was a perfect balance. I spoke first as leader of the whole community to make clear what would be *done* – what was going to 'come down'. I said simply that the incident was obviously disastrous, that our whole endeavor would quickly disintegrate if we had further such incidents, that nobody was to blame in this case any more than anybody else, that from this moment there would be a rule of no physical violence between any members of the community, to be enforced by expulsion for offenders whether they be staff or students, and that we would continue to meet together now until we resolved this conflict.

The students relaxed immediately and disbelievingly. A murmur ran around the room. They had expected the staff finally to unveil its power, now that there was a crisis, and prove that all the collaborative talk was bullshit. They had expected to have a fight and be beaten. They were disarmed.

But, being well-versed in the politics of chaos, they quickly imagined the next problem. The students nearest me were forecasting: "Tom and Regina never goin' to live in the same house as Jimmy an' them. They be out for each other every night."

Now our Vista Volunteer, Rick, spoke to the community. It had been agreed that he was the member of the community with maximum credibility to all, knowing the students more intimately than the staff and not being a staff member himself (although he had volunteered to be present all week and to cook). He also spoke in the students' idiom, which I could not yet even fully understand, much less speak.

Rick repeated and filled out what I had said, reminding the students of what they'd hoped for and still needed out of the program, using examples from the streets to illustrate how damaging vendettas arising from false pride could be, citing my action as final proof that this program was different. His rap, picked everyone up with his urgency and re-inspired them, just when the darkening evening and the prospect of having to start from scratch to prepare a delayed dinner threatened to intensify the gloom.

When he felt he had regenerated some possibility of hope, Rick pressed to the conclusion that on the spur of the moment seemed to him the most feasible. He insisted that for the sake of the whole program all the participants in the fight join him outside in order to work through their bitterness to a reconciliation. 'Let's go!' he ended, turning to the door.

Into the moment of tense stillness that ensued, I called on everyone else to help prepare tonight's dinner, trying to stir up as much common activity as possible. I could see the participants in the fight using the commotion to cover their exit, while eagerness to quell hunger pangs knit the rest of the group into a more smoothly functioning unit than I had yet seen.

In retrospect, Rick's last action seemed a stroke of genius. The community had not yet developed to the point where it could have helped the intensive confrontation required among the participants. And, in front of the rest of us, the participants would probably have sought refuge in their wounded pride. Yet the matter needed immediate resolution. None of the combatants would likely have taken the first step towards a peaceful settlement. But by their willingness to step out the door and face one another they all implicitly took that first step together.

All I know about that little meeting is that Rick began by insisting that whatever was said belonged only within that group at that time and he never wanted to hear any stories about what went on from others. Just as everyone sat down to a cold supper supplemented by hot dogs, the little group reentered the dining-hall, and Rick announced shortly that everyone had shaken hands. The dignity of the event spoke for itself. Everyone, students and staff, was amazed.

As I had said to the parents four evenings before, this really would be a different kind of school.

■ ■ ■

The next evening we traveled to the Newport Jazz Festival. The trip both ways and our time at the Festival were utterly tranquil. One of the performers was a guy I'd never heard of before with a terrible, uninterpretable, whiny voice and harmonica and guitar whom all of us – black and white, student and staff alike – disliked. His name was Bob Dylan. But there was also a woman named Joan Baez whose voice was thrillingly pure and fine.

■ ■ ■

Looking back over that first week, I can see that I experienced and trusted an intuitive sense about when to 'take charge' much more than I ever had in situations with the staff during the spring meetings. Whether it was a matter of formulating an assignment for my tutees, or of pushing towards a governing structure despite chaotic meetings, or of making instantaneous decisions during Thursday's conflict, I did not become paralyzed by the apparent inconsistency between unilateral leadership on the one hand and a commitment to collaboration on the other, nor by the apparent inconsistency between a need for action and a need for inquiry. Both were needed all the time in the right blends, activated from a post-cognitive, non-dual awareness.

Put differently, I seemed to realize that week, without reflecting about it, that most, if not all, of us were not yet fully capable of pure collaboration…And that there were ways in which I (or someone else, such as Rick, the Vista Volunteer) could structure situations that preserved and even enhanced our collective capacity to collaborate in the future far more effectively than refraining from a strong initiative would have done.

Or, to put this yet again differently, a particular person, such as Rick after the fight, may take what appears to be unilateral leadership at a given moment because he succeeds in expressing a common aspiration. Or, to put it still differently, there is a principle or spirit of collaboration that a single person or a minority may sometimes have to defend against the momentary impulses of the majority. I had felt in this position at our general meetings the first two mornings of the week.

As the reader may imagine, these were not the last of our "exciting" meetings or of our difficult conflicts. Progress was made in all sorts of unexpected ways as well, however. For example, our volunteer doctor discovered that half of our students required eyeglasses, and we financed them with some of the money originally budgeted to 'travel expenses for lecturers.' Between the new eye glasses and the interesting reading and writing classes, our students on average improved five grade levels in reading skills by the end of the summer.

Another delightful unexpected success occurred when our quiet art teacher and her charges produced an end-of-session art show that stunned parents, staff, and students with its glorious color and composition. Spontaneously, numerous sales were made, often the first money the students had ever legitimately earned. I still have my first art purchase ever (I think I paid a whopping $10 for it). My painting by Billy Deptula is of a very large flower in a dessert... that reminds me of the drawings in St. Exupery's ***Le Petit Prince*** *[The Little Prince]*).

During the following year only two of our 60 likely dropouts actually did drop out from school, cutting New Haven's dropout rate in half. And students improved their grade averages by two levels on average (e.g. from D to B).

■ ■ ■

At the end of the summer session, I dragged myself onto an airplane to meet my mother at an ancient peasant farmhouse in Italy that she had recently bought and was 'furbishing.' For the next three weeks, I spent up to 18 hours a day sleeping at the home Mom named "La Fratta." One could sit under an olive tree on the terrace at any time of day and simply watch down the hill, across the valley, and into the two ridge tops and the changing horizon beyond... The patterns of light, shadow, and color flowed across the landscape like a Monet series of haystacks or cathedrals.

Or one could read a long science fiction book like ***Dune*** or ***The Einstein Intersection*** until one's brain threatened to congeal...

■ ■ ■

In my absence, New Haven erupted in riots... Setting the tone for a bitter 1967-68 school year of disruptions in the city's high schools; and, in the nation's political arena, the assassinations of both Martin Luther King and Bobby Kennedy. (Endnote 8)

Chapter 6

The Three-Ring Circus, 1968

During the following school year (1967-68), I entered into an entirely different, much more fragmented rhythm, held together only by my conviction that all my activities served a similar end.

First off, I was living in the most unpleasant year-long place I have ever inhabited before or since, an apartment with Morris and Rob from the YUB core staff. Our space was floored in linoleum and furnished with various dental cabinets, depressingly reminding us of its prior use. Then there were our contributions (or lack thereof) to the scene: our graduate student lack of furniture or any form of adornment for the walls, except for Morris's posters of Marlene Dietrich, Lauren Bacall, Sigmund Freud, and Ho Chi Minh. Rob's contribution, as I learned in more detail 46 years later, was to absent himself as much as humanly possible. Put differently, my very good relationship with Rob did not improve because of our shared rooming situation that year.

Morris was not a cleaner, and the other two of us were out almost all the time... So, the dirty dishes and glasses and pots and pans filling the sink in the kitchen at the far back of the apartment was a definite No-Fly-Zone for guests, except for three or four times during the year when we cleaned up and gave a big party.

The party I remember best was in honor of Hannah Arendt, with Hans Jonas also in attendance, along with many of the leading Yale philosophy professors, as well as another dozen or so graduate students and Upward Bound staff members. Arendt with her cigarettes and her friendly but challenging conversation about the human capacity for vision and action – for birthing new possibilities, not just following orders – left an indelible portrait on my mind that the relatively recent (2013) movie about her controversial book ***Eichman in Jerusalem*** further intensified. I must confess, however, that for me the highlight of that evening occurred at around 2am when all the professional philosophers were long gone... and the Beatles just-released ***Magical Mystery Tour*** was playing on the turntable.

In the meantime, I was also discovering just how often Morris was drunk, and just how often when drunk he wanted to climb into my bed at midnight... Requiring me to lever him in turn into his own.

During the days, I was taking the full graduate student load of four courses each semester, with papers. Also during the days, I was working at Upward Bound, securing new funding for the next summer, and going through the program design and staff build-up for the second session, not to mention meeting with our students every other Saturday morning throughout the year.

I was also devoted to researching the core staff's experience of the program and understanding how the first year's Upward Bound experience ought to influence our approach to the second year. In addition, I was commuting to the Gurdjieff Work in New York two and sometimes three times a week, including most Sundays. On the side, I was hosting a group of some dozen graduate students from around the university, in an improvisational drama evening every other week.

My Three-Ring Circus

At that time, I can remember liking to think of my life (rather grandiosely, but also with some sense of humor) as a three-ring circus – thinking of the three rings as being concentric to one another.

In the innermost ring, I was trying to find some more valid, more awake, subjective state – a kind of attention that experiences one's own thoughts, feelings, and sensations objectively, impartially, and simultaneously instead of losing oneself in whatever thought or feeling is foremost. That ring was symbolized by my relationship to the Gurdjieff Work, where no one was supposed to talk unnecessarily.

People stood like humble, anonymous lampposts with eyes to ground in the waiting hall of the Gurdjieff Foundation in the Upper East Side brownstone. Once or twice I saw Bill Murray there, the most humble, anonymous, and still of us all. Years later Murray contributed to the legacy of Gurdjieff and Ouspensky via the wildly successful comedy ***Ground Hog Day***, a kind of adaptation of Ouspensky's novel ***Strange Life of Ivan Osokin***.)

During the mostly silent New York meetings, I would at times be aware of the soft sound of myself breathing, feel the presence of energy in my entire spinal column, taste the liquid in my mouth, feel the occasional spoken words trilling in the aviary of my night-mind, emptying backward toward the non-dual attention at the source of thought and action. At other times, my back would hurt, my mind would flit among the women I was attracted to, others' voices and ways of presenting themselves would grate on my nerves, and the moves and pauses of the lead student, my spiritual teacher, would feel almost menacing, in spite of his soft and frequently-jovial voice. How could he be so damn aware all the time? What could make anyone want to do that? – I mean really: all the time?

Another Work activity was "Movements" – sacred dances created by Gurdjieff and the Russian composer Thomas de Hartmann, to re-present the archetypal action of universal laws of consciousness, energy, and matter. I can attest from experience that these 'movements' are literally impossible to do, unless you are seeking a very special kind of awareness of the body, unless you are feeling toward a deepening wishing, and unless you are using the mind in a very unaccustomed, purely mathematical way. My mind and body seemed especially spectacularly uncoordinated during most of these movements classes…

What were we attempting to study? My older friend and fellow student in the Bay Area, Jerry Needleman, put it this way in his early book ***A Sense of the Cosmos***,

> *Time, energy, (and) causality are part of me. Time – whatever it may be – pervades my body, my emotions, my experiences,*

everything that is in myself. And whatever energy is, it is obviously my life and movement, my power in all senses of the word. As for causality, can it be studied apart from observing in myself the forces that influence my own existence?

...In the great spiritual disciplines of the world, the path of self-knowledge is precisely the study of time, energy and causality in oneself. (p97)

In my imagined three-ring circus, all of these "inner ring," 1st-person self-study activities of the Work itself were supposed to support my more paltry efforts to become more fully present when on my own during all the other times of the week.

The Second Ring of the Circus

The second or middle ring of my life could be described as the relationship between my thoughts and feelings and my actual behavior in any social setting. My graduate work with Chris Argyris in Individual and Organizational Behavior symbolically re-presented the second ring of my personal psychodrama. Here, in classes and in my own research, I was focusing primarily on the relationship (and discrepancies) between my own values, on the one hand, and my actual enacted patterns of behavior on the other (as revealed by tape recordings of meetings). I was also reviewing all the empirical research and theorizing in our field intended to illuminate these questions. Gradually, I was coming to see a very general regularity in individual, organizational, and societal development – that at each scale one could trace an evolution from an age of *dependence* to an age of *independence* to an age of possible *inter-independence*.

In particular, I was asking how I and the core staff at Upward Bound could generate more creative, productive, collaborative, inter-independent relationships among ourselves and throughout our small community of teachers and students, when all of us were more accustomed to predominantly authoritative, dependency-generating organizing, or predominantly collegiate, independence-generating organizing. The core staff and I engaged in a series of research meetings that increased the trust and intimacy among most of us, as well as our sense of shared vision – in short, our sense of working inter-independently. And those meetings also led me to fire one member who could not seem to listen to or work productively with the rest of us. This turned out to be a great lesson for me because, although I was scared of taking such an irreversible step (to generate such conflict), this person found a job that suited her much better within a week and came by to thank me deeply. Meanwhile, the rest of us breathed a big sigh of relief.

Chris Argyris was at the forefront of the field in theorizing about how to intervene practically in organizations and how to use knowledge about how senior teams are actually strategizing and performing to get them to improve their strategizing and performing. It is truly difficult to do justice to the degree of Chris' influence over my thinking and acting. So many of his ideas grounded my work at the time and later. For example:

- the idea that persons increase their sense of psychological success only when achieving goals that they have set, not when achieving goals others have set for them;
- the idea that the true sign of high self-esteem is the capacity to help others raise their self-esteem;
- the idea that attempting to unilaterally protect someone else from some 'truth,' based on the inference that it will hurt them, is patronizing and can radically misfire; and
- the distinction between our 'espoused theory' about how we act and our actual 'theory-in-use,' which might be quite incongruous (as I had first learned when my Elihu friends refused to work with Chris).

In the realm of practices, Chris introduced me to:

- the very possibility of real-time inquiry about a conversation or work project in the midst of it...

- the practice of balancing advocacy and inquiry in conversation if it is to become truly mutual and is to reveal and potentially transform the deeper patterns of trust and power in a situation...
- the practice of holding informal, voluntary 'intellectual evenings' in the informal setting of one's own home... and
- the practice of recording conversations in order to be able to study participants' (including one's own) actual practices.

The Third Ring of My Circus

The third and outermost ring of my life, as I then envisioned it, constituted the arena within which my performance effected outcomes intended to be of value to me and others.

At the beginning of my second year in the doctoral program, I seemed to be progressing as expected in my scholarly life. I was also doing well in terms of outcomes from the point of view of earning my own living. And, although it had seemed a close call all the way through the Upward Bound summer session, we seemed to have succeeded in winning the hearts and minds of most of our students by creating an unusually collaborative kind of organization that facilitated personal transformation.

As the year after the first Upward Bound summer unfolded, however, my sense of success in co-ordinating the three concentric rings of my circus declined significantly. Nothing seemed to be progressing nearly as smoothly as one might hope, let alone with the timing and artistry of a three-ring circus performance.

I've already noted that I in fact rarely practiced the Gurdjieff attention work except at specific Gurdjieff Work activities. Nor was my graduate work in Organizational Behavior advancing smoothly. First, I dropped out of my second statistics course rather than finishing it. Next, I intervened in the departmental firing of a secretary by the new department chairman who was taking over from Argyris. My intervention did **not** get the secretary re-instated, but **did** get Chris angry at me for butting into the big boys' business. Finally, in the late Spring,

I failed my Qualifying Exams. (I was asked to write a long paper the following fall on each of the three questions I was regarded as having failed.)

Moreover, if the first summer of Upward Bound was an extending, draining, almost-always-nearly-failing-but-finally-succeeding 'comedy,' then the second winter and summer of Upward Bound turned toward tragedy, including the dual tragedies of the assassinations of Martin Luther King and Bobby Kennedy.

Not only was my three-ring-circus not really going well from the point of view of its outcomes, but the very image of my life as three concentric rings altogether omits the central emotional process for me of that year and my resolution of it: namely, my personal loneliness, leading to my engagement, and my wedding. Near Christmas time, I turned toward my former girlfriend from next door in Washington, even though we had split the prior year, and even though I had been the initiator of the split. After several dates toward the end of that fall, more promising than the ones before, I asked her to marry me. She agreed, and we celebrated our wedding in early June, 1968, at the National Cathedral in Washington.

Because of my commitment to Upward Bound and to living the rough life, I had arranged for my wife and myself to live in one of the student dorms for the 7-week program – an arrangement not calculated to optimize the growth of quiet intimacy between us. The following fall, my wife found little connection with the Gurdjieff Work and soon discontinued her attendance. The decisive moment occurred about half way between New Haven and New York, in the parking lot next to the hockey field where she'd just played while I watched. She told me she was returning to New Haven, not continuing to New York with me now or again. No, the marriage was not starting well, but we were both deeply committed to talking things through and spent untold hours seriously dedicated to making the marriage work. One thing that did *not* work from our wedding night on, but which we did *not* talk about, was our love-making, to which we both brought equal amounts of inexperience – she stiff; me over-excited, early-ejaculating, and deeply embarrassed.

The Second Spring and Summer of Upward Bound

As already foreshadowed, the second spring and summer of Yale Upward Bound in 1968 was a time when I learned how small a leaf is a personal mission and how small a branch is a visionary school — even one with some considerable special identity to many of its students, summer faculty, and core staff — when a broad national and global social lightning storm is burning down one center city after another around it.

We did do some very good planning with our returning students during the year. For one thing, we decided to move the program outside New Haven to the Quinnipiac campus, in order to separate ourselves more from non-program friends and give us a better chance to concentrate. Also, Quinnipiac was less expensive than Yale, permitting us to pay our extra-large staff a little more. We also decided, students and core staff together, that the staff should have full control of discipline for the second summer.

These were not easy decisions to make, and when they were announced at subsequent Saturday meetings, the students who had not been present when the decision was made immediately objected. This led to repeated conversations, since everyone's informed commitment was significant. The students themselves often took the lead in remaking the arguments. Why give the staff "all the power" (full control of discipline)? For two reasons: 1) we returning students should be ready by this summer to really concentrate on our studies and should want to put less energy into just keeping the program going, since we now basically trust the staff; and 2) because we do not entirely trust our own discipline to concentrate more on our studies, we want the staff (whom we now know, from our first summer's experience, are on our side) to be tougher on us than a student/staff discipline committee is likely to be.

...But the tug-of-war of a rapidly polarizing social environment around racial issues and the Vietnam War tore this fragile new communal identity between the core staff and the returning students to shreds. Martin Luther King was assassinated the night before our first spring meeting of Yale Upward Bound staff, teachers, resident tutors, and advisors. Black groups called a meeting on the New Haven Green, starting two hours before our Upward Bound meeting. I was there, tears streaming down my face, yet also experiencing an unprecedentedly dark, foreboding, thunderstorm mood among blacks.

The crowd of several thousand was perhaps two-thirds black, a bad omen to begin with, had I but reflected about that at that moment, in addition to all the different things I did reflect upon and weep about. The blacks concentrated around the rostrum, where only blacks spoke, shouting the most incendiary rhetoric I'd ever heard. A fierce sense of unity, a menacing elation, seemed to grip the blacks, making the isolated white mourners on the fringes feel all the more displaced. Although many blacks and whites had left by the time I left at 12:00, none of the black members of the staff were present at our meeting when I arrived.

When the meeting began, there was still only a minority present, all white. Forty-five minutes of subdued, somber, paralyzed conversation later, the black majority arrived, the meeting on the Green having altogether dispersed.

As one white resident tutor later remembered that first staff meeting:

> *The meeting really began with a rejection of a white offering by a militant black tutor... It became a sort of black inquisition into white feelings... Bill raised the issue of black nationalism's effect on the program, and I suggested, in connection with the interchange in which I saw whites being punished by blacks, that the issue of continued communication across racial boundaries was crucial to me. This was seen as an 'admission' of weakness by some of the black tutors, but we*

were unable to explore the dominance-submission implications of that perception ...

We lurched through the spring meetings from one crisis to another. One huge difficulty turned out to be: sharing with new staff members how the school was evolving. They struggled to grasp such paradoxes as the fact that the program appeared less collaborative than the previous summer (e.g. an all-staff discipline committee for the coming summer), but that this very decision had been made collaboratively with our returning students. (Of course, our forty new students had also not participated in our subtle collaborative decisions.)

The second and even greater difficulty turned out to be the increasingly implacable hostility with which one of our returning black tutors in particular now viewed any white initiative. It was very hard for me to believe that Ischmael could have changed so much. He was a somewhat small, very bright, and almost unbelievably kind, shiny-eyed young man from Pittsburgh, whom I had first gotten to know as a Yale Summer High School student. After his admission to Yale, Ischmael had played a highly constructive role as a resident tutor during the first summer of our program. But now he treated me and other whites as poison (my name became "White Devil"). More and more of us too slowly came to realize that *he* had become poisoned with hate. (And if this language about poison sounds melodramatic, let me mention as a tragic postscript that Ischmael left Yale in the following year, before graduating, joined an armed black group in Chicago, and was shot dead by police less than two years later.)

As the second summer session approached, I was pleased by the decisions made with the students and the staff about the curriculum, the daily schedule, and the disciplinary procedures. But I was simultaneously terrified by the racial polarization of parts of the staff, and the fact that few of the new staff viewed themselves as active, experimenting learners.

Having been chosen as a staff member and resident tutor again, Ischmael volunteered to arrange the tutorial groups into the different resident halls. Before anyone had imagined what could happen the students and staff all found themselves racially divided – blacks with black tutors, whites with white tutors – when our second summer began. Everyone felt tricked, since Ischmael's strategy was clearly unilateral and non-collaborative. Nevertheless, many felt the division between blacks and whites might be positive in terms of developing, not just black pride, but also a more constructive inter-racial conversation. In the end, we agreed on racially-integrated girls' groups and racially-separated boys' groups, with the chance to reconsider as the session progressed…

To my unutterable relief, the first three days of the summer program ran infinitely more smoothly and with fuller attendance at everything than ever occurred the first summer. Moreover, I was no longer constantly besieged by messages of imminent chaos. Nor was I kept awake almost all night, as I had been the first summer.

"Injustice" and Collaborative Catastrophe

But this placid beginning turned out to be a mere lull before further storms. By the end of the week, we managed to create a true collaborative catastrophe. On Friday afternoon, the new all-staff Discipline Committee made its first decisions: to suspend two students for two days each. Minutes thereafter, Jimmy – the very fellow who'd launched himself into the punching match with the tutors the summer before, but who had since truly become a model member of our community – abruptly returned to something more like before, as he entered our first student-staff full community meeting that I was leading.

Interrupting our proceedings, Jimmy shouted that an injustice, contrary to all the school's principles, was being perpetrated by the Discipline Committee, and that he was representing the aggrieved parties now (you can see that he had learned, as we say, how to use his words, not his fists!).

Despite my best efforts to regain control of the meeting, yet consider this new issue too, I could not get other faculty or students to speak strongly on behalf of the Discipline Committee and why there were no students on it. I missed the moment when I needed to trump Jimmy's authoritarianism-in-the-guise-of-injured-inquiry with a more legitimate authoritarianism of my own on behalf of earlier collaborative, student/staff community decisions. I eventually called for a vote, believing the Discipline Committee would be affirmed. To my horror, I found that the majority of the students and some of the tutors, a clear majority overall, voted against the Discipline Committee decision.

The students returned by bus to New Haven and to their homes for the weekend…And the furious faculty adjourned upstairs to the faculty lounge, cold pizza, and the first of its Friday evening staff meetings. Almost everyone including myself, felt that a worse injustice had just been done than any the Discipline Committee might have committed. Indeed, the disciplinary issues themselves had not been debated. Instead, the vote was actually against the notion of an all-staff Discipline Committee. I was angry at everyone else for not strongly supporting our collaboratively agreed-upon policy. And everyone else was even angrier at me for the same thing. The meeting went on – ungraciously, harrowingly, and exhaustedly – til 11pm. What were we going to do? Certainly, my need for a lot more practice in leading/facilitating volatile new communities – in spite of my success after the student-staff fight the previous summer – was glaringly revealed.

In the following weeks the morning classes and tutoring meetings remained well-attended, but other elements of the program began to unravel. The ceiling tiles in the dorms were easily removed from their brackets, and a wave of room thefts began to occur. False fire alarms brought fire engines after midnight two nights in a row. My wife was not sleeping well, and I was once again hardly sleeping at all.

A pitched battle nearly occurred one afternoon between our practicing football team and two truckloads of the college's grounds crew. This incident persuaded the college business manager to cancel the program. Only a direct call to the college president and some emergency meetings saved it.

The next thing we knew New Haven youths began driving the ten miles out to the program at nighttime to join in the mayhem. The staff decided we must end the residential part of the program after the sixth week, hoping to hold day classes in New Haven the seventh, but unsure anyone would show up.

On the last Friday of the residential program, a resident tutor heard knocks on his ceiling and remained quiet in order to catch the culprit. As the ceiling tile was removed, he found himself facing from above the faces of the two students suspended the first week, along with two 'visitors.' All four climbed down into his room, advised him not to report them, and began to hit him when he would not back down. He escaped, and we called the police to send a car. The four rude youth at first cockily said there was nothing we could do to them, but then agreed that, rather than await the police, why not accept our ride into a black community house in New Haven and meet with a black community leader we knew and trusted? Another call asked a police car to meet us at the community house.

When we got to the community house, I waited outside for the community leader to appear, then entered when one of our students whom I had known both summers called from the door that he was inside (I still had a little work to do on developing my distrust meter; come to think of it, I'm still slow on that one). Once inside, I found a dozen or so youths ambling toward me from various directions asking hostile questions, twirling pool cues, one holding a chair. With an instinctive effort not to run, I calmly said I would be glad to leave and edged toward a side door, squeezed out, got hit by something in the back of my head, and stumbled out to the sidewalk involuntarily sobbing, wheezing, and bleeding.

The requested policeman was on the corner, facing the other way. Two minutes later my friend and Associate Director, Jim Walsh, drove up, and in another few minutes we were racing back to the Quinnipiac campus to join the no-doubt-angry final staff meeting. On the way, Leon, the black student whom I had still believed in enough to let him trick me into entering the community house, tried to explain how I had become his great hero because of my action. From the driver's seat, Jim intimidatingly shouted Leon down in his anger at him and at me for going in, in spite of my promise to him that I would wait for police presence. Bleeding from the back of my head, what could I say? I still seemed to be acting like the numbskull who, as a 12-year-old Boy Scout, had jumped off the log into the creek head first.

■ ■ ■

We held classes the final week in a church auxiliary in New Haven. I had been so demoralized by the events of the previous Friday that I couldn't imagine many students would actually show up, but in fact that final week was astonishingly well-attended, productive, and peaceful. Twenty students passed make-up exams in subjects they'd failed the previous spring, compared to only four the first summer.

I made an anguished speech at our 'graduation,' Thursday evening, in Dwight Hall at Yale, before our final day. It was about the difference between the unilateral-power values of the 'street' and the collaborative-power values of a 'community of inquiry.' I begged all present to ask themselves to what degree we each believed in both and to what degree we each had learned from our struggles together. In spite of my intense emotional involvement with this final opportunity to influence what we each learned from one another, I doubt anyone remembered the speech long. The staff was by and large negative about it, saying it was depressing rather than uplifting, theoretical rather than practical.

■ ■ ■

It had been planned all along that I would 'retire' after the second summer in order to write my dissertation about the first two years of the program. Yale decided to hire as my successor a conservative black teacher a generation older than me, with a law and order orientation, to drum basics into the students.

The next summer session was indeed quiet. But, in a later review of the files, I found that all the faculty evaluations of the program were predominantly negative, such as this one:

> *I was given the impression that the overall program was to be structured and skills-oriented... During the first few days it became evident that these impressions were not correct. Although nominally required to attend class, to study in the evening, and to observe a curfew, students were not penalized for not doing so. Almost two weeks elapsed before the first full staff meeting. ... The trends begun the first few days continued until there was no academic program. ... Teachers, tutors, and administrators blamed each other for the failure.*

Apparently, the changes in the educational philosophy, in the age, and in the skin color of the director did succeed in making it quieter, but not in teaching more basics. (Endnote 9)

Interlude

My Grandmother's Death

My wife and I were house-sitting Bill Coffin's home in New Haven, as we searched for our own apartment in early September of 1968, just after the second summer of Yale Upward Bound. My brother Jim knew where we were, so Dad reached me there by phone, sounding truly shaken, to tell me of Dee's sudden death. He asked me to drive down to Washington immediately, as I of course wished to do.

When I arrived in Washington, I learned that Dee had committed suicide by climbing onto a chair on her balcony in order to thrust herself over the rail of her eighth story nursing home room onto the cement driveway far below... She had had an eye operation that did not succeed, and she had an aversion to becoming blind and dependent.

What I understood right away was that it seemed to me to be her right at that age (91) to make such a choice – to actively engage in the final transformation of her lifetime. My father felt guilty for not having been attentive enough to prevent what happened, but that did not seem to me to be the point, especially as he had been the most attentive son any of us knew of.

Only much later, did I come to think how sad and ironic it was that even Dee, our great conversationalist about matters of the spirit, could not, in our society at that time, speak openly with her community of closest friends and family about her feelings at this point. Our culture of silence about death, which in most families continues to this day, prevented discussion of this matter and any potential decision to celebrate her transformation beyond this life with us in a friendly, communal way, rather than struggling and acting alone.

One source of solace – for Dad in particular – did reach us within a few days. Dad received a handwritten letter (dated 9/10/68) from our cousin, theologian Rosemary Radford Ruether. It reflected Dee well, highlighting how her final act was very much in keeping with the dance she danced in life:

> *I hope* (wrote Rosemary) *this little message will not come as something unwelcome or intrusive, but as a tribute to a relative of mine with whom I've always felt an affinity. Even though we were separated by a long generation, Alice seemed to be a special ancestress of mine, a kindred spirit. We both insist and protest against being "taken" by circumstances beyond our control. There is a little rebelliousness about us that spoke to each other. I remember when I visited Cousin Alice two years ago on 28th Street, I felt an angriness and impatience about her that I commented on to mother in a letter. Her knees were falling apart on her and it didn't just make her sad; it made her mad. Her spirit shouldn't have to fall victim to biological forces in that way.*
>
> *I felt a funny premonition; not of anything specific, but just a general sense that dying would be hard on Cousin Alice; that it wasn't the kind of thing she was going to resign herself to. Since there seemed to be no choice except to resign yourself to that last obliteration of the spirit in which you become less and less "you" and more and more just a dying body, that haunted me very much.*
>
> *Then the knees seemed to get fixed up and the sense of crisis that I felt at that time passed. Then this summer when I heard that she had not been able to see after the operation and according to reports was being "very grumpy about it," I felt that same feeling of empathy, for I felt this grumpiness was*

not just an old lady's petulance but was the expression of that same rebellious spirit, that refusal to take it "lying down"; that sense of rebellion against the finite condition which makes the spirit the last victim of the body.

So when Aunt Sophie called a few days ago to report that Cousin Alice had "fallen accidentally over the rail," I felt immediately, although without any proof at the time, it was a conscious response to a question that had been in the air. I have been thinking a lot about this subject lately because similar decisions have also been taken by other friends of ours with incurable diseases in recent months. It seems to me that part of being human is a certain transcendence of the "Finite," of the "body," or whatever you would call it. It is what makes man who is finally mortal both noble and tragic.

As man has developed, in more and more areas he has refused to be simply the passive victim of circumstances; the forces of procreation, weather, food supply; all these things that just "happened" to man in the primitive state became more and more something that he consciously chose. Religious institutions have tended to be conservative about that; to see it as a "blasphemy" for man to assert his own decision and control over matters that "should be left in the hand of God"; but in more and more areas man has transgressed that line and taken into his own hands things formerly thought to lie "in the hands of God." It seems to me that as medical technology makes death itself more and more a drawn out process; still not averted, but perhaps worsened by being prolonged, it becomes more and more an option for us to make our own choice about it at that point when they know that they have "seen and done" everything that they can do, and there is nothing left but a last capitulation to the processes by which the body itself finally fails. At that point to make death not just a resignation, but a personal decision, is the humanizing of the last enemy. I hope people will learn to respect the vague feeling of "shame" or "guilt."

My feeling for my venerable cousin is one of sadness at such a moment, but touched by a certain awe or admiration. She was always a bit of a terror and it is a not unfitting completion of her life that when she had decided that she had "had it," she wouldn't just resign herself to it, but took death by the horns and met it. Cousin Alice, Hail and Farewell.

Love, Rosemary

I want to add two epitaphs to Rosemary's 'Hail Alice.'

One epitaph concerns my father who took a quarter century to do so, but who then not only edited, but also, from their weekly letters to one another and his calendars and diaries, completed my grandmother's memoirs, which she had named ***Ships and Shoestrings***. She had reached only her 71st year in her own written accounting for her life when she died. Dad described her final 20 years. The final typescript was crafted by my brother's daughter who carries Dee's name — Alice Coyle Torbert. Hail Dad and Hail Alice, twice over!

The second epitaph concerns Rosemary who, though still alive as these words are scribed, has not been able to speak since her stroke a year and a half ago, after a long career as leading Catholic theologian of feminism. Although speechlessness is a spiritually ironic condition for Rosemary, I do not doubt her capacity for turning her daily life all the more toward source and presence simultaneously. Hail Rosemary, twice over!!

Chapter 7

Struggles with My Graduate Work 1969-1970

In the fall, following my qualifying examination failure of the previous May...following the semi-violent end of Upward Bound in August...and, most recently, following Dee's death...I retreated to write papers to make up for my exam failure and to puzzle about the meaning and sequence of events during my two semi-organized, semi-chaotic years at Upward Bound. My three make-up papers all passed, and one of them was eventually published in the *Journal of Applied Behavioral Science.*

My next academic requirement was a 'special area paper,' on a topic of my choosing. I studied the many different theories of individual and group development which suggested that people and groups go through historical developmental stages, and compared them to events at Upward Bound. I remember creating a long list of 143 events at Upward Bound along one side of sheets of paper, including each spring's staff and program development cycle and each summer session as subcycles. Then I showed the stages described by the various developmental theories on the other side of the paper, trying to figure out which theory seemed to account best for the actual events.

The entire process of this study was very meaningful to me because there had been so many events I didn't really know how to understand, and about which I was still hoping to learn how I might have acted in a more timely fashion – not least, of course, that cataclysmic Friday meeting at the end of the first week of the second summer.

The simple rules for the 'special area paper' were that the student's dissertation committee must approve the topic (as my committee of Chris Argyris, Richard Hackman, and Tim Hall did). Then, you could do as much preparation for writing the paper as you wished and have as many notes or books near you as you wished when you began. Finally, you were to devote no more than one day (that you committed to ahead of time) to its writing.

As the day to which I had committed approached, my preparation gained intensity until finally, one night long after I had gone to bed, I awoke around 3 a.m. in the morning and returned to my pages of events and theories to continue my puzzling. Suddenly, an hour or so later, the idea for a way of organizing the events crystallized in my mind. I quickly began to see the entire two years of Upward Bound as having a certain sequential rationality to them. I next examined each distinct subprocess within the two years. I thought I could see them each replicating the same sequence of historical stages in miniature ("wheels within wheels").

My excitement over this discovery of order within apparent chaos led me, two days later, to type out my examination answer, starting at midnight, with so much pent up energy that I succeeded in typing forty-four pages in that single day, with time out to see a movie in the early evening.

Two weeks went by without my hearing how I had done on the exam. In those days in that department that seemed like a long time, so I inquired about it and was told that the paper itself seemed excellent. The delay in getting back to me was due to uncertainty about how to penalize me for having violated the one-day rule on writing! It had not occurred to any of my faculty committee that forty-four pages could be written in a day. My immediate outraged innocence was apparently persuasive in overturning my committee's collective assumption, and my graduate career lurched forward once again.

The theory of development that had ultimately seemed to me most closely related to what happened at Upward Bound was Erik Erikson's theory of individual/ interpersonal development. I had had asked myself what Erikson's individual stages (Birth, Trust, Autonomy, Initiative, Industry, Identity, Intimacy, Generativity, and Integrity) meant more generally and how they might apply to an organization. Also, how would they plausibly be named in organizational terms, if the different organizational cycles at Yale Upward Bound were any clue?

Before I got to those organizational names, while I was trying out different ideas and phrases, I began to notice some similarities in Erikson's names for his stages. Most obvious was the similarity among his three stages called "Autonomy," "Identity," and "Integrity." Clearly, all had something to do with discovering one's boundaries and treating oneself as separate or distinct.

But how were autonomy, identity, and integrity also different from one another? Gradually, I figured out that the distinction had something to do with 'Autonomy" being about the young child discovering his or her physical, bodily autonomy. "Identity" referred to the young adult developing a distinctive cognitive-emotional, social identity. And "Integrity" referred to an elder toward the end of a lifetime of spiritual and practical inquiry attempting to align vision, theory, practice, and outcomes — attempting to act with ontological integrity.

Likewise, Erikson's names "Industry" and "Generativity" sounded related. I could see that both had to do with productivity, but the first implied productivity in culturally-already-defined ways, whereas the second implied productivity in culturally-inventive ways. Erikson cited Einstein and Gandhi as exemplars of Generativity (and then, of course, there are all those mothers of the world who seek to raise culturally-inventive children).

"Initiative" and "Intimacy" also sounded alike, but how? The first, I learned from Erikson, refers to the period when children take on language and social roles... The second refers to when adults discover peer/ sexual/ spiritual love together (if indeed they ever do). Thus, both have to do with encountering new realities beyond oneself.

Arranging the similarities and differences in the right sequence led to a 3 x 3 figure (I show the names of both the Eriksonian stages and the 'Torbertian" action-logics, the latter in italics):

	Relational experimentation	**Successful environmental manifestation**	**Self recognition**
Physical/ behavioral	Birth *Impulsive*	Trust *Opportunist*	Autonomy *Diplomat*
Social/ structural	Initiative *Expert*	Industry *Achiever*	Identity *Redefining/ Transforming*
Spiritual/ historical	Intimacy *Alchemical*	Generativity *Ironic*	Integrity *Elder*

Looking at the events of Upward Bound over the entire two years, as well as during each of its subcycles, I gradually named the organizational analogues to Erikson's stages as follows:

	Relational experimentation	**Successful environmental manifestation**	**Self recognition**
Physical/ behavioral	Conception	Investment	Incorporation
Social/ structural	Experiments	Systematic Productivity	Collaborative Inquiry
Spiritual/ historical	Foundational Community	Liberating Disciplines	???

(Endnote 10 offers summaries of how Upward Bound events illustrate these organizational action-logics and how each organizational action-logic can be more generally depicted.)

My change from effective leadership at the end of the first week of the first summer, to ineffective leadership at the end of the first week of the second summer was probably due in part to my not being directly involved in the first fight, but at the center of the second. It was probably also due in part to there being no existing organizational structure to defend the first summer. Also, the first fight was not inter-racial, but the second one, between Jimmy and me, was. Moreover, the political climate had changed from 1967 to 1968. Finally, we were all new to YUB in 1967, but half the students and faculty were new in 1968 and did not share our organizational history. The community as a whole had not yet sufficiently mastered the Collaborative Inquiry action-logic to fully succeed.

In later years, this theory of organizational development became very useful to me in specific instances of leading, of consulting, and of designing courses. For example, the notion that an organizing process will face a threat to its survival at the early Incorporation action-logic (see Endnote 10), as was true at the end of the first week of each Upward Bound summer session, later helped me, again and again, to make a special super-effort at such moments.

I also used the theory to guide me on specific projects, such as taking and entering a new job: first, be sure there's a shared vision between yourself and the organization (Conception); next, negotiate an appropriate salary (Investments); third, upon entry take care to learn the organizational culture (Incorporation); only then, make unique contributions (Experiments); after that, guide a team to success (Systematic Productivity); etc.

Another orienting feature of the theory was its highlighting of the alternating movement between the centralizing action-logics (Conception, Incorporation, Systematic Productivity) and the decentralizing action-logics (Investments, Experiments, Collaborative Inquiry). I realized that the field of organizational development as a whole had grown up around helping huge Fortune 500 organizations (e.g. Esso, Ford, IBM) move beyond Systematic Productivity in a decentralizing direction, so it rarely occurred to o.d. consultants that a given organization (e.g. Digital Equipment Corporation) might need to move in a centralizing direction. Thus, DEC later died despite (because of?) having the highest concentration of o.d. practitioners of any company in the world).

The Next Crisis

Although I had by now passed my Comprehensive Exams by writing the three papers, and had also passed the Special Area Exam as just described, the departmental faculty was apparently not happy with my overall performance and attitude. I first found this out when I got to listen to the faculty's taped annual review of me toward the end of March of my third year. (This taping of live faculty assessments of doctoral students' performance was an organizational innovation introduced by Argyris and, so far as I know, historically unique to our doctoral program for a short time.) The departmental secretary told me that the other four third-year students' evaluations were on one side of the tape, while mine took up the entire other side.

The half hour of the faculty's evaluation session dedicated to me focused on the dual themes of why I was so unruly and why I wasn't living up to my potential.

The evidence offered for my 'unruliness' included: 1) I had failed the Comps; 2) I was supposed to be taking an independent research course with one professor, but he had yet to see me, and it was now two months into the semester; and 3) I was trying to get out of having to pass a statistics course, on the basis of already having a book in the publication process that demonstrated significant statistical acumen.

Moving on to the evidence in support of my 'underachievement,' that evidence included: complaints by three different professors that I had written only one excellent paper in the past year; and concern that I was proposing a thesis that could not possibly be scientific because I was studying a setting in which I myself was a principal actor. How could I possibly avoid being biased?

I could immediately see that this conversation spelled trouble, no matter how close to, or far from, the truth particular statements of fact were. It was clear to me that I would have to kow-tow to the faculty in some way if I wished to continue in the program – even though I felt sure that the patterns they saw were not really valid.

Why do I speak with such certainty about the faculty's assessment not really being valid? Am I merely reacting defensively? See what you think after I offer the following evidence, pro and con. With regard to the failed comprehensives, my view was that this issue had been resolved by my successful writing of later papers. (On the other hand, I do get that this could constitute a legitimate part of an overall pattern of questionable performance on my part.)

With regard to the independent studies course: back in December, when the professor and I had agreed that I would do this with him, the professor asked me to set our first meeting for the first week in April, based on his work schedule. That meeting occurred the week following my having listened to the tape recording. I reminded him of our arrangement (which he had had on his calendar all along). He apologized for his forgetfulness at the faculty meeting... which, at that point, I truly appreciated. Nevertheless, his complaint about me had already been woven into the faculty's collective story.

As for the three professors complaining about my lone excellent paper of the year, they were in fact referring to three different papers (two of which later became journal articles), although they had assumed they were all referring to the same one.

With regard to my request to be exempted from the statistics requirement, one was allowed – indeed encouraged – to request 'equivalencies' for prior performance in the relevant area. I had been perfectly ready to comply with whatever decision the faculty made on the matter. Under the circumstances, I withdrew my request for an Equivalency and completed a statistics course in my final semester with an A.

> (I found a peculiar kind of poetic justice in the irony that I learned no new statistics at all in this course. I had already covered all the work up to the mid-term exam twice before, so, knowing I'd better do well on this part, I concentrated and

received an A on the midterm. A few weeks later, the course was interrupted by the unprecedented Yale shutdown during the period when the Bobby-Seale-Black-Panther murder trial occurred in New Haven that spring of 1970. Afterwards, students were given their choice of accepting their mid-term grade as their final grade, or of taking an additional test based on the material in the second half of the term if they wished to try to improve their grade. You can probably guess what my choice was!)

From my point of view, the only really important issue in the faculty's critique of my performance was the one concerning my dissertation. This seemed totally unjustified to me... But here I at least also felt safe... Protected as I was by the agreement Argyris and I had made as part of my entry to the program to support me in my new-paradigm-exploring attempt at action research.

At the same time, however, I realized for the first time that others were really hostile to such exploration. One of my fellow grad students pointed out that, with my book on labor and leisure, as well as several different kinds of book chapters and journal articles already in production, I was ahead of some of the junior faculty in the all-important publication realm. Also, I was doing paradigm-challenging, not paradigm-conforming, research. If you factored in as well my easy access to Argyris, who was the current senior full professor and recent department chair, these sociological facts made me a likely subject of disapproval and envy, this student thought.

Had I had any self-protective instincts, I would have gone to speak with Chris about the whole situation. But all I could think of to do was to redouble my energies in writing a first draft of my dissertation proposal for him (the draft became a hundred pages long). The paper was a philosophical and methodological exploration of how action and science in fact continually interweave...And how we can more intentionally try to get them to interweave in ways that optimize the validity of our data and the efficacy of our actions. I illustrated my arguments with a qualitative empirical exploration of how action and research actually interwove at Yale Upward Bound. I hoped that, rigorously honed through further drafts, this paper might become, not only the methodological section of my dissertation, but also a document for the department as a whole to discuss at one of our monthly evening meetings.

Argyris was a very careful and critical reader, and I expected hard criticism of this first draft. What I didn't expect was what I got. He failed the paper outright and without any textual comment, communicating that I needed to find a new dissertation topic. Failing a *draft* seemed completely illegitimate to me, and it had never occurred to me that Chris would renege on our original agreement, to which I had devoted at least half my time for over two years. On one level, that felt like a betrayal, a sort of throwing of my carcass at the faculty's feet. (Forty-five years later, I learned at a doctoral program reunion that the other faculty had been taken aback at the draconian nature of Chris' action.) I had already told myself I was going to have to kowtow to the faculty somehow. But this seemed more like hara-kiri.

In any event, well-shocked indeed, I gave myself the weekend to feel toward and think about "What next?" Because my primary commitment was **not** to joining the academic fraternity, but rather to pursuing the very work I was being asked to stop, I very seriously considered dropping out of the program. Whatever my decision might be about that, I began by committing myself to writing a book about Upward Bound and the theory of historical stages of organizational development, as soon as possible. Perhaps it would be improved by being unfettered from dissertation requirements?

And indeed, I did write the first several chapters of such a book that very summer in Italy, and the book, with a final chapter on the nature of an "action science," was eventually published by Wiley Interscience in 1976 – much the better, I believe, for not having been written in "doctoral-dissertation-speak."

My New Dissertation Study

Having resolved the issue of how to manage the Upward Bound study, I next realized that I did not have an immediate alternative direction to follow, and decided that, in the absence of a clearly preferable alternative, it was important to finish successfully what I had started, both for myself and for the Danforth Foundation that had so heavily invested in me, while offering no constraint at all.

I had also realized over that weekend of reflection that I could define a new dissertation that took into account a new set of governing variables, in addition to my requirement that it concern a topic of deep interest to me. Now, the dissertation must also be completeable-in-nine-months, and must use quantitative, laboratory experiment methods more familiar to the department. Then I would certainly have kow-towed in full to the faculty, and could potentially get two books out of my graduate career, not just one.

By the end of the following Tuesday, I presented my dissertation committee with a new 20-page dissertation proposal for a social psychological lab study of two groups in different learning environments. I would be testing whether and how the two groups learned in a transforming way from their different experiences. I would be collecting phenomenological data (via interviews about what they were experiencing during and in between our meetings), behavioral data (via quantitative analyses of the meeting tape recordings) and attitudinal data (via questionnaires with fixed 1-7 rating scales).

With no delay this time, my committee approved the new proposal twenty-four hours later. It was as though I were suddenly speaking in their language! And they did add the bemused comment that "it sounds fine, but it doesn't sound like Bill Torbert." "Wasn't that precisely what you wanted?" I responded – very much to myself and under my breath. And apparently it *was* precisely what they wanted, for I encountered no more difficulties with the faculty during the remainder of my graduate career.

For my new dissertation, the question I was asking myself and trying to learn about from those who participated in the experiment, was "Why is it so difficult to learn major new truths from experience?" What had struck me during my three years creating and directing the two summer high schools for students from disadvantaged backgrounds was *not* how hard it was to work with the students (who were often reputed to be "the toughest kids in the system" or "impossible"). Rather, the surprising thing to me was how hard it was to work with the very-well-educated staff members who might have been expected to be more open to learning from experience. Instead, in the press of demanding daily events, they often seemed to me to become increasingly entrenched in their pre-existing worldviews and habits.

(Of course, I was entrenched too, if I could stand to begin to see that my own unrelaxed hyper-alertness combined with my fear of conflict was the part of my own experience I was having trouble learning about and transforming. You will see evidences of my continuing struggles with these patterns of mine in the chapters ahead.)

The field in which I was doing my graduate work " –Individual and Organizational Behavior" – was full of optimistic talk and rather loose theorizing about how people can learn from experience, not just incrementally, but also transformationally – born-again-edly. Moreover, I too believed, and wanted to continue to believe, that people can learn something new and true and transforming from their own experience.

Yet, contrary to this espoused value of transforming learning ... My summer high school staffs, I myself, and my graduate department faculty (in their refusal to let me stake my own future on a new way of interweaving research and action) suggested that *in practice* none of us is too excited about learning something that may challenge and transform our assumptions about ourselves, about valid research methods, or about how to handle young folks who seem to violate rules we've made together.

Based on these experiences, it increasingly seemed to me that an adequate theory of learning would have to explain both how self-transforming learning from experience is *possible* and, at the same time, why it is so *rare* and difficult to induce. This, then, was the task I set myself in ***Learning from Experience: Toward Consciousness***.

The study produced, among other things, a new theory of learning — learning through self-recognition — which included but transcended behaviorist learning through external conditioning and cognitive learning through problem-solving. The study also advanced the concept of the four ontological territories of experience and three types of feedback from which we can learn. (Endnote 11 and Appendix A)

One irony of this study is that, despite its title and subject, it is, as my doctoral dissertation, the most purely 'academic' of all my books (published in 1972 by Columbia University Press). Another irony is that it is dedicated – how not? – to Chris Argyris.

Chapter 8

Unlike a Horse and Carriage

Meanwhile, as I pushed to complete my new dissertation on 'Learning from Experience' in the final months of my near-decade at Yale, my wife and I were suffering manfully and womanfully together. We shared a beloved dog (named Hubinger after the New Haven street we lived on). We shared the pleasures of tennis, mountain climbing, swimming, and skiing. We shared a delight in one another's families and our families' history of friendship with one another, since we had met outside one another's back doors over a decade earlier. And...we shared an earnest belief in talking things through.

With regard to this last point, we were delighted to be included in extensive interviews, occurring around the country, on how married couples managed their relationship, and hoped we'd provide an inspiring example of a not-easy-but-committed partnership. A year later, to our great surprise, we were offered feedback. (The surprise about receiving feedback is due to social science studies' frequent claim that they will offer participants feedback, followed by 'forgetting' to do so ages later when the analysis is done and something is written.) We learned, with uncomprehending shock, that, across some 30,000 couples' interviews, there was a strong <u>inverse</u> relationship between how much couples talked to each other each week (about anything) and how long the marriage lasted. *The less they talked to each other, the longer the marriage lasted.* Stunned, we concluded that it was hard to imagine that many of them talked in as disciplined and open a way as we did!

Now, in long-term retrospect, it's not clear that we were well-informed about, or fully understood, or could express our own feelings, particularly about matters of sex and attraction...as three drawn-out episodes concerning the boundaries of the marriage began to illustrate.

The first episode occurred when we found ourselves at a large dinner party one evening, with Jane and her husband as another invited couple. This was the first time I had seen Jane in over two years, since she had told me that her abusive husband was too strong for her (at that time I did not yet know of his threat to kill me with a broken bottle). The party was seated at a long dinner table, with me placed next to Jane, while my wife and Jane's husband were seated at the far end of the table.

Although constrained by the social situation, Jane and I did have an effervescent conversation. My wife could see and feel the laughter between us. She turned very cold as we left, and when we got home began weeping for fear I would leave her.

I acknowledged that I continued to feel love for Jane, but tried, gently and patiently, to reassure her that I loved her as well, that I had decided to marry her in spite of this other feeling, and that I had no intention of leaving her for Jane, nor any intent of seeing Jane again. We talked...and we fought...and we wept all night long and into the morning hours.

As the morning continued without resolution, beyond exhausted I remembered a friend once saying that if all the different things you're trying aren't working, you should try the last thing you would ever think of doing in this situation (thus, theoretically, freeing yourself from the grip of your false assumptions about what will and won't work). Right now, I thought, that would mean getting angry at my wife.

I could not imagine how getting angry would reassure her of my love. Nor could I imagine what I had to be angry about. Then I remembered that I had been teased about never getting angry. Maybe I can *never* imagine why I should be angry, I reflected, but maybe I actually *am* angry without realizing it. Maybe I am rationalizing away an anger I'm not letting myself feel. Not even knowing what I would say, I started making an angry roaring sound, and, to my surprise, heard myself yelling at her that she didn't trust me and my love for her. That felt totally true to me.

She immediately quieted down, began to weep in a different, reconciled way, as did I, and we were out of the cycle. After that, we experienced a new mood of softer openness to one another that lasted several months.

One of the things we had been talking about, given the times in which we were living, was whether opening our marriage could strengthen it (I was reading a book named ***Open Marriage*** at the time). I was in favor of doing so, for several reasons. I believed in multiple, strong, non-possessive, mutually open friendships, with marriage as a special ongoing trust and commitment, including the joint commitment to one's children. I did not believe in brief, secret, possibly commercial sexual trysts or affairs. I thought we could find both more friends and new ways of approaching one another erotically if we allowed ourselves to discover what intimacy with others and in other groupings besides coupling meant and what it could teach us about our own sexual-emotional-spiritual intimacy.

My wife claimed she didn't need more friends, and that brief, secret sexual trysts would probably be less dangerous to the marriage than ongoing, open friendships. Nevertheless, I pressed for a measure of openness, and she agreed to let me visit two women friends in Vermont, one of whom she knew better than I, for a weekend.

Gamboling on a Vermont Mountaintop

The two women and I had started our time together by climbing a small mountain and meditating in a clearing at the top, before beginning to speak about our experiences and aspirations. This whole conversation, over 20 hours, led us to propose a foundation ("Foundations Incorporated") where all members would both "give" and "get" support for one another's creative endeavors.

While still at the beginning of our time together, in the clearing atop the hill, one of the women brought out a pipe and a little bag of marijuana, to my surprise, and we smoked together. Because I had never smoked before, except for three cigar puffs at the end of the undefeated soccer season at Andover, the inhaling was a somewhat painful initiation for my throat. I coughed several times, before I learned to inhale in a slower, more gradual, and more relaxed way. At first, meditating away in my most determined way, I could feel no "effects" of those first "tokes" at all. But after a little while one of the women suggested we get off our asses and onto our hands and knees, and play about like animals.

As soon as I turned around like that, all of my bodily sensations and emotions became vividly present to me, running up and down my backbone. My images and ideas seemed like distinct tear drops, and a more powerful attention embraced these inner "tears," as well as all of nature around and under me, and both women, and the many subliminal messages passing among us. All this flowed through me in a splendid, liquid, wondering silence…

We rolled about, smelled the earth, sounded our voices in various ways, building a basic sensual trust in one another's intentions and respect. Here was an active inquiry! This state (very much like an LSD experience, as I later learned) lasted throughout dinner and for an entire night of exquisitely intimate touching and conversation about our affinities and alonenesses. As we moved, we chose carefully and explicitly what limits we would maintain and why (no nudity, no intercourse).

Throughout the experience, I could feel viscerally how my four years of micro-efforts in the Gurdjieff Work had taught me something about how to dis-identify with each particular thought, feeling, and sensation, enhancing the shared inquiry among the three of us, and prolonging the inner and intimate journey.

Each of the three of us, the two women and I, took on a next task after the weekend, in furtherance of our initial shared vision. One was to establish the legal basis for our foundation. The other, having several favorable connections for doing so, was going to explore ideas about, and sources of, funding. I, as the social scientist, was to document our vision and to supply a kind of 'Minutes' of our meeting.

When I returned from the weekend, I tried to share the sense of the very deep encounter I had had with the two women, along with an invitation from all three of us to my wife to join us next time. I was shocked by her initial response of fear and dismissal, but hoped that her feelings would evolve with further attention.

I quickly performed my duty of writing up and sending off to my two women friends a summary of our time together and of our initial conception of Foundations Incorporated. To my dismay, I received no response. Nor would my wife engage in further conversation about the matter. Feeling wounded from all sides, I saw one of the women several months later and learned that she had called our home to talk with me and been told by my wife not to call again because she did not want me involved with them in this way.

That my wife should feel this way was by this time not so surprising, given her initial response to me after the weekend and her avoidance of the matter thereafter. But that she should unilaterally cut the communication between me and them without informing me seemed illegitimate to me. But, true to my dislike of conflict, I did not pursue the matter. Thus, though miraculously conceived, the new foundation was aborted very early in its development. We did not overcome the threat to the organization's survival at the Incorporation stage (though it did not even occur to me then to apply my new organizational theory to the event).

■ ■ ■

Earlier during that same spring, when I was completing my dissertation, I had been interviewing for jobs the next fall, with the great good luck of being able to consider a joint appointment in management and education at Northwestern, as well as a position in education at Columbia's Teachers College, in management at Case Western

Reserve, and in business at Southern Methodist University. I chose SMU because it was engaged in a major innovation about how to educate its students to become more self-directing and entrepreneurial.

In spite of her parents' feeling that it was my wife's job to follow me to my first faculty position, my wife did not like that I accepted the least prestigious and furthest away offer from Southern Methodist University. Generally angry at me during this period, she began to say she was considering divorce.

Bethel

Over that summer, the Danforth Foundation was generous enough to support me one more time, to attend the nine-week Applied Behavioral Science Internship program far north in Maine at Bethel.

My wife and I went together. She signed up for three weeks worth of programs, one titled "On Becoming a Woman" and another promising a two-week deep encounter experience guided by a well-known elderly couple. After the first program, my wife seemed a lot more outgoing and happy, and now agreed to experiment with an open marriage agreement. We realized that although we might each be open in principle, we would have to discover how we felt about our initial experiments and be prepared to redefine limits as we proceeded. So, for the time being, we had agreed to open our marriage.

She did in fact "fall in love" (her words) with another man during the ensuing two weeks, and they spent whole nights of very intimate time together, but, as in my case in Vermont, did not make love to one another in the coital sense.

At some point during those same two weeks, the wife of a couple we both knew well called me to see if she could visit me. That couple too was exploring open marriage; indeed, the four of us had discussed our feelings about doing so, and the other couple had decided to do so before us. Mave and I spent an exquisitely slow and gentle evening together, making love with one another in a profoundly harmonious, weeping, inter-being way that I had never before come close to experiencing and for which I remain grateful to this day.

Once again, the denouement between my wife and myself was painful. After proudly sharing her new love with me, she seemed disoriented by my true pleasure on her behalf... as though she had been expecting (hoping?) I'd be jealous. After she introduced him to me and the three of us spent a morning together walking in the woods, with me liking him a lot, she seemed to lose interest in him, and I never heard about him again.

In the meantime, when I followed her story of love with mine, she was very upset that our friend and I had made love. I had absolutely no feeling that I was about to run away with Mave, nor did she vis a vis me. As my wife and I passed through New Haven on our way to Washington and then Dallas and SMU, I managed to persuade her to join me for a very good conversation with Mave and her husband. But I soon learned the conversation had not transformed my wife's feelings. When I reached Washington, one day behind my wife because I had been filing my dissertation at Yale, something else had happened.

To understand what that was and how it affected me, it is important to know that we had started our marriage with the crazy idea that we could be open about how our relationship was going with our parents (a crazy idea that actually worked with my parents, and that I continued to enact with them for many years to come). But. But. There are so many 'buts' in this story! But my wife and I had agreed some months before that we would no longer share our difficulties together with *her* parents because her mother in particular became distraught when we did so.

Nevertheless, when I arrived at her parents' home a day after she did in Washington's August heat, I found a frozen atmosphere. I could tell immediately that my wife had told her mother I had slept with another woman. And I soon learned she had left out the details about our joint process of opening the marriage and her own love affair. Instead of offering the kind of support my wife had hoped for, her mother had become completely infuriated at me.

In our room, upstairs on the third floor – sometimes screaming in suppressed voices, often weeping – while her parents engaged however they did on the second floor, and the four of us met on the first floor when we met – I decided it would be wrong to tell 'my' side of the story to her parents. To do so would only continue the practice we had decided not to continue, a decision that seemed supported by the present debacle. To tell the fuller story might also drive a wedge between my wife and her parents.

At a certain point, it became clear that I was called downstairs for a conversation with her father. I apologized to him for causing him and his wife –my earliest 'alma mater and pater– ' so much pain.

At the same time, I agonized about the misunderstandings I was perpetuating by protecting the harmony of the daughter-mother relationship. So tense and wounded did I feel that I sought out my own parents, who were still serving in Washington at that time, for a conversation. With them, for the first time, I allowed myself to mention that, not only my wife, but also now I was beginning to wonder whether we should divorce.

Then, as my wife and I walked out the door of her parents' home for the three-day drive to Dallas, I hugged her mother goodbye, trying to begin the mending process. As we began to move back from one another, she whispered into my ear, "You bastard."

The Trip to Dallas and SMU

As my wife and I drove from the August heat of Washington down through Virginia and into the August heat of Tennessee and Arkansas, you can bet her mother's last words lingered in my heart and mind. But what I was most aware of was the electrical shocks down my left leg, which made me get in and out of the car with a pantomime of gradualness.

These sciatic shocks seemed to emanate from yet another one of my numbskullian actions, this one occurring during our time at Bethel. We had hiked to a place called "Step Falls" with many of our friends. "Step Falls" was a place where you could slide down certain rock formations, smoothed out by the flowing water over the millennia, and be launched into a short flight, landing in a pool below. My very tall friend David Brown decided to slide down one of these funnels, and my driving-trained imagination imagined his mass gaining speed and flying past the pool onto the rocks below.

I stationed myself at the pool's far side to offer a buffer if needed. In the act, he definitely overshot the pool. His ass caught my shoulder, and he continued, landing virtually unscathed on the flat rock beyond. But the impact of our hit drove one of my feet deep into the pool, gashing it bloodily. This wound healed soon enough, as the deeper wound, the rupturing of two discs at the bottom of my back, began to announce itself increasingly prominently.

After two weeks in Dallas, the sciatic jolts from the two ruptured discs started assaulting me even when walking evenly down the business school's marble corridor. But the jolts were hurting less and less because the leg was becoming numb.

This did not seem like an altogether constructive direction of development, so I had a back operation during the third week of classes, which initially left me with no control whatsoever of my legs. We will return to this point in my physical history anon…

■ ■ ■

As my wife and I drove toward Texas, the second thing I was most aware of was the combination of excitement and anxiety with which I was approaching this new and much-sought-after assignment. I knew that however brave an effort Yale Upward Bound may have been, it had definitely not been a clear cut success (ha!!!). In this next job, I had to go beyond promise to accomplishment. The accomplishments I counted had to be convincing, first and foremost, as successes in conventional terms to all the key stakeholders in the setting. Else, neither the organizing process itself at SMU, nor my hopeful career at or beyond SMU, would long sustain themselves. Whatever developmental bonuses post-conventional *Liberating Disciplines* sorts of organizing achieved for students and staff, these accomplishments must not impede conventional success.

I thought I knew the key: I had to be willing and able to blend my unusual and relatively well-honed ability to share power and to generate mutual power and inquiry, with the appropriate (but for me counter-intuitive) use of unilateral power to establish an overall authoritative frame and sense of goal-achievement among participants. Only so were they likely to experience enough sense of psychological safety and success to gradually become more deeply committed to the transformational learning process.

My newly-to-be-activated use of unilateral power could be entirely legitimate. It could come partly from my new social status and organizational role as a "superior" – a faculty member and team leader. I would, after all, be "Professor Torbert" for the first time ... though I also fully recognized the advantage I would gain with students of that era if, after a few weeks, I began asking that they call me "Bill" (as I actually preferred).

My newly-to-be-activated use of unilateral power should also derive from the personal authority gained from my real-world leadership role at Upward Bound, as well as from my study of lived group dynamics and from my experiences in the Gurdjieff Work. At that time, my self-assignment to exercise authority and to place high value on conventional success felt like a difficult challenge. I knew intellectually that a blending of unilateral and mutual power is a valid and strategic approach to the use of power. But I was afraid I would once again miss opportunities at the actual moments when assertion of my personal and role-defined authority was required.

■ ■ ■

On that drive down to Dallas and during the nights we stayed at a motel in Dallas til we found a ranch house to rent, fifteen minutes by bicycle from campus, the third thing that was bothering me was my marriage. It probably wasn't as painful as my electric sciatic jolts, nor certainly as exciting as my immediate work future seemed to me; but then how can one compare physical pain or anticipatory pleasure with emotional suffering??

I was particularly feeling the tearing contrast between my increasingly heavy heart with regard to my marriage and my wife's brightening optimism. She had said for six months that she would stop complaining about going to Dallas once we actually went, and, to my very great surprise and semi-consternation, she did stop complaining. Capable briefly of cynicism for once, it seemed to me that, once I told my parents I was beginning to consider divorce and then told my wife that she was not the only one considering it: presto, her attitude about the marriage transformed into positive initiatives. For whatever reason, even though I welcomed her changes, once I had allowed myself to imagine taking the initiative to separate, my emotions reversed. Suddenly, I found it difficult to look at her or touch her.

Once in Dallas, we would go for a week or two with me becoming more and more distant from her, even though I could see that she was now acting more positively than before. Then we would have a real meeting. Painfully, I would tell her how I was feeling and she would tell me how she was feeling. We would have a reconciliation and be able to be together lovingly for a short time. But by the next day I would again begin to feel estranged, and the cycle would repeat itself. After the third of these cycles, she again began to talk about leaving.

I now secretly hoped that she *would* leave. For although I had thought of separating, and the emotional side of me now wished to separate, it seemed to me like a complete betrayal of the vows of marriage and to be basically unconscionable. To separate would be an admission of weakness of resolve and would in any case be unjustifiable: the commitment had been for life, had been eternal.

So, even though I was thinking and feeling separation, I was not proud of myself for such thoughts and was not ready to act. Nor was I proud of the thought that it would be easier if she took the initiative to leave. We will return anon to this third strand of the story too...

■ ■ ■

My final worry on that trip to yet another new world and new beginning was that I knew there was no Gurdjieff group in Dallas at that time. I would lose the support of those weekly meetings and frequent Sundays, a loss that, in my youthful rush, I did not sufficiently mourn then. I had already planned vacation trips to the Northeast at Christmas and spring break and out to the San Francisco area in the summer. At those times and places, I would find my teacher, so I would be able to work with him for periods three times a year. My inability to attend Work meetings in Dallas (and thereby rediscover the innermost work that I so easily forgot) was frightening enough to get me to sit quietly on my own more regularly than ever before…

Chapter 9

Pat Canavan and Our First Weeks at SMU

Luckily and hearteningly for me, my best friend in the graduate program at Yale, Pat Canavan, was driving down to Dallas separately and would join me as a new faculty member at the SMU Business School. Although we were close friends and members of the same profession, Pat and I were very different stylistically. Pat wore long, electric red hair and faded jeans, the conventional countercultural costume of the time. I wore my hair shorter and dressed in a casual, collegiate fashion, respectful of local custom. Pat made an immediate impression on people by his energy, his warmth, and his joyous, abstract monologues. Whatever impression I made was less immediate: people sometimes noted my honesty in awkward situations, my accuracy of perception, my general good-naturedness, and my goal-orientedness. Pat was charismatic and likeable. I was honest and reliable, and perhaps impenetrable.

Both of us chose to begin our faculty careers at the SMU Business School because we regarded it as showing a strong institutional commitment to a confrontative, experiential learning process among faculty and students. The primary evidence of SMU's commitment to a new kind of learning was its choice of Jack Grayson as Dean two years before. Jack was energetic, visionary, and practical. He had already articulated a new and exciting philosophy for the school. The new philosophy emphasized the need for a new kind of education to prepare students to become *initiating entrepreneurs* rather than *passive bureaucrats*. We could already see concrete faculty commitment to this rhetoric in a faculty vote to eliminate all previous course requirements at the school (i.e. accounting, finance, marketing) and to substitute just a single required course to help students make the transition from passive, reactive learning styles to active initiating styles. (Of course, the point was **not** that students should not take accounting, finance, and marketing, but rather that those courses should be exposed to market feedback of their efficacy and that students should think through why they were choosing [or not choosing] them.)

The practical side of Grayson's new philosophy was that its emphasis on entrepreneurship and action-oriented learning appealed to the conservative, free enterprise values of the Dallas business community. The Dean's persuasiveness in public speaking and his ability to organize attractive mixed-media presentations to market the school was already generating new financial and political support. For example, it soon attracted a $40 million grant from a brash young CEO named Ross Perot, who two decades later ran for President of the United States.

Setting: The Superior, Peer, and Subordinate Cultures

When Pat and I came to SMU, we realized that we were not entering a utopia devoid of conflict. Southern Methodist University was a relatively conservative institution with a relatively conservative student body in Dallas, a relatively conservative city. Football, fraternities, and sororities still dominated SMU's active social life when I arrived. Indeed, the changes at the Business School, which so far had affected the faculty more than the students, were so out of character that a number of faculty members had vehemently resisted the Dean's initiatives. At one point, led by a Real Estate professor, they had gone over Dean Grayson's head to the President of the University to seek Grayson's dismissal (unsuccessfully).

One reason we chose to join the SMU faculty was because of the way they were dealing with the conflict generated by the ongoing changes. In short, they did not try to hide it from us. Unlike most universities where I interviewed for jobs by going through a succession of one-on-one interviews and then giving a presentation, at SMU I was invited one evening to help design a course as well as some research to test its effectiveness. Then the next morning I sat in on a tense faculty meeting of the Organization Behavior area. Toward the end, I was thanked for bringing a conflict I observed into the open in a way that made it address-able by the department. These experiences gave me confidence that persons were really struggling to work together differently... Not merely packaging the same old individualistic, competitive activities and manners in with a new "collaborative" language.

I arrived at SMU in late August, 1970 with a very clear idea of the social role I wanted to take during the next phase of my life. After two years of reflection about my previous leadership effort at Yale Upward Bound, I was ready to try again... But with a very different sense of how to try. Whereas before I had acted as though society represented a contract among free and rational persons – its injustices representing aberrations, however severe... I now viewed society as distinctly pre-rational (primarily as a raw-knuckle contest between Opportunists, Diplomats, and Experts). I now also regarded almost all adults as distinctly unfree and unaware of their lack of freedom. Often, persons seemed to have internalized within themselves the very social structures and procedures they professed to despise. Still, though the camel seemed larger and the eye of the needle smaller... I believed in the possibility of a community dedicated to loving education action.

My new sense of society as predominantly pre-rational suggested a tripartite political strategy aimed at three groups of persons – those whom we consider to be our "superiors," those with whom we are working as "peers," and those whom we or they regard as our "subordinates." In this formulation, the ultimate aim of cultural, political, and personal development is to generate inter-independent relationships among mutually influential peers. But the manner of developing the educational process will vary radically, depending upon which of these three classes persons and teams initially appear to belong to.

In retrospect, the ***Superior***, ***Peer***, and ***Subordinate*** cultures at SMU seemed quite sharply delineated. The Board of Trustees and the Business School Foundation, dominated by Dallas businessmen such as Bill Clements (who would much later become Governor of Texas) and Ed Cox (who would much later have the Business School named for him), represented one face of the ***Superior*** culture. We might call this the rather demanding and perhaps sometimes rather arbitrary "father" archetype. At the same time, the norms of the central administration and staff represented another face of the ***Superior*** culture – more like the 1950s "mother" stereotype. The central administration maintained a gracious, traditional southern family atmosphere. The primary virtues-in-practice were warmth ("Y'all come back soon now, y'hear!"), politeness ("Yes, ma'am!"), and avoidance of open conflict ("Now, cum'on y'all, I don't think we have to raise our voices!"). Competence, scholarship, and honesty, on the other hand, were generally honored at a polite rhetorical distance.

Meanwhile, the student body at SMU generally exemplified what I refer to as a ***Subordinate*** culture. Coming from protected, well-to-do backgrounds for the most part, these students viewed college as part of a socially expected routine preceding marriage or a pre-planned job. Courses, classes, and knowledge were the castor-oil of pre-adulthood, to be ingested as painlessly and passively as possible. Football games and parties were the main meal. At best, many of them felt, one might find a few teachers who were good enough showmen to make class time entertaining.

The leadership of the Business School, however, was operating much differently from the assumptions of either the ***Superior*** or the ***Subordinate*** culture, much like what I am referring to as a ***Peer*** culture. Certainly, Jack Grayson and his associate dean, Gene Byrne, and the OB Department chair, Craig Lundberg acted and felt like older brother colleagues to me... Not at all like parents.

Role, Task, and Leadership Style

Because of my rather unusual degree of practical experience creating experiential learning environments during the previous five years, as well as a book chapter I'd published with Richard Hackman in ***The Changing College Classroom***, I had been asked to become faculty coordinator for the new required course for undergraduates that was to commence in the fall of 1970. It was to be a huge course: during my two years at SMU we had enrollments of 240, 412, 360, and 340 each semester. We were setting out on an apparently self-contradictory process of batch processing uniquely creative entrepreneurs!

To team-teach this monstrosity, Craig Lundberg had recruited Pat and me from Yale and had also recruited three other members from the pre-existing SMU faculty – one a former dean in his retirement year, forty years older than me – as well as five students to serve as teaching assistants. Other than myself, Pat was the only member of the incipient ten-person staff with any deliberately developed skill in helping people in groups to become collaboratively self-directing...And we were the two outsiders!

So, the task was triply huge: (1) we were being asked to undertake a delicate and little understood human process; (2) we were being asked to do so on so large a scale that the faculty could not hope to have significant contact with, impact on, or control of individual students; and (3) the "we" who were being asked to do this job were a largely unskilled team that would meet one another for the first time only two weeks before the first session of the course, with no philosophy, let alone design or syllabus, for the overall course yet.

I felt I had learned many things in the two years since my last major leadership effort at Yale Upward Bound that would enable me to be a more effective leader this time around. My painful, digested leadership experience at Yale Upward Bound showed me that to *suppress my* power was not an effective way to model and encourage others to exercise *their* power responsibly. It also showed me that neither principle, nor digested experience, founded most persons' preferences. In the terms I'm using in this chapter, we needed to invent a mode of organizing that spans the gap between organizing dominated by superior-subordinate relations and organizing permeated by peer relations.

I had named this kind of organizing *Liberating Disciplines* when I had constructed my theory of organization development action-logics after the Upward Bound program. But because Upward Bound only reached the edges of the *Collaborative Inquiry* action-logic, I could not yet really describe either *Foundational Community of Inquiry* or *Liberating Disciplines* in any empirical detail.

I didn't drown in worry about the impossibility of these tasks, because I had also learned a good deal about the importance of humor and informal leadership for building a sense of trust and community within a staff group over the past two years since Upward Bound. At Upward Bound, I had tended to plunge grimly and willfully forward in the face of obstacles, becoming disappointed on the few occasions when I felt little support from my staff. I was unwilling to pay much attention to staff problems because, I thought, the staff should require no special attention; it was being paid to do a job.

At that time, I did not yet recognize the developmental challenges facing not just students, but also staff members. At Upward Bound, my approach turned the staff into part of the obstacle rather than the main resource for dissolving the obstacle, making me feel more isolated and unapproachable than I in retrospect wished I had been. Allowing so little room for serendipity, mutual creativity, or refocusing and reframing on my own part, I, like so many others, had made leadership a harder and lonelier job than it need have been.

Now, my two highest priorities as the coordinator of the new required course at SMU were: (1) to take a half-hour "vacation" for myself during working hours each day; and (2) to create a regular weekly occasion when the staff could gather informally, drink beer together, and discuss whatever personal or organizational dilemmas we were encountering. With this background and in this mood, I approached the first meeting of our "team."

The Staff Meetings to Create the Course

The first day's meeting of our ten person staff went very well. We spent most of our time introducing ourselves and explaining why we had decided to take part in this effort. A sense of warmth and of shared mission began to develop. At the same time, however, the meeting made me nervous because it revealed just how distant most of the members were from anything like the skills and understandings Pat and I had about how to generate self-directed learning and increased action effectiveness.

The first test of my supposed new style of leadership as an SMU faculty member came much more quickly than I would ever have expected, bright and early on the second day. Suddenly, I found myself hearing my one sure friend and ally, Pat, arguing against any structure whatsoever in the course. He believed we should simply form the students into groups and ask them to choose what they wanted to do, consulting to them as they met problems along the way. I was sure that most students would feel utterly at sea under these conditions and that most of these, in turn, would react by resentment and withdrawal rather than by active inquiry.

I felt betrayed that Pat, the one person I had counted on as an ally, should be proposing such a course of action. At the same time, I was very scared of confronting him and fighting seriously. My fears, which I doubt I could have articulated at the moment, were that a fight between us would cause the loss of his friendship, would undermine the future of the course, and would end up with me utterly alone. These very unarticulated fears reminded me of my recent learning with my wife that *Fighting can express commitment to a person or a principle*, not just rancor, and that *avoiding a fight can itself generate distance and discord*.

So, after an eternal minute or two of intensifying internal agony, I finally summoned the courage to challenge Pat severely. Our argument flared into loud voices. We attacked each other as well as one another's ideas, trying to illuminate how each ideology reflected the person's total style and presumed blindness. After a few ineffective efforts to stop us, the rest of the staff sat back, somewhat aghast at the level of conflict occurring in this normally saccharine southern culture.

After forty-five minutes of back and forth, our fight ended in a manner so surprising to me that I could not have imagined it: Pat yielded. He suddenly looked across at me with just a moment's pause, and then announced in his same buoyant and confident tone that I was right and he was wrong – that he had not been thinking very clearly about the characteristics of the students we were to deal with, nor about the size of the course (240 students). I was astonished and confused by his sudden capitulation, but he thanked me warmly, and it was immediately evident that our friendship had not merely survived but deepened.

Nor were these the only positive outcomes. I found that I had somehow communicated my ideas and convictions much more clearly and convincingly to our new colleagues during our argument than I had been able to do the day before during our introductions. As a result, what had threatened already to become a split familiar to me between the "pro-structurers" and the "non-structurers" transformed itself into a common commitment to the still-vaguely-defined notion of creating "Liberating Disciplines" — structures that would generate learning that would make the structures obsolete.

Another positive outcome – the most important from the point of view of my own personal welfare and development – was that the fight and its outcome totally eradicated the nervousness and anxiety I had felt after the first day. Instead, I felt at once powerful and at the same time supported and understood by the staff. I had finally experienced my power in balance with the environment—my visioning, confronting, mutually-transforming power establishing an increasingly mutual relationship with others, rather than dominating or withholding itself. Once I first found that mutual sense of dynamic balance, I found it easier and easier over the decades to find it again in any particular relationship or group in a given institutional culture. But it could still sometimes be difficult for me to find anew in different settings.

Testing and Transforming Relationships on the New Team

Our planning sessions continued each morning for the next week. The scrap between Pat and me seemed to have relaxed the whole team and given us confidence that we could reach decisions together. Twice during those days we fundamentally altered the overall organization of the course. Rather than niggling over details, we concentrated on defining major goals and processes for the course and on developing a sense of one another's managerial styles. To do the latter, we set aside time at the end of each meeting for feedback of our impressions of one another and of how the meeting as a whole had gone.

Through this medium, I found it possible to confront Ed, one of the student assistants, for whom I felt an almost instant instinctual dislike. Ordinarily, I would have distrusted my own feeling, would have awaited more data to confirm or disconfirm it, while working hard to be fair and not to show my feeling, and probably would have become increasingly resentful about Ed. By describing my feeling so early, I could do it with real tentativeness about whether it would turn out to be more 'telling' about him or about me – with a genuine sense of inquiry addressed to him and to other members of the group.

Our initial exchange revealed that Ed stage-managed his life to minimize the painful awareness that, not just I, but many people, reacted negatively to him. The irony was that I was responding negatively, as were others in the group, to precisely this sense that he was stage-managing his self-presentation. From there, it turned out that Ed needed no urging to change his approach. He had actually been deeply dissatisfied with his non-solution and craved an alternative; but he had no model of experimentation and feedback, nor any experience of support, that could help him take appropriate risks. The staff group came to serve this function for him (and very soon, with the astonishing serendipity that the charisma of personal development seems to generate, a lovely, calm, serious, Hindu woman entered his life as well). He, in turn, offered us an extraordinary dedication, initiative, and inventiveness for the rest of the semester.

When it came time for each student-assistant to affiliate with one faculty member and one section of the course, Ed and I chose to work together. We felt comfortable doing so, and we apparently succeeded from the students' point of view, since our section reported the highest average level of overall learning among the five sections.

Next, my concern soon came to focus particularly on Aaron Sartain. Aaron was the dignified yet amicable former dean of the school, an objective and kind father figure, whose willingness to work in his retirement year in this undefined new course with nine other persons, none of whom was anywhere near half his age, was itself a remarkable gesture. His presence offered our staff a potential sensor of, and reconciler with, "old guard" concerns about the course itself and the new directions of the school in general. I very quickly conceived a liking and respect for Aaron, but at the same time distrusted my tendency to respect older persons of authority without test. During our early staff meetings, he seemed content to take a relatively passive role, though he always commented willingly when questioned. I wondered to what extent Aaron really understood and shared our growing commitment to challenging students to practice the skills of self-direction. Would his teaching in fact forward this aim? Or would it at best merely exhort students toward self-direction in lectures that in fact permitted them to remain passive?

With heart in mouth, I brought myself to say something like the above at one of our meetings and was rewarded by a wonderfully open response from Aaron. He said that he supported the aim of the course, but did not know how to achieve it. He was somewhat skeptical of the emphasis some us placed on learning from feedback within groups, but he confessed he had never tried such an approach and was at once scared and eager to work directly with groups. He knew for sure only that he had worked before in large introductory courses at the school and that they had invariably failed to stimulate students.

Aaron's openness immediately humanized him for us, making him much more Peer-like and much less of a Superior, more approachable than olympian. Even though we had no solution for these problems, and even though what had previously been private fears about vague possibilities were now established as public facts, the ironic effect was to calm us and raise our spirits. Indeed, the conversation with Aaron had established not only that *he* did not know how to help individuals and groups, but also that most other staff members were in the same boat.

In light of these acknowledgements, someone suggested that we, the staff, should perhaps write 'Learning Papers' each week following a format we had just designed for the students. In these brief, one page papers, the author was to describe some aspect of his or her behavior in relation to the course during the previous week, then the feelings associated with the incident, then some theoretical generalization, drawn from course readings, about the relative effectiveness of the action, and finally a prescription for some future experiment one could try in order to become more effective in similar circumstances.

We agreed that Pat and I would read over the staff papers and serve as consultants in cases where staff members were experiencing group leadership problems. Thereafter, I found myself in the curious and moving position of reading weekly papers that documented significant learning on the part of a man nearly forty years my senior. Without quite realizing what we had done at the time, we had invented a *Liberating Discipline* both for the students and for us.

In the final days of planning the course, the staff learned that, in addition to the general irony we faced of *requiring* a course that was to teach students how to become more *entrepreneurial*, we faced an additional irony this first semester. The entering junior class, which believed it had already completed all pre-major requirements the previous May, were now required to take this new course, named A.S.1 (Administrative Seminar 1). We were to work our way back, semester by semester, toward requiring the course of entering freshmen. Clearly, we needed to choreograph some events so unique that they would speak to this unique quandary of requiring a course beyond all expected requirements and transform this potentially deadly contradiction into an enlivening, informing, empowering, and liberating irony.

The First SMU Course Meetings and the Research on Those Meetings

We could influence where the first meeting of the course would be held, so we scheduled it for the university's ballroom in the Student Center – one small signal that something new and different was afoot. Next, we evolved a unique schedule of events for the first two weeks of the course, leading up to students' choices of areas of concentration during the following eight weeks. The very first of these events was a really strong experiential signal that however prosaic the name of the A.S.1 course might be, the experience itself would *not* be prosaic.

Pat Canavan started the first class session by asking the assembled 240 students how they felt about taking another required course. Laughter and muttering were followed by a few brave shouts of "Angry!" Pat openly agreed that he would feel that way too. Then he invited everyone to surface this anger in a mass roar, in order to make its energy available to us. There was initial trepidation and resistance, as is the way of such things, and the initial 'roar' amounted to little more than a few disparate squeaks. But Pat expertly and jokingly challenged and jollied us along, and all together we gradually transformed those squeaks into a series of increasingly enthusiastic and impressive group roars that brought other denizens of the Student Center to the Ballroom doors to see what was going on. Pat concluded, in a mock academic voice, that rarely if ever in the history of organizations had a 250-person organization so quickly developed fully coordinated production that simultaneously managed to advertise itself so well!

Next, I took the microphone and proposed that the course was going to teach them to learn from their own experience. It was virtually certain, I said, that they did not know how, intentionally, to learn from their own experience. In all probability, I continued, no previous academic experience in their lives had had either this mission or this effect. Immediately lowering the lights, I asked students and staff to close their eyes and mill among one another without speaking, seeking to learn from their experience what their usual strategies for interacting with others under unknown conditions were. Were they timid or aggressive? Exploratory or defensive? Were they embarrassed, fearful, or relaxed in direct contact with others?

This brief period was characterized by tense outbursts of laughter, wisecracks, and persons who kept their eyes open. But it was also most often mentioned in their next week's learning paper as a producer of insight. Shortly, Pat asked everyone to lie down on the floor and imagine themselves inside the cocoon of their past lives. To help them, he asked everyone to remember the circumstances of their eighth year, to relive inwardly the feelings and details of the first particular incident that came to mind, and to exchange stories with the person they found themselves nearest. Then, he asked everyone to return again into their own cocoons.

By now there was a sense of quiet, concentration, sharing, and willing cooperation throughout the dimly lit ballroom. Pat asked everyone to scan their past lives for the most striking and meaningful learning experience, whether bitter or sweet, they had ever had. After a few moments of silence, he asked all those for whom that learning experience had occurred in a classroom to raise their hands. As he noted, no hands rose.

After the first two meetings of the course, we analyzed students' learning papers and offered the following comments in a report to both the students in the course and the whole faculty of the business school:

> One-third of the students commented about the impact of the course on them already, even though such comment was not directly part of the assignment. About half the comments were straightforwardly and strongly positive, such as:

For some reason, it (the first session) just struck me right. I even looked forward to the next session! I'm proud that our business school would undertake such a venture.

■ ■ ■

It will probably be the most beneficial course I will ever take as to my getting along successfully in the business world.

The other half of the student comments indicated that the course varied sharply from their previous experience, sometimes creating conflict within them. Here are three students' comments on the initially unusual, unexpected, confusing, or negative impacts of the first two sessions on them:

The course is different from the traditional learning experience.

■ ■ ■

To be honest, I'm not sure what the course is really about.

■ ■ ■

I will admit I didn't care for these "sense experiments."

All but two students who report initially negative reactions also report that experiences in the course have already led them to self-questioning and changed attitudes:

I did not particularly want to take the course and was even more sure of the fact after the first meeting. Then, on closer look at what had taken place that evening and when we broke into smaller groups, my attitude toward the course ... changed.

■ ■ ■

My first impression was that the course was a farce and wouldn't work. I was turned off. At this point of writing, I've swung around and am anticipating a fantastic experience, especially around the topic of communications.

■ ■ ■

At first I was quite negative, but later realized that that was probably because I was self-conscious and embarrassed. My second impression is a mixture of optimism and curiosity.

This early, relatively positive feedback about the course was especially significant to the staff because eight of ten staff members had never before attempted anything like this and were naturally anxious about the outcome. Learning from the experiences of everyone present as clearly and concretely as these papers helped us to do gave us the confidence to continue strongly.

In general, the five different eight-week concentrations that students chose among the third week, with their common features such as weekly Learning Papers, turned out to be significantly successful as well. In response to a course evaluation the week following the concentrations, students rated themselves as learning a good deal more than in an average course – 4.8 on a seven-point scale (where 4 means "same as in an average course"; 7 means "extraordinary learning compared to an average course"). (We soon learned from using the same scale in other courses that students were perfectly willing to assess a course below 4.)

More specifically, 90% of our students felt they were learning more about interpersonal process than in an average course; 84% rated themselves as learning more about their own personal learning style; 77% felt they became more self-directed than in an average course; and 74% noted learning more about how to act effectively.

At the other extreme, 82% reported learning fewer facts than in an average course. In terms of theory, career insights, and business skills, students were evenly divided between those who learned more and those who learned less than in an average course.

On the overall question about amount of learning, students' responses varied systematically depending on their choice of concentration. The highest average learning rating for a concentration was 5.8 and the lowest was 4. This data provided good feedback to the faculty members responsible for each concentration.

These quantitative results about responses to the course after ten weeks were again pleasing to the staff, as the earlier results had been. In particular, we were aware these statistics would be important to convincing other faculty that we were generating significant student learning. But we ourselves paid much less attention to them this time because we were now so enmeshed in the course – so involved in re-framing it as we progressed from week to week and so involved in responding to the particular dilemmas of individuals and groups. Also, the Learning Papers, along with our after-class staff meetings and our after-meeting beer drinking, was keeping us apprised of developments virtually as they occurred.

The weekly Learning Papers were also perhaps the best single example of the 'conflict cycles' to which Liberating Disciplines consign participants until they begin to engage in authentic learning from experience. At first many of the students just described some incident from the prior week's class, without describing their own behavior or feelings, nor a theory from the reading, nor a future experiment. They would get such a paper back with a shocking "0." Alarmed, they might look at a couple of classmates' papers that received a better grade and quickly conclude that the key to a good grade was to use the word “I.” Doing so might, or might not, raise their grade on the next paper to 25 or 50, still disastrous. By now they’d begin looking for better sources of feedback (such as the syllabus, or, heaven forefend, speaking with a staff member). By the fifth week in the course, virtually everyone would be getting 100 on the papers, and their interest would have fundamentally changed from seeking a grade to seeking staff members’ qualitative, written feedback and to doing some behavior-changing learning. (Endnote 13)

Chapter 10

Tangling with Texans And Losing To the Superior Culture, 1970

Our difficulties with the Dallas and SMU ***Superior*** culture came over us like a tornado. At the outset, all there was to it was Pat's inimitable and energetic way of living. Pat came to SMU from six months during which most of his energies had been devoted to a group named Cosmic Laboratories. Aided by musical instruments, various media, and plastic structures, Cosmic Labs created large scale spontaneous happenings for organizations and communities, with the objectives of reconnecting persons to shared visions and to one another.

Who was Pat? He had been a pale, pinched, muscle-y, crew-cut Irish-American mathematician and furniture mover when he arrived at Yale only four years before. Now he was an expansive, long-electric-red-haired organizer, accustomed to a nomadic, aesthetic, open, collaborative, uncertain way of life. Upon his arrival in Dallas, he quickly transformed his diminutive, box-like, grey, windowless office at the Business School into a fascinating den. A colorful parachute decked the interior. A string of ties replaced the door. A stereo tape deck provided additional atmosphere. Well before there were supposed to be any students on campus, one could often find eight to ten of them spilling out of his office door, engaged in excited conversation. (I know, because I had to climb through them to reach my own diminutive, grey office just beyond his at the corner of the narrow corridor.)

Having learned how to live in his Volkswagen, Pat decided not to rent an apartment or house. Instead, he commuted among the homes of faculty families, sometimes cooking and babysitting for them, inspiring impromptu parties two or three times a week, organizing a touch football game on Sunday mornings among some dozen of the preteen children, and generally connecting people to one another and to the dream of a joyous learning community to a startling degree.

To celebrate the beginning of this new culture we were joining in creating, Pat conceived of a series of "Disorientation Activities" to complement the more formal orientation and registration activities during the week before classes started. With the support of the Business School administration, he lassoed members of Cosmic Laboratories from New England and members of the SouthCoast architectural commune based in Houston to organize (if that's the right word) the event.

For three days the Business School was besieged by long-haired paratroopers with rainbow bandanas who: transformed the student lounge to the discomfiture of the janitors; built an enormous plastic structure on the lawn in front of the school to the discomfiture of the local fire marshal; led hundreds of students in chanting at night to the discomfiture of the campus police; cracked raw eggs on one another's heads to the discomfiture of some observing faculty; achieved favorable local television publicity; and generally succeeded in disorienting a large number of persons to the great enjoyment of most.

Even before this event, however, Pat had succeeded in disorienting someone enough to have the central administration investigate his background for possible connections to S.D.S. (Students for a Democratic Society, one of the militant, leftwing groups of the late Sixties). The spirit of Pat's work was completely contrary to the dour, self-seriousness of S.D.S., so no such connections were discovered (and he had none). But the central administration did discover that Pat had filled in his background information form in an unorthodox way, listing his religious belief as "Zoroastrianism."

The Provost, who happened to be a professor of ancient religions, invited Pat in for a conversation, presumably intended as a low-key grilling and warning. Pat happily complied, transforming the conversation into a high-brow discussion of his beliefs, which were indeed well described by Zoroaster's doctrine of the relatively independent deities of good and evil – Ahura Mazdah and Ahriman – and the role of humanity in engaging with their interplay.

As their conversation flourished, the Provost introduced Pat to other administrators, and Pat thereafter counted him as a friend. Nevertheless, I once thought I detected a wee bit of discomfort on the part of the Provost as I saw him walking across the campus with Pat's arm draped easily over his shoulder.

As these vignettes indicate, Pat was becoming a well-known campus personality, even before he taught his first class, so the campus newspaper interviewed him and ran an article about him and the changes at the Business School over the masthead of its first issue. In the article, Pat told why he was excited about joining the Business School faculty, and what the school was trying to do. The photo showed him in his office, bare feet on desk, hair flowing, parachute in background. At one point in the article Pat was quoted as declaring that "traditional education is shitty."

This disrespectful characterization of traditional education, along with the photograph and the article as a whole instantly became a focus for organizing dissent to Dean Grayson's innovative program. We heard the next day that the article was being xeroxed and handed around at executive meetings of downtown businesses. Then we heard that some members of the faculty were soliciting negative letters to the dean from businessmen at breakfast meetings.

The day after that Ed Cox, the head of the Business School foundation, backed by Bill Clements, the head of the SMU Board who had just been appointed Nixon's Deputy Secretary of Defense, told Jack Grayson something to the effect of, "We're not going to tell you what to do – just what the consequences of your choices will be. If you keep Canavan, the school loses all financial support. If he stays and changes his image and behavior, the result will probably be the same. If he leaves, we'll see what we can do downtown."

Our Response to Their Response

I heard this news at a more or less continuous informal open meeting occurring in the dean's office on the morning that I was to enter the hospital for the back operation to scrape out the two ruptured discs that were pinching my sciatic nerve. The atmosphere of the meeting when I entered was utterly gloomy, except for Pat who maintained his good spirits throughout the event. Everyone seemed convinced that there were no alternatives — that if we fought for Pat the whole experiment would be destroyed by lack of financial support. Initial comments (and later non-action) by the President and Provost indicated that they would not defend Pat or the principle of academic freedom in this case.

I viewed the situation very differently, coming from the infinitely greater academic freedom that a privately-well-endowed university like Yale generates, compared to a school that has virtually no endowment and is dependent on an annual drive in the business community to balance its budget. It seemed to me that this backroom, power-play atmosphere directly violated the university's primary mission of generating valid, public information; that it also directly violated the principle of academic freedom; that it also directly violated the ethical and institutional responsibility of the head of the Board; and, finally, that it directly violated the way of "doing business" that our school wished to stand for. Moreover, firing Pat for uttering a four-letter word that got published seemed to me a ridiculously unjust outcome of the particular circumstances of this case. As I said something like this at the informal meeting in the dean's office, the atmosphere in the room changed.

But although others began to speak more hopefully, I noticed that they had little sense of what kinds of initiatives to take. My view was that, first, the Dean ought to confront the tactics of the foundation head as totally unacceptable and contrary to a university's practice (the tone could potentially vary widely, even verging on an apologetic "I'm sorry, Ed, that's just not possible"). Second, the Dean ought, with our help, to arrange a series of small educational meetings between Pat himself and businessmen, acknowledging the gap between cultures and seeking to reach across it. Third, these meetings could be videotaped and edited to become the basis for a positive publicity effort. And, fourth, the Dean ought to make it clear, if necessary, that if any parties tried to resolve the conflict by unilateral power rather than by mutual education, he would escalate the stakes by making the power-play public.

This strategy evidently sounded unfamiliar, delicate, and way too risky to the Dean and the six or seven others present. For the first time, I saw a limitation in Jack Grayson's style. Brilliant, imaginative, sensitive, persuasive, and incredibly hard working as he was, he seemed afraid of openly confronting the superior culture and its aura of unilateral power. He, like most people, apparently thought of power as the unilateral capacity to get someone else to do as one wished. Because he clearly did not have as much of this kind of power as Cox, Clements, the university president, or the provost, he evidently felt he did not have the power to confront them. He did not seem to have experience with, or a visceral appreciation of, the possibility of reframing situations and dramatically transforming the power equation by the very act of public inquiry. (This sounds very patronizing of me toward Jack, as though I knew so much better. But of course, at that point in my young professional life I myself was early in my learning of this art of exercising *revisioning* and *praxis* power [see Endnote 13].)

When Jack Grayson later read my interpretation of his leadership style at this point in the Canavan crisis, he respectfully disagreed with my assessment. As he wrote back to me when I sent him an earlier version of this chapter:

> *Though I heard your arguments when you were here surrounding the "Canavan Affair," I certainly read carefully what you wrote here. I still think that the course that I followed was*

probably the best in the long run for the school. You don't have all the data. Also, I don't think you've had enough experience in dealing with very large scale and small power blocks beyond the university campus. Washington certainly taught me a lot about it! You may be right – who knows? But I don't think so.

At the time, Jack wanted to keep the whole problem as quiet as possible for fear that publicity would utterly alienate these two powerful men – Clements and Cox – and other potential supporters of the Business School. Consequently, in my view, "our side" gave up its power before the encounter began. The group of six or seven kept talking day and night while I was in the hospital having my back operation, and some contacts were made with other businessmen; but even when they were somewhat sympathetic, they also saw all the power on the "other side" and concluded that even if we were basically right, the atmosphere was so poisoned that keeping Pat would disastrously reduce the school's financial support.

■ ■ ■

Meanwhile, at the hospital, I had returned to consciousness but was not yet able to walk… The muscles had been cut away from the spinal column, so my legs dangled like a puppet's when they raised me to a sitting posture. It took a call to Bill Coffin at Yale before I began feeling a smidgen uplifted, even a mite ebullient. As usual, Coffin had a bagful of humorous, insightful, and polarizing stories and epigrams, which somehow reaffirmed and reinvigorated my sense of the situation.

"Don't ever draw your gun on a Texan," he said. "It makes him mad. But you'd better be sure to have it lying on the table as you talk…" And: "Look, you've got the ethical initiative. As long as you've got it and take it, you don't have to worry. You're in the driver's seat." Coffin went on to talk about his previous visits to SMU and his confrontation at a decorous, lilly-white sorority dinner, served by black-help, where he raised the issue of integration at the table, including the servers in the conversation... to the immense embarrassment of his hostesses.

Not afraid to fight when basic customs were attacked, some of the young women accused Coffin of acting in extremely bad taste. To which he replied, "That seems to be a basic difference between us: you choose taste over truth when you see a conflict between the two. I believe the truth is always in good taste."

■ ■ ■

As colleagues visited me in the hospital, relaying the latest news, I relayed back Coffin's stories. They made my points so much more provocatively than I by myself could. Then, my hospital visitors and I would plan various initiatives that persons could take. They would enter the hospital room dispiritedly... and they would leave energetically. This was encouraging...

But a few days later it would turn out that they had talked together a lot more and had taken none of the initiatives we had discussed... This pattern convinced me, after three repetitions, that we weren't sufficiently prepared, as a brand new, aspiring ***Peer*** culture in its earliest stages of development, to meet this challenge – ourselves not yet sufficiently educated in the politics of speaking truth to unilateral power as a way of generating mutually-transforming power.

Some members later blamed our political failure on Jack Grayson's weakness, or on the central administration's moral paralysis. But I view the responsibility as much more widely shared. Frankly, I'm glad I was in the hospital. Not only don't I believe that I could have organized our side successfully... I might well have aggravated our failure by taking initiatives on which we might not have fully followed through... and our ability to learn and accomplish all that we did in the following year and a half might have been sacrificed.

Ritual Sacrifice

Pat made it clear from the start that he would be willing to resign if that was the best solution for the school, and Jack ultimately did ask him to do so. Because of his own joyful equilibrium throughout these events, and because of the favorable publicity he and the school received, Pat's ritual sacrifice to the ***Superior*** culture had a sort of jujitsu effect of weakening its legitimacy and therefore lessening its capacity or motivation to attack our experiment again. At least that is how it seemed at the time. We did not know then that Cox and Clements had simply shifted their action a little further off the public stage.

Within weeks of this time, without any forewarning or personal initiative on his part whatsoever, Grayson received a personal telephone request from President Nixon to come to Washington to take on the newly created role of Phase II Price Commissioner. Reluctant to accept this offer because he was so deeply committed to the transformation of the SMU Business School, Grayson sought the advice of Cox. Cox told Grayson that one could not refuse to serve one's country. So ... off went Grayson to Washington.

What neither Grayson nor anyone else at the school knew was that Bill Clements and Ed Cox had decided they no longer wished to work with him. Through Clements' connections to the Nixon White House, as the new Undersecretary of Defense, they arranged the offer that Grayson could not refuse. Cox and Clements were confident that Grayson would encounter other opportunities in Washington and would never return to Dallas. (I learned this story years later from a man with a nationally respected public record of integrity who heard this version from Cox himself at Cox's pool side at the time of the events recounted here. Both that man and I were members of the Harvard faculty when he serendipitously told me this story.)

Grayson was, in fact, very well received by Congress, the press, and associates in Washington. Nevertheless, he remained committed to the program at SMU and returned. He never did receive the pledged support from Cox and eventually resigned and founded the American Productivity Center in Houston.

Cox and Clements were not entirely quiescent as they awaited proper hegemony over the SMU business school. Yes, Cox had become Chairman of SMU's Board when Clements went to D.C. as Undersecretary of Defense. And yes, they'd eventually gotten rid of Jack as Dean, even if he'd made a brief return appearance. But that was not all. In 1974, Cox encountered considerable controversy at the university and local levels when it became known that he had manipulated the resignation of the university's president, Dr. Paul Hardin. Cox had sent the trustees an announcement of Hardin's resignation asking them to accept it. Though surprised by the request, they did. Simultaneously, Cox told Hardin that the trustees had voted in favor of his resignation and asked him to accept their decision. Though surprised by the request, he did. The double deception was eventually uncovered and aired in the newspapers, but efforts on the part of some other members of the Board to change the decision were unsuccessful.

In 1980, the Southern Methodist University Business School renamed itself the Edwin Cox School of Business in response to his $10 million gift. This fact in itself represents nothing more than business as usual among business schools over the past fifty years. Many have been named after a major donor. The fact that Cox had originally pledged the $10 million a decade earlier was little known and less remembered. The additional fact that at the time of the donation in 1980 the business school's dean's office at SMU sported a plaque on the wall that read: "The Golden Rule: He Who Has the Gold Rules" may be interpretable as no more than an unremarkable example of Texas humor.

Not to be outdone by his buddy Ed Cox, Bill Clements encountered considerable controversy in 1987 when he was Governor of Texas. At the state and national levels, NCAA officials and the public became aware that two years earlier in his role as a trustee for Southern Methodist University, Clements had authorized improper payments to S.M.U. football players. These improper payments led to the suspension of the S.M.U. football team from NCAA play.

The moral I have learned from this part of the SMU story is to take care not to perturb the ***Superior*** culture until you, as a member of a ***Peer*** culture that designs and enacts *Liberating Disciplines*, are ready to play the politics of truth seeking and truth speaking under 'battle' conditions. For once you have perturbed the ***Superior*** culture, it is not likely to compromise the matter and settle for winning just a battle – receiving just a ritual sacrifice. It will strive to win the war and to eradicate all sources of threat.

■ ■ ■

Back at home after my back operation, but still unable to walk, I held a birthday party for Pat to which some forty people came. Since he had given us so much energy, we decreed that he should lie passively and receive from us. So, he was hugged and kissed and passed from group to group, carried about the house and yard, and then ritually buried in the middle of the den. We raised a funeral lamentation, which moved some to tears and others to embarrassment, and we expressed anew to one another our dream for our still embryonic learning community.

Commuting from Vermont to Dallas to California, Pat would thereafter reappear every few months to spend a few weeks with me and visit with our friends. (Eventually, Pat became the head of organization development for the Digital Equipment Corporation in Europe, and then moved to Motorola, where he served in many roles, including Senior Vice-President for Global Governance until the time of his retirement in 2008.)

In the meantime, I just felt all the more determined. I could feel how the A.S.1 course was succeeding as a *Liberating Discipline* for building a ***Peer*** culture among the staff and for transforming the ***Subordinate*** culture of our students. I could also feel how much more there was still to learn about how to do that. And learning how to build a thoroughgoing ***Peer*** culture seemed to me a precondition for successfully engaging in a politics of truth seeking and truth speaking with the ***Superior*** culture.

At the same time, my motivation to research and publicize both our errors and our effectiveness increased still higher, for I now believed even more strongly than before that this was the appropriate pre-emptive defense against attack from the ***Superior*** culture. I also increased my customary caution, no doubt inherited from my father, against behaving in public in a flashy manner. (Endnote 15)

Chapter 11

Blocks to Creativity

In this chapter, I want to turn to the shocks and reversals that peers generate among themselves – educational shocks and reversals – shocks and reversals associated with increasing dis-illusionment and awakening.

You may recall from Chapter 8 that I was feeling allergic to my wife during my first fall at SMU and that because of my repeated withdrawal, she was again considering separating. At that point, we had both attended a weekend executive workshop together at the Business School. The workshop, for Business School faculty and students, was testing a new executive development methodology called "Blocks to Creativity." Through some initial paper and pencil tests, each person identified where he or she stood in relation to fourteen different "Blocks to Creativity" with names like "Reluctance to Let Go." Each of these blocks could, properly, be a *building* block to creativity, but might be functioning in one's own life as a block *obstructing* creativity. Once each participant identified several blocks that he or she wished to change from blockages to building blocks, we approached large cardboard "blocks" with those names, each containing various exercises relating to that block. These exercises both illustrated how we were blocked and provided opportunities for experimenting with new actions. (These exercises offer another example of *Liberating Disciplines*.)

After a short introduction, my wife and I and the 23 other participants each wandered about the large space, occasionally consulting with one of the facilitators, or inviting several of the other participants to join in some exercise that required more than one person. I chose to work with the block called "Reluctance to Let Go." Here the notion was that some people just keep worrying a problem, attacking it mulishly again and again from the same perspective, unable to detach themselves from it or from their particular version of rationality. Such persons cannot gain the distance to see what is really going on, nor the relaxation to act in a balanced fashion. Often they can't let go of a task enough to delegate authority; or, by trying to hold too tightly and possessively those with whom they would like to be intimate, they may repel them.

When I chose this block, I was thinking of my difficulties in truly delegating rather than doing it all myself. I was not at that moment thinking of my marriage. (Nor did it occur to me that my wife could be seen as sharing this same block; nor that "reluctance to let go" may characterize the attitude of many persons on the verge of developmental transformation, a large part of oneself not wanting to let go of one's existing way of relating to the world.)

The exercise that I came to in this "Block" involved choosing some pressing problem in one's life and throwing some coins which would determine where to look for an answer in an ancient Chinese book called the ***I Ching***, or Book of Changes. I knew vaguely of this book, that it contained commentaries on sixty-four different hexagrams with names like "Difficulty at the Beginning," "Breakthrough," and "The Wanderer." How you threw the coins supposedly pointed to what hexagram would help you address your current dilemma. I knew it was somehow a highly respected book, yet the procedure seemed to me pure chance, utterly arbitrary, and superstitious.

The description of the exercise acknowledged that this might well be one's initial reaction, and that certainly the procedure was not rational in the Western scientific sense. Stepping back, the directions emphasized that the point of doing the exercise was not necessarily to accept and act on the "answer" one received, but rather to experience the difficulties one had in letting go enough even to do the exercise – even to try a fundamentally different approach – even to consider accepting help from a completely unanticipated direction, completely outside one's own control (except in the sense that one's action of throwing the coins influenced the response one received).

I could not recognize my extreme skepticism about the value of this whole procedure as itself a symptom of my reluctance to let go of calculative thought. But (again reluctant to let go) I was determined to be a good Boy Scout and follow through on the exercise. So I asked myself, "What's the most serious problem I have now?" The answering question sounded back loud and clear "Should I remain married, or should I separate?" I threw the coins, went through the process of locating which hexagram they indicated, and found myself facing a text entitled "Endurance."

"Endurance" seemed a most ambiguous answer. Since all my predilections for the past months had been to separate, "endurance" could mean that I should endure in this intention and actually do it. On the other hand, it could also clearly mean to endure in the marriage. I read through the entire commentary (two to three pages). It was full of provocative imagery, as the following excerpts indicate. And, to me, it continued to be full of ambiguity. An immediately striking 'coincidence' was that the main image of the hexagram was that of marriage:

> *In the sphere of social relationships, the hexagram represents the institution of marriage as the enduring union of the sexes ...*

This passage, I thought, made it clear that endurance, in this context, meant that the marriage should endure.

But as I read on, I saw:

> *Thunder rolls, and the wind blows; both are examples of extreme mobility and so are seemingly the very opposite of endurance, but the laws governing their appearance and subsidence, their coming and going, endure. In the same way*

> *the independence of the superior man is not based on rigidity and immobility of character. He always keeps abreast of the time and changes with it. What endures is the unswerving directive, the inner law of his being, which determines all his actions.*

"Keeps abreast of the time and changes with it" implied, it seemed to me, that change was okay. Not the external marriage, but the "inner law" of my being was supposed to determine my actions.

The words and phrases did have a certain grandeur and dignity about them. But I was irritated by the ambiguity and by the nagging feeling that this arbitrarily selected text couldn't possibly mean anything or be the basis for action, especially in regard to something as important as my marriage. At the time, I did not notice that my entire interpretive set was empirical and scientific. I was attempting to locate an answer empirically, in the world outside myself, in the text. And I expected this answer to be internally consistent in terms of Aristotelian logic. I had not expected to believe the answer I got, but I had at least expected a clear answer.

I then asked another nearby participant in the workshop who appeared to be between tasks to help me. She said she would read the text out loud to me. I could not see how that would help at all — I had wanted a 'more objective' opinion from her. But I lay down on a couch, closed my eyes, and listened as she read. And lo and behold, as she read and I relaxed, it became very, very clear to me that what it was saying was that I ought to get out of the marriage.

Even as this powerful message was beginning to circulate within me –nonetheless shocking for coming so gently and definitely from within me as a kind of felt sense – I also began to see, like a second wave overlapping the first, that this "answer" was what *I* wanted, was *my* answer. By responding to my question in a different language and metaphorical framework than I had been using, the text was helping me go beyond my 'objective' weighing of pros and cons, beyond my own ambivalent layers, to accept some deeper feeling or intuition which could be a truer guide – not because it was more *objective*, but rather because it was more truly *subjective*.

The wider framework of the "Blocks to Creativity" exercise was helpful too, because it suggested that I needed to let go of my rationalistic-empirical, left-brained approach. The point was not that objectivity was wrong and condemnable, but rather that it needed balancing with subjectivity. Put differently, I could be objective about neither objectivity nor subjectivity if I could not let go of – detach myself from – each. In my effort to achieve a generally justifiable answer, I had been blocking myself from seeing, experiencing, and accepting the main fact, close at hand. This fact was that – generalizable or not, justifiable or not – *I* wanted to end *this* marriage.

Tangling with My Wife and Myself

My wife and I went home for the evening. I was so scared and upset that I couldn't speak. I was choking on the words. We almost spent the entire evening watching television. But that scenario seemed too demeaning even for someone as craven as I then felt. Moreover, I rather quickly realized that my emotionality was partly yet another symptom of my reluctance to let go. For I was not "merely" letting go of my marriage. During the second reading of the hexagram, I had already come to terms with that. I had already accepted that I wanted to let go of my marriage. In what sense, then, was I still reluctant to let go? The responses came quickly now that I was genuinely questioning and genuinely listening for new answers, as I had begun to do earlier that day when I lay on the couch. Instead of thinking deliberately, I was listening 'into the dark,' allowing new insights to fly in the aviary of my night mind.

One response that flew through was that I was reluctant to let go of my usual way of getting answers to my questions. With someone like my wife, with whom I wished to interact as a peer, I wished to reach a consensual decision about our marriage, based on facts and principles that we could both agree on. I could never have envisioned making the decision unilaterally with the guidance of such a peculiar non-empirical, non-rational book as the ***I Ching***.

A second response was that I was reluctant to let go of my self-image as a good boy who succeeded at all the important things in life, including the hard work of figuring out what the important things really are. For divorce is not rationalizable. One has genuinely, unalterably 'fucked up.'

As these responses came, they simultaneously legitimized themselves. I had undeniably learned something important from the ***I Ching*** exercise, so the guidance of the book *was* clearly of value, at least in this instance, and I might as well accept that. Also, I had admitted to myself now, without equivocating, that I wanted a divorce, so clearly I *had* messed up in a serious, adult way and I might as well accept that too. But these realizations did not end the internal conversation.

Did separation and probable divorce also represent leaping into a metaphysical void? If I could break the most solemn and binding promise that two human beings in this culture can make to one another, was I sowing the seeds of an ultimate futility and hopelessness for myself? Was I embarking upon an ultimately cramped and debilitating relativism that permits only temporary and selfish "marriages of convenience"?

Finally, painfully, I said out loud that I wanted to have a conversation. We turned off the TV, and I told her what had happened to me during the day and that I now wanted to take the initiative in separating. Once again, my wife's whole orientation immediately reversed, from being on the verge of leaving herself, to seeking to save the relationship.

She read the hexagram from a copy of the ***I Ching*** that she had in the house, unbeknownst to me. And, perhaps unsurprisingly, she interpreted it differently from me, hearing its message as a clear statement that we should endure in the marriage. But by now I was comfortable with the notion that there was no single "right interpretation," so I tried to explain to her why her interpretation did not influence me.

Next, she wanted to talk about this decision at length with other friends and counselors. I agreed to one long conversation with another older married couple, both of whom had previously been divorced. I was now so sure I wanted to separate, however, that I refused to continue such conversations because for me they represented evasions.

A week after the workshop I left our home for a small room in a boarding house. At Christmas, she returned to New England. A year later we completed our divorce. She went on to blossom in many ways, achieving a doctorate, becoming a professional, exploring other relationships, remarrying, having children. And, after some years of careful distance, we more gently re-explored our caring for one another.

I have never experienced one moment's doubt that my decision was right for me. For many years, I believed I would not remarry, preferring informal communal arrangements, or, later, a more deliberate commune as ways of seeking true peer relationships. But life continues to evolve in unanticipated directions, so, still later, I found myself more than a decade into my second marriage, with three sons, and two mortgages.

Through this experience, the ***I Ching*** gained the status of a sacred book for me, a reliable liberating discipline. I consult it sparingly, with a deep and quiet pleasure. It always leaves me with a clear taste for how narrow is my ordinary access to myself and how incomplete is the rational-empirical scientific method for gaining access to the world of personal, social, and spiritual experience and timely action.

The rational-empirical scientific method operates within a given paradigm, within a given set of assumptions. *Liberating Disciplines* like Blocks to Creativity and the ***I Ching*** are somehow trans-paradigmatic. They can help us to see beyond our previous limits and assumptions, can help us reframe the dilemmas we experience. Other such *Liberating Disciplines* include Socratic conversations, Christian prayer, Freudian or Jungian dream analysis, Sufi whirling, Hassidic stories, Buddhist meditation, the Hindu yogas, Tai Chi, and more. Because different persons begin with different kinds of indigestion, anxiety, and incomprehension, some of these approaches will transform your experiencing more effectively than others.

The validity of a liberating discipline for oneself is determined by its continuing role in revolutionizing one's experiencing – one's sense of search, one's sense of oneself, one's sense of the wider world – and in increasing the integrity, mutuality, mercy, and justice of one's actions. The danger is that a person will become addicted to one particular discipline, shrinking it to a taken-for-granted paradigm, rather than continuing to expand to meet the unique revelation of each new moment. We must cultivate, and then give up, "brief habits," wrote Nietzsche.

Jill

When I had come back to Dallas from my Christmas vacation up north the first year, I found myself teaching my heart out (to put it in a way that seems at once very naïve and very unfashionable to say, and yet perfectly true to my feelings at the time). I was also engaging actively in the politics of the department, the school, the university, and the nation. For example, I played a significant role in salvaging the integrity and efficacy of the "Nature of Man" course at the university, as well as spontaneously taking a joint leadership role with students during a campus strike against Nixon's and Kissinger's bombing of Cambodia. I was also editing my ***Learning from Experience*** dissertation into its Columbia University Press published version. And I was wondering how to relate to women, given my new condition of being not just separated, but committed to exploring what non-possessive loves felt like and entailed.

Very soon, I was seeing Jill, the college-aged daughter of a faculty member, every other week or so, in a relationship that felt so good I couldn't believe it. She was quiet, but I loved to listen to her. She was also bright and inquiring, so our conversations could be lively and contentious, as well as soft and whispery. We loved the same music (Janis Joplin, James Taylor, Cat Stevens, Credence Clearwater...) She was easy to the touch and entrusted her body to mine. She was also an artist, very private, independent, not giving herself away totally to anyone, thank you very much, in that early-feminist age... We were thus instantly at one with one another in our heavenly sense of non-possessiveness, as well as in our occasional oceanic inter-weaving-ness.

And then there were the students whom our staff chose, and who themselves chose in turn, to serve as consultants to our student teams. Different ones of them, as well as members of the faculty, gave parties almost every weekend, during which the energy-link within our A.S.1 staff group – whether dancing, or talking, or meditating, or playing some game – was often intense (though never exclusive of anyone else at the party who wished to join in). It seemed there was a kind of collective eros at work. Some of these students married one another; some became professionals in related fields; some, along with some of the faculty, became lifelong friends of mine. One — Bill Joiner — entered the Gurdjieff work, followed me to the Harvard Ed School for his doctorate, and later wrote a significant book in my same field, titled ***Leadership Agility***.

I said before that the campus had missed the 60s, but the 70s arrived in good time and in full swing. Feminism was in flower, indeed Gloria Steinem – in cowboy boots, jeans, black dancing top, and leather jacket – was the first public persona to parade her story through our newly renovated Business School auditorium during that winter.

The summer between my two years at SMU, Jill and I travelled all about the country – from Herb Shepard's island off Maine to Craig Lundberg's Spirit Ranch in northern Washington state. I was working on two of my books and penning an ode to "Making Love As a Lifetime Act." Jill was making jewelry and throwing pottery.

Earlier in the summer, before both the Maine island and the Washington ranch, Jill and I visited Ron and Peggy Blunt in Princeton. I'd gotten to know Ron and Peggy at Yale, when Peggy taught at Upward Bound, and they joined me in the Gurdjieff Work. Later, they asked me to serve as godfather for their first daughter.

Over the course of our week together in Princeton, it slowly became clear that our foursome, in all its permutations, shared an unforced ease, warmth, and delight. I had known that Ron and Peggy did not hold an ideology of marital sexual exclusivity, and I had enjoyed Peggy's openly provocative comments toward me. But no occasion of full sexual intimacy among the three of us had heretofore evolved. Now, it felt to me as though an occasion of sexual intimacy among the four of us *was* evolving.

On the final morning of our stay, Peggy and I found ourselves talking in just this way, happily convincing ourselves into just such an initiative, with the added pleasure of knowing just what we were doing. Suddenly, it occurred to both of us that we had no idea what Ron and Jill were doing just then. With playful horror at the possibility that we might be merely discussing what they might be enacting, we snuck upstairs and found them: in the shower together. This was too propitious a signal to be misinterpreted (!), so we immediately doffed our clothes and joined them, amidst great hilarity and affection. Eventually, the four of us dried one another and draped ourselves atop the large bed in the adjoining room.

There seemed to be no question but that we were all unhurriedly intending a languorous, love-making leave-taking. Nevertheless, I knew Jill to act perhaps a bit more agreeable at times than she really felt, as well as a bit slow to speak her reservations; so I asked her how she felt as the newest acquaintance in this group. Her response did not break the pleasurable mood and could easily have been interpreted as assent to whatever was to come next, an interpretation that certainly fit my sense of inertia and of desired acceleration. But her response was, at the same time, to my ear, a little passive. Even though it seemed somewhat redundant to me to do so, I pursued my initial question more explicitly. Would she be comfortable with – did she wish – love-making among us?

The brief pause that followed was the dis-illusioning answer, though she reluctantly also spoke a little to say that, really, no. With sighs and glances and touches of regret, but without recrimination, all four of us reversed our inertia. The two of us gradually dressed and packed and took our leave.

In the car on the way to Philadelphia, I explored with her what her reservations had been. She told me that her mother and step-father had gone through a tumultuous period of group sexual experiences that ended with their divorcing their former partners — a period during which she experienced the adults as treating one another cruelly and selfishly — and that that taste and fear had flooded her as we lay atop the bed. I was so grateful then that the scenario our foursome had ultimately enacted together was one of mutual caring in resisting sexual desire – one of seeing love – rather than of mutual blindness in submitting to sexual desire.

■ ■ ■

When we returned to Dallas for the fall semester, I asked Jill to move in with me. She could certainly have a room of her own, I suggested, perhaps more private than her room at her mother's home. She tried it out, ambivalently. A couple of weeks after she came to live on the waterbed in the room on the other side of the bathroom from me, she also became attracted to another guy, a musician.

He was an attractive young man to me as well. He already seemed to have an acquaintance with his own aesthetic being and soul. In short, I was open to exploring a trio relationship among us. He, on the other hand, very straightforwardly (and non-hostilely) wanted her and not me, as he told us late at a supper I'd arranged at my home.

Jill loved us each, and her ambivalence and suffering rose... Until I finally decided for her that she should not live with me. Instead, she found an apartment with another woman friend, became the other fellow's girlfriend during that year, and remained friendly with me at a distance. I was not angry with either of them, but I suffered a sense of loss long and deep. Making love as a lifelong act of mutual inquiry and mutual power was proving to be a complex commitment that could make one intensely vulnerable and anguished, as well as wonderfully harmonious. (Endnote 16)

Chapter 12

Continuing Experimentation with Liberating Disciplines

Our choreography of the A.S.I course for its second 'run' during the spring semester of 1971, directly addressed the limits we had encountered during the fall and included many major changes. The course had become so popular that four hundred and twenty persons signed up for it; the Business School attracted more students overall from other university departments; and the university subsequently increased the school's budget. For this and the following versions, we selected 16 to 20 of the very best students from the previous term to serve as consultants to the various teams, and the staff team as a whole became more and more of a ***Peer Culture***, with the student-consultants having already experienced one incarnation of the spirit of the course and with weekly two-hour classes ourselves to keep the course under constant assessment and re-design, not to mention our by now sacred ritual of a long voluntary session each week after the evening class at the nearby student "watering hole."

In general, the second semester went very well, and we were astonished at its conclusion by the quality of many of the projects, such as:

- the student run coffee house that made a big profit;
- the steel foundry action research team that instigated a significant organizational change at that company, increasing retained earnings; and

- the team that brokered a new neighborhood park in a low income section of Dallas through delicate negotiations with residents, local businesses, and city officials.

We made additional changes as the course proceeded, but then one failure, the third week before the end of the course, made me momentarily despair. The team-evaluations and the self-evaluations, which counted significantly in the final grade, were occurring that evening. As the session proceeded, I began to hear more and more stories from students, teaching assistants, and other faculty of rigged, superficial, or otherwise invalid evaluations by groups. I began to feel that our objective of creating a structure that guided students toward responsible, adult goal-setting, action, and evaluation, weaning them from dependence on the pre-defined structure, had made no impact whatsoever, despite the repeated assertions by many of the students themselves that it had.

I remember sitting in my small office as I heard these reports, feeling glared at by the overhead light and feeling as though I were inside a nightmare, the victim of forces greater than whatever paltry allies I might have. The course was virtually over. We had no more leverage. One of our primary systems intended to engender reflection and self-correction was itself being subverted.

In this moment, perhaps just to get away from the glare, I closed my eyes, put my head down on my arms, and tried, much against my depressive inclination, to sit with myself quietly, prayerfully if you will. Breath and pulse entered my awareness, as well as thoughts and feelings. I allowed it all without focusing on any of it, feeling a gradual diminution of the nightmarishness and a rising gratefulness to the source of this blooming attention…

> *I was reentering the present. "We never keep to the present," Pascal tells us. "We recall the past; we anticipate the future … We are … so vain that we dream of times that are not and blindly flee the only one that is. Thus we never*

actually live, but hope to live, and since we are always planning to be happy, it is inevitable that we should never be so (Pensees, #47)."

Reentering the present is always confusing: there never seems to be any reason to do so; the time never seems right – either there's not enough time, or there's nothing going on, so why bother. Once I begin to detach from, and thereby make contact with, my body, thought, and feeling, there is so much to attend to; yet, again, there is no clarity what deserves attention. The gradual effect of sustaining this exercise, however, is to create a kind of gravitational field, like a black hole sucking time toward it, until the past and the future congregate around the rim of the present, exhibiting their relation to the present rather than distracting me from it ...

I began to remember some of the principles that had emerged over the previous nine months. One was to take whatever appeared to be a block or barrier to progress and redefine it as a building block. Another one was, when in a jam, think of the last thing I would ordinarily do and try it out.

Instead of giving up, as I may too easily have done on other occasions, I decided to fight. With this decision, the calmness that had supplanted the nightmare began to turn into anger, and the anger began to turn into an unusually intemperate message to the students, which describes more particularly what was making me, now, so angry. Even before the end of class, most of the message was written. After review by the staff, it was amended, duplicated, and handed to the students the following week, Career Night, along with the sparse announcement that all evaluation decisions reached between groups and staff members the previous week were null and void, to be renegotiated after discussion of this message on the final night one week hence. Here is the conclusion of my angry screed:

> How about this for a final example: a student surprises his group early in the term by revealing his deep Christian convictions, his sense of being able to talk to and be sustained by God. Although some of his earlier behavior had seemed insensitive to others, making them feel somewhat distant and wary of him, his personal revelation draws others closer to him. Thereafter, however, he gradually withdraws commitment from the group, ceasing to attend many meetings. Finally, at the time of peer evaluation, he apparently colludes before the meeting with two other members who have participated minimally to rank themselves as having contributed most to a healthy group process, simultaneously ranking those who have invested most in the group as having contributed least, presumably hoping to achieve an average ranking similar to others by this tactic.
>
> Perhaps, after years as a behavioral scientist, I should be a bit more blasé about the fact that persons' behavior regularly contradicts their ideals, as in this case; or, as an educator, maybe I should just admit to myself that none of us influences very many students deeply (there is plenty of research to reassure me on this point). I find it much more hopeful, however, to respond with anger.

On the final night of the course, the auditorium was jammed. I was determined to say whatever I could to make the groups converse honestly later that evening and finally calculate how their present lifestyles (what, in retrospect, I have named the ***Subordinate Culture***) related to the practices encouraged by the course. I was determined to keep us all cooped up in that large, warm room until some connection occurred among us, even if it was unequivocal mutual rejection.

In what mood the students entered, I'm not sure. Staff members were tensed toward their roles with the groups, for I had insisted ferociously that they unrelentingly confront any group that tried to short-change the evaluation process, and we had role-played several possible scenarios. Certainly, the mood was different from earlier in the semester. I now knew some two hundred of the students personally, many quite intimately from intensive interpersonal relations weekends, so I was looking into many faces I knew and cared for, meeting many eyes. By this time, my anger was less central in my feelings than my desire to challenge the many students who I knew had genuinely tasted and valued the experience of speaking and hearing truth to take the necessary risks in their groups to reawaken the taste of truth again tonight.

After all my preparation for this moment, I did not know what I was going to say. When I picked up the microphone I found myself filling everyone in on the conversation I had just had with my faculty colleague Roger Dunbar over dinner about our sense of the successes and failures of the course, of the strengths and weaknesses of the students and the SMU culture, and of our hopes and fears for the future. From the very first words I knew that I was finally talking to everyone in the room. I was relaxed, meeting their eyes and feeling their listening.

The Positive Feedback

Afterwards, as the students left the auditorium for their group meeting rooms, the "Christian" who had colluded to rig his group's peer evaluation in his own favor made his way up to shake my hand, thanking me and saying he certainly deserved whatever was about to occur in his group now.

The staff celebration at the pub that night was long and merry. Everyone had good news to share of groups coming to full accountings, even when difficult, of their semester's activities. I would hardly claim that this occasion changed many persons' lives or values noticeably, but I do believe that such events touch a deep and often hidden sense in persons of the dignity of hewing to a truth at once personal and objective – a sense which may be quickly forgotten again – but which each calling forth makes more accessible to the next call.

Ultimately, no safe, foolproof technique guarantees the self-correcting capacity of a person or social system. There is no guarantee whatsoever. The beauty of self-correcting systems can never wholly supplant the ugliness of self-destructing systems. The beauty of self-correcting systems can never be 'safely' institutionalized apart from particular persons deeply committed to the ongoing vigilance and initiative required to exercise the power of balance. Self-correcting systems are always vulnerable to demise.

The quantitative student assessments of the spring were very positive. Students rated themselves as learning *more* than in an average course in the areas of self-direction, action competence, awareness of interpersonal process, and awareness of personal learning style. They also judged that they were learning significantly more in general in this course than in their average course (and it is worth noting that most of the courses at the school that used the 'learning-compared-to-your-average-course-this-semester' measure were rated as delivering less than average learning). On the other hand, only 9% of the students rated themselves as learning more "facts" than in their average course, and only 20% rated themselves as learning more "theory." To us, these limited findings indicated that the course was generally succeeding in generating outcomes congruent with its purposes.

We received another confirmation that the impact of the course was widely experienced as positive when one of our faculty members was chosen the Outstanding Professor at the Business School.

The Negative Feedback

Despite the just-mentioned forms of positive feedback, a significant proportion of the senior faculty of the school was **not** feeling like we were learning together! When we sent them our fourth long report of the year on our work on behalf of the school and met with the faculty to discuss it, the debate was lively indeed. While most of the new faculty and several of the senior faculty were supportive or at least constructive in framing the debate, a significant group of the senior faculty was only too happy to use our own data to attack us.

During the conversation five criticisms of the course emerged:

1) it was not hard enough; there were too many A's;
2) it was too frustrating for students; many did not seem to know what was expected of them, nor how course activities related to business skills;
3) there was not enough emphasis on facts and theories;
4) the emphasis on working in groups in the course was generating conformity rather than encouraging individual entrepreneurship; and
5) there was too much emphasis on 'learning' issues in the course and too little on 'business.'

Even though we disagreed with most of these criticisms, the course staff decided to try to restructure the course for the fall of 1971 in such a way as to respond to *all* the criticisms, thus testing both their validity and our efficacy at the same time. For example, in response to the criticism of too many A's, we changed the grading system altogether to an "Honors," "Satisfactory," "No Credit" system; we reduced the percentage of the grade given over to self – and team-assessment results; and we reserved "Honors" grades for truly "A" work. By the end of that fall semester, 20 of the 360 students had dropped the course, 52 received "No Credit," the vast majority received "Satisfactory," and 36 received "Honors" (by contrast, half the course had received an A or A – the previous spring).

At the same time, the overall end-of-semester ratings from the students improved that third semester over both previous semesters. And, in terms of our two weakest ratings the previous spring, the number of students who regarded themselves as having learned more theory than in an average course rose from 20% to 67%, to our satisfaction, and the number who regarded themselves as learning more facts, though still a minority, rose from 9% to 33%.

The course faculty reported the latest data at a full faculty meeting, particularly thanking those faculty who had critiqued us the previous spring for helping us to improve the course yet again. In particular, as a result of taking seriously their critique that the grades were too high, we had learned something important about how to use the grading system to increase learning.

To my amazement, without a word of acknowledgment, let alone any congratulations, the Old Guard once again launched into a critique, this time without reference to any of the data since the data did not support them. I responded that the course staff could hardly be expected to accept critiques based on single comments by students or no data at all, if other members of the faculty were unwilling to take seriously the quantitative and qualitative data we had collected. In response, one of the senior faculty complained that my statement was "blindly antagonistic." Other faculty burst out in spontaneous laughter at the projection and unintentional irony of his comment. Given my years'-long effort to overcome my conflict-aversion, I found this as satisfying a piece feedback as I'd ever received.

In spite of our excellent success during the third semester, we once again radically transformed the course for the fourth semester, when one of our staff came up with a much simplified version. This new version worked well too.

The End of My Time at SMU

But now new forces were at work. In the spring of my second year at SMU, I was invited to apply for an associate professorship at the Harvard Graduate School of Education. At the same time, the senior faculty cabal that had opposed the A.S.1 course (and seemed to oppose it all the more the more our research data showed its efficacy) went back to work, proposing that the school eliminate all required courses. At this point, of course, A.S.1 was the only required course.

Contrary to my initial intentions when I flew to Boston for interviews, I accepted Harvard's offer. Although I hated to leave the excitement and friendships at SMU, I looked forward to learning more about developmental theory from well-known scholar Larry Kohlberg at Harvard. I was also drawn to the spectacular diversity, competence, and social action orientation of the Ed School's graduate students, who included a significant percentage of Blacks, Hispanics, Native Americans, and international students. Moreover, I realized that I would be able to join the small Boston group associated with the Gurdjieff Work.

When I met with Rosabeth Kanter, one of the friends I had made at the Bethel program two summers before, now an Assistant Professor of Sociology at Brandeis, we found we shared a wish to create a communal home. And, not least, in a single weekend visit to Boston, I attended two parties with more old friends and more women of my own age than I'd met in two years at SMU.

■ ■ ■

For me, the two-year period at SMU was a more intense period of success, empowerment, and transformation than any similar length of time before or since in my life. I believe that I mastered both the theory and practice of designing liberating disciplines in relation to the ***Subordinate*** culture. I also broke through to new levels of understanding and practice in relation to generating a powerfully collaborative, creative, and productive ***Peer*** culture. In this arena, however, I certainly did not attain mastery, and the learning continues to this day.

Finally, the events surrounding Pat's early departure and the end of AS1 as a required course made me inescapably aware of how deeply embedded ***Superior*** cultures become and why. To protect their own power (as they understand power in its unilateral sense), they are viscerally motivated to protect their assumptions from inquiry. The transforming learning celebrated and encouraged by a culture of true ***Peers*** is enormously threatening to ***Superiors*** at the early action-logics (Opportunist, Diplomat, Expert, Achiever), so they easily become self-justifiedly hostile to ***Peer Culture*** and to the later leadership action-logics.

Whatever I may have learned about ***Subordinate Culture*** and how to transform it, I learned much less about how to deal successfully with ***Superior Culture***. And what I did learn was more about defense than about offense – "stay under the radar initially" [unlike Pat] – "attract conventional badges of success" [the teaching award]). The one offensive strategy we clearly practiced was to "do research on the collective action you are leading and publicize its results." But our way of enacting that strategy influenced the ***Subordinate Culture*** more than the ***Superior Culture***.

If that two-year period was intense and transforming for me, I think it is safe to say it was also transforming for the SMU Business School in a permanent fashion, even though some of the particular innovations did not last. Two years after my departure, some of the basic concepts of action learning, such as contract-based projects, were in fact diffusing rapidly and visibly throughout the school to the point where students now expected to chart their own careers both within and beyond the school rather than to follow a pre-defined set of requirements. One course – taught collaboratively by members of the marketing, management science, and organizational behavior departments and based on projects – attracted 170 students. Members of the finance and accounting departments had completed a self-paced, video introduction to those two subjects, had experimented to their satisfaction with the use of teaching assistants (starting with a former A.S.1 teaching assistant), and over half of the entering business students were now choosing this method of instruction. Two A.S.1 faculty members continued to teach the Action Science course I had introduced during my second spring term at SMU, expanding it to three sections with over 100 students. A Life-Planning Center had been created and about 200 students a year were choosing to go through a career planning process as one of their courses.

In faculty and administrative matters, the school was also becoming increasingly contract and project based. The yearly Faculty Action Plans that the acting Dean had announced before I left had become institutionalized. Faculty members chose which department and which program they wished to belong to (!) and developed their action plans with that chairman and that program director. Also, the school moved from a pattern of late submissions of budgetary and instructional data and projections to the university, to becoming the earliest to submit its budget and other documents.

The emphasis on action learning was proving attractive to both students and businesspeople. Both the number of students and the amount of funds being attracted to the school were increasing. In a year (1974) when there was a faculty hiring freeze in all other schools and departments at the university, the Business School was scouting the country for 19 new faculty.

On a less visible level, my conversations two years later with faculty, both in the course and not, and with former teaching assistants, revealed a continuing digestion of the initiatives from the earlier time. (Thirteen of them read and critiqued the first draft of my later book, ***The Power of Balance: Transforming Self, Society and Scientific Inquiry***, about that period and about different kinds of power.) One former teaching assistant said, "A.S.1 was such a shock to my system that I spent most of my senior year recovering from it and integrating it all. I really did – that was a very dormant time and I felt like the school was a lot quieter, which was good for me."

Several faculty members, some of whom had not been on the A.S.1 faculty, spoke of applying the action learning approach to more and more areas of their professional and personal lives. As one of them (*not* on the A.S.1 faculty member) said, "The idea that you came into the system and diagnosed some of the motivating forces and then drew up a model, designed a strategy, hammered it out with others, acted, observed, revised, acted again — that model is a fascinating perspective for me to see the events through. I didn't see the events through that perspective at the time. I wish I had, but I didn't."

In the "invisible" realm, however, there was also something about the continual quality improvement process that A.S.1 had enacted that had since disappeared. "We're getting very, very good at doing what we were doing two years ago," one former A.S.1 faculty member reflected. "And these new faculty are very competent. They'll relieve some of the overload. But the new blood has not been expanding our range, adding whole new perspectives."

The dean was finding it more difficult than he had anticipated to get many of the faculty to take the initiative necessary to craft personally and organizationally useful Faculty Action Plans. "This kind of organization depends on the various individuals and groupings within it to take initiatives," he said, "but instead people keep asking me how much authority they have." At the same time, the faculty with whom I spoke unanimously viewed the dean as using the Faculty Action Plans and the new Program Directors as ways of achieving tighter top-down control over the system.

Another former A.S.1 faculty member put it this way: "There are now more visible symbols of external control and fewer of getting in touch with your own power, which is what A.S.1 was really about. The external part of A.S.1 — the contracts and projects — got diffused to the rest of the system. But the internal part — the consciousness — has disappeared except for a few individuals. I think the people who have already felt their power still experience a lot of freedom in this system, but those who haven't see a lot of controls."

A former teaching assistant added, "There's no longer an active support system welcoming anyone who wishes to search for who she is and where she's going." And a faculty member concluded, "People have always respected one another's skills here, and that makes it a good place to work. But once there was a kind of awe, a going to learn, going to the mountain, each to the other." (Endnote 17)

Section III – Stranger and Stranger

Chapter 13

Moving On to Cambridge, the Channing Place Commune, and Harvard 1972 – 1976

After many a farewell party in Dallas with faculty and student friends, Stavros and Helen and I shared the driving of my old car and a rental truck up to Cambridge.

I knew the road well, having by now made the car trip back or forth from Dallas to Washington, New York, and Boston a full eight times, counting this haul. From Texas through the corner of Arkansas, then the long way through Tennessee and Virginia. Maybe a stop in DC to visit my friend Mark Foster, usually a visit with my spiritual teacher in New York, where time itself might, briefly, stop ... And on to Boston.

What with a nap every third round of driving, and Stavros and Helen to talk with at meals, the trip was a lot more fun this time than when I drove it alone. Stavros and Helen had been students at SMU who played the consultant role in the AS1 course. They were becoming friends of mine who would remain friends after we reached Boston. In fact, they would be rooming at low rent at 6 Channing Place, the communal home off Brattle Street that it turned out, after my two long-weekend visits to Harvard in the spring, a group of us bought.

As his name suggests, Stavros was Greek. He was entering the Harvard Business School doctoral program, but would soon drop out, in favor of joining the spiritual community surrounding Chogyam

Trungpa Rinpoche. My other fellow-communard-to-be – Helen – was a very bright young woman who was graduating from SMU without a clear next step. She was also sleeping with me on occasion, with the enlightenedly-explicit mutual understanding that we were not, and were not seeking to become, exclusive partners. Rather, we belonged to a new category of love I was trying to define and embody with men and women "non-possessive mutually-beloveds who practiced *coitus reservatus* and other limiting yet liberating commitments in the sexual, the relational, and the spiritual sense.

■ ■ ■

The dream of a communal home had become a reality more quickly and easily that spring than I could have imagined. Rosabeth Kanter led the local search for the home, and we each brought in two other persons. To my Stavros and Helen, she matched her new husband-to-be, Barry Stein, and the infinitely pleasant and laconic Harvard Social Relations professor, Phil Stone.

I had visited Rosabeth twice during the previous two years since our nine weeks at Bethel together, sharing a little of her deep grief since her first husband's suicide in his office at the Harvard Business School. This would have been a colossal shock for any young married person to take, and her suffering included an added piercing question about whether their mutual competitiveness – both of them in their first year of teaching and scholarly publishing at the time – she doing very well, he less so – might have played a role in his suicide.

There had been four suicides at "the B-School" that year – two students and two faculty – so I thought that the institution deserved its due share of the credit. It was my pleasure throughout my academic career to cordially hate the Harvard Business School, as too self-servingly and uninquiringly allied with the power-elite of unreconstructed, unconscious capitalism. (In recent years, I have come to admire its difficult initiative, driven primarily by women faculty, to rebirth the HBS culture into a gender-mutual, action culture.)

When I had first visited Cambridge, considering the Harvard job, Rosabeth and I had discovered that there were a good dozen or more very large, but down-at-the-heels, Victorian homes in the Cambridge area at good prices. Apparently, no mere nuclear family could afford heating such a large expanse of high ceilinged rooms. Or if they had the money, why go to the trouble of refurbishing these old places?

We chose 6 Channing Place, just off Brattle Street, a lovely 15-minute walk to and from my office at the Ed School in Harvard Square. In what very quickly became known as the Channing Place Commune, Rosabeth and her new husband, Barry, would take the big wing of the second floor, giving them an entire apartment to themselves, complete with library, bathroom, and guestroom. Phil Stone also made a healthy investment in the down payment, and he took the other side of the second floor (two rooms and full bath). Stavros, Helen, and I would each take one of the three rooms on the third floor with a shared full bath.

Everyone was happy with his or her or their space. And in addition, we had a magnificent, more public area on the first floor, with a large living room, very handy for large parties, and a much more cozy library with TV, where any or all of us hung out regularly, with lots of close friends for the big Celtics and Red Sox games. There was a spacious yard on the side, where Stavros and I played palette. In spite of all these delectable places, the one I loved perhaps best of all was the deep old-fashioned bathtub on the third floor, where my back would relaxingly crack when I slid into its steamy waters.

I had little capital to contribute to the down payment – only $5,000 – but was willing to pay more than my share of the monthly mortgage and happy to contribute sweat equity as well, all of which would increase my financial equity. Thus, I gained great satisfaction later that summer, repainting the dark corridors on all three floors and the stairway walls, transforming them from deepest evergreen to sparkling white. The following summer I helped a professional re-shingle the outside. By combining our different forms of equity, we were able to live like minor princes and princesses, whereas on our own most of us would have been renting delapidated third-floor walkups.

My $14,000 a year Harvard salary, bulwarked by our communal ingenuity and mutual commitment, seemed munificent to me, more than meeting my wants and needs. With the decision to hold a weekly meeting on Sunday evenings and to set up cooking and food-shopping rotations, our 6-person communal experiment began in August, after the papers on the house finally passed. So it was that once again it became relatively easy for me to heed my primary rule for the good life, which is to pay no more attention to the earning of money than is necessary to maximize the time one can spend on good work, good friends, and good questions – working, loving, and inquiring.

Communal members turned out to be of great help to one another on unexpected occasions. For example, Phil Stone turned out to be of help with regard to my first book, drawn from my undergrad thesis on blue collar workers' labor, leisure and politics. An ambitious Harvard graduate student took advantage of the fact that I included all of our coded data as an appendix for our book. Just as I'd hoped might happen, he set about re-analyzing the data. Eventually, as promised, the good student left off a copy of his paper at my office... along with a regretful note stating that his re-analysis of the data, using the latest Path Analysis parametric methods, had proved my more primitive, non-parametric statistical conclusions to be invalid.

Unless we had made computational errors, I could not imagine what could be wrong with our ordinal statistics, based on our ordinal data. My review of the numbers found no computational errors. Nevertheless, much concerned by this student's claim, I took my book and the student's paper to Phil, who very soon reassured me that my ordinal analysis was correct because the data were themselves ordinal in nature and could not bear the assumptions inherent in interval-level statistics, such as the Path Analysis technique the student had used.

One of the things this episode taught me is that the ordinal level of analysis is much more important in most of the day-to-day realms of human affairs than the interval level, even though interval level statistics have much higher prestige amongst statisticians. Ordinal analysis is more important for two reasons: first, because in most cases humans can only reliably make ordinal distinctions, such as "more/the-same/less," or "1st, 2nd, 3rd"; and second, because in our active roles, we are usually working with small numbers (say a six-member senior team trying to decide among three strategic alternatives), for which non-parametric statistics work best.

Summertime Wandering in Europe

That summer of 1972, before we moved into Channing Place, the three third-floor members of our incipient commune – Stavros, Helen, and I – had each decided separately to travel to Europe. Stavros travelled to his cave on the island of Ios. Helen travelled to France first. And I travelled to Mom's Italian farmhouse first, then on to my own personal, spiritual home – at St. Gilgen on the Wolfgangsee in Austria, and from there to Bulgaria for a week, where my father was now Ambassador.

I had brought some tabs of LSD with me, and, after two days of climbing and swimming and writing at the Wolfgangsee, I walked up the hillside in the forest, off any path, just as Don Juan counseled Carlos Castaneda to do in ***Journey to Ixtlan***, to what felt like my very own place. There, I 'dropped' the LSD, meditated for a time, threw the ***I Ching*** coins, and asked about my course in life.

The hexagram I drew shocked me because it was the second time in a row that I had come to it, of all 64 to which I might have been guided. The hexagram is named 'The Wanderer.' (Eventually, I drew this same hexagram 4 of the first 7 times I threw the ***I Ching*** – such a statistically improbable event that it is highly unlikely any other human being has ever done so.)

"The Wanderer is always polite because always a visitor in others' homes and lands," I read. This characterization of me was an incredibly apt description of both my Foreign Service childhood and my current itinerant academic life right up to this very moment in an inn in a foreign land. At the same time, it was a tremendously frustrating message, since I was hoping for some clearer, more permanent, more inspiring focus.

Next on the hillside, I entered into more prolonged and more stunning Gurdjieffianly-inspired meditations than usual. Then, I slowly rolled my back against the hillside as the tide of chemically-assisted imaging rose, and invited myself to dream my own vision for my future.

Closing my eyes, I actually fell into a sleep and saw myself painting the walls of what I knew was to be my large third-floor room at Channing Place. The ceiling I dreamed was covered by a billowing gold silk cloth like an Arabian tent (later, in the actualized version of this dream, this role was played by some inexpensive yellow cotton spreads). The walls I dreamed began in forest green at the bottom and gradually transformed to gold on the way up. On the one wall of the room that had no door or windows, there was a long diagonal slash of red. And, in the dream, I was manipulating an extraordinarily broad brush to make a short, violent black stroke on the other diagonal.

I awoke slowly and sweetly on the hillside while it was still light, holding the image of the dream as a precious gift. I was also full of relaxed determination to return to Cambridge and create what I had seen. The determination coursed through my body and felt lion-like, and I rolled about some on the forested hillside carpet of moss and leaves.

The green evolving to gold of the walls of the dreamed room felt like my idealized (and only very occasionally actualized) sense of my embodied self – green and alive within my body, like now in the forest on the hillside, with a golden light of attention flowing through my thoughts, feelings, and sensations of my embodiedness, and thence out (… and back in again through vision, touch, listening, breath, and smell).

Was the long red stripe in the dream image the suffering of a heart torn between attraction to human experiments in love and attraction to a non-dual source of attention itself? Or was it (less grandiosely!) the suffering of a lonely boy, a little traumatized perhaps by losing all his friends again and again as a child, each time his family moved on, now wanting to keep them all for the rest of his life? And did the thick black stroke in the painting bespeak unintended interruptions and black discontinuities of attention such as we all experience? Or some more ominous shadow yet?

From this full-bodied, curled-up contemplation, I aroused myself, sprang to my feet, shook the leaves off, and ambled down the hill, keeping the fluid, lion-like, Lucy-in-the-Sky-with-Diamonds feeling for the entirety of the next 24 hours. As I contemplated my experience, I came to feel the time had come to act – not like a "Wanderer," but like the "Master of My Own Home and My Own Life" as symbolized by painting my room.

Upon my return to Boston, and after turning all the halls in the house from dark green to white, I went to work painting my own room. Turning the walls of my room into a smoothly changing color from pine green base to golden ceiling was a much harder job, however, showing me a little of the demand of true craft. The two brush strokes from the dream were even harder to accomplish. I had to construct special brushes and paint pans, and do some rehearsals in the old garage, before the morning came when, after a meditative and martial arts preparation, in a kind of waking dream state, I completed the enactment of the red and black slashes from the dream onto the wall of my room. However unprofessional and unabidable the paint job may have appeared to others, I was extremely satisfied with – nay, proud of – my artistic creation.

Although our communal experiment lasted throughout my four years at Harvard, we interrupted our weekly meetings and cooking schedule after the first year when we dispersed for the summer. And we never again resumed meeting regularly.

The Harvard Ed School

My sense at the time, in moving to the Harvard Ed School, was of having made the right strategic move, both professionally and personally. I should come to a place dedicated first and foremost, as I was, to learning... and to learning relevant to a truly diverse (internationally, racially, economically, and gendered-ly) group of adult activist-scholars. I should come to Harvard at a time when revolution was still in the air, when Chris Argyris (who had moved from Yale to Harvard) and I could become colleague-peers, when I could and should learn from the best theorist-empiricists Harvard had to offer, and when I could try out my commitment to timely action on a larger stage.

That I would meet women of my own age – women who were not my students, and who were in possession of their own sense of identity and power – was a key decision-variable. So was the fact that I would be participating in the creation of a communal home that half of the participants, including me, could never otherwise have afforded to live in. Key too was that I would be able to participate weekly or twice-weekly in the Boston Society for Experimental Studies (the local mask for the Gurdjieff Work meetings).

At first, the Harvard Ed School felt like a perfect fit for me and my concerns. I was becoming increasingly interested in developmental theory. At the Ed School I could learn from two old lions of developmental theory and research, Larry Kohlberg and Bill Perry, as well as two emerging young titans, Carol Gilligan and Bob Kegan. Moreover, the students were multi-cultural, motivated, leadership-oriented, bright, and experienced. I was a popular teacher with large classes and many doctoral advisees. I also published three books and wrote a fourth in my four years there, along with a sprinkling of journal articles. So, in some ways, the place did work for me.

But for many reasons, the Ed School felt less and less nurturing as the years went on and I experienced more of its deep structure. First off, I was hired as an Associate Professor on a five-year contract and told that there were no open tenure positions, no matter how well I performed. Since I didn't believe in tenure, this did not disturb me at first. But I gradually realized that, as an untenured faculty member with no long-term future there, I was not about to have an influence on the school as a whole – unlike the SMU Business

School, which welcomed my influence when I was even younger and more junior.

Moreover, unlike the rest of Harvard except the Divinity School, the Ed School had virtually no endowment funds. The lush amounts of annual federal research funds available in the 1960s were suddenly running dry in the stagflation of the early 1970s. In spite of the overall funding dearth, however, each senior professor wanted to continue his or her own research program, rather than collaborate with one another – since no one else was good enough for anyone else to bother collaborating with!

At first, I was glad to take on more and more students as doctoral advisees, until I realized that senior faculty refused all but those who directly reinforced their own research. Also, although I (truly!) loved nothing better than to read drafts of colleagues' papers and books and offer extensive editorial responses, I began to find that most of them somehow never got around to reading mine.

Faculty meetings, I soon learned, were meaningless exercises because many senior faculty would miss them, effectively prohibiting any sense of collective vision and strategy – let alone action – from developing. This left the poor dean to negotiate with them individually in regard to any actual decision. It was as frustrating a confederacy as our original 13 states became in the decade following the Revolution. Perhaps partly because of the resource squeeze, and perhaps partly because of being the very acme of modern academia, Harvard was also sometimes a viciously and small-mindedly competitive place.

I was not amused. I was deeply identified with the notion of creating wider and deeper communities of inquiry in educational organizations of which I was a member. This had been possible to some degree in so many of my prior organizations: at Elihu, at YSHS, at YUB, at the graduate program at Yale, as a Danforth Fellow, at SMU, and in the Gurdjieff Work. I became somewhat depressed that the chance to have any such influence appeared so small at Harvard.

Intimacy and Inquiry with Friends

If the Ed School as an educational structure seemed wanting to me as a transformational cauldron, its students were nevertheless a treasure trove of bright, activist men and women of all races and nationalities, almost all of them older than me (I was now a grand old 28). Dot Uhlig is just as one example. More colorful than all her fabulously colorful artwork that I can see from my spot here typing in my home now, Dot was fifteen years older than me, a social services leader in Massachusetts, and an artist. During a long evening that was just right, we became one-time lovers, continuing as friends through the years thereafter – also just right... Right up to the exquisite and extravagant 80th birthday party on Cape Cod that her three children, put on for her and her wealth of friends.

I was clear that I was not seeking to marry, nor seeking any exclusive, possessive relationship, but rather multiple, committed friendships with men and women, many of whom became good friends of one another as well, all constructed on a communal base. I also felt sure I would want children in my thirties and that committed personal and communal covenants would provide the right kind of nest for them, freed from the exclusive – and therefore often overbearing – influence of just one or two parents. (I had no complaint about my parents in this regard, but I was amazed to find, during these early years of intimate conversations with friends about one another's life histories, how rare my experience of gratitude for my parents seemed to be.)

Every other month or so, a Yale group of young philosophers, including Morris Kaplan, Tom Schmid, Seyla Benhabib, Don Johnson, and Jay and Heather Ogilvy would motor up 91, 84, and the Mass Pike, from New Haven to Cambridge to meet with the likes of a Gadamer, a Habermas, or a Nozick. I and others would go down to New Haven on alternate months.

If many of those moments when we met were intellectually demanding and stimulating, I capture a different set of emotionally rawer Cambridge communal moments in a letter to my parents:

Morris was here most of August on vacation, but also out of a job again and unsure where next to look or even to live. He was also drinking again, which makes me more nervous than anything else anyone else in the world can do, even when he is drinking moderately, which for the most part he was.

As usual with Morris, his presence brought flocks of old friends to the house, and we had some great parties, Tom Schmid and Seyla coming up from New Haven, Bob Anderson coming over from his basement apartment in Boston, Jim Walsh coming down from Lynn where he is now Director of the Community Action Program.

Finally though, Morris went on a binge, and we had an incredible scene when I discovered him drunk just before he was supposed to entertain Jim and his two daughters for dinner, so I blew up at him and made him promise never to drink here again.

At this point Jim walked in, got angry when he found Morris drunk, and started back out, only to run into Joanna (my 'sister,' Joey Hiss) *returning from vacation. Morris asked Joey gently enough from upstairs for help in "drying out," but she needed to prepare for a consulting trip to Kansas the next day (and anyway she gets even more upset than I at Morris' drinking because of her problems with her parents' alcoholism).*

Joey and I went to say hi to Paula who was staying at the house temporarily, but when we knocked lightly on her door we heard her sobbing over the phone, so we turned away just as Celia entered to go to dinner with me. Celia and I have been working together this year on a de-segregation program she runs and that I am research director for, but this evening she wanted to talk to me about her daughter whom she discovered the week before has gotten deeply involved in drugs ...

Ah ... the communal life!

After hopefully shocking Mom and Dad just a little with this relatively chaotic, emotional story ... I evidently also wanted to prove just how capable and concerned and responsible I was, so my letter continued:

Everything's now better. Joey went off and did fine. Morris dried up while I stayed at home with him the next day and is back in NY though still without job. Paula was going through a terrible schism with her former husband who was still her closest friend, but whose new woman was jealous of Paula, so he told Paula he couldn't see her again (all of which I found out much later that evening). We had some long conversations that helped her. I predicted her husband and the new woman would not last three months. In fact, it's already over.

I've also talked a lot with Celia these last weeks, and I'm afraid the next years for her daughter will be terrible, but momentarily things seem better ...

To a significant degree, I believe, Morris became a full-fledged alcoholic because of his difficulty recognizing and coming to terms with the fact that he was gay, a difficulty he shared with his entire gay generation who came of age a decade before Gay Liberation became a consciousness-raising political movement. He had sought out counseling for his alcoholism during the years when he completed Yale Law School, and he had been taking 'antabuse,' a pill that (perversely!) poisons you if you drink alcohol anytime during the 72 hours after taking it. But every few months, Morris would stop taking the pill and leap off the wagon again 72 or so hours later.

The scariest event for me was the next time he came to Cambridge. He was very definitely "on the pill" at the time and therefore "safe," since he had promised me he would not go off the wagon at Channing Place. At dinner together at a nearby Japanese restaurant, Morris ordered a Virgin Mary. The Japanese waitress did not quite understand and in fact brought him a Bloody Mary. We found this out when shortly, after two sips, Morris suddenly smiled stupidly and said, in an oddly slow, but deliberately coherent, fashion that he thought there was vodka in the spiced-up tomato juice. This comment was followed instantly by his neck giving way, his head falling onto his shoulder, and his body as a whole lounging absurdly to one side, just prior to slithering altogether to the floor. I yelled "Ambulance" in a voice I seem to know how to summon on the rare occasions when it is necessary ... and soon the ambulance was there.

That night at the hospital, Morris very nearly died from those two sips. As I watched, holding his hand, his temperature sank through the floor; his body was shaking in delirium tremens or whatever it was; and the medical team gave him a major blood transfusion. The next morning he came home to spend two more nights at Channing Place. By Monday morning at breakfast, he allowed as how he felt himself to be a well man once again, and grateful. Morris' genuine opening at breakfast, and his sense of strength in speaking of himself as "well and grateful," emboldened me to speak. I said quietly that I too was grateful that he had not died; and then, contrary to my planning, broke into tears as I angrily yelled at him that I would not ever invite him back or visit him if he did not go to AA when he got back to New York. Neither of us had ever heard me speak to him as though from a senior place like that...And he agreed to take me seriously.

I did begin checking by phone within days of his return to New York, and I can report that he did ***not*** go to AA right away. He spent a couple of weeks shilly-shally-ing about, driving me mad ... First, it was because of his having heard of a nice country place to recuperate. ("***Money???***") Next, he was irritated that no one at AA would come to pick him up and take him to the meeting ("***You committed to go. Goddamn it, Morris. Taking yourself is the proof.***")

He did, to his credit, acknowledge over the phone the importance of making that commitment himself. And then he did go, in person and on his own, to his first AA meeting. At least in big cities like New York, there are regular AA meetings at regular times and places, and anyone, new or regular, can go to any one of them. It being New York, Morris made his way around to the nearest meeting, and later to the Legal-Aid-related meeting (since he worked at Legal Aid at the time). But soon thereafter he found his way to a nearby gay AA meeting with a very attractive redhead. Not only did Morris' drinking stop, without using the antabuse pill, but his gay liberation process suddenly accelerated enormously.

Three months later, I happily accompanied him to give his 90-days-dry speech at his AA meeting. He has never again had another drink. After fifteen years as a Legal Aid lawyer, Morris was appointed to the philosophy department at SUNY-Purchase. There he teaches to this day and is well known for such publications as his book ***Sexual Justice***.

What an enormously demanding privilege it is to accompany a lifetime friend through a transforming crisis like that, just as he had, a decade earlier, accompanied me at Yale through my crisis with Jane. (Endnote 17)

Chapter 14

Sufi Jester or Harvard Professor?

I will share just three stories about moment-to-moment challenges of acting in a timely way while I taught at Harvard, and the first is one by a student about me.

In what seemed like a surprising and odd coincidence, when I was originally writing this 'Harvard' chapter, I suddenly found the following story by one of my students of forty-plus years ago. It was in an attachment to an old e-mail, which I read for the first time:

> *Bill Torbert was a Sufi jester masquerading as an associate professor of organizational behavior. Bill was dating the black vice dean of the school. He was scheduled to pick her up for dinner from a meeting, which always ran late. She asked him to rescue her. It was Halloween.*
>
> *Bill always wore jeans, never wore ties. At the appointed time, he interrupted the meeting wearing a pinstriped suit and a beautiful paisley tie, just a touch loud. After all in the room faced him, he undressed, revealing a tight fitting Superman costume. Then he swept the dean off her seat and carried her out of the meeting. A trailing admirer retrieved the suit.*
>
> *He was well over 6 feet tall. He looked burly, but was thin. His large domed head was bald, a fringe of hair covered the perimeters. His lower lip protruded when he was in thought.*

His face was plastic, moving from fierce to handsome to child-like. He had a gift for silence, and listened very well.

Bill illuminated the cyclical nature of human organizing efforts. He made visible to our eyes the behaviors that cause decline and ascent. When I began my career as a consultant, I relied on the processes that I learned from him.

Appointing me one of his teaching fellows, he gave me a wonderful lesson in moral courage. At the end of my section on a Friday, I announced a paper was due the following Monday. A half dozen students corrected me. It was a week from Monday. "No, no," said I, with complete confidence. "This coming Monday." Almost everyone groaned. I ignored their groans and dismissed the section.

Sunday evening, Bill called. Over the weekend, half my section had complained to him. Many students cancelled their weekend plans to complete the paper by Monday. By Sunday, most knew that I was wrong. Their lost weekends had been unnecessary. Bill told me that I risked losing the section, unless I did something.

Panic swelled until it seemed to occupy all of me. My fingers tingled, my throat tightened. I took a deep breath, and retreated to my yoga space in the bedroom. Before I started my yoga, I defined the question I wanted my unconscious to work on, 'How do I turn this apparent defeat into a victory?'

My yoga completed, I knew that I had to acknowledge my error, the justness of their anger, and the unfairness of my mistake. Then I had to apologize sincerely. The more I did this with an open heart, the better my chance of salvaging my leadership position.

Bill met with the section leaders as a team for an hour before the sections met each week. My panic rose near the end of this meeting. I said that I could not face my section. I was too afraid. Bill said that if I didn't, he would. That pushed me over the rise. I got up, went into the section, did my acknowledgements, and expressed deep regret sincerely.

I was stunned by the section's response. Writing about this, 30 years later, tears roll down my cheeks. The section embraced me. Several commented how few leaders do what I had just done. This was confusing, on the one hand. Confessions had always led to unpleasant consequences. This felt wonderful. I looked up and saw Bill at the door, a great grin covering his face. He shook my hand, hugged me, and left, never uttering a word.

Learning to Trust (Not!)

The next thing I knew, a very good student – one who had taken my previous year's version of the large course "Organizing: Practice and Theory," and who was now playing one of the teaching fellow roles for the large class – chose to focus his doctoral dissertation on the topic of "Learning to Trust." At the Harvard Ed School this process begins with a Qualifying Paper that reviews the relevant scholarly literature. I served as chair of the QP committee, with Chris Argyris and a well-known professor from the Divinity School as the other two committee members.

With some dispatch, the student produced a good first draft, with ample reference to both Chris' work and mine, as well as many others'. After the student responded to my comments on his first draft, his next draft seemed to me excellent and certainly worthy of being read and commented on by the other two committee members. After that, assuming the paper passed, there would presumably be two weeks or so of revisions, and then on to the dissertation itself. But this typically-correct forecast proved seriously off-base on this occasion.

One illustration of learning to trust in the student's paper concerned an interfaith meeting of theologians. Martin Buber and a Catholic theologian generated a moment of increasing tension about whether Jesus was a Christian or a Jew. The tension further escalated into a silent staring at each other. Then they dissolved the tension without another word by rushing into one another's arms.

The student suggested that by relating empathically to this story, one could imagine the possibility of learning to trust in ways that went before and beyond words. He used this illustration to propose that a fully adequate theory of "learning to trust" must take into account two distinct concerns. One is the cognitive Argyrisian concern for developing consistency between our "espoused theories of action" (what values we say guide our behavior) and our "theories-in-use" (what our actual patterns of behavior in conversations look like). People who "walk their talk" inspire trust.

In addition, however, the student wrote, an adequate theory of learning to trust must also include a trans-verbal, trans-cognitive, embodied dimension of trust as well. The paper referenced my ***Learning from Experience*** book (the one that had been my second dissertation with Argyris as my Committee chair) as an example of a theory that did so, citing its notion of a possible kind of trans-cognitive "attention" or "consciousness" that can simultaneously experience itself, one's thought, one's present sensation/action, and the outside world in mutual intercourse with one another .

The student was asking, "Can we imagine that both the Jew and the Catholic are aware of their surroundings ("outside world"); aware also of the confrontation the two are enacting ("one's own behavior"); and also aware enough ("intentional attention") of their different thoughts and feelings ("thinking") to be, at least momentarily, disidentified from their doctrinal commitments?" The student was further, asking, "Can we imagine both the Christian and the Jew realizing in the moment – and seeing in the other's eyes a similar realizing – that they can enact a different ending than expected to their argument, an end that enacts the love supposedly at the heart of each faith, an ending that builds trust across the distances between faiths?"

Argyris responded very critically to this example of the "wordless hug," arguing that we could not know for sure whether Buber and his co-inquirer resolved their conflict, or merely sidestepped it – whether they increased their mutual trust, or simply avoided showing their decreasing trust. Was this a romanticized image of trust that obscured the actual investment required to overcome difference? Worthy questions indeed, the student and I both agreed, and certainly no single case proves anything in general. But proof was not the author's point in this case. The author was asking his readers to use the story to help us imagine only a *possibility*, not to argue how empirically prevalent that possibility is, nor to prove that this instance was a definitive example of learning to trust.

The third reader and I passed the paper 'With Distinction.' With pages of commentary, Chris failed it. The student wished to respond to Chris' critique and did so, presenting a carefully revised paper, reviewing additional literature. Once again, two of us passed it 'With Distinction.' And once again, Chris' failed it (the rule was that all three readers had to at least pass it). According to the Committee on Degrees, this circumstance (two faculty twice voting Honors and one faculty twice voting Fail) had never before arisen.

Now, as committee chair, I felt it to be my responsibility, with the student's concurrence, to ask the Committee on Degrees to appoint a new third reader. This was done. A prominent scholar outside the school read, commented on, and approved the paper, the matter officially concluded. The story thus ended happily in the sense that the student now had official permission to proceed with the dissertation. But he had in fact used up all his doctoral funding on the extra five months this process required. Thus, he returned to his Midwest home with a good new job, but no doctorate, and little, if any, trust in Argyris.

But... let's pause and rewind. I have described these later, pragmatic outcomes of this "learning to trust" episode, before presenting what was for me the dramatic climax of the story and crux of the matter. I've presented the later outcomes first because I want to put the outcomes behind us, so to speak…And see what you think of the following, for-me-cathartic moment along the way.

To wit, before writing to the Committee on Degrees to request the change in the Qualifying Paper Committee – and after much thought about unexpectedly finding myself in a situation where I felt obliged to use my 'legitimate/ institutional' authority (my *logistical* and *productive* powers) as committee chair on behalf of the student in a unilateral way, if necessary, 'over' Chris – I told Chris that I would like to set a time to meet with him about this.

That very moment, when I was simply trying to set up a future time to speak, became the moment when I suddenly found myself tested by Chris as never before. This moment occurred in the fourth floor common area of the Gutman Library where Chris and I happened upon one another amongst a number of students and other faculty. As I attempted to set a time for a meeting with him, I suddenly found myself very much *in* a very emphatic discussion, as the other people in the area silently slipped away. We were really blowing at each other, maybe a little like those Chinese chaps that stamp a foot as they squat down and "throw a glance" at their opponent – a glance that sometimes knocks one or the other of them down.

For twenty minutes or so – twenty minutes that felt to me like Jacob's whole night with the angel – we wrestled each other verbally, each of us feeling required each time we opened our mouths to re-frame and de-legitimize the very ground the other asserted we stood upon. Chris would argue, say, that the student had not made an original contribution to knowledge; and I would respond, say, that this was not a requirement for this review of the prior literature; the dissertation itself was where the original contribution is expected. I had always been pretty good at joining Chris on his terms in rapid conversational swoops and loops back and forth between content and process, analysis and prescription, historical analogy and likely future consequences. But his terms and timing now contradicted what I took to be my prior responsibility to the student in this particular matter.

He asked that we talk further, and I agreed, but said I would act on behalf of the student now and write to the committee immediately. Like so many productive scholars, both of us can be mulish on occasion. In this case, the two of us spent no less than four excellent-but-insufficiently-tasted luncheons at the Harvard Business School Faculty Dining Room battering one another with arguments, without any sense of resolution.

I grant that I must now be telling you the *Learning to Trust* story one-sidedly, in part to convey how much I needed to hold my ground at the time. But my point is not to one-up Chris in this retelling. Indeed, my point is not about what happened outwardly at all, but rather about what happened inwardly to me.

I am trying to describe the unromantic, but nonetheless miraculous process of spiritual transmission that can sometimes occur between brother and brother or between a master and former apprentice as they approach new, increasingly peer-like experiences. Let me see if I can put words to this peculiar Alchemical experience that occurred within me and that goes far beyond words (even when, like then, words are one aspect of what is going on)...

Chris has said that he gets close by fighting. He is very Greek, very agon-istic, in this way. Like Socrates, and like my friend Stavros, Chris likes to pick a fight early, likes to win it (of course), likes to show how this victory enhances a much greater good, such as justice or integrity, and likes to recruit you to his vision and his disciplines through his uniquely crafted combination of unilateral and mutual power.

As you have been learning in this book, *getting close by fighting* is emphatically ***not*** my "native" style. I am much more of a sissy. Like my father, whom I tried so hard to be unlike in this characteristic, I am predominantly a Diplomat – sometimes by strategic foresight, sometimes by default – eager that we (whoever the 'we' currently is) have a good time together.

Nevertheless, let me tell you: In the case of our 20-minute verbal struggle over the *Learning to Trust* paper (somewhat like my struggle with Pat Canavan at SMU), we managed to create a situation together where I felt I had no choice but to stand and fight, in whatever sort of dodging, weaving, tai chi, sissy manner I could manage to invent on the spur of the moment. On that occasion, asserting and holding my ground rather than 'suing for peace' was victory enough for me – not so much over him as over myself. For me, there was a feeling of the two of us having met fully on that occasion and of having strongly tested one another, in peer-like fashion. By virtue of constructing a new kind of boundary between us, I experienced a sense of spiritual empowerment. Collaborative inquiry does not lead to consensus in all cases by any means; sometimes it leads to new boundaries.

What did Chris' and my strong confrontation and then our lack of constructive resolution around the "learning to trust" issue mean? Was my willingness to fight and win a power "battle" with him a sign of my coming of age as a warrior of mutually-inquiring, mutually-vulnerable, mutually-transforming power, able to appropriately blend-in more unilateral forms of institutional-role power in service of a more widely just outcome? Or was it a sign that, though Chris was good at creating relatively mutual conversational situations in settings where he had primary control (as a teacher, or department chair, or as a scholar/consultant), he was less mutual – more dominative – in his exercise of intellectual and institutional power in everyday settings?

Or: was this unresolved struggle a sign that Chris would inevitably continue to feel alienated from me, now that I had begun to work with an ontological theory of four territories of experience, an epistemological theory of developmental action-logics, and a growing toolkit of first-, second-, and third-person methodologies for action and inquiry that went beyond his methods. Might I not only continue his legacy, but also deserve independent attention for new contributions? The future would tell.

Standing Philosophy on Its Head

My final Harvard story concerns the time I was invited to address the Philosophy and Aesthetics Colloquium, a group that typically drew about a dozen Boston area philosophers to the Ed School and was sponsored by Project Zero, a research center led by the ever-more-well-known scholars, David Perkins and Howard Gardner. My sense is that I was invited because I had published an appropriately scholarly and sufficiently provocative essay review of John Rawls' ***Theory of Justice*** (summarized in Appendix A), and because, at an earlier session of the Colloquium, I had made some comments about the aesthetics of action, and the interweaving of aesthetics, ethics, and political power in timely action.

In any event, I was delighted to be asked and did some exploration with friends about what my topic should be. I also did a ridiculous amount of reading, writing, and thinking on my own, much of it related to Ludwig Wittgenstein's later investigations into the relationship between language and action – how language games are like all other games we play; how difficult it is to fully define increasingly abstract concepts, such as "game"; and how language, in live speech, is 'quasi-performative– ' in other words, is partly descriptive, but also partly a more or less artistic or politically apt action in an ongoing life-language game (see Appendix B).

I think I ended up with four titles for the talk, such as "What Kind of Knowledge Leads to Timely Action?" and "How to Aid Emergence and Avoid Emergencies." The title I most clearly remember is "Standing Philosophy on its Head" (borrowed from philosopher Richard Bernstein's talk at Yale some years before about standing Marx and Freud on their heads).

I also came prepared to reframe the Colloquium from the typical seminar-like monologue followed by a little question and answer period at the end… Into a full audience-participation event… but without forcing those present to be anything other than typical, quasi-anonymous seminar listeners, if that was their preference. Put differently, I came prepared to illustrate by what we did, as much as by what I said, a somewhat new kind of game for philosophy to play.

Somehow, the word had gotten out that this might be as interesting an event as my Harvard Ed School predecessor Richard Alpert used to pull off. (If the name Richard Alpert leaves you at a loss, it may be because he later became much more widely known as Baba Ram Dass.) Whatever the cause, there were a surprising 40-or-so people crowded around the walls of the small conference room at the outset. I had asked my friend, Tom Hickey, to video the event. And there he was with his shoulder camera plugged into the wall, with a long extension cord for mobility.

After I was introduced, I introduced Tom's function to the assemblage as a metaphor for our own individual, observing consciousness, which might be 'on' or 'off' at any given moment. The video camera could serve, I suggested, as a reminder to turn on our own inner camera again, should we find it off. (This was long before the era of Institutional Research Boards and, in any event, I was not thinking of using the resulting video for third-person research purposes; it was intended to support each participant's first-person research in the 'here and now').

In my introduction, I also invited participants to waggle one of their hands to remind themselves of their 'embodiment' as well as their 'consciousness.' In the meantime, their 'thinking' and their awareness of the 'outside world' were probably occupied, at least in part I suggested, by looking at and listening to me.

At this early point, there was quite an outburst of laughter at the marked discrepancy between the professional, faculty philosophers present, who were mostly seated at the long seminar table and who mostly did **not** waggle their hands... and the rest of the participants, mostly graduate students, who were mostly seated or standing around the walls and in the window wells and most of whom **did** waggle a hand for a little while and would occasionally waggle it more ostentatiously later in the seminar, as a public reminder to the group of the first-person research they could be performing in the present.

My first point, I said, and one way of standing philosophy on its head, is to claim that philosophy is not primarily an argument about what abstract ideas about nature, human nature, language, and number are eternally true. My claim, rather, is that philosophy is an inquiry into how timely one's action among others can be in each present moment (and how to determine the timeliness of actions). My intent, I said, was to illustrate how profoundly-emotionally-disorienting and behaviorally-challenging profound inquiry with a time signature can be. I went on to quote Kierkegaard, Nietzsche, and Wittgenstein ... In particular, I can re-enter my reading, with great dramatic pleasure, of the dizzying page from ***The Gay Science*** when Nietzsche's madman tells the villagers how lucky they are not to have heard yet of the death of God and of all "pre-given" value.

Comments and questions began to crop up early on during my presentation, and I would encourage short conversations, as well as offering some responses myself. Those in the inner circle around the table seemed to be finding the exchange somehow non-linear and irritating (if their glances down and away and their occasional grimaces were any clues).

At what seemed to me an appropriate point, while continuing to engage in the conversation, I slowly – and with some dignity and grace, as the video later confirmed – climbed on to the seminar table and brought myself into the standing-on-head yoga posture. This evoked prolonged laughter and applause from the periphery of the room and the beginning of some apparently-urgently-uncomfortable whispering among the official philosophers at the seminar table.

A few minutes later, one of the philosophers rose and, moving to the wall, pulled the plug on the video camera, stating that the decision to film the meeting had been authoritarian and did not have the agreement of the participants. After a several second pause of collective shock, a graduate student got up and plugged the camera in again, declaring that the prior action of unplugging the camera had been equally authoritarian and without the agreement of participants.

Now, several of the philosophers began questioning me in a rather hostile tone about what I was planning to do with the film. I said I had no future plans for the film; the filming was, as I had said before, a symbolic act meant to influence our present awareness. But, now that the question was raised, it seemed to me that the film of the session ought to become the property of the present group, since we were in effect creating it together by our actions.

At this point, to almost everyone's surprise, small groups of the faculty around the table began to collect their materials and leave the room together, as the rest of us continued to talk. None of the thirty or so of us who remained could understand why those who had left had done so. There were comments about how quickly this apparently innocuous action and inquiry process had turned into some kind of conversation-interrupting emergency for the philosophers themselves. Why had what was emerging turned into an emergency for one identifiable cohort of participants – just what one of the talk's titles meant to ward against?

Those remaining agreed as our next step to set a time to watch the film and try to figure out what had happened, inviting those who had left to join us. Although this seemed a positive path to me, I was simultaneously so perplexed about what was going on that I asked the group to continue on for a few minutes while I too left the scene to see whether I could find one or more of the philosophers to ask what had become so bothersome to them.

Upon my second turn down the corridor to the elevator, I stumbled into the whole group of philosophers speaking animatedly. They couldn't believe I was walking up to them asking them sincerely what they were upset about. They turned away sullenly, it seemed, unwilling to speak. After standing uncertainly for ten seconds or so, I said I would check again later, but in the meantime felt some responsibility to return to those still engaged in the inquiry.

The meeting concluded about half an hour later. As folks streamed out of the room, Howard Gardner (later author of a book on multiple intelligences!) came back in and approached me. Such an innocent 'sufi jester' was I that I actually imagined he was going to apologize for the philosophers' behavior, and I stuck my hand out to shake his, by way of meeting him halfway.

He did not shake my hand, but rather asked me for the film. I said I could not give it to him because those who had voted (and who constituted a large majority of the initial meeting) had decided it should be regarded as common property, which we planned to watch at such and such a date and time and hoped he and others who had left would join us for. In a strained, clipped, bureaucratic tone, he responded, as he turned on his heel to leave, "If you do not surrender the film to us within 24 hours, we will bring administrative action to bear."

Now I was even more perplexed than I had been before, except for a new clarity that whatever the problem might be, it was no joke from their point of view. I decided I'd better let my department chair, who was himself a lawyer, hear the story from my perplexed point of view right away, and get his advice. But before I reached him, I learned a good deal more about what concerned the philosophers.

I learned this from one of the graduate students who found herself following several of the faculty up the stairs of the neighboring building as they returned to their offices. They were talking about the possibility that Senator Proxmire (D-Wisconsin) might get hold of this film "with the kook standing on his head" and give their research grant what Proxmire called a Golden Fleece Award, which he regularly awarded to National Science Foundation grants that he deemed a waste of federal taxpayer moneys. For Proxmire to do so might doom the project's future funding. To them it seemed critical that the film to which they had not agreed be destroyed (and they apparently assumed they must exercise power unilaterally rather than share their concern with me).

At one point during the quasi-legal negotiations over the next week, I went to talk with the senior philosopher, Israel Scheffler (who was not among the NSF grant recipients). When I reiterated the proposition that I had had no plans for using the film after the occasion, he asked me, quickly and suspiciously, why then it was necessary to have film in the camera at all. That stopped me momentarily, and I responded that it obviously was not necessary. It had simply not occurred to me or to Tom to do it without the film. I could see a different kind of light enter his eye as he realized I was telling the truth and saw momentarily how many different assumptions he and the others had been making. Would that that light had grown more substantial!

Ultimately, however, an agreement was reached, whereby I sent out retrospective permission forms and the philosophers wrote in a special paragraph, giving their permission for the film to be seen *once only and only by participants, and thereafter to be destroyed.* None of the philosophers appeared at that viewing and the discussion afterwards, but almost all of the other original participants did, along with lots of popcorn and laughter.

At the time, I thought the incident would make a very good ***New York Times Magazine*** or ***New Yorker*** article, if there were a good enough writer to bring out both the comic and the mysterious aspects of this philosophical inquiry in action into the nature of timely action. Or, perhaps those of us committed to action research processes ought to have contested more seriously the proposal to destroy the film, on the grounds that it represented both scientific data and an early work in the performance art of timely action inquiry. Perhaps the philosophers did deserve a Golden Fleece Award, **not** for inviting a fool to question basic assumptions of current philosophy and of conventional philosophical discourse, **but rather** for their small-minded response to a *creative inquiry* event.

But such responses seemed too heavy for what had begun as so light a form of play. Moreover, by this time I had become rather cynical about making any unnecessary effort in Harvard's direction.

■ ■ ■

As I was walking the dog in the park this morning after finishing the foregoing story last night, what I recognized as most surprising to me about this event was how completely unmoored I increasingly felt in that most conventional of institutions (Harvard) while I was there. In Dallas the transformational change alchemy was centered in my collaborative work at SMU, with reverberations among the faculty and the whole school. Moreover, in Dallas all my friendships were SMU-related... In Cambridge, by contrast, the transformational change alchemy was centered in my personal, communal, and spiritual friendship initiatives, as well as in my own classes, but otherwise did not affect the faculty or wider school at all, except on the small occasion retold in this last story.

Harvard's president, Derek Bok, came to a faculty meeting at the Ed School in the winter of my fourth year there. The meeting was unusually full, as the full professors came (for once). Bok discussed the drying up of federal research funds and the need for the development of a case statement on behalf of fund raising for the school as a whole, given the lack of success of professors' individual attempts to raise research funds. He asked the full professors to collaborate on developing such a case statement.

A long silence ensued. Finally, one professor asked what kind of support the president could offer for such an effort. Another long silence ensued. Then, with grave courtesy, President Bok responded, "I would have imagined a sense of professional responsibility and pride might have motivated the effort." Stunned by the moral force of his quiet rebuke, I imagined others of the full professors would leap to transform the tenor of the conversation. But not one did so. Instead, a few more senior members of the faculty offered a desultory series of what I can only describe as whining complaints before the meeting ended.

This event galvanized me to resign the next day, effective at the end of the spring semester. If the president could have no influence on the school, then certainly I, a mere junior faculty member, could not expect to. It did not seem 'on mission' (whatever my mission was) to continue in this role. Oddly, at just the moment when I was at the very acme of early career success in professional academia, I became defiantly and depressively unmotivated to do anything conventional to further that success (like apply for another job, or write for publication).

But I did find that, upon my resignation, my overall depression immediately lifted, signaling that I had made the right decision for me, even if I had no idea what my next step would be. (Endnote 18)

■ ■ ■

As a postscript to this chapter, I offer an e-mail from a student of that time that arrived out of the blue by e-mail several days ago.

> *Sent: Saturday, October 29, 2011 12:12 AM*
> *To: William Torbert*
> *Subject: Thank you*
> *Googled you after decades. Longfellow left, late afternoon.**
> *I believed you. I got it. It worked . . .!*
> *Actually, I did thirty years without drinking the Kool Aid*
> *(And it wasn't Gardner's influence). Thank you.*

* Place and time of large "Organizing" class

Chapter 15

The Boston Society for Experimental Studies

Still another fractal of my living inquiry in those years occurred through my membership in the Boston Society for Experimental Studies, the official name and mask of the not-for-profit organization that represented the Gurdjieff Work in Massachusetts. The president of the Society for Experimental Studies (BSES) was Minor White. Minor was in his sixties, one of the major American photographers of the mid-century, and a professor of photography at MIT. I was officially the vice-president of the little-known BSES.

Dorothea Dooling – the founding publisher of ***Parabola*** magazine and a direct student of Mr. Gurdjieff at the very end of his eventful life – mentored the group as a whole, visiting each month from the senior group in New York. In Boston, the group was much smaller – never more than fifty over the next seventeen years of my participation.

It was quite a shock, when I first arrived in Boston, to somehow find myself 'promoted' from one among many hundreds in many "Group 3"s of the Gurdjieff Work in New York to one among four in "Group 1" in Boston. Why did that happen? In part, I suspect, because I came as a direct student of the man who now led the Gurdjieff Work in the US. In part, perhaps, because of my Harvard status. Perhaps in part too because I had visited many different Work communities around the US during my travels of the past six years, from Los Angeles to San Francisco to Seattle, to Denver, to Rochester NY. In largest part, however, my 'promotion' to Group 1 probably occurred simply because there was no one more experienced in Boston. Even Minor was slightly 'suspect,' having spent years as a student of Zen before finding and entering the Work quite recently.

It turned out that I seemed to have a talent for sitting in front of silent groups til someone raised a question from his or her inner, first-person efforts of the week and in the moment...and then for responding in a way that that person and others seemed to find credible, demanding, or juicy. I found two kinds of guidance in this role: first, the examples of all the leaders I had by now encountered in the Work, whom I knew well enough to know I shouldn't be "copying" any of them; and second, to speak from my own inner listening toward the source of attention as I listened in the group, rather than from anything more mental, hypothetical, or pre-planned. This haiku emerged from and fertilized such listening:

Listen Now

Sound and silence:
Related as branch tip is
To trunk and root of tree?

I can now boast about this 'talent' without too much fear of egotism, because I later somehow lost it and spent years mostly observing my dry inadequacy in that same seat in front of a group.

Although the BSES group was small overall, there were plenty of soulful characters and colorful or prickly personalities. I would call Minor the archetype of 'colorful' personalities, even though his long hair was white, his eyes the palest, wateriest blue, and his body vegetarian gaunt. He was utterly without pretension and both his laughter and his capacity for silent listening and movement were deep.

Mrs. Dooling, by contrast, became a kind of archetype of prickly personalities for me, a kind of unsatisfiable Mother-in-Law. In addition to Minor and Doro, there were folks from all walks of life, such as the musician and sound recorder Jimmy Metzner who later hosted an NPR program called "Ear of the Universe" and who wrote and performed the theme song for my first post-Harvard organizing effort, the Theatre of Inquiry.

I first met the later-well-known New Haven architect and rock musician, Barry Svigals, and the even better-known Boston bronze sculptor and back-up singer, Peter Haines, when they showed up at the beginning of a year of meetings in the fall of 1974. In the silence at the beginning of the meeting, I recognized Barry right away because he had taken my left fullback position on the Yale soccer team during the several years that a rag-tag team of us graduate students would try to give the varsity a good scrimmage now and then.

At the end of the meeting, Peter and Barry introduced themselves to me, and I enjoyed momentarily playing the mystical savant, appearing to guess facts about Barry's background before giving away the real basis for my knowledge. Barry's voice and guitar later led many a night of rock and roll singing among the brothers and the sisters – not least many years later at the tenth anniversary of his own architecture firm, of which Peter Haines and I are among the founding advisory board members.

Peter, for his part, lent me his sculpture studio for certain hours each week when I later started the Theatre of Inquiry... Still later, I bid up Peter's prices for as many of his pieces as I imagine anyone else in the world owns, other than his brother... including his "Standing on Head," which graces this book's cover and for which I served as model.

For a time, Barry, Peter, and Minor sent one another postcards on the theme of "Lives I Never Lived." I remember clearly the photo of the ethereal Minor in a wife-beater t-shirt, flexing his non-existent arm muscle, with motorcycle chains hanging from his forearm. Here was truly imaginative research into the third dimension of time, the volume of all possibilities (a.k.a. the future).

In addition to the Boston meetings, I spent long Work Weekends in Armonk, New York from time to time, as well as Work Weeks each summer in San Francisco. During the summer of 1974, I spent my usual month or so in San Francisco at the Gurdjieff Work and then in Mendocino at my brother's and Theta's goat ranch. Later, in August, I drove up to Lake Sunapee in New Hampshire to visit Jay and Heather Ogilvy. On the way (with no drug-enhancement whatsoever) a kind of name appeared in my imagination, just about where the rear view mirror was in the car. The name was:

Nun. How was (am) I a n/n? And what did the slash through the u mean? Was I a nun in the sense of a servant/sister/mother/lover Mary – of Jesus?

Was I a Buddhist sister of compassion? Or a n/n like... Hildegard of Bingen, the medieval Sybil of the Rhine? Hildegard was a woman of ecstatic spiritual experience and transmission, but also among the first senior managers in the west, as the abbess of a convent. Like me, she seemed to crave both organizational efficacy and mystical experience. (There's a great 'old' movie about Hildegard, played by the same lead actress as later also played Hannah Arendt in *Eichmann in Jerusalem*.)

But also N/n, with a slash through the "u" to emphasize that it was none of those either. Not "Nun," but "None." If outwardly I was a Harvard professor, a social scientist, a student of students of Gurdjieff, an explorer of trio and group intimacy, a mountain climber, a soccer player, or a napper... Inwardly I was none of those things, nor anything else I might imagine myself to be. The vast majority of the time, I was no more than my fleeting impressions of the outer world, or an occasional inner sense of my body breathing or in motion, or amidst fragmented thoughts like these.

I was impressed by the comic meaningfulness of this symbol and, over the next months, came to adopt it, by repetition, as an inner mantra for myself. It was a name that for many years I told no one. It was supposed to function as an inward liberating discipline, reminding me to let go of any images I might be carrying about myself, including this name itself – any images that might be spellbinding me from a more active, continual listening into the four territories of experience…

I did write a whole story from Nun's perspective some years ago, in honor of giving up the name as a mantra. N/n's story was about a series of experiences in San Francisco with his spiritual teacher in that same summer of 1974.

N/n opened his eyes slowly. He was resting comfortably on a hardwood floor, gazing up, up into the concerned faces of tall, elderly strangers far above.

Without urgency, questions occurred to him… Where was he? What had happened?

Looking beyond the faces, which so far appeared clueless to him, he could see no background whatsoever. The faces were all surrounded by a faint white glow emanating from everywhere, as though we were all in some angelic realm.

The faces began to thin out. Now he could distinguish the sound of a faint shuffling away of stockinged feet, in the direction of a stronger light and a fresh breeze. He breathed in more deeply…and the pleasurable fresh air chased away some of the pleasurable lassitude.

Gene: sixty-ish, yet catlike; a tai chi master as well as a teacher of Gudjieff's Sacred Movements; the only Movements teacher other than Jeanne de Saltzmann who moved him.

With his long, generous, quilted and quiet face, Gene now knelt beside him. And Alice, Gene's gnome-like, bird-like, seventy-six-ish wife of the joy-Fierce blue eyes hovered just beyond. Gene and Alice were prominent among the strange attractors that drew Nun here each summer.

In this enclave of extravagant reserve, where each surrounded herself in an effortful silence – sometimes suffocating, sometimes crystalline, sometimes parody-like, sometimes paradisical – Gene and Alice moved with grace in their own attentive quiet mood and pace.

Alice's was the darting grace of uncompromising spontaneity, even in the stillest sitting. You could see it in her smallest movements, as her legs crossed themselves in front of a cushion – they were not accommodating themselves to a pre-determined posture, they were sensing toward a perch they would like to keep …

Gene's was the easy grace of uninterrupted practice of his craft. He imparted the gestures of the dauntingly demanding dances of this school in a rhythm so smooth that even N/n could find it within himself to find timed movement and mindful observation of the math – even Nun, whose principal experience in such classes with other leaders was knotted humility …

Even N/n could, in Gene's presence, find the source within himself from which such movements celebrated communion – the communion of the bottoms of the feet and the top of the mind – the communion of dumb matter and conversant energy – the communion of yearning and discerning – the communion of t'ai and chi.

Gene's eyes now mildly appraised Nun, who responded in kind. Gene's hand reached behind N/n's neck, his fingers testing the pulses there, as he brought Nun into a sitting position.

Now, sitting, N/n was recalling the claustrophobic silence in which the 300 closely gathered persons had stood, erectly awaiting the offering of the day's common inner task, before the diaspora toward their different outer tasks. Nun was supposed to work with the roofing team. He realized that at this very moment he was probably missing the instructions about how to set the Spanish terra cotta tiles.

He moved to rise, but Gene soberly held him still. He relaxed and again breathed, more deeply.

What had happened?

This dance hall was the only room on the estate large enough to accommodate all the participants in this week of work, and even so only if all stood close and breathed shallowly. The large room was windowless, entirely clothed in luminous white of variable intensity, depending on the setting of the rheostat that controlled the ten thousand light bulbs behind the seamless cloth. They had all stood wonderfully silently for longer than any of them could have expected (maybe ten minutes). Then the leaders had entered single file through the narrow path, til they too stood silent – Gene, Alice, Isaac (a.k.a. Jerry Needleman), and Lord Pentagon.

Alice had led us on a short awareness-expedition into our own bodies – "tasting our tasting" and other such delicacies. Then it was Isaac who this day had given us our daily task. What was it?

N/n realized he had already forgotten it. Of course, the idea of the daily task was to remember it and practice it continuously as one went about one's outer tasks. But, of course, the experience of the daily task repeatedly began with the realization that one had forgotten it. What was the task?

Oh, yes. "Whenever you touch something, follow your attention through the sensation in your arm and hand, into what you touch. Follow what you are offering and what you are receiving." Nun reawakened to the fact that Gene's two hands were still offering him warmth and support.

"Do you think you can stand up now?"

"Yes."

And he could.

But the standing felt different. He felt relaxed and distended rather than compact and determined as he usually did, when not feeling rootless and afloat, or otherwise. Roofing was going to be an interesting task!

■ ■ ■

John Dark approached the small group remaining in the dance hall, "Lord Pentagon would like me to take you to his room."

John was one of N/n's favorite people. You weren't supposed to care whether you liked the people you were working with. In fact, irritating people were more likely to "wake you up." The point was to be aware of what you were offering and what you were receiving in each exchange, whether you liked it or not, committed to 'conscious labor' and 'voluntary suffering.' Nun had decided to be unembarrassed about his feeling of animal affection for John, for Gene, and for Alice.

Anyway, John had really taught him something the previous summer when they were demolishing the old shed in order to build the new, larger craft studio. N/n had been pounding ineffectually on the imposing cement wall when John had happened by. "What you need for a job like this," John said, taking the sledge hammer and swinging it back, "is a little mindless violence," a sentence he aptly punctuated by reducing the wall to rubble with a single powerful blow.

What impressed Nun most, though, was that he himself could perfectly well have delivered the blow had he had the simple presence and courage to size up what was actually required. It was apt violence, timely violence, mindful violence.

"Wow, what a crash!" said John. "You fell like a tree in the forest. You should have seen everyone jump! I can't believe you found the room to fall without hitting anyone ... Pretty good way of getting Lord Pentagon's attention," he chuckled. N/n just hoped he wasn't about to be sent home. What a thing to do at 7AM on the first morning of the week of work!

He involuntarily reviewed some of the other times he'd fainted – the first and only time he'd ever gone to a Catholic service, when he smelled the incense – and then later at his own first Communion in the Episcopal Church.

He'd worried a bit at the time that God was singling him out for his sinfulness, but he felt a little sinful even thinking that, because he knew the real problem was that he and his friend Ricky had stayed up til 6AM on their overnight together, before his father dragged him off to the Communion service. A sin no doubt, but unlikely to be grand enough to have caught God's special attention, even if he really does know when each sparrow falls.

In any event, God had let him go through with a less ceremonial communion at a sparsely attended early morning service a few weeks later, so he had finally caught up with most of his classmates who had had their confirmation or B'ar Mitzvah the year before.

Not that all his fainting was so overtly religious. He used to faint occasionally as a child, usually when he went to the bathroom before sunup. And, he'd had a great fainting spell, again in the bathroom, this past year after a loud fight in his 135 person "Organizing: Practice and Theory" class at Harvard with a very bright black student. Each was confronting the other for acting in an authoritarian manner. When the student would yield the floor to no one else, Nun had finally asked him to leave the class. After a long, tense moment, the student turned to the rest of the class, shrugged as he gestured toward N/n, said "See?" and walked out. Nun held his tongue and, after the door closed, only shrugged. The class, led by the other blacks, applauded.

But N/n mourned the loss of the student. That night, he awakened from a nightmare with severe indigestion, reached the toilet bowl headfirst on time, fainted in the wake of his success, and then almost instantly reawakened yet again, this time screaming because his foot, calf, and thigh had all locked simultaneously in a massive cramp.

■ ■ ■

Lord Pentagon stood at the door in his colorless clothes, as thin and straight as a conscious walking stick. But to Nun's astonishment, as soon as he'd closed the door on John's retreating form, he became as voluble as N/n's great aunt.

"So good of you to give everybody a shock like that right here at the beginning of the week," he chortled, as though they were in league together. (Lord Pentagon was not known for 'chortling,' nor for being 'in league' with anyone).

He brought out two cut glass goblets, dropped two cubes of ice in each with silver tongs of ancient wrought that held N/n's attention an extra beat, and poured. "No one understands when to drink the Glenlivet," he prattled on, "Nor how little of our cousin's gift is necessary," he added, as he dispensed no more than a few drops-worth of the MacKinnon's Drambuie to each. N/n knew only that he hated Scotch as much as he enjoyed these attentions.

"People drink when they are scared!" Lord Pentagon suddenly roared in a stage whisper, "scared of meeting themselves, or scared of meeting others.

"Preposterous!! Alcohol embodies the mind – properly subordinates you. Cannabis reminds the body – properly uplifts you. But neither shocks you properly unless you are exercising your attention at the moment.

"A toast to all who were exercising at the moment of your fall!"

Lord Pentagon raised his glass, and Nun joined him with the smallest possible sip. Even so, his lips burned and his gums froze. At least, the taste reached no further.

"That's right," intoned Lord Pentagon, observing N/n searchingly, "Many small sips. Follow each. What is offered? What is received? Take several between each toast. Yes, now," he urged, as Nun made only the most minute gesture of acknowledgement.

Taking the glass again, N/n could already feel a clear distinction between his physical reluctance to drink and his emotional eagerness to participate in whatever foolery Lord Pentagon was fomenting. He risked a slightly more generous sip. Now, the fire reached the back of his mouth, and he became sensually aware for the first time ever, of his missing tonsils.

Meanwhile, Lord Pentagon is concluding, telling Nun that he should find the translation team on the second floor, where Lady Landismere, Clement Hipsey, and a French woman, who understands the Tibetan original, are translating The Life of Milarepa. Lady Landismere, he tells N/n, was a one-time-young friend of the aging Evans-Wentz, the original translator of Milarepa into English. Clement Hipsey Nun knows from the New York group. Clem graduated from Yale a few years ahead of him and is now a banker and an art critic who is particularly familiar with Bacot's excellent French translation of Milarepa.*

N/n is to join these three, not work on the roofing.

* Eventually published as The Life of Milarepa by Lobsang P. Lhalungpa (NY: Dutton, 1978)

With these events, an intense week of inner work began for me. I had come to California almost fleeing from my relationships with women, only to be seated all day long each day at a table with a young French woman who seemed both somehow deeply wounded and fatally attractive to me.

Since my separation and divorce, several women had touched me deeply. I had tasted different flavors of joy and pain and discovery, always freshly astonished by the blindness and naivete of my longing, by the turbulence my presence generated in their lives, and by the endlessly complex vicious circles we would gradually discover ourselves to be enacting.

I knew there must be a relationship between the passions of the flesh and the passions of the spirit. Otherwise, life could only be miserable. The search for this relationship brought moments of majesty and moments of despair, but, so far in my life, no permanent engagements in intimate inquiry with women of my own generation. I yearned deeply for deep, continuing friendship; knew somehow instinctively how to find it among a wide variety of men; knew less, if anything, about how to find it among women.

During the past year, two painful relationships of almost identical shape, despite the radical differences in the two women, had turned me into a monk, fleeing to this "monastery" of inner work, seeking sheer detachment from my own passions.

Here, the four of us were working around a bridge table covered by a Tibetan shawl with deep, formal colors. The multiple versions and languages of ***Milarepa*** and the most recent typescript we were editing alternately inspired and confounded us, as did our own occasionally-observed egos.

Hour by hour and day by day, we attempted to penetrate the young Milarepa's experience of compulsion by, and liberation from compulsion by, the fires of black magic and earthly desire. For me, the triangle of different attractivenesses ... Of the book, of the French woman, and of our elevated, four-way conversation about the meaning of these words generated a near-continuous dynamic that temporarily freed my attention from its ordinary passivity and torpor.

Then, each evening I was privileged to hear the words of our peculiar master, dead now a quarter century, read aloud into the silence of a public practicing inner and outer listening. All, in that concentrated state of inward and outward listening, seemed directed to my particular condition – these words in particular:

> *"There is one exit only…from inner emptiness and a meaningless death…to have outside myself, so to say, a 'never-sleeping-regulating-factor…'*
>
> *Why should (God)…send away from Himself one of His nearest, by Him animated, beloved sons, only for the "way of pride" proper to any young individual, and bestow on him a force equal but opposite to His own?*
>
> *…I refer to the "Devil."*
>
> *This idea illuminated the condition of my inner world like the sun, and rendered it obvious that in the Great World for the possibility of harmonious construction there was required some kind of continuous perpetuation of the reminding factor.*
>
> *For this reason our Maker Himself, in the name of all that He had created, was compelled to place one of His beloved sons in such an, in the objective sense, invidious situation.*
>
> *Therefore I also have now for my small inner world to create out of myself, from some factor beloved by me, an alike unending source.*
>
> *There arises now a question like this: What is there contained in my general presence which, if I should remove it from*

myself, would always in my various general states be reminding me of itself?

Life is Real Only Then, When "I Am"
G. Guyrdjieff NY: Triangle Editions, 1975

In my own case, it seemed clear to me that my desire for absolute intimacy – for surrender of personal judgment in a mutual rhythm – was the factor I needed to remove from myself, if I wished to cultivate a never-sleeping-regulating-factor.

Yet the doctrine of plucking out thine eye if it offends thee (or even if it just gets taken momentarily by something attractive) never much appealed to me. Tantric spirituality made more sense to me, even if few have ever mastered its practice in everyday life.

■ ■ ■

Toward the end of that Work Week, I felt that I was able to hold the question about my inclination toward mutuality and intimacy in a more ongoing, revealing way than any question I'd previously held. During the question period after lunch, heart throbbing, I spoke. My direct teacher, in his late seventies at the time, uncharacteristically attacked me in the strongest possible terms, but just the barest raising of his mild voice (which somehow made it infinitely sharper, yet also, to my taste, comic). As he cleanly cut away my outer personality with his comments, I began to weep with joy. From within my breast a molten, sun-like glow began to radiate.

During the following day, not two or three, but a dozen or fifteen people came up to me separately to tell me how sorry they were that I had received such rough treatment, but that they had felt as though he was really aiming a great gift of a lesson at each of them personally during that event. (I listened with amazement at the wider scope of my teacher's timely action and said nothing in response.)

Near the end of the Book of Job, God finally speaks to Job after all Job's suffering and questioning. When God finally speaks – when He becomes, as Aquinas would say, irrefutably self-evident to Job – he does so in what those who are not prepared can hear only as an unnerving roar. He 'thunders' at Job from 'a whirlwind.' But Job talks back and ends by saying, "I had heard of thee by the hearing of the ear, but now my eye sees thee, and I melt into nothing." After this, God turns on Job's three friends and tells them, "you have not spoken of me what is right, as my servant Job has."

So, I conclude, Satan got God and Job to experience one another directly in conversation, as Chris Argyris and I experienced one another directly in our (metaphorically) "thundering" conversation in the public lounge at Harvard – though in our case neither of us "melted." Likewise but differently, my Gurdjieffian teacher and I had experienced one another directly in conversation, and 'I' did melt. (Endnote 19)

Chapter 16

The Inner Chapters Driving School

I had been writing and receiving long letters that summer from both Jason Longstaff, one of my teaching fellows to whom I'd become close the previous year, and his wife Lee, whom I had just met toward the end of the spring. The fact that they were married, and the fact that I had no desire to interfere with their intimacy and their marriage, seemed a fortunate circumstance helpful to our avoiding absolute intimacy. Also, as I gradually learned, Lee could have imagined nothing more unpleasant than "absolute intimacy," and to this day likes nothing better than to cultivate her own garden. Perhaps because of her unusual degree of self-containment, I did not find myself fatally attracted to her as I had been to so many other women like the French woman decoding Milarepa.

The story of my relationship with Jason and Lee continues the following winter. At Christmastime 1973, I was reading Chuang-Tsu's ***Inner Chapters*** out loud to calm down a rather raucous party at Channing Place. (Chuang-Tsu is said to have been a student of both Confucius and Lao-Tsu.)

One of the ***Inner Chapters***' innermost stories tells of the King's Butcher. This Butcher becomes so renowned for being able to butcher meat without ever needing to sharpen his knife that even the King hears about him and visits him out of curiosity.

"How do you do it?" asks the King.

"I follow the natural grain," replies the Butcher, "letting the knife find its way through the many hidden openings ... There are spaces between the joints. The blade of the knife has no thickness. That which has no thickness has plenty of room to pass through these spaces ... "

The assembled party animals at Channing Place fell to commenting on what useful guidance the ancient Chuang-Tsu offered for contemporary Boston drivers. Since one can never count in Boston traffic on anyone obeying the traffic signs or signals, nor on the exercise of any norms of civility, let alone of driving competence, it's best to drive slowly, size up the joint, find the spaces between, and move into them, taking a path no one else is taking at this time.

Unnoticed, one woman slipped out the door and into the frigid midnight air. Forty-five minutes later, she exploded back into our communal home, cheeks afire and in high-spirited mirth. It was Lee Longstaff. As her story tumbled out, we learned that – after two years of depending on Jason to drive her everywhere because of two minor accidents and her subsequent fears – she had just driven all around Cambridge, including the dreaded circles, as well as in and out of parking places, following the simple principle of driving only into the empty spaces!

This was a double-loop change of strategy on her part, from the defensive to the offensive, with further ramifications. Within weeks, Lee's new assertiveness netted her a much-better-paying-and-more-interesting job, moving from librarian to business consultant at a major consultancy – the now long-lost Harbridge House, then right at the corner of Arlington Street across from the Boston Gardens.

From these events was born The Inner Chapters Driving School, for which I have since served as sometime director. The ICDS specializes in teaching persons to overcome their lingering fear of driving, whether they already have a driver's license or not. It also teaches licensed drivers who have first learned only with an automatic shift how to drive with a manual shift as well.

■ ■ ■

The following September, Jason drove Lee and me up to New Hampshire to his cousin's summer home, where our group of teaching fellows was to meet for the weekend, in preparation for that fall's version of my big course, **Organizing: Practice and Theory**. The rest of the group was arriving by noon on Saturday.

The trio ride up had been an exciting combination of deep conversation and pleasurable physical mutuality. Jason is a great storyteller... Lee a great critic and comic. There was also a more than merely comfortable sense of trio physical closeness, with Lee in the middle, Jason's left hand lightly on the wheel and his right even more fully relaxed on her left leg, with my left arm around her other shoulder, my hand possibly tickling Jason's ear now and again. Lee had some special way of welcoming and absorbing such intimacy without multiplying it.

That night, after a wonderful pasta-dinner-by-Lee and conversation-by-all-three, I was taken by surprise when Jason, in a very relaxed, confident, and generous way, invited me into bed with the two of them. After a delightful period of three-way massage and foreplay, I maintained just a bare sense of touching each of them once they got going. I was soon, on that very first occasion, impressed and overmatched by their athletic love-making...

After their whirl, the three of us lazed around together for a while during that kind of lull when everything feels at one if there is genuine mutual passion and commitment... Then Lee and I began to nuzzle each other, and Jason went off for a shower before I could even formulate for myself how self-conscious I would have been had he remained during our first full exploration of love-making together. I was much relieved to be able to be able enter my dance with Lee more gradually, establishing our own rhythm in awakening one another's deep presence.

Over the following year and a half, Jason and I also each developed an occasionally sexual relationship with other women in our friendship constellations. This was all open, sometimes bringing five or more of us to evenings together, in an atmosphere of enough spiritual and relational inquiry to create a reliable stew of trust and intimacy across a rather wide net of friends.

Jason, Lee, and I planned a trip to Europe together during the summer of 1975, visiting England, Scotland, my spiritual home at the Wolfgangsee, and Mom's farmhouse near Lucignano. Jason returned to the Boston area to take up his new Assistant Superintendent position there a week earlier than Lee and me. He met us at Logan airport when we arrived, and they dropped me off at Channing Place ... Where, prior to final preparations for my courses, I lapsed into a sleep of 24 hours or so.

This reverie was finally interrupted by Lee's phone call to tell me that Jason had dropped her too at their apartment...And then proceeded onward to a studio rental he'd gotten for himself. I was thunderstruck by this news and incredulous. I had seen that Jason's spirits had dipped during the last two weeks the three of us had spent together, but it had never remotely occurred to me that he might separate from Lee.

A few weeks later, Jason returned to his and Lee's apartment from his studio. The three of us discussed deeply what was going on, both in our three distinct duos and – over two weekends that we reserved for meeting together – in our trio. We were all equally clear that this was not a case of Lee and I preferring one another and becoming a couple at Jason's expense. Neither Lee nor I wished to become a couple at that time; and neither Jason nor I experienced tension with one another.

The problem seemed to be that Lee and Jason's relationship had been partially anchored by a mutual co-dependence that Lee had begun breaking beyond when she began driving again and then when she transformed her career trajectory from librarian to consultant. Now that she was not feeling dependent, the ways in which Jason was emotionally dependent on her grated on her and called forth her educated tongue.

Desperate to know how Lee really felt, Jason one day found her deeply private journal. What he read in it could not have heartened him ... Regardless, he then failed to replace it precisely as he had found it. Upon her return home, Lee realized instantly what had happened. She felt violated and enraged. Jason tearfully confirmed his sin and apologized. But she turned completely cold on him from that moment, announced her separation within weeks, and rented her own apartment as of January 1, 1976, our nation's bicentennial.

Jason's and my friendship remained remarkably deep and steady. Over the next twenty years he moved away from Boston, but we met once every few years, usually for a weekend, or at least overnight, with delight in our idiosyncratic trajectories and conversations.

■ ■ ■

Unlike Jason during and after our European trip, I enjoyed struggling with Lee. It seemed only to enrich all the other shared pleasures of our relationship: our dinners, the growing circle of mutual friends, our meditation practice, the humor, the sex. She entered the rest of my life easily and allowed me my privacy as well (no mean feat, since I myself did not often – let alone continually – recognize my desire for a purely first-person, personal sphere).

Our relationship was Platonic in the real sense: fully erotic, not just sexually, but also spiritually – its primary genius, from my point of view, a playful conversation that graced us with ever new recognitions.

She aroused no fantasies in me. To look at her was simply to see her distinctness, her independent life – her intelligent green eyes, her relaxed mien, her many-colored autumn sweater, her slightly stooped Italian-peasant-shoulders, and what I thought of as her 1930's hairdo, parted, short, and wavy.

I felt no magnetism in her presence; quite the contrary, I experienced a greater spaciousness, a quiet call to attention, from which apparent emptiness ever new and energetic epiphanies shaped themselves. There was no habit or presumption in our relationship then. Each time we met, we wondered whether it could begin anew; and wondered all the more as we experienced it each time so begin to do. (Endnote 20)

Interlude

Minor White's Death

The winter and spring of 1976 marked the death, not only of my Harvard career and of Jason and Lee's marriage, but also of my older/ elder friend in the Boston Gurdjieff group, Minor White. (As I write this, I am now ten years older than Minor was at his death at 66.)

Minor is the first person I have known and loved who literally died in inquiry among friends. Minor's friends included his younger colleagues at MIT and in the Experimental Studies group, the young photographers who lived with him each year apprenticing, and the staff at ***Aperture***, the photographic journal he had founded. For Minor, all the communities of social practice to which he belonged were simultaneously communities of inquiry. Here is how that inquiry evolved as he approached his death.

On my birthday, in February 1976 at the outset of my 33rd year, I was at Minor White's home in Arlington, just outside Boston, as he continued to recover from his heart attack of early December. Abe, one of the young photographers who lived with Minor that year, had pulled Minor's tongue out of his throat and gotten him to a hospital. Then a lawyer who had only recently met Minor got himself named executor and stopped all work on Minor's publications while Minor lay in a coma.

No one really believed that Minor would return to us this time, so the fact that he had made no will, thus leaving his lifework to the whims of this unknown lawyer, disturbed us deeply. Although Minor was reported to have opened his eyes occasionally by the time I came to visit him in the hospital, no one had yet elicited a sure sign of recognition from him.

He was, of course, in "intensive care." Machines hovered all around his bed, connected to him by all manner of tubes and straps at wrist, arm, throat, and scalp. The pale, emaciated face, framed by his long and wispy white hair, the hospital bed, and the hovering machines horrified me. What chance had life in this monstrous environment?

His eyes opened and, as they touched mine, I began to weep and to speak what I must say to him, on the chance that he could understand. He too wept and, with a lurch, ripped his arm up from its embalmed position to grasp my hand. He could make no coherent sound, only gurgles, but we communicated fully. Old enough to be my father, he and I were nonetheless brothers. My preparations for his death faced me with my own mortality – with the smallness of my own time – with my adulthood – as no other moment yet had.

But then Minor began to return to us. By mid-January we had him home, with one of us by his side twenty-four hours a day to help him sit up and move to the bathroom, to help him keep to his complex schedule of pills, to shield him from phone calls and visitors, and to talk him back to our world from the shadowy images with which he had spent the previous six weeks.

Again and again I returned to his simple, silent home with the high ceilings. Minor slept much and alternated, when he spoke, between vagueness and a sharpness I had never before seen in him. He knew that this time was a gift, not to be used in merely continuing his previous work, but rather in bringing it to an end, intentionally. In his weakness, something in him that had always sought expression was now concentrating itself instead.

As winter passed into spring, we occasionally brought our group meetings to his home and could feel the new edge of his silent alertness cutting through our preoccupations. In June, his heart's muscle weakened again, and he returned to the hospital for his final hours.

Does a life have meaning beyond its mute gestures? Is there a preparation for death that concentrates a faculty capable of reaching, through death, a permanent engagement in inquiry? Doctors' practice today is to drug their patients into insensibility in order to spare them pain. Minor's practice, by contrast, was to suffer voluntarily in seeking an alertness that could survive death.

Our quiet efforts to influence the well-intentioned doctors had no effect at first. But when all his vital signs assured the doctors it was his last day, they with-held the drugs, and Minor spoke directly to each of us sitting and standing about his small room. To me, he said, "You have prepared yourself carefully for leadership and you have now completed that preparation. But beware. You know what happens to leaders: people like nothing better than to leave a leader high and dry."

Each of us went up to his bed for a final farewell. Then Mrs. Dooling invited us to rest with Minor, awake to our state. After a blissful hour in a kind of silent waking dream utterly unfamiliar to me, I again heard Minor's voice, a croaking whisper through the hiss of the tube swallowing the saliva in his mouth, asking one after another of us what we were thinking about. As each spoke, Minor would respond, until we had all met one another again and again taken our leave.

Nevertheless, the next day Minor continued to live. Now half a dozen of us alternated sitting with him. In my last week at Harvard, simultaneously moving out of my office and completing a controversial report on the school desegregation effort in Boston, I could stop at the hospital for only three or four hours at a time. Minor, so weak he could not move, so weak he could scarcely whisper, was continuously restless, wanting to know the time, then realizing he meant his own time; wanting to be lifted into a sitting position to see better, then realizing his seeing must now move in the reverse direction, inwardly, toward the source.

People from all over the world were beginning to converge on Boston for his funeral, but he had not yet completed his preparation to die. On Tuesday his kidneys ceased to function. Blood poisoning and death follow within six hours at most, the doctors told us. Still, he continued his undefinable struggle through the night and then throughout Wednesday, telling us that day, "I've seen the other side, but I can't seem to find the right boat for the crossing." Although I had never before heard this formulation as part of one's shortly-before-death preparations, it richly evoked the River Lethe in Plato's Myth of Er, not to mention Buddhist myths of the possible transformational journey through death.

At 4 a.m. Thursday morning, some kind of transformation occurred – Minor relaxed, announcing that he now knew the time and saying "See you at 7." Without wanting to take his words literally, we nevertheless gathered about his bed at 7 a.m. Nothing special occurred; he continued to breathe. Throughout that day he spoke only to his closest companion. That evening I was having a farewell supper with my philosopher friend, Bob Anderson, at my home, sharing my whole experience with Minor. As he listened, touched, and spoke of the two deathbed scenes he was reminded of – Jacob's and Socrates' – summer thunder suddenly filled the hot, clear sky. It was 7 p.m. Within minutes, I received a phone call that Minor had just died. (Endnote 23)

At his funeral, I described our experience in these words:

We are brought together this morning, as we have been brought together in different groups and at different times before, by Minor White. This past week some of us have been privileged to be at his bedside as he consciously completed his preparation to continue his search through death. He showed us in a new way that liberation from fear of death can be achieved – that through a work in the body the spirit can be liberated.

I feel I speak with deepest knowledge when I say that Minor does not require our mourning. Instead, we will honor him if we now listen to the life of the body and the life of the spirit in ourselves – just as he attempted in his photography, in his life, and at his death – as we hear the teaching of the New Testament about life in the body and life after we die to our bodies (I Corinthians 15, 20-28, 35-52).

(Endnote 21)

Chapter 17

Circling from Boston to the Bay Area, The Bicentennial

I was flying to San Francisco again after Minor's funeral, as I had been doing most of the prior six summers, to participate in Gurdjieff Work activities, as well as to write at my brother's ranch in Mendocino. The only difference was that this time I had no idea where I was going after that. In dying to my outer work, might my inner Work accelerate?

Before I left, Lee solemnly gave me a 5x7" black journal, full of empty pages. I suppose this became my transition object over the next six months. Certainly, I've never again written so much in it.

Lee giving me the black journal was in fact quite challenging and somewhat daunting to me. I was quite aware that my college diaries had never amounted to more than a few obscure descriptive phrases, and that I had never since had the discipline to keep a regular, or even an occasional, meaningful journal. But if ever I was confused and needed to talk with myself, that time was now. Lee was the good journal writer, but now she was asking me to think carefully about us. They say that girls reflect and boys repeat. Lee was asking me to reflect. There was, one might say, a time signature on this period of uncertainty between us, and the Black Journal was its symbol.

In any event, I decided to try for a daily practice of journaling, beginning during my flight from Boston to San Francisco:

July 8, 1976

Minor White is dead and buried.

I have left Harvard with the same relief I have felt ever since deciding to resign a season ago.

I have bid Lee farewell with the same puzzlement I have felt ever since beginning to wonder a season ago about our future.

What must I now learn? What must I now write in this black journal she has given me?

In any event, here I now am on the way – on the way to California, on the way to a future whose shape I can in no way discern.

And yet . . . the stewardess steering down the aisle towards me with sweet rolls and orange juice, the haziness of my own eyesight encroached upon by mucous-swollen glands – not to speak of the tears my exhausted yawns are evoking – indeed, the very lack of feeling with which I boarded the plane an hour ago for this round-trip without destination . . . All make me wonder what subtle taste assures me that this air-path is the way.

My intent has not yet solidified. My vision does not yet put everything in question. My attention only rarely listens deeply into the world, or touches or moves it.

■ ■ ■

I did receive a clue two nights ago about the direction I must now take, after thirty-two years of seeking earnestly to live well.

I had already, for about a year, been sniffing around the notion that, to combat my many years of thoughtless do-good-ism, I must now become deliberately and consciously bad – a bad actor. (A bad actor in tension with a thoughtless do-gooder might, I narcissistically divined, provide just the sort of comic relief civilization currently requires.)

On this hot summer evening two days ago, as I sat nude in meditation with Camilla, the woman whose presence teaches me most about the interplay of body and spirit ... such metaphysical thoughts resolved themselves into a precise sensation of direction, like this:

I sat motionless, sensing the energies crowding my back, amused by the babylike corpulence of my belly, and wracked simultaneously by an unarticulated wish to flee this posture.

At which moment Camilla murmured quietly, "You look more comfortable now than I've seen you in a long time."

Shocked, I replied, "I see that I do not know how to be comfortable," and dove into my memory for aid.

■ ■ ■

I found myself eight years old on hands and knees happily digging a tunnel into the cool dark earth in the basement of the house being built next door to us, in Vienna.

In the next instant, motion ceased. The vacuum created in playful oblivion imploded, the earth knocking me, relaxed, from my knees, embalming me completely (as the now-descending plane now embalms the man).

Struggle out of the question, on one plane I immediately resigned myself to my fate and gracefully gave up the ghost. When my brother and my friend Andy pulled me out by the feet a few moments later, I was intellectually relaxed and at peace – the incident soon forgotten.

On another plane – from which I had segregated my attention until this evening with Camilla – when the sand tunnel collapsed, my buried body froze with claustrophobia and anxiety. I had thereafter shunned the relaxed posture into which gravity had frozen me, I now realized, and had tried my best to act angelically instead.

With Camilla, I saw that I must now rediscover my fear of death if I was to act badly (or in any way artfully, for that matter) rather than merely to re-act angelically. And if I was to rediscover my fear of death, I must suffer my claustrophobia and my frozenness and re-enliven my comfortableness.

■ ■ ■

On yet another plane, we are about to touch ground as I think these thoughts. I awaken momentarily from my reverie and seek to refine my new aim of becoming comfortable by observing my present condition through it.

I realize first that I am in fact incredibly uncomfortable. Vast distances of dense gauze separate the pinpoint of my thought from the outer universe. My breathing is shallow, my ears and nose are stopped up. Now that I am no longer going any particular where, I have all the time in the world to see that my habit is to accept such discomfort – to see that I have no automatic strategy for combating it.

I voluntarily take a deep breath. Involuntarily, I first cough and then sneeze explosively. Then, semi-voluntarily, I blow my nose. The woman in the seat next to me stirs momentarily.

THE ***ROAR*** *OF THE BIG JET ENGINES suddenly fills my ears. The other passengers come to life again before my eyes. This world is mine! And I've made it: the air craft lands in San Francisco, wheels spinning, ground-air, ground-air, ground-air…*

The Black Journal Continues…

I instantly failed in my goal of writing on consecutive days. Nevertheless, I was still keeping track of something from each day. My second journal entry reads:

July 12, 1976

First (way back on July 8), I spend the afternoon pacing the colorful and relaxing San Francisco streets searching, sans success, for a $2,500 car on sale for $800…with an occasional break to call acquaintances (none of whom are home).

Refreshed, I spend the night at an inexpensive downtown hotel – the strobe full-color-spectrum light across the street winding through my eyes, whether open or closed, broken by Casablancaish black and white dreams and night mares.

Exhausted, I rent a car in the morning and begin a tour of the Bay Area. First, I travel north to the jacussi action of the waves sucking in and out of the rocks off Point Reyes beach, as I swirl in place underwater. Next, I drive into the jacussi action of the wind swirling me around Mt. Tam in a wide tai chi dance.

In the evening comes the climax: the jacussi action of Junior Walker and the All Stars percussion, with the crowd's full-throated accompaniment.

Maya has brought me to the concert. I've met Maya but once before (at a Channing Place party where we hoe'd quite a row for a minute or two of foot stomping dancing).

Maya is in the midst of writing a book about how wonderful her mother is, but has just discovered in the past week, through her writing, that she hates her. Maya has also nearly been killed four times and says that she has learned some not-very-flattering things about herself when faced by death: that she bargains with the god in whom she does not otherwise believe, and that she becomes hysterical.

Junior Walker fills the small concert hall with the solid sound of his saxophone and the disciplined, staccato, ham-fisted resonance of his voice – a militant, masculine call to life – to which the crowd responds with a roaring rush on the stage. The choreography of antic emotion.

Later, neither I nor Thou is in the least bit frantic to enliven the other, though our bodies seek one another out. So, we sleep the night together, like kittens in a litter, utterly comfortably and completely unerotically.

Sunday morning I head straight up Rt 101 to my brother's goat ranch in Mendocino. Already, less than two days away from home, longing for a home-nest with a ferocity I have never before seen in myself.

After that, there is quite a pause before my next journal entry two weeks later. During that time, I've been building a grape arbor behind Jim and Theta's home. The arbor is intended to grant their bed, brought outside for the summer, a sense of nest-likeness or privacy. They have not themselves felt this arbor necessary, though they are now declaring it an added pleasure.

During this time, I have also begun crafting my 1978 ***Journal of Higher Education*** article on "Educating toward shared purpose, self-direction, and quality work: the theory and practice of liberating structure." It is a special pleasure to be moving back and forth between the physical construction of the grape arbor and the intellectual construction of the theory.

Travelling a few miles toward the coast, Theta, Jim, and I have also spent a memorable afternoon and evening with the solemn Redwoods, the true Ents of our world (along with their cousins in New Zealand). Coming back to the ranch, we pick our way up the far side of the ravine from the wild blackberry patch that the goats love to eat around. We approach the fiery pinks, purples, yellows, reds, and greys of the peeling bark of the Manzanita trees. Soon Theta herself peels off to do the milking, then Jim disappears to do the dinner prep.

Late in the evening, after much further communal pleasure, all in their kitchen, Theta leaves us to retire outside to the now-absolutely-black-night-sky and to their bed behind the grape arbor... and Jim now brings out a colossal stogie that he says will help turn the end of the acid trip into a smooth landing. We smoke a puff or two (I've always remained extraordinarily sensitive to this natural miracle and have long known that two tokes are enuf)... My experiential world enters into an unprecedented condition, where each moment truly does seem eternal, certainly with enough time to have dozens of reflections on and of and through each (as though each moment were its own developmental octave in multiple dimensions, occurring simultaneously).

Jim and I, each rocked back on a substantial chair, are laughing our loudest at one another's stories of our childhood and parents, both constantly surprised by the other's divergent point of view of specific moments ... When Theta suddenly appears in the kitchen door against the absolutely black night background, clearly distressed, asking Jim to come outside immediately. I will not soon forget the double or triple eternity when Jim wavered between the two of us, first unwilling to leave his chair, then framing himself against the black in the kitchen door, with his arms up against the top corners of the frame, still unwilling to leave our conversation, but finally disappearing at Theta's next call.

I myself waited for four more eternities of inquiry, fear, and hesitation, giving them some moments to themselves, before deciding that I would join them ... However and wherever they might be. First, I descended two steps from brightly lit kitchen to midnight ground. Now blinded, I literally felt my way with hands out front toward the grape arbor and their bed. After but two or three steps, I stumbled right into them hugging and weeping.

Theta, whose parents both died by the time she was eleven, had felt panicked by Jim's and my fraternal intimacy. Did Jim perhaps love the goat ranch and me more than her? My arms had enfolded them both by now and we were all weeping and hugging and speaking together. I am grateful that I could listen to my intuition about what to do in that moment so that a friendship rather than a wall could grow. Since that time Theta's primary complaint about me is that I don't visit them often enough.

July 31, 1976

For discovering the secrets of nature, Tiresias was turned into a woman.

For entrusting the lessons of his two-natured experience to the gods, Tiresias was blinded.

For foretelling the future to man, Tiresias was disbelieved (but involuntarily obeyed).

What sort of knowledge do we seek? That of the blind seer or that of a grounded doer?

August 13

At the Academy of Management meetings in Kansas City …

I guess I'm growing into this profession. I felt I knew a lot of people here among the thousands.

Great dinner with the 'Yale mafia,' now spread to the four winds, but as a result so much better a network!

Craig Lundberg's symposium 'Galumphing Toward an Action Science' seemed to be 'my' moment. (The symposium was named, after all, in celebration of my new book, Creating a Community of Inquiry, where this oxymoron ["action science"] is first coined):

The other guys – Craig, Herb Shepard, Karl Weick, Ian Mitroff – seemed to feel I was 'hot' at our preparatory luncheon just beforehand, so they stepped back a little, and I stepped up a little at the occasion itself.

There was a big crowd – folks standing around the walls and seated in the aisles. It was my first (big crowd). Usually, in the symposia I participate in, it's a question whether the crowd will be as large as the panel. … Better yet, there was, throughout the event, the kind of blending of laughter, conversational ease, and intensity of questioning that I like.

Am really looking forward to the long weekend of intellectual autobiographies at the Illinois Institute for Advanced Study with Pondy, Weick, Vaill, Mitroff et al in the fall.

I returned from Mendocino and Kansas City to Boston in August, and my dear friend from Upward Bound days, Jim Walsh invited me to a grand, everyone-bring-to-share party one weekend. It was held at the communal home he managed, in return for living rent-free, on the tiny peninsula of Nahant just north of the city.

Lee and I had decided to take a break until either one of us was ready to check in next, and I must confess I was sorely tempted by the occasion of Jim's party to call her. But this felt very immature. I had decided nothing yet, so I should await the dawning of a decision before contacting this person I loved, but did not know whether I wanted to commit a lifetime to. I felt a duty not to call her until I knew, having been so egregiously wrong the first time I married. That children were explicitly included in the near-future this time made it even more serious.

What I did already know was that I was ready for children and that I would love to have them with Lee. What I didn't know was whether I wanted to commit to the exclusivity explicit in institutional wedding vows, when I was still imagining a continuing wider community of mutually-beloveds.

In the meantime, I did go to Jim's party in Nahant. His communal home was a magical place for me in those years, a kind of California (where I always feel more at ease) in Boston, a place where I might often encounter one or both of his two daughters from his first marriage, whom I had known since they were four and two, as well as many other common friends, not least his fellow communards, many of whom (like me) still come to his parties to this day.

I was on time for Jim's party and ahead of everyone else, except a few fellow communards showering or dressing upstairs. In the kitchen, alone with Jim, I blurted out my sadness that Lee wasn't with me. A very peculiar, Cheshire-cat-like smile slowly spread over Jim's face. He spared me further curiosity by informing me that Lee was coming too, a surprise announcement that caused tears to force themselves into the corners of my eyes and a sudden confusion of wet laughter... He had invited her separately, and when she hesitated because I would be there too, he had said she should come to see him, irrespective of whether I came.

She did come. We had a very sweet reunion (I can still see her sitting on the porch railing at one point), and we concluded we should stay in touch whenever we wished henceforward, rather than waiting til whenever to get in touch (these two may sound the same to you, but they somehow sounded worlds different to us).

What to do next? Whatever Lee and I decided about ourselves, it felt likely that I should relocate eventually in California in the Bay area, where the familial, intellectual, and spiritual elements of my life all seemed to prosper. Why not buy a second – or third – or fourth-hand VW poptop camper and wend my way once again more slowly across the country, seeking the company and counsel of friends as I travelled, and aiming, once again, if at anything and anyone, at ending up at Theta and Jim's goat ranch in Mendocino?

First, I headed to Mrs. Dooling's home in Mt. Kisco, NY, for a night.

Oct. 9, 1976

I arrive at Mrs. Dooling's in Mt. Kisco late morning and go running to shake out the car.

The storm which earlier pent me up now seems like sheer celebration.

Deliciously drenched by sweat and rain, I shout at the storm, and the storm bellows back at me. Leaves and gusts all about, I run and run and run... until finally even my head begins to clear.

When Mrs. Dooling arrives, she immediately challenges me with questions while preparing lunch. What am I doing now? Yes, but what is my aim? Why have I come to visit her?

I reply with a sort of civilized stolidity, forcing honesty, struggling for presence, repeatedly putting myself down with some humor.

I say that I want to try to speak (and write and act) in a way that can create a new vista for many people. Saying that straight out embarrasses me, makes me feel vulnerable, stupid.

Into this wound, she flatly grinds her immediate response: "The Work is not to be used as a tool for becoming famous and changing the world."

I Find myself defending myself against the implication that I believe that ***I*** *could use* ***the Work****.*

Later, I say that Lee is interested in the Work and Doro counters, conversation-deflatingly that everyone means such different things by the Work.

I miss the opportunity to ask her what she means by that; instead I catch myself showing off that I too have observed how narrow and particular is my own vision of Work.

■ ■ ■

I seem to want to have her think well of me, to be regarded as a "good boy," and I seem to be disturbed by her testiness.

Yet my aims certainly deserve the most suspicious questioning, so why should I feel hurt when someone else advances some of the same questions with which I confound myself?

I evidently ask the questions of myself in the hope of making myself more credible to others. Why don't I know more deeply that these questions are shaping my life in an increasingly peculiar way which will make it increasingly in-credible to others?

Mrs. Dooling's prickliness also manifested itself after she asked me to write an essay review for ***Parabola*** on E.F. Schumacher's ***A Guide for the Perplexed***. This book is Schumacher's much-less-well-known sequel to his famous book ***Small Is Beautiful***, one of the spiritual/economic sources of the early environmental movement.

I wrote the review, submitted it, received her thanks by post, then read the published piece, perfectly pleased til the final sentence. There at the end, however, I found that the final inquiry I had posed the reader was now followed by an answer. Not only wouldn't I have made that particular answer, but, more importantly, any answer by the author of the review ruined my intent of leaving the reader with a question. To me, the answer substituted the ideology of the Gurdjieff Work for its practice.

When Doro and I next met, after discussing the issues she wished to raise, I asked whether I might discuss the recently published review with her for a moment. She acceded to my request, and I told her, in the same quiet voice we were using, how angry I felt that, after my final question to the reader, a final sentence had been added. I neither held that opinion, nor wished to express any opinion. In the world of scholarly publication, the exercise of such unilateral editorial power would be considered unethical.

She replied in fine temper that my biggest issue was my egotism – her words were "your enlarged organ Kundabuffer." I said – coldly – that her action contradicted a scholarly freedom of expression to which I was committed. A silence ensued. I rose and yielded my place to the next person with an appointment to speak with her.

What I had found particularly fascinating about Schumacher's new book was that it divided the macro-world of the planet as a whole into four qualitatively distinct "territories of experience" (mineral, plant, animal, human), just as, in my book ***Learning from Experience***, I had divided the micro-world of each person's awareness into four qualities (awareness of the outside world [mineral], awareness of the sensation of one's own body [plant], awareness of our thoughts or feelings [animal], and a quality of attention that can embrace and include the other three awarenesses [human]).

The review began:

> *All people throughout history have shared certain dilemmas. One such dilemma permeates everyone's life at every moment. Yet this dilemma is rarely felt directly, even by geniuses. Even more rarely does someone address this dilemma directly, thereby cultivating awareness of it.*
>
> *The dilemma is simply that our knowledge of what is occurring at any given moment in our lives, conditioned as it is by cultural habits of attention and modes of thought, must be inadequate to what is actually occurring . . .* (the review continues in Appendix C)

Next, I visit Morris in New York City, intentionally timing it so I get to join him giving his virgin speech at AA, after ninety days on the wagon.

Then, I head down to Washington, as a final check-in with my source-place and source-family before heading west to discover my future. The irony that my destination is, once again, the familiarity of my brother's place does not occur to me at the time.

Dad has retired since serving as Ambassador to Bulgaria, and Mom and Dad are living in an apartment on Sedgwick Street just off Connecticut Avenue, within blocks of where our family lived when I went to Sidwell Friends. One of the week's fun moments is when, with both Lee and my first wife present, we get Mom and Dad to devote part of their "Hour of Charm" to trying out a marijuana pipe with us. The summary? Mom was eager in anticipation, anxious in the moment of lighting up ("What will this do to me?"), and then uniquely shrill in her denials that the mj was having any effect on her. Dad was noncommittal in advance, calm in the moment of inhaling and passing on the pipe, and delightfully euphoric both in his noticing of sunset colors refracting on the wooden table and in his purring when I massaged his neck.

The next afternoon, as Lee and I walked in Rock Creek Park, she provocatively accused me of being in the midst of dumping her without having the guts to say so. She had been sure upon arrival that this would be our last time together.

I had continued to be transparent about feeling absolutely unsure (just like a man) about what I would do. But now I was truly angry at her (and aware that I was angry at her!) for assuming I was acting dishonestly. My voice dropped very low, and she knew I meant it. Addressing that unusually clear, direct, loving anger toward Lee felt very good, expressing as it did my continuing engagement with her, amidst all the other signs of my ambivalence, temporary distancing, and detachment.

Maybe all of that is why – later that last night, that last night that Lee and I knew with any certainty that we would ever be together again – maybe that is why, later that night, Lee's and my love-making brought us both to such howlingly-emotional climaxes.

Heading West

From Washington I headed west toward the University of Illinois at Champaign-Urbana, where Lou Pondy had called a small group of us together – including Ian Mitroff, Peter Vaill, and Karl Weick – at the Institute for Advanced Study to share and learn from, to challenge and to contribute to, one another's intellectual autobiographies. During our long weekend together, it was refreshing to hear, for example, how free of expectations to publish Peter Vaill felt. Instead of scholarly articles, Peter insouciantly wrote reflective essays that didn't get published until much later when they were very well received in book form among the scholar/practitioner crowd). Peter also played the piano and sang... and could get a crowd of peers dancing and singing with him. I thought I was relatively relaxed about when and how to publish, but Peter set a new standard!

Lou Pondy had started off as a physicist and Ian Mitroff as an engineer, and it was fascinating to hear how each had come to confront the assumptions of their initial ways of doing science. Lou became a close personal friend of mine until he tragically died of cancer way too early nearly a decade later. During that time, he experienced the euphoria and the suffering of adult developmental transformation (as well as the transformation of his paradigm of science), a profound process which he shared with me and others as it was occurring. Then, he would quickly convert his philosophical, theoretical, and empirical experiences into journal articles (and he was prolific), thus sharing his wondering with the whole management-academic profession, of which he was a leading light. Lou gave me a daguerrotype of an Illinois farm that today hangs on the wall of the staircase to our third floor. I often stop there for a moment to mourn Lou's early death and breathe in his still active vitality, good humor, and fierce dedication to going where his inquiry led.

Ian, the engineer, has written many books (of which I recommend first and foremost his ***Subjective Side of Science***, about the Apollo moon scientists' hypotheses and how they responded to the first real data from the manned and unmanned moon landings). One of Ian's later books (co-authored with Ralph Kilmann) played a special role in my own education because it helped me gradually to understand better what kind of social science I practice. That book of theirs is named ***Methodological Approaches in the Social Sciences*** and was published two years after our "Gallumphing Toward an Action Science" symposium in Kansas City and our time together at the Illinois Institute. It distinguishes among four very different types of social science, based on Carl Jung's differentiation between Sensation (empirical data) and Intuition (grand theory) as ways of experiencing reality, and between Thinking (detached reason) and Feeling (passionate listening and action) as ways of making decisions.

The "Sensing-Thinking" type of social science that tests specific hypotheses with empirical data is the most common of the four kinds. "Intuitive-Thinking" science is the second most common, offering grand, unifying conceptual schemes (e.g. Hegel, Freud, Parsons). The other two types of science, based in Intuitive-Feeling and in Sensing-Feeling, were much more rare at that time, probably well under 5% of all original work. According to Mitroff and Kilmann, Intuitive-Feeling science offered normative theories for guiding action, such as Chris Argyris' intervention theory, which they used as their exemplar of that type.

When I reached this point in their book, I was, frankly, disappointed. I had thought that, with all Ian's knowledge of my work – based not only on our multiple meetings now, but also on a number of multi-page, single-spaced letters of mutual, intellectual appreciation and critique of one another – he and Ralph might have chosen as their exemplar of the Intuitive-Feeling type of science my own ***Creating a Community of Inquiry*** book, with its integration of Argyris, Erikson, and my own organizational development theorizing in the attempt to understand the Yale Upward Bound program.

Nevertheless, I continued dutifully on to read the final section of the book about what they contended was the rarest type of social science currently – namely, Sensing-Feeling science. I knew I would be interested by the rarest type, whatever it might be, and whoever its exemplar might be. To my genuine astonishment, the exemplar turned out to be my Upward Bound book. Ralph and Ian argued that my new "action science" approach represented a Sensing-Feeling kind of social science, one that is more likely than any of the other three types of science to explore the lived experiences and action choices of oneself and others in their (our) 1st – and 2nd-person voices. That was certainly characteristic of my close descriptions and analyses of my own and others' participation in the Upward Bound program.

At the time, I loved being singled out for recognition like that, by peers I respected so much. Nevertheless, I thought Ralph and Ian had gotten my place in their typology wrong. I thought I was more

Intuitive/Feeling, with a sense both for individual experience and for wholistic 3rd-person normative/descriptive theories... Indeed, given my Aquarian astrological sign, I prided myself on my excellently balanced (!) approach among the four types of science (having collected and quantitatively analyzed many different types of data in my first two books about labor and leisure and about learning from experience.

Even though I've gone on (with collaborators) to do dozens of quantitative studies and to develop the highly reliable and valid psychometric measure called the Global Leadership Profile, I have also, long since, changed my mind. I now agree with them that what's most distinctive about my work is my listening to what is *unique* about each of us participants, about our relationships, and about our institutional settings at *particular present moments when we can take potentially timely and transforming action*.

Karl Weick, another member of our long-ago, 1976 fraternity, was another kind of unique. Take a look at his short 1969 book, ***The Social Psychology of Organizing***, and you'll see what I mean. In direct contrast with my own debt to so many profound mentors, Karl felt little influenced by any of his teachers. I found it difficult to imagine how anyone could have the innate confidence to be so original as he. I had had the first of several long, adventurous, intimate conversations at dinner with him at the Kansas City meeting. There was no fear, constraint, or presumption in any of these conversations. He shared a humility before the unknown that I treasure. Although Karl is a much more successful and well-known scholar than I am – working with case studies of others, not of his own actions, and describing what occurs in qualitative, narrative terms and third-person language – he too is describing an action inquiry process that people can take on as a first – and second-person process – not basing action on prior knowledge and one's habitual tools, so much as "dropping one's tools" and acting into the unknown, then inquiring what outcomes occur in this particular context, then deciding what to do next. Further confirming Mitroff and Kilmann's assessment of me as a Sensing/Feeling scientist, Weick later referred to me as an "ear naturalist."

Although Karl couldn't in the end make it to the event, our meeting at the Illinois Institute for Advanced Study represented a key moment in my professional development. Having become somewhat distanced from Chris Argyris, it was a very good feeling for me to be developing a more peer-like community of inquiry within the profession, opening my horizon to just how variously my colleagues operated. More than that, given my current, de-institutionalized status, I was perhaps the most grateful of all of us for this opportunity for deep sharing of our intellectual, spiritual, and moral foundations...

■ ■ ■

From my experience in Illinois, I headed south and west to stay over with a friend in a doctoral program at Colorado College, then drove further south into New Mexico.

November 11, Eagles Nest, N.M.

It is cold.

I drove much of today hunched over to sight through the small clearing at the bottom of the iced-over windshield.

I keep getting the shivers when I enter warmth (probably body compensating for last night's liquor, though I didn't feel hung over in a direct way).

Amazing the narrow range of human comfort.

From Eagles Nest and Taos I rose slowly into the Rockies the next day. Uphill the old camper couldn't beat a steady 45mph. I spent nights in Arizona and then Los Angeles, but by now, though I skip both sweet and perplexing experiences on the way, I was pointing hard again toward Jim and Theta's goat ranch in Mendocino. (Endnote 22)

Chapter 18

To Theta and Jim's Goat Ranch and then Circling Once More

You've already read about how fast I drove up 101 four months earlier in July in the rent-a-car to reach Jim and Theta's ... so you're probably getting a bit of a sense for how the Wanderer and the Homeboy are tangled up in me and were vying for predominance during my second and much longer drive toward Yorkville that Bicentennial year.

This time I drove the pine green VW camper the last stretch up 101 from San Francisco through to Santa Rosa, on to Cloverdale ... Then slowly up the winding road to Yorkville, bearing right on the dead-end, dirt, oxbow road. I shifted into 'park' in front of the former town dance hall – now Jim and Theta's home. Once inside, it was good to see the artistic patchwork of old boards of different size, different shape, and different texture (mostly redwood, oak, and pine) that now constituted the interior walls of the dance hall. These boards I had found around the property and installed just a couple of months ago.

November 21

At the end of the road again. At Jim and Theta's goat ranch, after a long day's drive far into the night.

This morning I felt dizzy. But eating a big breakfast at the Oaks Cafe, carrying my sleeping niece Laura on a walk up hill and down vale, then playing soccer against Hopland in that hay field (what a miracle that the game should be today) ... until I mis-twitched my knee ...

Later taking a hot bath, sitting by the fire, eating a delectable dish of red tomatoes, green noodles, and liver and onions, calling my "Cheeka" on the telephone, and telling her I would fly into Boston Wednesday night in time for Thanksgiving with her family whom I will be meeting anew ...

Have, all together, left me feeling satiated, full of peace, no longer in struggle. Because Lee could not decide whether I had won or lost, I suggested we call it a "tie." And since I didn't mention my intention to propose a permanent engagement in inquiry, I actually don't think she noticed my first-ever intentional pun.

■ ■ ■

Will anything ever again require me in the way I have been required til now? The question occurs to me, have I ever before felt this quality of peacefulness? I really cannot think of any time ... though I have no desire now to press my memory, as I usually would, to assure this computation.

Instead, I am remembering Anna writing in Dorris Lessing's ***The Golden Notebook*** *that the good times generated no writing.*

My mood now shows that her point is well taken, so much so that I am writing almost in defiance of it, to give myself something to remember if (even "if" can be a courageous word) I should emerge from and forget this holy stillness and silence.

But I am writing too from a joy, an imploding joy that leaves nothing but a point of emptiness, an emptiness which yields all things their tones and shadows, this writing one of those shadows.

The state I inhabit has none of the character I attribute to profundity, nor any of the tension and alienation I attribute to seeking.

I am merely at home, my brother in his silence seated by the other lamp; neither of us requiring nor required.

Two days later, I drove my trusty VW camper to the San Francisco Airport's long-term parking area (a costly decision, it turned out, since it stayed there nearly a month). Then I limped like an old-fashioned cripple to my plane and circled back to Boston once more for Thanksgiving with Lee's Italian family.

Back in Boston Once More

The next three weeks in Boston might be said to have passed like a blur, so much happened before I found myself back in California again, at the goat farm again, this time with Lee, for Christmas, and this time, improbably, with my parents there as well.

Lee picked me up at Logan, and drove us to her apartment for a long, long night of communing. We touched each note of the octave in turn... Laughter... Tears... Heartfelt conversation... Me offering my vow to remain engaged in our inquiry forever... Love-making... She, through smiles and more tears, coyly asking me to wait til morning for her response... Then deep sleep, interrupted repeatedly for me by the discomfort of the 'mis-twiched" knee, only slightly dulled by quadruple doses of aspirin.

In the morning, Lee told me that she had really not believed I would ever make a commitment to her, and that I was so much trouble she really hadn't been sure she wanted us to be together either. But she had known that she wanted my child, whom she presumed she'd bring up alone. So, she had not taken her birth control pills before our 'final' meeting at my parents' home six weeks before. Then, a week before she heard from me that I was flying back to Boston, she had learned she was pregnant. She had spent a long evening with our closest friends, convinced that she was not going to tell me about the baby – against their stout arguments to the contrary. Now that I had unexpectedly shown up, she wanted to make it absolutely clear that she did not want to force me into a partnership based on some sense of duty. She released me from my vow of the previous evening and invited me to reconsider the whole matter.

I had already reconsidered as she spoke. After all, I had made my vow freely, not under duress. And I had already felt that I was ready to help bring a child into the world. As a result, the peculiar synchronicity in our interactions over the past six weeks, leading to the present moment, felt like a genuine miracle to me. I had no doubt I would have wanted to co-parent my child, even if I had learned about Lee's pregnancy before I had made up my own mind to commit to her. But if that had been the sequence of events, she might never have been sure of the quality of my caring for her.

So, I re-offered my vow, and over the next days she wrote me a corresponding vow of her own. In the meantime, there was Thanksgiving dinner at her parents' home. As Lee said, her parents easily reduced her to hiccoughing aphasia. Over the years she and they had cooperated in coming to a working relationship whereby she told them nothing and they asked nothing. Consequently there was a big backlog of ignorance on their part when it came to me.

We decided not to make any dramatic announcements during Thanksgiving dinner. Lee strove to keep the whole encounter casual, and succeeded well beyond my expectations. Her parents were cordial to me, but there was something in their attitude which would be more appropriate to "Impecunious Hitchhiker Unexpectedly Brought Home By Scatty Eldest Daughter To Share Thanksgiving Dinner." We left there in the early evening, riding a trough of anticlimax.

We decided we would return to California to try to make a life there. Lee gave two weeks notice to her company, which was not happy about her leaving (but which nevertheless *was* happy to promise her job back should we later return to Boston).

We put her apartment up for rent. She went to work every day. Friends helped me pack everything. And we said hello and goodbye to our vast ménage of friends, necessitating several going-dutch evening banquets at Joyce Chen's restaurant.

Once in California, we wrote her parents a letter announcing the advent of the baby.

Doctor of (Apartment) Management

Flying back to San Francisco together, we rescued my VW camper from longterm parking, and set out apartment-hunting. From Noe Valley to the Castro, to Oakland and Berkeley, our search went on and on. There were few places at anything like "our price," and we lost out on two we bid on. In despair, because Jim Walsh would be arriving in the U-Haul with our furniture in the next 48 hours, we paradoxically gave up serious searching altogether and drove out to Tiburon just for the sake of the view (apartments there were well beyond our price range).

Lee asked to stop by the side of the road on the way into Tiburon to deal with a little morning sickness, so I checked in at the real estate office that happened to be right there. After being told by a secretary that they had no vacancies, the owner came through the door and announced to his reps that they needed an apartment manager for one of their Tiburon properties, forgiving half the rent. This sudden opportunity rang a loud bell in me, empowering me to quickly persuade them that my doctorate in management made me just their man, with a good deal of laughter about just how practical a PhD can be!

Thus it came to be that we began living above our meager means in an apartment in Tiburon with a great view of the bay, just in time to receive our few sticks of furniture from Jim Walsh. (As we later learned, we were also only a few blocks from the home my spiritual teacher was renting that winter, a home we visited more than once in the following months, as Lee cultivated a kind of bantering relationship with him.)

Mom and Dad flew to California for Christmas and New Year's, and all of us celebrated at Jim and Theta's ranch. Lee and I slept in the large wood-stove-heated living-room-dance-hall-creamery, tucked into our own niche behind the Christmas tree and the piano. We collaborated to create a candles-on-tree-and-big-fire Christmas dinner, with home grown lamb, root vegetables, and Mom's Yorkshire Pudding. All four Torberts were together for Christmas for the first time in eight years... The three Torbert couples were together for the first time ever...And for the first time the two babies (Laura and the neonate within Lee) represented the new third generation.

In me, a depth of family feeling flowered anew. After a long generation of silence within the family, Dad turned instantly into a very funny family *raconteur*. In a series of epiphanies, I found myself directly touched once again by his laughter and my mother's thoughtfulness. I suddenly realized that I had buried such tender feelings below a slightly cooler love nineteen years ago when I had first gone away to school at Andover and found myself separated from my family by a whole ocean at Thanksgivings and Christmastimes.

"The baby"

By now Lee and I were starting to "go public" about the baby. I ended a New Year's message to friends,

> *And now still another sacred message has floated our way across some ocean, as though in a bottle from some unknown haven, like a benediction on this magical time: we are going to have a baby! It is so perfect that I can hardly bear to think of it directly; we are both so ready to love this child and so scared by the occasional knowledge of the inconceivable enormity of this act (whose consequences one must, above all, not presume to foresee); yet so without reservation have we each and both*

entered into this act, that it comes to feel as though all three of us are in a womb together, approaching a cosmic birth.

Except, as it turned out when we attended our April Fools Day amneocentesis appointment, it was all **four** of us in a womb together! Yes, you've guessed: it was, and it still is, twins (though seven years later they gained a third brother who is now bigger than both of them).

But these were, and are, not just any old fraternal twins, or even regular old identical twins. No. In what we were told occurred about once every 84 times in twin births, they are "mirror-image opposite" twins (in 2020, Google says about one of seven sets of twins are "mirror-image opposites") . This means that one is right-handed, the other left-handed, one is more emotional, the other more intellectual, and that's just the beginning of it! (Forty plus years later they retain their distinctive temperaments: the one sleepy, jobless, and living on his own; the other an active professional, married with two children, and a musician. They highlight for me the striking distinction in human development between one's relatively stable temperament and one's relatively changeable character.)

On May 31, 1977, I sent the following hand-scribed, one-page letter to some 90 friends and family:

Dear Friends,

GOOD NEWS! Lee has borne us twin sons on May 23 –

Michael James Torbert, 4lb.s, 5oz.s, 4:36pm and

Patrick Cassettari Torbert, 4lb.s, 9 oz.s, 5:40pm

They were were born on just the day Lee had anticipated a week before. Lee labored hard for the final five hours, with me by her side, and a dozen doctors and nurses in outer orbits. The delivery was natural, and she was high for a day and a half afterwards. I was exhausted.

We had a short period of sadness and worry because Patrick had pneumonia symptoms and had to be tied into various machines. We could not hold him and it looked terrible, but it was not pneumonia and he is now fine.

In the early days, the two have markedly different temperaments, Michael the sleepy philosopher, Patrick the little man of action, as feisty as can be. Lee returned home Sunday the 29th, and we impatiently await bringing the boys home later this week.

As for the rest of our lives, I did not get the one job in the Bay Area for which I had a strong chance. I am scheming to start my own business/school, "the theatre of inquiry," in Boston, but that requires a small amount of capital which I do not now have. At this point, nothing about our economic or geographical future is certain. We have by no means yet taken root here.

What is certain about our future is that four of us will love discovering it together.

In joy, we send our best wishes, Bill and Lee

As hinted at in this letter, since my next chance for an academic job would be for one starting a year hence, and since Lee could retake her former job in Boston and act as our primary provider for the coming year, we were now veering back and forth between coasts in our minds. In any event, I wanted to try out something more radical in the way of learning environments, both for myself and others. I was conceiving a new organizing idea – The Theatre of Inquiry – hoping that it, along with the Inner Chapters Driving School, could net me a little income to supplement Lee's in the coming year. (Endnote 23)

Chapter 19

The Theatre of Inquiry, 1977-1978

As soon as I had sent off the short note about the birth of the twins, I set about composing a longer letter that I sent to some two hundred friends, asking them to invest their advice, criticism, and support of all kinds to help transform "The Theatre of Inquiry" from my 'Conception' stage of organizing to our 'Investments' stage of organizing.

What turned out to be our last month in the Bay Area was a trying and confusing time, as indicated by the early paragraphs of my July 18 letter to Mom and Dad:

> *As Dad said in his earlier letter to me: Whew! These last two weeks have really been something. Looking back on them now, they seem incredibly difficult. But at the time, they simply seemed necessary, even filled with insight. The external conditions included: (1) letters and phone calls coming in in response to my letter, each individual one an absolute delight, but altogether arriving only by dribs and drabs; (2) an abortive trip to both of Jim's and Theta's places over the July 4 weekend, cut short after an unbearable night of twins-screaming in Yorkville; followed by (3) over a week of almost constant breast feeding by Lee, climaxed by 22 feedings in one 24-hour period; and (4) my participation in an intensive Gurdjieff Work Week. I went to two days of the Work Week, after getting up twice, as usual, each night to help feed the boys, leaving the house at 7:30 each morning and returning after 11pm each*

night. Upon finding Lee surrounded by babies and drowned in tears when I got home the second night, I ceased going altogether (a decision I could never before have imagined making).

Up til then, Lee had maintained ferociously that we must not feed them formula too, or they might leave the breast. Since then, we have fed them everything we can get our hands on – breast, formula, or cereal (true Torbert men, it took them each exactly one bite to learn to eat from a spoon) – and we are all faring much better.

And them twins am a-growin: both over six pounds now! And their legs are beginning to propel them, Patrick's propelling him on his first header off the couch last week, Michael's pushing him three feet along the bed last night to where he could nurse on Patrick's forehead.

As to Jim and Theta, they continue great. In the past week they have decided to change what was developing into a killing pace, by not trying to build a house on their new land this year, but just moving there in a trailer. They have still not finished the Yorkville place. In fact, when we were there it was once again embattled by construction. The parts that are finished are really finished well though, and I have no doubt the whole thing will look superb when they do finish. But, as usual with these mundane things, it takes more time than anticipated. Jim just reported discovery of an additional water source which will help a lot …

As for me and Lee, we stretched ourselves and the twins yet further, by agreeing when Jim and Theta implored, to go on up to their new land just past Ukiah then and there, after the night of twin-screaming. This episode along with many others is teaching us gradually (and is especially teaching **me**, *especially gradually) that we are an entirely new four-person-animal, born again, with entirely new limits, not necessarily meant to be stretched and broken just now…*

So… Back we flew to Boston at the beginning of August, with the twins. Once there, we camped happily at the home of some friends who were away at their wilderness camp for the month. By September, we secured a perfectly serviceable first floor apartment in a pleasant Belmont neighborhood. We returned with renewed appreciation to partying with our old friends and, in my case, to meeting with the Gurdjieff groups on Friday evenings and frequent Saturdays. Starting September 1, Lee was also working 35 hours a week. We had a babysitter for 30 hours a week, and I took up the slack in terms of shopping and child care.

In response to my Theatre of Inquiry letter, eighty-one friends had offered some $4,000 in funds, as well as at least that much again in key in-kind gifts. For example, sculptor Peter Haines offered to lend me the front display room of his sculpture studio in Cambridge for the "Action Workshops" I was planning. One of my staff friends at the Harvard Ed School decreed that, as a former faculty member, I was qualified to reserve the Longfellow Hall auditorium for free for my projected, monthly Public Performances. Jill, my woman friend from Dallas now living near Boston, along with her husband, volunteered to be my printers if I would pay for the paper for publicity flyers. Robbie Gass, a former student and already widely known as a spiritual music-maker and couples retreat leader, lent me his address list. Yet another friend lent me his company's conference room for my evening Business/School meetings.

I was both moved and emboldened by these responses… Including the criticisms. Philosopher and futurist, Jay Ogilvy, wrote to me, courageously and caringly, that I sounded as if I was planning a career as a guru, and he frankly advised against it and would therefore **not** invest in it. I didn't think that's what I was planning, but I definitely appreciated the dangers of the guru role, as well as Jay's commitment to me in responding as he did. He had in fact invested in my project with his double-loop, warning feedback.

Michael Rossman (Berkeley Free Speech Movement leader, mathematician, flute player, and author of ***The Wedding in the War***, as well as the glorious "Music Lessons") warned me that I shouldn't be starting this enterprise – school, theatre, scientific experiment, business, or whatever it really was – **alone**. This was the post-heroic, androgynous, anarchic, queer, ***collaborative inquiry*** phase of human history, wasn't it? Where were my direct collaborators?

I took Michael's formulation of my dilemma even more seriously than I did Jay's. I didn't mean to become a guru, as Jay feared; but I did mean to work and play collaboratively and inquiringly, as Michael feared I was already **not**. But by this time, with my 81 supporters, I did have a rich band of different kinds of collaborators, including, ironically, Jay and Michael. On the other hand, it did become true that none of these collaborators was more than occasionally engaged; so I did not have fulltime collaborators.

Later that fall, my spiritual teacher followed Jay and Michael by sending me one of his handwritten letters, offering me a third warning about the danger of the wrong kind of success:

> *I have no doubt that your Theatre of Inquiry will go like a house on fire unless you hold strictly to the rules so admirably stated by Ouspensky of not being in a hurry to share with others ideas and methods of which one only has as yet a superficial understanding. I very much wonder whether you will be able to restrain yourself in this respect, Bill, and I wish you were not so far away. Because in the long run, it will not work for you – you have been too close to be comfortable as a popularizer, merely. And although from time to time it may appear otherwise, I don't think there will ever be a firm "market" for work of the kind we are interested in. Of course, I don't want to be cutting myself off from anything that is really creative, that*

is really your own, in what you are attempting. In fact, I don't want to be discouraging in any way. But I think I had better speak out now in support of that part of yourself that has not given up altogether the idea of earning your living in the world in a more or less conventional career setting and that regards the present adventure as an interim measure.

What a privilege I enjoyed, in the willingness of this wise man to concern himself with my choices. The Gurdjieff Work was about spanning the distance between the material and the spiritual, the distance between the early and the late developmental action-logics, not about becoming a guru who works only with volunteers. After tasting his message again and again over the following several weeks, I wrote back:

Dear Lord P.,

Thank you for your reply to my last letter. It has spiced all my activities these past weeks. I should say immediately that in supporting that part of me that would prefer "a conventional career setting" you give further prominence to what already feels like a large part of me. Indeed, I often think of my present efforts as an interim measure, and I only hope that it will be the sort of interval that makes all the difference. I continue to speak and write for academic settings, am seeking foundation support for a doctoral internship program that would link Harvard, BU, and MIT to The Theatre of Inquiry, and in general regard this venture as another in the series of organizing experiments, like the Upward Bound and SMU years, that contributes to my social scientific work.

The fundamental difference in this case, as I see it, is that I am no longer working within any framework that I can take for granted. Far from seeking to popularize anything, I find myself challenged to become clearer and clearer about what is peculiar to my own approach, beyond whatever influences I have accepted and continue to accept, and beyond any mere synthesis that may occur through me.

In any event, however superficial my understanding may be, I do know that a house on fire is not the process in which I am interested. I seem to be creating a condition which calls me to rethink what I am doing at closer and closer intervals. While I cannot yet speak directly about what is creative in my approach, I do know that my interest in our continuing dialogue is more active than ever. I want to keep you informed of what I am doing and deeply appreciate your willingness to respond.

You Are An Actor

So, after mentioning its name so many times, what was The Theatre of Inquiry?

In his song about it, which became a Boston radio commercial for Tol, my Ear-of-the-Universe friend, Jimmy Metzner, put it this way:

You Are An Actor

You are an actor
You put on your mask
You ready yourself for your task:

You'll be playing a stranger again,
And as long as you've asked
You're in – The Theatre of Inquiry

In front of the footlights and behind
In and out of the dialogue
Going on in your mind

Where is that listener
You've been trying to find?
In The Theatre of Inquiry

Is there a present
To pull out of the past?
Is there a feeling
To make it last?

Just what is this role
into which you've been cast
In The Theatre of Inquiry?

You're playing the fool
You're playing the sage
You're acting just like a child
You're acting your age

All of a sudden you're on center stage
In The Theatre of Inquiry

True enough, that song is a tease, but then so was the organization that inspired it. Here's how the postal flyer read – the multicolored one that went out to some 5,000 Boston area households, inviting readers to engage with a new set of inquiry activities – weekly "Action Workshops," a "Business/School," and/or a new Theatre of Inquiry "Public Performance" each month. According to the flyers:

"ACTION WORKSHOPS – Studying the art of living inquiry on a personal scale; weekly 90 minute meetings. Each group of eight persons will seek to recognize and practice a kind of thinking, feeling, and sensing that permits inquiry-in-action – inquiry in the midst of daily errands, interruptions, crises, and moments of leisure. Physical and mental exercise, massage,

meditation, chanting, role-playing, and conversation will all enter into the search for a disciplined, relaxed, questioning attention that encompasses both the inner and the outer worlds.

"BUSINESS/SCHOOL – Studying the art of organizing business and professional endeavors; weekly 150 minute meetings. The group will form a company, deliver a product or service, and learn how one's own behavior, as well as various decision-making, legal, and financial procedures, can facilitate or obstruct inquiry, creativity, and organizational effectiveness.

"PUBLIC PERFORMANCES – Studying the drama and politics of living inquiry; monthly. Act I each time will introduce the audience to the spaciousness, color, and intrigue of the historical origins and archetypal characters of The Theatre of Inquiry. Act II will invite (but not require) the audience to actively participate in inquiry exercises. Act III will be a conversation among those present about how an atmosphere of inquiry can permeate our world's institutions."

The flyer also included brief quotes from Schiller ("*Man is only wholly man when he is playing*"), from Thoreau ("*To be awake is to be alive. I have never yet met a man who was quite awake*"), and from Wittgenstein ("*We are asleep ... Our life is like a dream. In our better hours we wake up just enough to realize that we are dreaming. Most of the time, though, we are fast asleep. I cannot waken myself! I am trying hard, my dream body moves, but my real one doesn't stir.*")

Apparently, Schiller, Thoreau, and Wittgenstein were quite attractive to the Cambridge intellectuals and Newton therapists the mailing targeted. By the end of January 1978, four Action Workshops were purring along with 29 participants; the Business/School enrolled 13 for 13 weekly sessions; and the first Public Performance sold 89 tickets.

Pricing was not my strong point: the Action Workshops and the Business/ School cost $10 per person per session, and the Public Performance tickets went for $2 a head. Pragmatically, my family financial situation called for higher prices, as did any financial strategy that understood people's actual preference for high-class performances, measured initially by how much they cost. If I had charged $10 per head for the Public Performances, $20 per session for the Action Workshops, and $25 dollars per session for the Business/ School and attracted the same number of participants, The Theatre of Inquiry (and my family) would have done a whole lot better financially, with no one feeling the worse off.

Some 70 or 80 folks, including my parents, had come for the eats and drinks and conversation to the ToI founding party at Peter Haines' sculpture studio, and they were enjoying all three. I had been circulating during the first 45 minutes, meeting and greeting and hosting, along with Peter and the dozen or more who initiated themselves as fellow-hosts. Then I disappeared into the back, doffed my suit and tie, revealing white tights, donned a white skull cap and a black stocking scarf, climbed onto one of the steel girders, and reappeared slowly and unnoticedly above the party.

Stationing myself in Danny-Kaye/Court-Jester-like fashion with weight entirely on the back leg, left toe and ball of foot touching girder in front, sensibly but weightlessly, I emitted an Austrian yödel. The satisfying response was a quick silence and uplifted-visages. I offered a short monologue on the ToI vision, probably a little less stilted than the following written reflections from the later foundation-statement:

> *"...Action is that peculiarly human kind of behavior that relates an intention to an effect... not merely obeying a predetermined definition of the situation and predetermined norms, but rather questioning and potentially changing them as well.*
>
> *Historically, a few active inquirers – Confucius, Gautama, Pythagoras, Jesus, Mohammed, Dante, Marx, Darwin, Freud,*

> *Einstein – have framed the universe within which the attention of subsequent individuals and whole civilizations has moved.*
>
> *…What these great inquirers of the past also have in common is their failure to organize their work with others in such a way as to encourage a widening public to develop a similarly inquiring attention, disciplined and free, penetrating and receptive.*
>
> *In the absence of a kind of organizing that encourages the questioning of fundamentals … religious, political, and educational initiatives become contorted into their opposites. Thus, Dostoevsky's Grand Inquisitor crucifies Jesus at his second coming in the name of his own church. Thus, Marx's theory of political liberation is used by Stalin to justify one of the most repressive, totalitarian regimes in history. Thus, John Dewey's pragmatic philosophy becomes the basis, not for more schools like his laboratory school at the University of Chicago, but rather for a colorless cant that affects few teachers' actual practice.*
>
> *We cannot expect significant improvements in elementary, secondary, or college education until the human race discovers how to create a kind of public institution – a kind of* Theatre of Inquiry *– that encourages its adult members to develop an inquiring attention …"*

My short monologue transformed into a halting dialogue, increasingly triangulated by silences. Everyone was getting a little tired of craning their necks, or else a little restless about not knowing in what direction to look now, when really they'd been having a great time just before these tense moments. In a rare public intervention, my father broke the (creative?) tension by speaking up to say with a chortle, "Well, why don't we all just get another drink?" Everyone laughed and happily complied, the earlier hubbub quickly resuming, everyone relieved to be relieved of wondering what constitutes an inquiring attention.

My first Action Workshop was populated almost entirely by folks who were already Candidates-for-Lifetime-Friendship with me, and all of whom had come to the "Coming Out" party. One of my friends had started a sign-up sheet and gotten seven others to sign up before the end of the party.

So, one way or another, by the skin of its teeth, The Theatre of Inquiry successfully met the challenges of the Incorporation stage of organizational development.

The Action Workshops

Thereafter, folks coming to the hour-and-a-half/week Action Workshops in their "exercise, dance, or meditation clothing…" would enter Peter Haines' single-story, brick, industrial building, on the then down-and-out side of Cambridge nearest MIT, through it's threatening, metal front door. They would find themselves emerging into the largely-empty, "display" studio, with the exposed ceiling girders that I'd recently managed to stand on.

Peter was then a close to penniless artist and sculptor from Columbus, Ohio. He'd been a Marine in Vietnam and then a Harvard MBA student. When his mentor, the famed HBS professor Tony Athos, proposed he do a painting as his final project, Peter veered from business toward becoming an artist. A quiet man, Peter has mainly let his work speak for him since then, which is why I feel so well accompanied by him in my own home now: my twenty-four different pieces of his work – woodprint monotypes and bronze sculptures – give me versions of him to gaze at and touch in the first floor and bedroom of my home. As previously mentioned, this includes the bronze androgynous merman standing on his head on the cover of this book, for which I was, thirty years ago, able to serve as model… making it yet another peculiar emanation of our friendship.

Once you got through the front door at Peter's place and into one of the Action Workshops, you found exercise mats and cushions spread about rather randomly. It wasn't clear what you were supposed to do. Spasms of conversation, meditation, dancing, massage, or wrestling were apt to break out at any time. The dilemma of not-knowing what to do next was intended to be continuous. You were of course supposed to **act inquiringly** – to take action ... to lead ... to perform in such a way as to help generate a good time.

When my friends who constituted the first Action Workshop complained that the meetings seemed very discontinuous because they could not understand what we were supposed to accomplish, I suggested that, as a Liberating Discipline for the next three sessions, they become an advertising agency with me as their client. In that way they would have recognizable roles and a recognizable purpose. Moreover, their questions about the The Theatre of Inquiry would be legitimized by their function as an ad agency. I would tape record the first two 'advertising agency' sessions and offer some kind of analysis at the third session about the degree to which we were succeeding (or failing) in "living inquiry" together and in discovering, through their ad agency masks, new ways to introduce The Theatre of Inquiry to others.

The group was enthusiastic and met early the next time to discuss together how they would proceed. When I arrived, I discovered them seated behind a table with name cards, ready to role play. Interestingly, they were pretending we didn't already know one another, so they became quite discombobulated when I responded to their early questions, not only by answering as best I could (e.g. that I thought that ToI wasn't as much a product as a deep adult experiential learning process), but also inviting them to use all of their experience of the Theatre of Inquiry so far to help address our advertising question as well.

About halfway through our first advertising meeting, Peter – perhaps the least verbal and least scintillatingly bright of the group in conventional terms – impressed me once again in a new way by being the first to begin to formulate an expanded version of what was going on among us:

> *We've been brainstorming, in effect, as to what is the best way to get that product across. We're all assuming that we know what the product is, and my sense of what we're here to do today is to get as well understood as we possibly can – what is it? What is this product? What are we trying to advertise? Then we can talk about methods and brainstorm media and all the rest. But I would suggest, and I'd like to see how other people feel about it, that we spend this last half hour really trying to zero in on what is the product that we're talking about.*

As had happened years before in Morris' Yale Summer High School class on Kafka, some members caught on more rapidly than others to the larger 'game' within which the role playing was occurring, while those others began feeling betrayed by their comrades, who seemed to them to be forsaking the role-playing roles they'd agreed to for a 'real' inquiry.

When the hour allotted for the role play ended, some members were feeling cheated — "It's not the money, it's the idea…" An even more emotional conversation ensued, ending with me saying to laughter by all, "I want to create a situation where you participate in discovering how to get your money's worth. I mean, if **I** give you your money's worth, I will not be giving you The Theatre of Inquiry." After the laughter and a pause, I concluded, "I've done as much as I possibly can tonight. But I certainly will stand by that promise." And after more laughter, I added, "Maybe that will be the advertising campaign right there." One of the more euphonious members of the group began warbling "If I give you your money's worth, I won't be giving you The Theatre of Inquiry…" to more laughter…

Although there were some close bonds within this group before we joined in the eight-week Action Workshop, the bonds certainly drew closer after our unencipherable experiences together. No other moment touched me as deeply as the session in which Peter brought all of us to tears by sharing his Vietnam experience, including a nighttime firefight in the forest when no one in his platoon but he survived.

Talk about Stirring Occasions: The Business/School

The Business/School was in some pragmatic ways the most successful of my Theatre of Inquiry experiments that year. I attracted thirteen participants and we met for thirteen weeks (yes, that's $1,690.00 at my prices). To my eventual delight, seven of those thirteen folks actually started their own business the next year. Moreover, six of the seven businesses lasted longer than mine. (Ah... how many of my students have since gone beyond me as well!) When I checked four years after that, four of the businesses were still operating locally.

The Business/School was also the most fun of my Theatre of Inquiry experiments. With no capital to build the communal Roman Bath we envisioned just off Harvard Square – we instead developed "Stirring Occasions" – a party-consulting company that would put on the party you really wanted. We hosted two weddings and two other occasions, serving and changing costumes and roles in all the ways agreed to beforehand with the hosts. People loved us at the time (and I can actually say this with some objectivity because I myself was never present at the actual "stirring" of the four money-making "occasions," but heard afterwards from several of the guests each time).

Not only was the Business/School a modest success in these various ways, but it also provided me with the single moment that was most spiritually, theoretically, and practically meaningful to me as an example of how to prepare for and then take timely action. This "epiphanic moment" occurred between the third and fourth meetings of the Business/School and then during the fourth meeting. As suggested above, we had entertained several other business possibilities before landing on Stirring Occasions, and we had done some real business feasibility research on each opportunity. I had set the end of the third meeting as the time by which we would choose our mini-co-entrepreneurial venture. But in fact what we managed to do by then was to decisively *eliminate* all three business ideas we had explored up to that time.

We agreed to meet for an informal, bring-something-to-share supper the hour and a half before the next meeting, with the explicit intent of brainstorming creatively during that time, so that we would be more likely to reach resolution on a business to start together by the end of the fourth formal meeting.

As the week wore on – in between changing the twins diapers, delivering grant applications to foundations, conducting three Action Workshops and perhaps another three Inner Chapters Driving lessons, preparing for the next Public Performance, and applying for academic jobs (which were beginning to seem hard to get now that I was finally serious about getting one) – I became more and more anxious about the next Business/School meeting. Realistically, it seemed pretty unlikely that we were going to come up with the right thing in one meeting, given we had just failed to do so in three meetings. But if we didn't, I wasn't sure I could hold the group's commitment for further meetings.

One very, very early morning, after feeding and changing the twins, I decided to try to map out where our business process was, in terms of the developmental organizational action-logics I had discovered after the Yale Upward Bound program a decade earlier. I hoped that trying to clarify for myself where our enterprise was in our collective developmental transformations would engender new ideas about how to help us transform positively during the fourth meeting.

The Business/School had obviously passed through the 'Conception' and 'Investments' action-logics, since we were already 'Incorporated' in the sense that we were meeting together. To become fully and ongoingly 'Incorporated,' however, we needed to complete precisely what we were trying to do: namely, settle on a business to enact.

That didn't tell me much that I didn't already know. Could I be more precise? Could I perhaps tease apart sub-stages of development between Investments and Incorporation? I figured that we (the initial members of the Business/School) had started in to the Incorporation action-logic when we started our first meeting, so perhaps that could count as the Conception sub-stage of Incorporation. Next, maybe the research time we had invested could be considered the Investments sub-stage. Our three modest business plans might embody the Incorporation sub-stage. We had actively experimented with different ways of comparing our plans against each other (the Experiments sub-stage?), and had ended the third meeting by reaching a negative version of the Systematic Productivity sub-stage, when we decided against all three. Next, in deciding on a decentralized supper for the beginning of the upcoming meeting, the group as a whole could now be interpreted as sharing leadership at the Collaborative Inquiry sub-stage.

This tentative analysis of an inner octave of change seemed more useful for design purposes. What might moving this sub-process beyond Collaborative Inquiry to the Foundational Community of Inquiry sub-stage in the course of our next meeting mean and entail? What kind of leadership action might I take, and when, during the next meeting, in order to help us complete the Incorporation stage of the business/school positively?

The Foundational Community action-logic parallels on the collective scale the Alchemical action-logic on the individual scale, according to my version of developmental theory. To reach this way of "operating" or "performing," one must inquire and act in ways that are born from a listening into the dark ... beyond all that one knows ... as well as listening out to the already-defined world ... through all one's felt-embodied-senses. During my meditational jog in the park that morning, my mind returned to this question, not in an analytic, gnawing-on-a-problem sense, but in a receiving-a-vision-of-a-possible-future sense. I began with the feeling that:

> *If, by the end of the formal meeting we are to invent the right business for our learning –*
>
> *Then, the share-what-you-bring Collaborative Inquiry supper ought to transform between the decentralized first course into a shared dessert that I would bring, marking the movement from Collaborative Inquiry to Foundational Community.*

My 'visioning' imaged my acting in silence, seeking to observe how the conversational streams converged as the subgroups congregated around the dessert, which now appeared in my mind's eye as a large platter of cut fruits, with vanilla yogurt, strawberries, and a bowl of melted fudge nearest the center. I would silently gesture with the platter, inviting each of the subgroups toward the center of the floor, where I placed it. My waking dream suggested I was to remain silent throughout this time, long into whatever shared conversation developed, in a kind of ritual observance of the sacred birth of whatever business/ educational process we invented.

I didn't get any better brainstorms before the event, so I turned up at the event with the dessert, committed to executing the above, bizarre plan to the best of my ability. I knew I shouldn't eat much and I wanted to listen in on the subgroups as well, so I circulated among them getting just a bite of this and that finger food from their plates, before going to the kitchen to arrange and present the dessert.

The diverse conversations about what business we might create all seemed to have been inspired by the Harvard Square Roman Bath idea we'd had to nix the week before on account of lack of capital. One woman was courageously suggesting that we promote mutual-massage-and-sex-parlors. One sub-group was developing a consulting firm. And the third was playing with the idea of a catering service named Party Smiths.

At this point, it's pretty easy for you the reader to see how the group as a whole – once it got together over dessert – might dream and laugh and argue its way to the idea of a Party-Consulting-company-that-will-deliver-the-party-you-mean-to-have (i.e. not just catering the food, but choreographing and facilitating the whole experience). But back at that time, it seemed a truly improbable, magical, alchemically stirring occasion to me, for it seemed so obvious that nothing I might have said or done (or not done) could have worked out better than my silent service of the dessert, even though, in an ordinary sense, it didn't seem as though I had had any influence on the occasion at all.

■ ■ ■

So, this result seemed miraculous – in some sense like the timing between Lee and me a year and a half earlier, in our decision to become at-one and at-four.

It also represented the first time I had used the developmental theory deliberately to try to invent a timely action. Moreover, it also seemed in some unfathomable way significant that both in this case and when I had circled so long before making my commitment to Lee, timely action was preceded and surrounded by an unusually attentive period of ***inaction***. Perhaps I was learning timely inaction at least as much as I was learning timely action, and perhaps both intentional action and intentional inaction are mutually, non-dually necessary.

In the long run, though, the most important part of this experience for me was that it gave me a stronger taste of how to engage in research into the volume of future possibilities. The meaningful future visions I'd occasionally had before (such as the vision of how to paint my room at Channing Place, or the vision of N/n) had had a somewhat happenstance quality to them. Now I realized that I could also, to some degree, precipitate such visions through my own physical exercises, emotional practices, and attentional disciplines of inquiry, including using the theory of organizational development as a design tool to aid my dreaming of futures while awake. (Endnote 24)

Chapter 20

The Dress Rehearsals for the Public Performance, 1978

At the beginning of February, I sent out a second flyer, this time in the shape of a letter on Theatre of Inquiry stationery on one side, with photographs of the first dress rehearsal of the Public Performances on the back. One of the photographs shows a large audience holding their arms out, with me (and a sculpture) on the stage doing the same. In another, you can see a guitarist on the stage, interpreting the effects of the performance in sound. Sitting in front of the podium, a mime mimics the audience's movements. A roving camerawoman (this time with no film in her camera!) "films" whatever arbitrary aspects of the situation her attention focuses upon. The overall event is meant to encourage 'four territory awareness' (effects, embodied sensation, thoughts, post-cognitive attention).

Imagine receiving this letter and the photographs in the mail. What would you think of it? Would you consign it to the bin before reading all the way through, or would you investigate further?

Dear Friends and Strangers:

I invite you to join this spring in any one or all five of the remaining "dress rehearsals" of The Theatre of Inquiry Public Performances.

Through a collaborative inquiry among all the participants ("and just what is a collaborative inquiry?" you may well ask), the Public Performances seek to discover and display the art of organizing. The art of organizing is not a pre-defined art like painting or ballet or a concert, but rather the art by which persons sculpt their time when they consciously act in concert. The art of organizing is at once the least known of all the arts and the master art – the art which, if practiced, determines the framework within which all other arts, sciences, professions, political aims, and personal desires are pursued.

The Public Performances are informed by two questions, which participants may come to share: (1) what kind of attention is necessary in order to "see" and influence the changing social sculptures in which one participates with others? And (2) what kind of public institution encourages its participants to develop the attention to play a continuing role in sculpting the definition of any situation?

The Theatre of Inquiry can be approached as entertainment, as a public school for adults, as a new genre of participatory art, as a social science experiment in which the researchers include themselves within the field of observation, or as a new form of government ...

However you approach the Public Performances, I hope you will come. Strange as they may sound, they are really friendly occasions. Moreover, these "dress rehearsals" aren't primarily for the sake of those of us who already recognize ourselves as actors in The Theatre of Inquiry. They are primarily for the sake of developing a new taste for, one might even say a new fashion of, public action – public action that encourages inquiry.

The details of when and where appear on the reverse side, which I would be delighted to have you post somewhere if you wish.

Sincerely, William R. Torbert

The dress rehearsals for the Public Performances were meant to attract the folks who came to them to go on to participate regularly in an ongoing Action Workshop or the Business/School, which was about to start. The title of the first Public Performance, seen in the photos, was "Creating a Community of Inquiry: In Science, Society, and One's Own Circle." In the first act, dressed in a three-piece professorial suit and playing the role of "thought," I defined a community of inquiry as one that encourages inquiry into all four territories of our experience – into outer appearances and sounds (like the musician's guitar-playing); into the act-ual practices of its own members (with the mime in front of the podium as reminder of their practices); into what thoughts are most relevant (my role), and into the nature of our own attention (re-presented by the meandering camera-woman).

The second act consisted of attention exercises, cultivating "4-Territory" experiencing among all participants... such as the arms-out exercise in the photo. The formal part of the evening concluded with a third act, consisting of a conversation among all present about just what kind of an event or game this was. At the end of the "show," any participants who wished to come were invited to continue the debriefing at a local bar.

The dozen old friends and new acquaintances who congregated at the bar – over scotch, beer, wine, seltzer, and a huge antipasto, agreed that although the occasion had had its share of interesting tastes, I had lectured too long and too abstractly and had not sufficiently helped the rest of the participants develop a shared sense of the significance of the occasion. I was advised to begin the next Public Performance by telling some exemplary stories instead of speaking so theoretically, and by involving the audience earlier in steering the occasion.

So, in February I did just that. Sitting in an easy chair with a lamp behind and a table next to me with a glass of water on it and manuscripts open, I began by asking all present to consider what a unique fraternity they were joining by choosing to be present tonight for this "membership trial." This elicited a bout of nervous laughter, but no further comments during a pause of some duration.

I explained next that I would read some stories that exemplify the mysterious combination of action and inquiry in the present – just what participation in The Theatre of Inquiry is intended to provoke. First, I offered a story you readers already know: the Inner Chapters story of Price Wen Hui's cook. That transformed into a story about the Inner Chapters Driving School and driving in Boston, concluding with the more general challenge we all face: of steering our lives well through the 6-dimensional space/time events in which we participate (Gravity, Levity, Extensity, Duration, Presence, Volume of Possibilities).

This story elicited laughter at various points, but no further comments during another noticeable pause at its conclusion... Until a woman spoke up from the back of the auditorium in a clear, sharp voice, telling her own story:

> *Waiting here for someone to speak, impatient and apprehensive, reminds me of the first dinner party I ever gave as a teenager for several older boys who were in college. My mother left a ham in the oven, saying it would be ready by nine. Everything else was prepared, but I could hardly hear the conversation during the first part of the evening for worrying about whether the dinner would come off.*
>
> *We are just approaching nine o'clock now, and I feel the same way tonight.*

When I opened the oven at the party, I discovered that the ham was as cold as could be: the oven had somehow never been turned on. I immediately turned it on and fled back to the party, knowing it was up to me. At ten o'clock, when the guests were visibly salivating, I served the ham half-baked. The boys all took seconds, and everybody complimented me about how delicious it was ...

Again laughter and again a prolonged silence ...

The next speaker turned to the rest of the participants and asked whether someone besides me could explain to him "What the hell is going on here?" Several persons volunteered responses, and I told further stories. But it is safe to summarize the rest of the evening as anti-climatic. At the "post-game wrap-up" in the bar afterwards, I was criticized for not really acting and not providing enough exercises.

The March "Dress Rehearsal" played to an audience of forty. Reflecting the feedback I'd received to "really act," I for the first time provided a playbill titled "A Dance in Time." The playbill showed three acts and three different characters in the first act, all of whom I was fixing to play.

Before the performance, when I was changing in my dressing room (the large 'Handicapped' stall of the Men's Room in Harvard's Longfellow Hall), I first suffered angst about how authentic it was to act a part, and then an intense fear of failure because I had not memorized my three different roles. Such was my stage fright that I leaned deep toward the toilet, very nearly vomiting and fainting. But not quite.

In the first scene of the first act I was, as usual, explaining what was going to happen ... When suddenly a harsh critic of my "intellectual, explaining personality" started leaping around shouting at "me" for believing after all these years that anyone else cares about my approach to these matters.

Red in the face, still roaring, and pacing back and forth, my "emotional, judgmental personality" continued to upraid the previous performer, until itself interrupted, after a slow twirl around... By a third side of me that emerged from the twirl with a white mask and a full black beard, somewhat bent with age – an old Southerner... Who, laughing, chides the previous two youngsters, gently reminding them of the years it took for the changing shape of the Mississippi to insinuate itself upon Mark Twain as he struggled to pilot it – our attention surely no less mighty and changeable a stream...

> *Ship channels are buoyed and lighted,"* the old Southerner read from Twain's ***Life on the Mississippi***, *"and therefore it is a comparatively easy undertaking to learn to run them. Clear-water rivers, with gravel bottoms, change their channels very gradually, and therefore one needs to learn them but once.*
>
> *"But piloting becomes another matter when you apply it to vast streams like the Mississippi and the Missouri, whose alluvial banks cave and change constantly, whose snags are always hunting up new quarters, whose sandbars are never at rest, whose channels are forever dodging and shirking, and whose obstructions must be confronted in all nights and all weathers without the aid of a single light-house or a single buoy... Why you can't never stop measuring and learning from this river so long's you want to have a chance of navigating into port.*

After a minute of silence, I asked, "What would it mean to inquire into the flow of your own attentional 'river'?" After a further minute of silence, I announced a 10-minute intermission, after which we would try a variety of attention exercises during the second act.

After that, the actor/audience conversation of the third act this time began with a series of questions of me. I responded to two as they were asked, then raised a question about the third question, but also ended that 'game' by "dismissing the class."

After a shorter pause than I was getting used to, a female audience member denounced the first two acts as neither entertaining nor seriously concerned, as she was, with other people's welfare. She called them narcissistic and meaningless. Attack and counter-attack continued among participants for a good while, until another participant named that game "the competitive, two-party system."

At this point, several participants testified to the triune character of good conversations such as we were currently, painfully, constructing – how conversations often begin in a rule-following mode, but then can become rule-recognizing during the event, as we had now twice become – first recognizing our resemblance to a class controlled by a single teacher and, second, discovering our resemblance to a two-party debate. After that, a conversation can potentially become rule-transcending-and-transforming.

The formal evening ended with the original critic asking again what the conversation was about, "Is there any substance to this conversation?" she asked piercingly. And, after a short pause, in a huskier, flatter, and even more scathing tone... "Is there a 'what' here?"

At the bar afterwards, I was given some credit for providing a little bit more genuine entertainment this time... which seemed to have lead to our best third act conversation yet. (Or was the better conversation just by chance?) But don't worry, I didn't just get *positive feedback*; I was also criticized for practicing a politics too much focused on mutual attention to the present occasion. This was a problematic charge because the main difference between most politics and Theatre of Inquiry politics is that most politics avoids mutual attention to the present occasion altogether, whereas the Theatre of Inquiry is attempting to introduce it. How much is too much at first? Evidently, I had not yet figured that out for this audience.

Nevertheless, I myself judged this third dress-rehearsal-for-the-public-performances a major improvement. This was in part because I act-ually act-ed. In part, also, my good feeling was due to our developmentally-transforming conversation in the third act. Twice we named and then transcended our conversation's prior boundaries – the best example these public performances had yet generated of the mutually-transforming power of the politics of collaborative inquiry.

The prescription I inferred from the post-game conversation for how to conduct the fourth dress rehearsal was... To dramatically enact a future vision of a politics of inquiry... And of the mutually-transforming power of collaborative inquiry that would increase popular support for achieving this vision.

Mass Age Mess Age

The fifty attendants at the April 1978 Public Performance receive a playbill upon entering entitled ***Mass-age Mess-age***. The three acts run from the future back to the present:

> **Act I** set ten years in the future, portrays the ToI Global TV show
>
> **Act II** set three years in the future, portrays the embattled ToI Press/Release Corps
>
> **Act III** is set in the present.

Act I of Massage Message

In Act I, set in 1988, a business executive enters his office, checks the stuff on his desk, dictates briefly into a pocket phone, then flicks the TV on, doffs his suit to reveal exercise tights, whirls slowly around several times, and is transformed into Justin Thor, the ToI International TV noontime “Physical Play” Host.

Justin speaks in many quite different voices as he leads three exercises, having reminded those in theaters around the world that they are welcome to fill the aisles. (At this point about 70% of the audience in 1978 move into the auditorium aisles.)

The first exercise “ –Find Your Own Particular Changing Gait” – is inspired by elderly and otherwise-challenged persons. At this point the auditorium aisles begin to undulate and poke about oddly... as Thor himself gallivants awkwardly on the stage, while reminiscing about how the non-imitative exercises he created in his own Adulthood

Initiation Play ten years before led to ToI International and to the United Nations General Assembly Proclamation, ironically passed in 1984, decrying all leadership behavior intended to induce anyone merely to follow, mimic, or imitate a single leader. How to lead exercises like the ones he is now leading, which invite exercisers' own creativity and widening awareness ???

The second exercise – Touch Your Toes & Reach for the Sky As Slowly As Possible – is inspired by middle-aged executives with lower back problems. Now the auditorium aisles move more quietly and calmly in a yoga-like way. Thor, moving more slowly than anyone else, reminds participants that the way to become a ToI International Host is to dedicate a year of one's life, sometime between the ages of 21 and 42, to performing and re-performing one's own Adulthood Initiation Play. Those that rise through regional cooperative competitions, chosen as most transformationally educational, may ultimately appear on ToI International one of the 365 days each year.

The daily ToI Global Adulthood Initiation Play occurs, of course, right after these physical exercises, from 12:30-1:30pm, which is why more and more businesses, government agencies, and not-for-profits are creating an 11:45-1:45 break each day for employee development purposes.

The third exercise – Lie on the Floor & Squiggle – is inspired by babies. Thor is squiggling on his back as he speaks, some in the aisles are too, though some return to their seats. As he continues to squiggle, Thor introduces Rocky Thunderhead of Ft. Wayne, with his play titled "Satyagraha." This is to be today's Adulthood Initiation Play.

The lights dim. Justin Thor exits.

After a silence just long enough to make the audience seriously wonder what will happen next, a tape recorder blares Rocky Thunderhead's introduction of his Adulthood Initiation Play, which moves, he says, through the three ages of humankind – the age of blood, the age of law, and the age of mutual inquiry.

The age of blood will be enacted by Teiresias, in whom, alone among humanity at that time, according to Sophocles, "truth is native…" The age of law will be played by Jederman ('every-man') from the German Medieval morality play of the same name…The age of mutual inquiry will be played by Jimminy Christmas…

As the recording ends, the lights rise. A robed figure with flowing white hair enters slowly stage left, eyes vacant, one hand grasping a gnarled stick, tapping…The other hand feeling about in the air…The head cocking itself from side to side to listen into the silence.

Gradually, as members of the audience cough or giggle, the ancient man (or is it a woman?) becomes aware of the presence of an audience. Slowly at first, but writhing about with increasing passion, he introduces himself and tells his story:

Teiresias, I,
Two-Natured –
Man-Woman.

Visioned saw I
Two snakes copulating
Made one eternal circle.

Fire and poison
Writhing in my bowels and back –
A sickening potion –
I claimed my peace
And slew the female
Rather than digest
That offense.

Zeus Thunderer
Transformed me then:
Woman, I
Digested woman,
Slew the male,
Digested both.

Appearing again as man,
Now inwardly one,
Eternal circle,
Fire, poison, and flesh,
Swallowing myself,
Exhaling worlds,
I spoke with the gods,
Fearfully but truthfully,
Equidistant from their folly
And that of humankind.

■ ■ ■

Later, Hera asked
What I alone can know,
Man-woman that I am:
Whether man or woman
Pleasures more in love?

Zeus said woman more,
She: man.

Woman ten times more,
I replied.

Enraged Hera,
Not yet mistress of her passions,
Blinded me then,
As I had earlier slain the serpent.

Driven so to inward I,
Zeus o'pes me yet again
That I may spy
Past and future,

Humankind as one,
Mother earth beneath my feet
And father in the sky.

■ ■ ■

Called to Oedipus,
I knew he could not hear my truths.

I saw and still do see
That ages must pass
Before truth can set man free.

Now man's blood is his truth
And in the coming age God's law.

Then Mammon too will take his turn.

■ ■ ■

Humankind wants its truths small,
Wants one small truth
To digest all experience.

Not until we wake again,
Not to blood alone, nor law,
But to the surprise of life

And the leisurely digestion of truth,
Will transfiguration after transfiguration,
Truth itself transfigured,
Take us at our every word and act.

The lights dim ... Teiresias retires stage right, tapping his way with his stick ...

In the shadow, stick and wig drop ...

The actor moves slowly around the perimeter of the dark auditorium, echoing the haunting call "**Jederman ... Jederman ... Jed erman ...** " (Every-man ... Everyman ...) from the play I had seen in Salzburg when I was ten. (The play, now in comic mode and named "Everyone," currently [2017] appears off-Broadway.)

Thunderhead had noted in his tape recorded introduction, "This distant call around the circumference of the theatre of inquiry symbolizes the gradual externalization of the gods and the passions during the medieval and modern ages of law and order, culminating in the death of god and the cold inquisitorial horrors of Eichmann's law-abiding mind during Germany's Third Reich."

Thunderhead's tape recording had also introduced Jimminy Christmas, the lead character in the next scene. Jimminy Christmas is a Martian Old One, here to correct the message of Michael Valentine Smith as portrayed in Robert Heinlein's book, ***Stranger in a Strange Land***.

In the next Theatre of Inquiry scene, Christmas says that because Valentine was but a young man when he left Mars to come to Earth, he had not yet recognized the fundamental difference between Mars and Earth. Although Valentine had understood how astral-levity bodies play in the light, he had still not been introduced to the interplay between the light and the dark – between levity and gravity. In consequence of his youth, the angelic, non-possessively-loving Michael Valentine created a polarization between the light and the dark.

This is why Valentine's gentle message of opening and non-possessive love got him crucified. The war that ensued in the 1960s and 1970s between proponents of widening mutuality (e.g. Civil Rights, Feminism, Prague Spring) and proponents of unilateral force (e.g. the

Vietnam War, Watergate, and Mao Tse Tung 'Thought') could only be won by the dark forces and the spirit of gravity, since those are so predominant among us here on Earth.

At this point, Thunderhead himself dressed as a Martian [red dancing tights and green cap with antennae]) – is jerked through stage door left, as if by incompetently manipulated puppet strings. Christmas is trying to speak through Thunderhead to the assembly, but has trouble making the unfamiliar vocal chords work.

What he eventually says, and how he and the participants interact, is unknown... Because neither Thunderhead's original performance of Satyagraha, nor any of its many re-imaginings and re-enactments in others' Adulthood Initiation Plays, have been recorded. Not repeating what occurs during one's participation has become a sacred commitment participants make, so that new participants come with a dramatic sense of inquiry about what is about to occur and about what one's own actions will contribute.

Act I is followed by a 15-minute intermission.

Act II of Massage Message

Act II is set in 1981, only three years in the future.

Trailed by a member of the Tol Press/Release Corps (Tol is pronounced "toy") with a shoulder-mounted TV camera...

Torbert (playing a future version of himself, of course) hurries in with a large bandage on his forehead, a handheld mike, and a "MUTUALLY-TRANSFORMING POWER" placard in his other hand. He thanks the audience for its courage in coming here tonight, given the attack from all sides against the Theatre of Inquiry "Political Parties" and its "64 Public Policies."

Next, the future-Torbert reminds the audience that they are full-fledged participants in this "action inquiry" process... With no special privileges accorded the professional press... Quite the contrary, indeed, the Tol Press/Release film crew acts as a fair witness in case of biased media reportage.

Before introducing Public Policy #13, to be discussed tonight – a policy concerning voluntary sex education of the 18-year-old cohort of young men each year by that year's cohort of 36-year-old women –

Torbert recalls how "The Theatre of Inquiry" first came to national attention a year ago. At that time, the media, frantic for new approaches to the growing economic dislocations and high long-term unemployment, had widely publicized the ToI policy recommending that governing institutions, led by state governments, create a 20-hour work week with shared jobs, some running 9am-1:15pm, others 12:45-5pm (the overlapping times permit in-person co-ordination between the two holders of the same job). The idea was to encourage wider employment, of course, but equally important, more collaboration, more entrepreneurship, and more leisure.

> *"For about three months, the press closely covered The Theatre of Inquiry. We received a flood of inquiries about how to join or create Trios, Action Workshops, Business/Schools, Adulthood Initiation Plays, Weekend Sextets, and other leisurely, mutually-transforming, adult education venues.*
>
> *"But network newscasters became increasingly antagonized by the ToI Press/Release Corps who, in interviews, insisted on having their own cameras present and on their right to ask questions of the professional reporters and to comment on the degree of mutuality being exercised in the present encounter.*
>
> *"As many of you know, when the next ToI public policy was released nine months ago, it recommended that the legitimacy of corporations be determined by the degree to which they are managed as collaborative inquiries. The accompanying text offered data strongly suggesting that corporations in general, including news corporations have quite low CIQs [Collaborative Inquiry Quotients]; it also offered management*

guru Peter Drucker's analysis that the source of corporate legitimacy is indeed questionable, given their power to influence both individuals and governments.

"This ToI public policy was first greeted by a week of media and corporate attacks on The Theatre of Inquiry, accompanied by the withdrawal of sponsorships. The few reporters who did try to continue to write neutrally or appreciatively about ToI found their articles unpublished and their jobs threatened. Since then, the Theatre of Inquiry has faced a media blackout and inquiries have declined radically.

"Let me get us started on tonight's conversation, First in self-study trios and then as a whole community, by summarizing the longer text of our new adult sex education policy very briefly. The policy vests all responsibility for its voluntary and decentralized execution each year on the cohort of women who are becoming 36 that year. (The inverse process [36-year-old men 'educating' 18-year-old women] is emphatically ***not*** *proposed.) We recommend a new computer mail system, recently invented by the government, to support scientific research to support this de-centralized sex education process.*

"The sex education occurs during a once a month evening meeting between one young man and two mature women twice his age. Both men and women may belong to more than one trio should they so choose that year or any thereafter. The meetings occur at venues of the women's choosing, and the man provides the dinner for each occasion. The general curriculum is learning how to engage in collaborative inquiry, establishing and respecting one another's boundaries, and exercising mutually-transforming power when changing boundaries in the domain of friendship, intimacy, and sex..."

Such were the future-presencing visions that wound their way through me and into quasi-theatrical expression in the Action Workshops, the Business/School, and the Public Performances during the winter and spring of 1978. (Endnote 25)

At Home

At home, the miracle of the twins' development was front and center. Here was my best grounding experience of all. They and I spent a lot of time on the ground, or at least the floor. These experiences provided the "Baby Squiggle" exercise for Justin Thor, of course, as well as such wonderful later photographs as the one of me in May sitting on our sofa, with Michael, "the sleepy philosopher" lying across my lap asleep as usual, while above him Patrick, "the little man of action," wide awake as usual, is stretching parallel, with his waist and torso on the palm of my hand. Not only all that: Lee and I were still getting in our sacred Saturday evening dates by ourselves.

Nevertheless, I was nervous enough about where my contribution to my young family's livelihood would come from in the near future that I picked up two speeding tickets within 15 minutes of one another on my way to Springfield to visit a foundation executive about a grant. (Let me tell you, the Director of the Inner Chapters Driving School felt well chastised indeed on that occasion. What kind of 6-dimensional driving of one's life was that?)

At the same time as I was applying for grants, I was also applying for what, that year, seemed like a very slow trickle of academic positions in the Boston area. I looked into both schools of education (BU) and schools of management (Bentley) – even some liberal arts positions (Hampshire). As winter turned into spring... And then, more ominously, as spring turned into summer... NO JOB. As the summer wore on, with Theatre of Inquiry activities in abeyance, our larder became more and more bare, and Lee's stress became more and more palpable.

Then we discovered Lee was pregnant again, in spite of her birth control measures. We were pro-choice, as a universal human principle, but closer to 'pro-life' in practice... thus thrusting ourselves into the torturous dilemma of whether we wanted to proceed with this pregnancy in practice. With the twins still stretching us beyond the limits of our capacities, and with too little income already, the timing could not have seemed worse for a third child from a prudential perspective. Nevertheless, we both felt wrong about taking a purely prudential perspective. So, we finally agreed, with many tears and fears, to have the child. Three weeks later, Lee spontaneously miscarried. We both wept all the more bitterly because of our simultaneous feelings of grief and relief.

So much about what constitutes timely action remains imponderable.

Chapter 21

A Few Clues About What Transpired Thereafter

As it turned out (thank goodness!), I did get a job as Graduate Management Dean at Boston College. Now, I was playing in the real-world theatre of inquiry. But of course, not everyone regarded us as 'playing' in this real world, and no one else regarded us as engaged in a 'theatre of inquiry.' My three-piece suit was my daily mask in this new setting.

In spite of the initial, yawning gap between my Ivy League/ WASP/ internationalist background and BC's Catholic/ Irish-Italian/ local culture, I had evidently learned enough about adjusting to different Superior Cultures to last happily at BC for thirty years, til my retirement in 2008.

Relating to BC's Superior Culture

With regard to what I had learned about relating to the **Superior Culture** of an institution, I recognized that I needed to actively seek out and cultivate close allies within the senior administration. This began with the close friendship that my immediate boss, Jack Neuhauser, and I generated from our very first meeting when we discovered our shared delight in Zorba the Greek... and gradually extended to the Academic Vice-President with whom I shared a Yale background; the Dean of Arts and Sciences who liked my diplomatic background; the Executive Vice-President, who, for some reason, was willing to have lunch with me several times a year; and ultimately to the President who was pleased to be invited annually to offer a history of the Jesuits at one of our MBA Integrative Activities.

Equally important, the **Superior Culture** at Boston College was saturated by the Jesuit Order, a truly late action-logic institution whose principles of *meditation-in-action* and *curae persona* (care for the person) are very nearly identical with the principles of first- and second-person action inquiry. Also, the Jesuits were, like me, much more committed than leading secular research universities to a balance between teaching and scholarship. Moreover, the community of Jesuits at Boston College and throughout the world, although unmistakably hierarchical in many ways, also cultivated elements of **Peer Culture** among themselves and with others. In these regards, my job was to take frequent opportunities to note in passing the concordance between my aims and the Jesuits'.

Nevertheless, only Jack Neuhauser became a fully-fledged friend and peer with whom I could share my various prior adventures like The Theatre of Inquiry. As I acknowledged in my later book *Managing the Corporate Dream*, in the teasing mode we had developed:

> *"(Jack) is militantly anti-theoretical in his managerial practice, teaches the virtues of waiting and unobtrusive action by example, disarms potential opposition and self-importance through humor and disillusioning candor, and in general functions in what, to this neophyte, appears for all the world to be a Zen master-like manner in the midst of the American executive scene. Like the ancient tree in Chuang-Tsu's story, he survives, and provides protection for all in his neighborhood, by appearing useless. Certainly, he is centrally responsible for the pleasures of my work over the past eight years and for the blossoming of the Boston College School of Management."*

I had to some degree been playing with the Clown/ Alchemical/ 'Authentic' archetype during my Harvard and Theatre of Inquiry period.

Now I was resolutely donning a mask of conventionality and organizational authority, attempting to enact the Masked Ironist archetype, playing a long game (an 'infinite game'?), looking for accumulating influence, rather than instant impact.

One data pattern that I believe supports my sense that I was practicing Ironist discretion much better than before I took the BC job is that for the decade that I hosted the weekly BC MBA Integrative Activities each Wednesday morning, I frequently wore dancing tights beneath my three-piece suit to emphasize to myself that the suit was a costume, part of my "act," part of my mask. Also, this way of costuming myself permitted me to do a kind of strip tease, if ever the timing and the leadership lesson should seem apropos. When I dressed like this at conferences or workshops far from Boston, the time did sometimes seem right; but never, I am proud to say, at BC.

Transforming the Subordinate Culture

Despite my care with regard to the **Superior Culture**, I did not forfeit my role of attempting to catalyze individual and organizational transformation with regard to the **Subordinate Culture**. Three years into my new role, the new "action-effectiveness" MBA program that my colleagues and I had painstakingly designed and implemented rose in the national rankings from below the top hundred to #29.

From the outset, I wanted to research the transformational efficacy (or inefficacy) of the redesigned MBA program as a whole through third-person action inquiry research over time, as well as through first- and second-person action inquiry at any given moment. With the help of a $100,000 grant from IBM in 1980, I undertook one of the two largest research projects of my life. The outline of its 3rd-person empirical design was that, with their voluntary agreement and the understanding that they could receive feedback on their own results, we asked each new cohort of about 100 fulltime MBA students at entry to the program, and again 21 months later as they graduated, to fill out what is today known as the Global Leadership Profile (GLP), the psychometric measure of a person's action-logic. We wanted to see whether, unlike most educational programs, our new, action-oriented MBA program generated true, measurable, developmental transformation in our adult students.

Our initial findings helped to validate the GLP measure. For example, developmental theory predicts that persons at each later action-logic are in some way more open to feedback than at earlier action-logics. As mentioned, we offered the opportunity for voluntary feedback to students on their GLPs. Was there any systematic relationship between a student's action-logic and whether or not they requested feedback? None of our students were scored at Opportunist. About 10% scored at the Diplomat action-logic, and none of them requested feedback. Nearly half of the students were rated Expert, and only one-tenth of them requested feedback. (Moreover, three quarters of the feedback sessions with Experts became rather heated dismissals by them of the validity of the instrument, rather than seeking to learn more about the theory or the possible meaning and action-implications of their score.) About 30% were scored as Achievers, and four-tenths of them asked for feedback and discussed it with some interest. Finally, all of the few who scored in the postconventional Redefining or Transforming action-logics, not only asked for feedback, but several of these were eager to continue the exploration during a second session. Thus, we had found a rare phenomenon in social science: a perfect 1.0 correlation between our two variables: the later the students' developmental action-logic, the higher the proportion of the sample seeking feedback.

In another sub-study we also found, as predicted by the theory, that persons scored at later action-logics organized their job tasks more strategically and delegated more inquiringly than those at earlier action-logics. This finding was based on a laboratory study where 49 participants worked through the same set of executive in-basket items, making decisions about each and offering a brief written explanation for each decision.

Likewise, a field study of 16 MBA first-year project teams showed that those teams (5 of the 16) with one member measured at the late

Transforming action-logic outperformed teams with no one measured Transforming in three ways: 1) in terms of grades on the two course projects; 2) in terms of members' perceptions of efficient time-use; and 3) in terms of members' perception of within-group support for own learning. (No one knew the students' GLP scores at the time when the outcome data were collected; thus, it was pure happenstance that the five 'Transforming' students all belonged to different groups.)

These kinds of findings very much confirmed the importance of helping MBA students, who measured predominantly as Experts upon entry to the MBA program, to transform to later action-logics through their educational experiences if they were to become more effective leaders.

This leads us to the critical overall question our research was designed to answer: whether our much-vaunted action-effectiveness MBA program was in fact generating developmental transformation in its students. We already knew that *no other educational intervention that had been tested by Loevinger's version of the measure had done so*. (Later research found that practicing Transcendental Meditation at Maharishi University generated developmental change in participants, but over longer time periods.)

At the end of three years of study, we found that the first two cohorts we measured at the beginning and end of their programs did increase their average developmental position very slightly, so there was a very small positive correlation, *but it only accounted for a small percentage of the variance and did not reach the .05 level of statistical significance*. We appeared condemned to join the legions of educational research studies that have shown the innovation studied made "no significant difference."

After several depressing days of digesting this deflating outcome of years of research and practice, it occurred to me to check how many of the eight second-year consultants in each of the two cohorts had transformed, compared to the rest of the class. Lo and behold, fifteen of the sixteen consultants were among the total of eighteen students out of one hundred ninety-three who had gone through a double-loop, transformation of their action-logic. In fact, one initially silent, mathematically-oriented Asian woman who was rated as an Expert upon entry to the program, and who received the lowest scores for group leadership from her teammates in her first semester, won a consultant role a semester later, and had vaulted through two action-logic transformations by the time of her graduation. The overall finding showed that volunteering to participate in the 2nd-year consulting role and the associated liberating disciplines accounted for 81% of the variance (according to Kendall's tau statistic) of whether a student's action-logic transformed during the program. These revealing findings comparing the 2nd-year consultants to the rest of the class suggested what is required for transformational learning.

First, liberating disciplines similar to those of the first-year BC MBA program are necessary. These include live team consulting projects to companies and not-for-profits; the Oral Presentation Competition during which each team displayed how it had worked with its client to all the other teams; the within-team feedback sessions; the mid-semester student assessments of the faculty and program which were fedback and discussed with the entire cohort; the Weekly Integrative Activities with their listening and action skills workshops, confidential conversations with CEOs; and more. Those first year "action inquiry" practices offered all the basic building blocks for working in a collaborative inquiry fashion. But, as the small rise in the average developmental position of each cohort as a whole indicates, while a necessary step on the way, all that was not sufficient to cause developmental transformation.

Rather, our data suggest that for such a transformation to occur reliably, a person would, in addition to the first year required curriculum, have to go through something like the liberating disciplines that the second-year consultants engaged in. These included much deeper-reaching forms of 1st- and 2nd-person research, such as writing one's own developmental autobiography [1st-person action research]. In addition, the 2nd-year consultants all participated in the 2nd-person action research discipline of studying their own personal and group tape recorded behavior in meetings, each member offering the whole group a ten page analysis of one of the meetings, before its next live meeting. And of course, the 2nd-year consultants also attended weekly meetings of four different 1st-year teams (two each semester), attempting to intervene rarely but effectively, in support of those teams leading themselves in more inquiring and collaborative ways [1st – and 2nd-person research in real time]). Yet another layer of this developmental web was that the 2nd-year consultants met with the 'CEO' of the organization (me) for two-hours each week to address practically, psychologically, and politically sensitive issues concerning the students, the faculty, and our organizational clients outside the university. Here, we were seeking to interweave attention to 1st-, 2nd-, and 3rd-person action research in a timely manner.

Beyond all the first- and second-year liberating disciplines, the consultants' reliable developmental advance points to a third key design element in organizational systems that support truly transformational leadership development: namely, the encouragement of the most competent and most committed students in the MBA program to **volunteer** for the consulting role. Anyone who wished in the first-year class could compete for the consulting role, and the multiple selection criteria were well publicized: 1) first-year academic average; 2) one's ranking by one's own team in peer assessments each semester; 3) consultants' rankings of the candidates they've worked with directly; and more. Thus, the roles were filled on merit and came to be recognized as an important element of the education the school offered.

Altogether, our findings demonstrate: 1) just how long (about two years) and how intense an engagement with liberating disciplines is typically required to accomplish an adult developmental transformation; and 2) just how much of a voluntary action inquiry commitment by the candidate for transformation is simultaneously necessary.

But none of this good, abstract, research talk gives the slightest hint of the passion and tears that entered into students' processes of self-discovery. From my own point of view, reading some fourteen long autobiographies annually for thirty years, by students whom I also saw in action during our audio-recorded consulting course interactions and then again in their roles as consultants to first-year MBA teams, taught me more about the variance and subtlety of developmental movement than all of our quantitative research findings. At the same time, the interweaving and mutual-reinforcing of the quantitative, qualitative, and in-the-moment-of-action types of research bred a level of confidence in the Collaborative Developmental Action Inquiry (CDAI) process that no single form of research possibly could have. (See end of Appendix 1 for more detail on the difference between CDAI and other social science paradigms.)

Establishing Peer Cultures at BC and Beyond

Much as I had at SMU with the undergraduate teaching assistants, I was able to create temporary **Peer Cultures** with the MBA 2nd-year consultants at BC; at their initiative, we created an Alum Action Inquiry group that met one evening every three weeks for five years. I was also able to establish longer-lasting **Peer Cultures** with the PhD students in Organizational Transformation, whom I later taught. We established... three such groups; one of them, consisting of three students and myself, met six times a year for ten years. Finally, the largest, most productive, and longest-lived (15 years) of these **Peer Cultures** at BC was the monthly 'Heart & Soul' faculty dinner and planning meeting of the interdepartmental "Leadership for Change" graduate certificate program.

During my later years of consulting (to be discussed below), with the strong support of two of the CEOs, we were able to approximate a **Peer Culture** in one organization's top management team and in another organization's whole work force from board through administrative assistants. Although we have no quantitative research to document that these peer-like environments encouraged more than ordinary personal development by the members, my qualitative observations suggest they did.

I also joined two other ambitious attempts to establish **Peer Cultures** in professional organizations during those years. In the first instance, I served on the board of the Organizational Behavior Teaching Society during the years when it was transitioning from its Founding Director, Stanford's David Bradford. In the second instance, I became a founding member of Peter Senge's Society for Organizational Learning, based on a constitution with three membership categories — researchers, consultants, and business managers — all peers. Within the larger Society, a smaller group of about a dozen business people, consultants, and academics, including Peter, Otto Scharmer, Adam Kahane, and I met for a day once every six weeks to share and contest experiences, intervention cases, and theories. (Perhaps these frequent meetings across a number of years played a role in making Otto's ***Theory U*** (2007) a kind of first-cousin of mine, with its four ontological levels and its emphasis on 'presencing' consciousness for transformational action.)

Consulting Roles, More Research, and Articulating a Developmental Model of Social Science Itself

After nine years in the Graduate Dean role, I felt my next big challenge was to learn whether the CDAI approach could help to transform other kinds of organizations through consulting interventions. The first thing I began to experience in my consulting was that I could use developmental theory with the same clinical intensity as I had when we were starting up the Business/School at The Theatre of Inquiry – that time when I had served the dessert silently as the group invented the party consulting company "Stirring Occasions." An example of me working for two days with a small software company in the mid-1980s can show what this looks like (see Appendix D).

My second biggest quantitative and qualitative action research project occurred during the 1990s and engaged the consulting settings I entered. It focused on five for-profit and five not-for-profit organizations in six different industries. Along with three other consulting colleagues, I consulted for three years or more to each, always starting from their invitation to catalyze and support organizational transformation. Most important from a sheerly practical point of view, the research results showed that we succeeded in seven of ten cases in supporting organizational transformation that grew the organization's profitability and industry standing. More important from a theoretical and empirical perspective, we also learned that whether the CEO and the lead consultant scored at the Transforming action-logic (or later) accounted for 59% of the variance (beyond the .01 level of significance) of whether an organization successfully transformed. To my knowledge, no other research has ever developed as persuasive a qualitative and quantitative data set about real-world transformational successes. (See Appendix E for a description of the validity tests performed on that 'ten organization' study to establish its credibility and significance, and to explain why the small sample size does not reduce the power of the findings.)

If you examine first the detailed consulting case in Appendix D and then the statistical results of the 10-organization study in Appendix E, you will receive a full-breadth qualitative and quantitative illustration of action inquiry in practice. You will see how CDAI can become a 1st-person research/practice for a consultant engaged with a client…And how that, in turn, can generate a 2nd-person action inquiry process among the senior members of a company…And how the senior management team in turn can transform the way the company as a third-person entity operates. The research conclusion is: the later the action-logics of the lead consultant and of the CEO, the more intense does the day-to-day inquiry become among the senior team and throughout the wider organization, and the more likely the organization as a whole is to transform.

Our most practical new learning from the '10-organization' study for our own future 2nd-person action-research-consulting (i.e. our live work with companies and not-for-profits) was… That, since the action-logic of the company CEO is so critical to the success of organizational transformation attempts (at least in companies of up to 1,000 employees)… We, as consultants ought to be putting much more attention on supporting the CEO's development, ***if*** the CEO measures at Achiever or Expert (as more than four-fifths of CEOs do).

During the 1990s, I served as Director of BC's new PhD program in Organizational Transformation, as well as Chairman of the Organization Development and Change division of the Academy of Management, the principal scholarly association for our field. In these roles, I saw all the more clearly to what degree my social science colleagues identified themselves as exclusively either practitioners of quantitative, qualitative, or action research, with little attention to studying themselves in action. They did not imagine themselves as integrative scholar-practitioners of first-, second-, and third-person research in action. As a result, I now began publishing more articles delineating a developmental theory of social science itself and highlighting the power of the late action-logic paradigm Collaborative Developmental Action Inquiry.

In the years since my formal retirement from academia in 2008, the leadership development theory, rooted in the Global Leadership Profile administered through Global Leadership Associates, has become increasingly popular among major corporations (often under the name 'vertical development') and has been the basis for numerous doctoral dissertations and other studies. The invention of Transformation Cards by GLA in partnership with the Center for Creative Leadership offers the opportunity to 'democratize' developmental theory.

By contrast, since 2008 the organizational development theory and the action inquiry practices that catalyze organizational transformation have attracted much less attention, except among the coaches and consultants GLA trains and certifies. One reason for this inattention is, no doubt, that only a very small minority of executives take on the discipline necessary for successful stewardship of organizational transformation — i.e. the discipline of attending to the four territories of ontological experience and the complex waves of single-, double-, and triple-loop feedback among them in real time.

Meanwhile, the developmental theory of social science and the late action-logic CDAI paradigm remain virtually undiscovered within social science. Can this final book of mine reach out to today's young social science scholars and seed in them (in you) a new vision of social science and social action?

Can we entertain the notion that the primary aim of social scientific inquiry may be – **not** to gain greater and greater certainty about the truth of some conceptual map of the world, as supported by various sets of empirical facts (though this remains an admirable secondary aim) – ***but rather*** to generate more and more moments of deep inquiry amidst our solo-and-inter-actions? Can we imagine a social science that generates more and more capacity for – and practice of – mutual exercises of inquiry, power, and love?? A social science dedicated to cultivating ***increasingly mutual timely action?***

This possibility is still a foreign notion to the vast majority of social scientists, not to mention the much vaster majority of social citizens. Nevertheless, any of them (any of you) is a candidate to become a junior researcher in this kind of social science and social action, if they so choose (if *you* so choose). The Postscript offers an example of a person so choosing.

Postscript

Each of the following three stories, about herself by a member of Bill's action inquiry community — one story about an elementary school experience of growing up in Iran in the 1980s, one about a college experience as a new immigrant to Canada, and one about an adulthood, professional experience — can be read simply as vivid transformational moments offered by a woman doing first-person research on her own experience, which gradually evolves into first-, second-, and third-person action research into one incident in the Palestinian-Israeli conflict.

Those readers who have read the Endnotes, which analyze Torbert's experiences in developmental terms, may also want to approach these three stories as 'developmental detectives,' seeking evidence for what action-logic is being exercised when.

The developmental commentaries in the Endnote for each story can then be read as confirmation or disconfirmation of one's own analysis. (Of course, one may either agree or disagree with the analyses we offer.)

Three Stories of Development in a Different Voice

by Aftab Erfan, Chief Equity Officer City of Vancouver

I.

I don't remember much about the social dynamics of grade one – partly because my first school year was cut short due to the intensification of the Gulf War, which ended a few months later by ceasefire in 1988. But I do remember the dynamics of grade two and grade three. More than anything I remember that there was an awareness of rank amongst us that early on. It was broadly understood that some kids at my all-girls elementary school had higher status than others.

At the very top of the pyramid was Niloofar, whose aunt was the school vice-principal, who therefore could presumably get away with anything. High up there too was Sahar, whose father was the chair of the school's parent advisory committee. And then there was Yasi, who joined our class in grade 3, her family having just returned from a couple of years in the United States (an unsuccessful attempt to settle in Los Angeles, I think). Her standing was connected with her sparkly shoes and her blue American tote bag featuring Minnie Mouse, and though we were supposed to loathe America we were all so mesmerized by her she was nearly untouchable.

I also had rank due to being a gymnast, not an exceptionally good one, but one who nonetheless represented the school in citywide competitions. In truth, my athletic advantage was a proxy for my class advantage, since I was among a handful of kids at my public school whose families could afford to send them to after-school gymnastics classes.

But my status in school came primarily from the fact that I was a top student, which sadly was evident starting in grade 2 given the competitive landscape of elementary school education in Iran at the time. There was a dominant three-tier system governing our social standing (and therefore our friendship circles too) determined by academic achievement alone: there were a handful of us in each class of about 40 who were the top students, a handful who were at-the-bottom students (uncharitably called "lazy students") and a big bunch of kids in the middle who were less visible in the drama of elementary school life.

Most of the drama took place in the interaction between so-called top students and so-called lazy students, sometimes because we were designated as class moderators and they were our disobedient charges, other times because we were paired together by the teacher and put in charge of catching them up on various lessons. One teacher divided our fourth grade class into groups of five to learn our multiplication tables over a full term, putting one top student and one lazy student in each group. She made our end of term grade contingent on the performance of every group member, which was a tremendously effective way of making the top students responsible for the learning of the lazy students.

Our fifth grade teacher came in with a different tack. She was widely known as a strict teacher, a disciplinarian, possibly the most feared person at the school. She was also a sought after teacher because her students did best in the national exams we all had to write at the end of the fifth grade to graduate from elementary school and get into a good middle school. She was known for her use of corporal punishment in the classroom – rarely but effectively. Anyone who hadn't already learned their multiplication tables, she reasoned, would have incentive to learn them after they were slapped on the palm of their hands with a ruler. She used the threat of ruler, more than she actually used the ruler itself, but I have never met anyone who ruled more effectively through fear.

My most vivid memory of the fifth grade comes from a rare day when the teacher had her ruler out. I was not in any danger of getting the ruler, of course, because I was the teacher's favourite and I was multiplying three digit numbers together in my dreams by that time. So I was relaxed as she lined up a group of girls in the front of the classroom and began to test them orally on their seven-times-eights and eight-times-eights. There was some entertainment value for the rest of this class in this production. We wondered each time someone opened their mouth if the right number would jump out, or if they would be in trouble.

A small group of kids sitting in front of me tried to whisper the right answer under their breath as a way of helping the student being examined, to the teacher's occasional demands of "NO Helping!" I was too much of an abiding child to consider joining them.

The drama in front of the room came to a peak when one lazy student repeatedly failed to produce the correct answer to seven-times-six. She was a scrawny little girl who stood out not only because she was a lazy student, but also because her family was Jewish (we all knew this since she was excused from our mandatory class on the Koran every Wednesday) and she suffered the nasty stigma of being a minority Jew. Affected by these stigmas, I thought of her as the kid who never took a shower.

The teacher gave her a few more chances to screw up before she finally came good on her promise of picking up her ruler. The class gasped. We couldn't look, but we also couldn't look away. The little girl started to plead with the teacher who was clearly making a scene of the whole thing, her ruler threatening to hit as she kept asking the girl to extend her palms further forward. I pressed my lips together, tasting not only fear but also the thrill of the moment. As she began to cry, I felt horrible for the girl, but I knew for a fact that the teacher was always right.

Just in the moment when the teacher was about to lower her ruler, something else happened. A new voice joined the pleading with the little girl. It was my cousin. My pretend-cousin, rather – daughter of a friend of the family I had grown up with. "Please don't hit her Mam, please. She will promise she will learn it for tomorrow!" my cousin was saying now, putting her body between the teacher and the little girl.

I looked at her in disbelief. My cousin was in the top tier of students, but only just barely. She was a top student, but she was not nearly as top as I was! She typically kept a low profile and her only special status came from the fact that she had a professional woman for a mom (very rare at the time). How she ever dared to stand up to the teacher was beyond me.

"She promises she will learn it, Mam," my cousin repeated.

"Yes, I promise, please don't hit" the little girl said in between tears.

Other small voices joined my cousin from their seats "Mam, please don't hit!"

The teacher still had her ruler up in the air. I thought she would push my cousin aside, but instead she started negotiating with her: "Will you practice it with her? Will you guarantee that she will learn it?"

"I will guarantee it. I will teach it to her myself!"

"And you promise to listen to your classmate and learn it all?"

I promise, I promise," said the little girl until the ruler was put away and everyone sat back down in their chairs.

As the drama came to a close I was more aware that the whole thing was in fact a bit of a theater, and that the third role, filled by my cousin, was part of the show. Perhaps there was no intention of actually hitting, only the intention of causing the pleading and the promising and the need for rescuing.

To this day I don't know how my cousin had figured out that the rescuer role was available for her to play – had she witnessed this dance in a previous class? Had she just been moved by her goodness to do it? What was completely unexpected but immediately obvious to me was that as a result of her action, my cousin grew in rank on the spot. In her successfully standing up to the teacher, she had gone from just being a top student to being a top student with the kind of authority that could save others. She became a beloved classmate and a confidante to others.

I was immediately envious of her and ashamed of myself for not having thought to pull the rescuer move. The reality is, I was blinded to its possibility by my status as the teacher's favourite. I didn't have the ability to double-guess the teacher or imagine that she would have wanted to be confronted. Ironically, I was disempowered by my own privilege. Over the years I was to have many experiences demonstrating that my closeness to a figure of power would limit me and come at the expense of closeness with my peers, taking away the range of what I could do and how I could connect. But that was the first time I could see it. There was more than one route to more than one type of power. (Endnote 26)

II.

"I love Italian," you declare as we approach Renaldi's Pizza, Home of Thin Crust Pies and Classic Italian Dishes.

"Sounds good," I say, even though I think it is silly to go out for Italian when it is so damn easy to make perfectly good pasta at home.

Food tastes good with you and I eat with ease. I guess I notice the ease because it hasn't always been there.

Like most women (and probably many men) my relationship with food is complicated. I'm a little addicted to sugar and to salt, and I'm absolutely not above eating for comfort when I'm sad and for entertainment when I am bored. I buy sweetened yogurt with cartoon characters on the container for my children because that is what they will eat without a fight. On more than one occasion I have had a crisis in the grocery store isle, because my partner and I could not agree on what was the correct food to buy – Local or Organic? Over-packaged or over-processed? Delicious or healthy?!

■ ■ ■

My most active struggle with food dates back to 1999 when I was 18 and a first year university student.

That was the year I tried to starve myself.

Instead of putting on the famous freshman 15, I lost at least that much. If I had seen a doctor I would have undoubtedly been diagnosed with anorexia, the most common psychiatric disorder for a woman in the age group at the time.

People often think that anorexia is about body image and the desire to get skinny or the fear of being fat. This definitely played a part in what I was going through in 1999, in the sense that I felt proud to be buying a size 2 dress and looking more like the models on billboards than I will at any other time in my life.

But my decision to stop feeding myself was far more complicated than that. It wasn't so much that I was fighting my weight; it was more that I was fighting food itself and the basic biological idea of the necessity of food.

Every night at 7pm I would watch my roommate and the girls in my dormitory go down to the cafeteria for supper, just before the cafeteria closed down at 7:30. I would think about joining them and then I would procrastinate, I would putter around and distract myself in my room until it was too late to join them. Once 7:30 hit I had no possibility of eating, so there was no danger of my hunger winning over my decision to not eat.

I would feel a strange feeling of triumph every night as I did this.

I would feel triumphant again in the morning when I would wake up and still be alive. It was as if I was saying to my body, "haha, look, I didn't eat and I didn't need to! You said I'd be dead, but I survived again!" Food, which I had grown up being taught was very important, was turning out to be not totally vital after all.

But why did I get into this game with myself? I wonder now, looking back at that time. The reasons seem clear.

That year was a tough year. I was homesick, having left my parents house for the first time. I was lost in the large sea that was the University of British Columbia, a place that didn't care about me and to which I felt no sense of belonging. We had immigrated to Canada three years prior, and I had barely managed to make myself an identity as an academic superstar in high school. I had been mildly bullied in my mostly-white high school but I had survived through superstardom. Now I was among thousands of new university students from all over the world, for the first time the social or academic ladder I was supposed to climb was not so apparent, I was disoriented, and I didn't know who I wanted to be. I had also just lost a best friend/first love/romance, and even though I was pretending I didn't care, I was devastated by the loss.

Somehow, what I put into my mouth felt like the only thing I could actually control in a world that was completely outside of my control. Denying myself food was a way of exercising my willpower and feeling dominance over my own body. It was enjoyable, in a way.

Anorexia was to actual starvation as cutting is to suicide. It was a taste. A flirtation with death. A chosen infliction of pain at one's own hands. It made me feel involved in my own destiny. It did wonders for me at the time.

I grew out of it eventually, as I felt more at home in my new surroundings. But something unexpected happened in this anorexic exercise too, which had more lasting effects.

While it would have never occurred to me at the time, I now wonder if my wrestling with my appetite was actually a symbolic way of wrestling with my ambition.

When I stopped eating and found that I could still stay alive, I also realized that I could stop feeding my achievement-oriented tendencies and that wouldn't kill me either. If food wasn't totally essential, maybe money, career, a social circle, a husband, and all the other supposed accomplishments weren't so essential either.

I had come into university as an ambitious over-achiever, a young girl who was going to conquer the world of science (I would of course not go into the social sciences or humanities because they didn't have as much status), and I was in a science honours program with a bunch of ambitious over-achieving kids, most of whom wanted to be doctors and astronauts.

As I willed myself to lose my appetite for food that year, I also willed myself to curb my ambitions. Being a doctor or an astronaut would have been amazing, something to write home about, for sure. But it seemed kind of meaningless to me – as did the social life on campus, centered around drinking and sex. It suddenly didn't seem necessary to work towards a high station in society, an important position that would sustain me and nourish me. I realized I needed and wanted very little of that.

So when it came to the end of the spring semester and I had to choose my major I chose the one scientific field that seemed to me to be directly about humans: the very un-prestigious bachelor of science in environmental sciences. Around the same time, I start dating my first real boyfriend, a young red-head, too shy to ask me out in person (so he wrote a love letter): the very understated mad-genius in my class who set up a private fireworks show on the beach for my 19th birthday!

I can't say that I have ever looked back. (Endnote 27)

III.

It's late in the day and it's beginning to drizzle. I'm walking through a little patch of forest next to campus to catch a bus home when my phone begins to ring. It's a university number and I consider just ignoring it, because I've given enough already today to this institution that half nourishes and half exploits me. I nevertheless pick up.

On the other side of the line there is a young woman who introduces herself as Anna, one of the executives of the Alma Mater Society, the under-graduate student government. "Dr. Erfan," she begins and I cringe at my official title that no one ever uses unless they really don't know me. "I was told to call you by Alden at the Equity Office. He thought you might be able to help us."

Alden is one of my allies on campus (before he leaves the university the next year). He's looked through all the departments on campus and has determined that I am, in his words, "the only person" who can hold space for really difficult conversations – which seems strange since our university prides itself as the kind of global campus where faculty and staff and students should be having difficult topical conversations all the time. In future years it becomes my mission to equip more people at the university with dialogue tools, but at this moment I am just kind of excited, because when Alden sends someone my way it's almost guaranteed to be interesting. And this one certainly is.

"As you know, we're about to have a student referendum on whether the university should sign onto the BDS movement," Anna tells me. I don't know anything about this, actually, because I am already one of those teachers who arrive just in time for class and leave as soon as possible afterwards, and don't get entangled in campus life. Thankfully I know what BDS stands for: Boycotts, Divestment and Sanctions against Israel.

Anna explains that any group on campus can initiate a referendum on a topic concerning the life of the university, if they can get enough signatures on a petition. In January this year, a Palestinian solidarity student group ran a successful petition, which requires that we now have this referendum on whether or not the university should boycott Israel. The voting is supposed to happen next Wednesday and the campus is totally polarized. She describes to me the tone of a series of articles and letters to the editor in the campus newspapers, which I will read once I get home, confirming her impression that we are on the verge of violence between Israeli and Palestinian students and their supporters. Will I agree to moderate some sort of conversation around this topic?

I pause on the side of the road, the rain now soaking my hair, as I consider the request, noticing immediately a sort of excitement in myself, almost right away accompanied by a feeling of "What's wrong with me? This is such a painful situation for so many."

A request to come anywhere near the most longstanding conflict of the century would have scared me off a few years ago. But I've had a few turns with it by now, from the relative comfort of 15 years in Canada, far from the actual deadliness of the Middle East.

Just recently I have facilitated a 20-hour process for the staff and board members of a local organization promoting queer rights that was forced (by its members) to make a decision on whether or not to join BDS. The conversation had been so difficult, I had lost so much sleep over it, thinking it would never come to anything. But at the end we had arrived at a consensus decision and a public statement. Even better, the working through the conflict had unified and energized the organization, bringing it together, not only intact but stronger than before. While we still had no idea how the statement would be received by the membership and the larger community, I was proud of the work we had done.

And here is Anna now, suggesting first that I moderate a panel discussion between four faculty members with different views on the topic. She expects a lot of students will turn up in the audience and suggests that we don't allow any questions from the students because it will definitely turn nasty quickly. I have to smile to myself at the naïveté of her vision. I explain to her that I can't in good conscience let a couple of hundred undergrads sit through a highly charged political debate without speaking a word, and then release them into the campus where they can get into fistfights and shouting matches. I suggest instead that I host a student forum: No faculty panel. Everyone who wants to speak gets to speak. I would need a room with a large open space in the middle so that we can move around as we have the conversation. I would also need a security guard outside of the room and a counselor sitting in the corner…

To my surprise Anna comes right around, agreeing to everything I am saying. I kind of wish she would push back a little. I often need the rub of resistance to know if my ideas are actually any good. I move spontaneously to arguing against myself, listing all the reasons I may actually be the wrong person for the job: I am Muslim by birth and automatically suspect of being biased, I am not up-to-date on the campus issues, I don't have time to get to know any of the parties involved, I am a teacher here so there are power issues, I am particular about how I want the process done and unwilling to compromise or collaborate, and I am expensive. I can tell Anna is a little taken back by my anti-selling strategy. She waits until I am done arguing with myself. "We don't have anybody else who can do this," she says with confidence. And I am hired.

I have learned to explain my facilitation work to clients procedurally, not conceptually. I will tell them that we will begin with some framing remarks, a brief introduction to who is in the room, then we will stand in a circle, someone will say something and people will move towards them if they agree and away from them if they disagree. If the room polarizes we work with the conflict, and at the end we will distill the learnings and insights.

I will never tell them the secret to how I make this all work, which is my attitude of non-attachment, sometimes called "neutrality". I don't tell people about neutrality because it leads to too much critical questioning (including a good one third of my PhD dissertation defense meeting a couple years ago). People usually will say that it is impossible to be neutral, and sometimes that it is immoral to be neutral. But I haven't found anything more powerful in the hands of a facilitator when there is real heat in a room. Neutrality means that I don't take sides in the conflict, that I reflect and amplify everything that is being said equally, regardless of how unreasonable or politically incorrect it may appear to be. It means that I believe in the truth of every single statement, and that I don't judge or correct anyone (unless of course people begin to get physically violent or cross some other obvious line — but this has nearly never happened). It also means I don't speak my own mind or try to formulate any great solutions. It is almost like I give up my own voice and become a megaphone for other people. Then sometimes they can hear each other, which is just what's needed to create a shift.

It turns out that becoming empty of voice, empty of opinion is incredibly difficult. For the couple of days before the BDS Student Forum, I do nothing but work on my neutrality. I pray and meditate, I ask my friends and colleagues for advice. But mostly I read through the student newspapers, finding every statement that challenges my neutrality, every person that scares me or worries me or excites me. And I use my techniques to take these situations one by one and work them until they have no impact on me, until I can feel a cool non-judgment towards the statement or the person.

The day before the Student Forum I work for a long time with my fear of who I think of as Muslim radicals: Muslim students who may come to the Forum and call it a fraud – because to be in conversation with Israelis is to be complicit in their crimes – and who will walk out and slam the door and write awful things about me in their next letter to the editor. I am scared of them and their ability to hijack the process, and I curse my mentor who tells me to go right into my fear. As I hang out in there at some point I hit a kind of mirror. I realize that I am a sort of radical. I have a habit of using strong and absolutist language when I am passionate about something. I have absolutely done my share of grandstanding and storming out in protest, slamming doors, standing for principles I have believed in. So much of my activist youth has been spent doing that. And as soon as I see it that way, my fear of the Muslim radical students melts away. They have a right to stand for their principles. If they storm out, it's not about me. It's their way of speaking, their way of having voice. If they can speak, in whatever voice is theirs, I have done my job.

No slamming of doors happens on the actual evening of the event. I walk into the Geography building where the session is being held, feeling centered but nevertheless with a lot of trembling in my heart. About 80 students and a handful of faculty and staff show up, which I think is pretty impressive for an event that was only advertised a couple of days ago. They sit with their friends and I notice a palpable unease in the room. Many of them are looking at their phones, perhaps to avoid eye contact with each other.

All I have done on the day of the event is embodiment exercises, mainly because I would freak myself out if I got any closer to the content. So as I stand in front of the room I am super aware of my physical presence in the space, and at the same time I have a spacy kind of feeling, almost like I am not there at all. I have a moment of thinking to myself, "I hope all my preparations were not bullshit!" Even if they were bullshit, I kind of have to go with them now. As I open the session I have an impulse to pray out loud. I pray that any good we generate in the course of our conversation will benefit the Middle East where it is most needed, and any suffering we generate stays here with us.

The group agreements and ground rules, which we take over an hour to draft together, are a good example of how ordinary and how extraordinary the night is, how serious and how light-hearted at the same time. The agreements are:

1. Try and stick to the topic.
2. Brainstorm burning questions before we start the debate so people can speak to each other's curiosities.

3. Acknowledge the right to existence for both Palestinian and Israeli people and the right to existence of the Palestinian and the Israeli states, according to the borders drawn in 1967.
4. If we go past 8pm, order pizza and the pizza options must include vegetarian, gluten-free, vegan, Kosher, and Halal!

By the time we agree on the last ground rule there is already a kind of ease among us. Part of me feels that we should quit right then because our job is basically done. But the process goes on, far past 8pm.

Participants' Tweets become an interesting record of what happens in the session. Some version of my opening prayer is reflected in a participant tweet from that moment (which I read the next day): "The facilitator's prayer: that something good comes from this session. My prayer: that I don't feel like shit by the end of the night." Another tweet reads "Packed room at BDS Forum. Who needs to study for tomorrow's exam, right?"

"AMS has already endorsed the No side, but putting on a good show tonight", another cynically observes. As we get into the conversation, sound bites continue to stream out onto social media. "Jewish students concerned about vandalism if the BDS referendum is passed", one tweet reads, referring to the many examples of serious damage to Jewish establishments on other university campuses where BDS has been adopted.

"Signing onto BDS = no more Coca-Cola? Not necessarily so", says another tweet, reflecting an eloquent statement by a young Arab leader who explains that there is no single set of requirements for what needs to be boycotted under BDS and suggests that a student committee representing both sides of the conflict can sit together and define the requirements. "The facilitator has got game!", declares another tweet, totally making me smile.

Within the first half hour of the session I do in fact feel on top of my game, once I can tell that the process will basically work as long as I stick to my simple structures and the discipline or hearing and reflecting everything I hear with neutrality. Within a few minutes of getting into the conversation the room is clearly polarized, with the Palestinian students and their supporters standing on one side, the Israeli students and their supporters on the other.

There is a large audience too – participants who refuse to participate and instead opt for fence sitting (a position I regret allowing but don't have the mental capacity at the time to effectively discourage). In a minute I will give the Israeli students the floor to speak for as long as they want, and once they are finished I will give the floor to the Palestinian students to do the same, then I let them respond to each other. In some sense it is scary to stand in a room so starkly divided, but I tell myself that we have merely made an already existing division visible so we can work with it. What's more incredible is that these students – including some who have lost multiple members of their families in the war, including several who have actually been soldiers in the war, possibly responsible for the deaths of those family members, are actually together in a room, talking.

The two sides of this conflict have not spoken to each for so long that they know almost nothing about each other, so every simple piece of information is nothing short of a revelation. The Palestinian students explain why they mounted the petition that brought forward the BDS referendum: they wanted to force a conversation about the conflict that is destroying their country. A young Rabbi says that he too wants conversation and describes the vision of the newly constructed Hillel House on campus as a place for peaceful dialogue. "Please come join us and talk to us", he sweetly invites.

Later, a young teary woman in hijab describes why it is unimaginable for her to walk through the doors of the Hillel House, why it would never feel like a safe place for her to have dialogue (and we can all immediately see what she means). The leader of Palestinian solidarity group brings into life the experience of being in a conflict where the two sides are so uneven in terms of power and resources: "We've hardly been able to explain our pro-BDS campaign on campus because we're running this on a budget of $300, out of our pockets.

On the other hand, you are able to hang a $4,000 banner on the side of the Hillel House to tell everyone to say NO to BDS! How do we even have a chance of competing with that?"

At one point in the night the Israeli students harp on their fear of violence against their community if the YES to BDS side wins, to which one Palestinian man responds: "If that happens, if anyone tries to do any harm to you, we will come to you and we will stand with you". As he says this the Palestinians come and stand with him, indicating their support of the statement. The moment is so powerful we all automatically pause. Then an Israeli man speaks: "And if you lose the referendum and get the backlash, we will do the same for you."

The entire experience is a little like that for me: on the one hand, no remarkable transformation is happening here; on the other hand, the fact that anything is happening at all is completely remarkable. People stay standing on their own side of the room. No one changes their mind and joins with their enemy. But they are hearing each other.

I linger a long time after the session is finished, shaking hands with over half of the participants who come up to me to say thank you. Anna tells me that the session exceeded all her expectations. "If it had gone any better we would have solved the Middle East conflict itself!" she tells me cheerfully and I think she actually means it.

As I walk to the bus stop now, I slowly let my neutrality cape drop away. Only now, as I find my own politics and my opinions again, do I feel truly impacted by what has been said in the session. I wonder if the YES-to-BDS side, the Palestinians side, to which I belong as a person with opinions, has any chance of winning in the referendum. I sense that it doesn't – and I am proven right on Wednesday, when BDS is rejected on our campus by a fairly wide margin. I feel sad about this. I wonder if my work would have had more integrity had I spent my time campaigning for the side I believed in, instead of convening but staying out of a conversation (though of course the latter was what I was paid to do.)

I find a seat on the bus and cuddle with my thoughts, my sense of accomplishment as well as my sense of letting myself down by choosing a profession that gives voice to others but not to me. Then I notice that the leaders of Palestinian solidarity group are sitting in the row in front of me, apparently unaware of my presence. I lightly eavesdrop on their conversation, hoping to hear what they really thought about the session. Are they disappointed? Do they know they are going to lose? To my surprise, they are talking about chemistry and marine biology, preparing for tomorrow's exam. (Endnote 28)

Endnotes

Chapter 1

Endnote 1

Early drafts of Torbert's memoir did not include this story because it was not an actual memory of his own. Later, when he had accepted the name **Numbskull** as a valid, comic naming of an archetypal pattern of his, and when he realized that the very process of his birth might have contributed to his persistent numbskull-ianness – he decided to relax from the discipline of including only his own direct memories.

Endnote 2

In these pages, we have seen what Torbert (and other developmental theorists) later dubbed the early childhood *Impulsive* action-logic at work: Torbert jumping off the laundry hamper; screaming and kicking for his mother when she first left him at school; and dancing wildly with the other students when the teacher left the classroom.

> ***Impulsive**: In general, the child at this action – logic has trouble sitting still and acts imitatively or according to whim.*

In the following chapter Endnotes, we will continue to apply Torbert's theory to his own development, in order to help readers consider whether and how it may also apply to them.

It is important to recognize from the outset that developmental theory is not a personality type theory (like, say, the Myers – Briggs inventory) that describes a supposedly life-long orientation (such as extrovert vs. introvert). Instead, it is a character-development theory that maps and encourages transformation to later action-logics through personal effort and cultural support. Anyone may cease developing at any of the action-logics, but we may use supports (parents, school, particular dilemmas, as well as the theory itself and its measure, the Global Leadership Profile) to focus on the new capacities we need if we are to practice our way into our next transformation.

A second basic aspect of developmental theory is that each transformation to a later action-logic involves changing the assumptions of the prior action-logic into strategic variables within the wider assumptive set of the later action-logic – a process which is anything but straightforward! In the process, we retain all the skills and competencies we learned at the previous action-logic, although we may initially judge them negatively, as Torbert did his *Impulsive* spontaneity for many years.

Endnote 3

As Torbert moved to Austria at age six, he also gradually transformed from the Impulsive to the Opportunist action-logic. Over the course of the previous pages, we find numerous examples of Torbert's unilateral Opportunistic behavior during his years in Austria. He punches another boy and steals a baseball glove – and refuses to regret either. He repeatedly steals money from his parents and is proud about his wiliness in doing so. He manipulates his teacher and class into promoting him to the highest rank in his sixth grade class. Altogether, probably the most constructive of his Opportunistic actions are his voluntary cement-hauling and brick-laying. This work actually constructs something real and useful.

> ***Opportunist**: Young Opportunists focus on gaining control of their relationship to the territory of experience we*

call 'the outside world' and begin to seek to win (or at least protect self from losing) in any way possible. The Opportunist exhibits a focus on concrete things, short time horizon; manipulation, deception, rejection of feedback, and externalization of blame; fragile self-control and hostile humor.

The older Opportunists become without transforming, the more they tend to treat luck as central; to flout power and sexuality; to lie for advantage; to stereotype others; to view rules as a loss of freedom; to punish according to 'eye for an eye' ethic; and to treat what they can get away with as legal.

In addition to behavior patterns indicative of a particular developmental action-logic, we have now seen several examples of different momentary experiences of some kind of expanded consciousness in Torbert's earliest years – his synaesthetic experience in the sandbox in Brookline; his sense of being "alone" and "extra" at the Wolfgangsee; his sudden sense of wider socio-economic awareness as he lay in the mud in Salzburg; and his gradually prickling conscience after quite a few episodes of stealing cash from his parents. As we encounter more of these momentary-consciousness-events, we will explore how to name them and what their significance may be.

Chapter 2

Endnote 4

Torbert's Washington years at Sidwell Friends School epitomize the *Diplomat* action-logic that wants to win by belonging, fitting in, and minimizing conflict. He seeks popularity in sports, with girls, and in elections. He becomes one of the three kings in a Christmas pageant and president of his class. The degree to which his self-esteem becomes subordinated to another's esteem of him is fully displayed by his months-long suffering when his girl friend breaks up with him. And his conllict-free relationship with his parents reinforces his diplomat-ic training.

> **Diplomat**: *the Diplomat tends to observe protocol; avoid inner and outer conflict; seek membership and status in groups; treat face-saving as essential and 'white lies' as a necessary tactic; work to group standard; speak in clichés, platitudes; conform; feel shame if violates a group norm; see hurting in-group others as a sin; use disapproval and shunning as a punishment; feel loyal to the immediate group, not to a 'distant' organization or principle; treat niceness and cooperation as positive moral behavior.*

During this period in Washington, it is worth noting one particular event that illustrates how a given action may interweave several different action-logics. When Torbert is crossing the stream on a log at Boy Scout camp and dives onto his head, one can see a 'full house' of action-logics intermingling with one another. There is a strong element of the *Impulsive* **Numbskull**; there is an element of the boastful *Opportunist* – wanting to be first and best in terms of a physical skill; there is an element of the *Diplomat* – wanting others' positive regard; and there is even an element of the *Expert* – trying to show he knows the right thing to do when he scrambles out of the stream and announces the troop should practice new skills and build a stretcher for him.

Finally, in Torbert's experience of the profound stillness of his grandmother, meditating in the shadows of her garden, we see, as we have before, an unanticipated, at-the-time uninterpretable, prefiguring moment of a late action-logic experience, a moment of being fully present in the present.

Endnote 5

From the moment of his arrival at Andover, Torbert finds a culture dedicated to challenging him to develop into the *Expert* action-logic, with its focus on logic and expertise to win. Throughout the previous pages, we see evidences of Torbert's movement from the *Diplomat* to the *Expert* action-logic. Starting with the very move away from imbededness in his family to the greater independence of traveling alone to boarding school and internationally to visit his family in Rome, he accepts and attempts to successfully master the school's various disciplines – failing at first in soccer, but gradually gaining confidence in his classes and receiving high grades. He even has a paradoxical transformational learning experience, when he transcends the total dominion of grades in Mr. Gierasch's English class by 'taking' the '3' grade on a paper as humorous rather than as ego-defeating.

> ***Expert.*** *Generally, the Expert is interested in problem-solving; seeks causes; is critical of self and others based on craft logic; chooses efficiency over effectiveness; is a perfectionist, dogmatic; accepts feedback only from 'objective' craft masters; values decisions based on merit; sees contingencies, exceptions; wants to stand out, be unique; develops a sense of obligation to a wider, internally consistent moral order as a positive ethic.*

Although Torbert moves relatively quickly beyond full immersion in the *Expert* action-logic into early *Achiever* experiences — especially his soccer team experience of efficacy through teamwork — it is important to recognize that the *Expert* action-logic remains critical to his academic and professional success in many daily ways throughout the rest of his life.

Chapter 3

Endnote 6

At Yale and then in his associate directorship of the Yale Summer High School, we find evidence of Torbert performing both at the *Achiever* and the *Redefining* action-logics. Torbert's Andover varsity soccer experience was his first full-fledged team experience, where success came from the collective coordination of individuals' *Expert* skills in an *Achiever*-like cooperative/competitive system. Once at Yale, his successful apprenticeship for the Yale Daily News became his second significant *Achiever* experience, later 'crowned' by becoming vice-chairman.

His oil exploration work in Somalia and his research across the Midwest and subsequent writing for his thesis on blue collar workers' labor, leisure, and politics also illustrate *Achiever* qualities. And his administrative experience at the Yale Summer High School his first year beyond college may well represent the height of his specifically *Achiever* action-logic experience.

> ***Achiever.*** *Long-term goals; future is vivid, inspiring; welcomes behavioral feedback; effectiveness and results oriented; feels like initiator, not pawn; appreciates complexity, systems; seeks generalizable reasons for action; seeks mutuality, not hierarchy, in relationships; feels guilt if does not meet own standards; blind to own shadow, to the subjectivity behind objectivity; positive ethic = practical day-to-day improvements based on self-chosen (but not self-created) ethical system*

At the same time, Torbert was beginning to explore the *Redefining* action-logic, which involves reframing situations with others in unique ways based on one's personal experience and inquiry. Torbert's *Redefining* adventures begin with his effort to determine his faith during his sophomore slump, from which he emerges through a personal experience of being born again, the first time that he is playing an active, if stumbling, role in his own transformation. That summer during his oil exploration work in Somalia, he feels the tug between simply obeying his boss' orders to continue the drilling line through the native village, or obeying a deeper intuition of what action is just.

That fall he becomes involved in civil rights activism in Mississippi, manifesting his growing attraction to difference and change in the wider society. This interest in difference again manifests itself in his study of blue collar workers in the Middle West for his undergraduate thesis.

At this time, he also begins to explore his blind or shadow sides, first by learning something about his use of unilateral influence in seeking to get his Elihu delegation to work with Chris Argyris. Next, he begins to learn about the Gurdjieff Work, hoping to generate a new quality of attention within himself that listens into the dark.

> ***Redefining****. Generally, the person entering the Redefining action-logic begins to realize that different people, including oneself, hold [and are held by] different action-logics and cultures, which are neither intrinsically good or evil. One also realizes that one can play a role in transforming (redefining, reframing) one's own vision, values, action-logic or team culture. As one's vision becomes more coherent and more determinative of the goals for one's action, one feels less like the Achiever chasing many externally-generated and mutually-competitive goals, for which there is never enough time, and more like oneself. One seeks independent, creative work that feels like one's vocation, focusing more on both the unique present and the larger historical context from which current norms have evolved. One begins to become more attracted by people's differences and by processes of constructive change than by similarity and stability. One takes a relativistic perspective, becomes less inclined to judge or evaluate, and influences events more by listening and finding patterns than by advocacy. And one begins to notice one's own shadow and negative impact.*

Chapter 4

Endnote 7

In the year after his graduation, Torbert engages a great many of his activities from a *Redefining* perspective. These include his conversations with his friend Morris, based in Morris' existential teaching of Kafka and their idea of a new kind of school that will study its own development as a community; his still more personal confessions to Morris about his ill-fated love affair with Jane; his entry into the Gurdjieff Work as a means of cultivating a relationship with the 'consciousness' territory of experience, on the 'spiritual' side; and, on the 'mundane' side, his actual attainment of a federal grant to create this new kind of school.

Chapter 5

Endnote 8

With the start of the spring advisory and recruitment meetings for Yale Upward Bound, Torbert first begins to attempt to function as a *Transforming* leader who not only co-ordinates an organization's productivity, but also its developmental transformations and those of its members…while simultaneously seeking out feedback that may generate transformational learning on his (or her) own part. We can see an arc in Torbert's own development into the *Transforming* action-logic. He moves from his initial black-and-white sense of unilateral versus collaborative leadership and of confronting versus avoiding conflict, to a much more nuanced interweaving of the two extremes at the time of the lakeshore fight at the end of the first week at camp. We will continue to see him seeking to master the *Transforming* action-logic in the following chapters.

> ***Transforming Action-Logic***: *Transforming leaders become attuned to implementing a distinctive vision, not just following Achiever-like habits and customs of*

> *organizing. They are process oriented as well as goal oriented; interested in dynamic theories of organizing; and creative at timely intervention for conflict resolution and/or for catalyzing personal or organizational transformation.*
>
> *Transforming leaders offer and seek both single-loop, goal-oriented feedback and double-loop, strategy-questioning feedback. They are aware of paradox and contradiction, and that what one sees depends upon one's worldview. They put a high value on a culture of individuality and responsibility, on unique market niches, and on action 'sculpted' to particular historical moments. They enjoy playing a variety of roles and engaging in witty, existential humor (as contrasted to prefabricated jokes). And…they are becoming aware of the dark side, of the profundity of evil, and are tempted by its power.*

Chapter 6

Endnote 9

In this chapter we see Torbert 'in over his head,' to borrow the title of Bob Kegan's much later book (*In Over Our Heads*, 1994). Kegan describes our struggles when our personal developmental complexity and our ability to act in a timely fashion in congruence with our values falls short of the demands of our role and the social context.

Starting the year with an inflated view of himself as a co-ordinated three-ring circus, Torbert increasingly experiences the lack of coordination among and within his different activities. The most striking and consequential incident is the Upward Bound community meeting at the end of the first week of the second summer. This incident is in many ways closely analogous to the fight and community meeting at the end of the first week of the first summer, but ends very negatively rather than very positively. Why?

As we shall see, this is a question that Torbert himself tried to answer when he developed his theory of organizational action-logics during the following year, as part of his continuing effort to understand and enact the Transforming action-logic (see Ch. 7). But we can already notice three differences between the two events. First, Torbert was not directly involved in the first fight, but is at the center of the second. Second, there was no existing organizational structure to defend the first time, but there is the second. And third, the first fight was not inter-racial, but the second one is more so.

Chapter 7

Endnote 10

The Yale Upward Bound program illustrates the theory of organizational development action-logics, as demonstrated in brief below:

> Morris' and Bill's conversations in the fall of 1966, as well as Joel Fleishman's conversations with the federal Office of Economic Opportunity, and then Bill's grant writing represented the *Conception* stage of Yale Upward Bound.
>
> > ***Conception*** *involves dreams, visions, and informal conversations about creating something new to fill a need not now adequately addressed; interplay among multiple 'parents'; and the development of working models, grant applications, related projects, or business plans.*
>
> Next, the OEO's decision to fund the program, Yale's choice of Torbert for director, and the first spring's meetings among advisors and potential staff represented the *Investments* stage.
>
> > ***Investments*** *involves 'Champions' committing to create the organization; early relationship-building among*

future stakeholders; and peer networks and parent institutions making nurturing spiritual, structural, and financial commitments.

The first week of the first YUB summer session at the camp, along with the student/ staff fight at the end of that week, represented the *Incorporation* stage and the organization's survival of a crisis.

Incorporation *entails the operation of the organization in a recognizable physical setting (and/or cyber-address nowadays), tasks and specific roles delineated; goals and operating staff chosen; products or services produced; display of persistence in the face of threat.*

Much of the rest of the first summer – when we changed rules and class designs often, often uncertain whether we were reaching our students – represented the *Experiments* stage.

Experiments *is a time in an organization's life when alternative administrative, production, selection, reward, financial, marketing and political strategies are practiced, tested in operation and reformed in rapid succession.*

The increase in student reading abilities and their performance in school the following year (better grades, and cutting New Haven's dropout rate in half), as well as winning a larger grant from OEO, represented YUB's *Systematic Productivity* stage.

Systematic Productivity *entails standardizing structures, and roles, usually in pyramidal terms; attention is strongly focused on procedures for accomplishing the pre-defined task; marketability or political viability of the product or* *service, measured in quantitative terms becomes the overriding criterion of success.*

Finally, the re-structuring of the program with the students during that year in between the two summers represented our entry into the *Collaborative Inquiry* stage. (However, the actu al structure for the second summer session [with the faculty more in charge] looked and felt more like the *Systematic Productivity* action-logic to the new staff and students.)

Collaborative Inquiry *entails explicit shared reflection about the organization's dream/ mission across the organization; open rather than masked interpersonal relations; systematic evaluation and feedback of corporate and individual performance on multiple indices; direct facing and creative resolution of paradoxes: inquiry-productivity, freedom-control, quantity-quality, etc.; interactive development of unique, self-amending strategies appropriate to this particular organization at this particular historical moment.*

(The final two organizational action-logics — *Foundational Community of Inquiry* and *Liberating Disciplines* — will be introduced later in the story, when Torbert learned more about them.)

Endnote 11

In this chapter, Torbert's discovery of a truly developmental theory of organizational development in his 'special area' paper, and his switch from one dissertation to another both exemplify strategy-transforming *double-loop learning* characteristic of the Transforming action-logic.

In his 'special area' paper, he went well beyond a review of the literature on his topic (incremental, *single-loop learning*) to formulate an entirely new theory of organization development, induced from the Upward Bound experience and deduced from the comparison to existing developmental theories.

In the case of his switch from one dissertation to another, he went well beyond a change in tactics to improve his dissertation to changing everything about the topic, the theory, and the research methods.

The reader may appreciate a slightly more fulsome description of the differences among single-, and double-loop learning at this point:

> ***Single-loop learning*** *occurs when feedback from the outside world (natural and/or social) leads one to change one's behavior in order to reach a goal. In this type of learning one is weaving together a pattern in durational time (time's 1st dimension), from the moment the goal is set, through the various efforts to achieve the goal and the feedback that reorients one's striving, until the time when the goal is achieved (or abandoned).*
>
> ***Double-loop learning*** *occurs when feedback leads one to change one's cognitive-emotional-sensory structure (i.e. action-logic) in order to reduce incongruities between espoused values and actual practice and to enact a higher vision and a more timely embodied practice.*
>
> *Double-loop feedback is much harder than single-loop feedback to offer artistically, to receive without defensiveness, and to correct for. This is because receiving double-loop feedback can involve transforming one's cognitive/ emotional/ sensory structure or strategy (one's ego), at least temporarily. This type of learning requires access to a different dimension of time – to presence in the present or the eternal now (time's 2nd dimension) – that allows one to see and compare two (or more) territories of experience at once. Although many persons*

have occasional unanticipated experiences of 'presence in the present,' few intentionally cultivate this quality of experiencing.

Torbert's final doctoral dissertation proposes four ontological 'layers of reality,' or 'territories of experience,' with which our attention can make contact. These territories of experience can be named:

1) *the outside world*;
2) *one's own current behavior as sensed from within*;
3) one's internal *cognitive-emotional-sensory structure*; and
4) '*consciousness*.'

We are ordinarily aware of only one of these territories at a time, and ordinarily we are not *conscious* (in Torbert's understanding of the term as post-cognitive, four-territory awareness). Only *consciousness* gives us access to all four territories of experience at once and generates the 'ultra-stability' that permits our *cognitive-emotional-sensory structure* to relax and transform when appropriate.

Chapter 8

Endnote 12

It seems that Torbert was inclined to engage in the same kind of 'collaborative inquiry' in his love relationships – his marriage in particular – as in his work relationships, as though the two realms are directly analogous. But an organization is, by definition, three people or more, with no lifetime commitment; whereas marriage is between two persons and no more, with a lifetime commitment. Also, Bill was studying the history and social dynamics of organizational innovations and he had some life-experience in organizations; whereas he knew virtually nothing about the psychodynamics of marriage and had no life-experience of being married. Thus, we might expect him to run into even more trouble innovating in the realm of 'opening marriage' than he did in the realm of creating a collaborative school. And trouble he certainly did run into.

Looked at from a third-person perspective, fifty years after the events occurred, it seems clear that Torbert had a strong inclination toward multiple concurrent, intimate, and lasting friendships, with both men and women, that continued throughout his life. This inclination toward multiple ongoing friendships with men and women included occasional, non-exclusive, non-possessive sexual intimacy with some women.

As we shall see, he did not learn how to sustain his first marriage. We find several vivid examples, however, of Torbert going beyond the double-loop learning that he did during his graduate student career at Yale, to doing *triple-loop learning* in particular instances during the marriage. — going 'out of his (conventional) mind' and into a deeper attention to his whole self. We point first to the two triple-loop experiences, and then offer a clearer definition of triple-loop learning.

The first example occurred when Torbert quite deliberately went 'out of his mind,' when his wife had not been reassured by a whole night's reassurances of his love. He erupted in anger that he had been unknowingly suppressing, and thereby broke them out of their unending cycle of unavailing reassurances. It may be a long time before one learns the effects of one's new action, but in this case, the effect on her was instantaneous. It sounds like Torbert was immersed in the Diplomat action-logic through the night and then opened all the way into the Alchemical action-logic when he roared.

His second triple-loop learning episode occurred when he smoked marijuana on a Vermont hilltop with two women friends. When he got off his ass and onto his hands and knees, he discovered a silent, 'conscious' super-vision that embraced all at once his thinking, his feeling, and his embodying. This experience also made unmistakably clear, by contrast, how narrowly-imprisoned in his merely-mental processes he ordinarily was. It sounds like Torbert may have had access to his Expert, Achiever, and Redefining action-logics as they climbed the hill at the outset of this new venture; and then catapulted into the simultaneous four-territory experiencing characteristic of the Alchemical action-logic when he got on his hands and knees.

> ***Triple-loop learning*** *occurs when feedback shakes the very foundations of one's sense of attention, intention, purpose, and integrity, or when feedforward (from intent through action-logic and behavior to effect) is so congruent as to generate a sense of integral serenity or at-one-ness. Triple-loop learning relativizes one's cognitive-emotional-sensory structure so thoroughly as to reveal a spiritual quality, a post-cognitive, post-egoic, presencing consciousness as its own distinctive territory of experience. Whereas single-loop learning alters one's way of doing (one's embodied action) and double-loop learning alters one's way of knowing (one's action-logic), triple-loop learning illuminates or alters one's way of being. Being, knowing, and doing become realigned. This can include awareness in the moment of action of one's current operating action-logic; and of the possibility of an alternative action-logic, which one may not fully understand or even be able to articulate. Nevertheless, in that same moment, one may find the capacity to commit to and enact the new, ill-understood direction. Triple-loop learning also radically opens the question of different possible futures and can introduce one to the volume of all possibilities (time's 3rd dimension — see later chapters for more examples of the three dimensions of time and Appendix A for further discussion).*

Chapter 9

Endnote 13

In this chapter we see the exercise of many different types of power by staff and students, associated with different action-logics. First, we offer definitions of the eight types of power that Torbert articulated only years later, and then we suggest what types of power were exercised in each major incident or process described in the chapter..

New Types of Power that Become Available at Each Successive Action-Logic

Opportunist: ***Coercive power*** *"Hard power"; using (the threat of) unilateral force to get desired results; believes that "might makes right"; only the right behavioral stimuli generate the desired responses.*

Diplomat: ***Charming power*** *"Soft power"; relying on charisma, seduction, diplomacy, covert manipulation, or self-disclosure to attract support (e.g. running for office)*

Expert: ***Logistical power***: *"Smart power"; use of logic, professional disciplines, systems analysis & institutional position or process to get something done.*

Achiever: ***Productive power*** *Actually producing a product or service valuable to self or others, most often in co-ordination with a team; welcomes behavior-changing single-loop feedback that helps reach goal.*

Redefining: ***Visioning power*** *Using imaginative, artistic, mutually-trust-building faculties and disciplines, alone in nature and with committed colleagues or friends in society; to create new visions of the future for a meeting, organization, etc.*

Transforming: ***Praxis power*** *Inquiring with others, to spot, articulate, and correct incongruities among vision, theory and practice, thus increasing individual, relational* *and organizational integrity, alignment, mutuality, transformation efficacy, and timeliness.*

Alchemical: *Mutually-transforming power* *1st-, 2nd-, and 3rd-person practices of vigilant and vulnerable presence to one another that generates power via love and inquiry; interweaves previous types of power (e.g. MLK and the non-violent civil rights movement). Welcomes paradigm-questioning triple-loop feedback.*

Ironic: *The power of liberating disciplines* *Generates third-person structures, occasions, and constant feedback processes that disrupt habitual individual and group patterns, resulting in personal development, enhanced collaborative leadership at all levels, and improved organizational efficacy; structure-changing double-loop feedback especially welcome. Founding leadership practices deliberate irony; designs tasks incomprehensible and un-doable without reference to accompanying processes and purposes; and premeditates and pre-communicates structural evolution over time. Requires a leadership team open to inspection of its own designs and practices and capable of interweaving all the types of power and feedback in (relatively) timely ways.*

At the outset of the intense process through which the course staff exercised self-disclosure, support, and confrontation with one another during the two weeks before the course started, Pat's and Bill's argument about the overall structure of the course demonstrated the exercise of peer-like *visioning power*, *praxis power*, and *mutually-transforming power*.

The later conversations with Ed and Aaron also demonstrated peer *praxis power*, while other conversations not directly reported primarily used *productive power* to create the specifics of the course structure.

Once the course begins with the meeting in the ballroom and the experiential exercises, we see an even more complex interweaving of types of power. For example, Canavan used a combination of: *charming* power (his seductive, amusing invitations to roar in anger); *logistical* power (his legitimate authority as a faculty member), and *re-visioning* power (made mutual by the students' enthusiastic response).

With the learning papers that ask students to reflect on their own action-choices, along with the research reports to the students themselves and to the school's faculty... we begin to see for the first time something about what the power of *Liberating Disciplines* means, with its design of continual opportunities for experiential learning, and its constant cycles of feedback on individuals' actions and on the performance of the course as a whole.

These feedback cycles sometimes occurred in real time, such as when Pat Canavan incited students to shout their anger in the first class meeting. Sometimes the feedback cycle occurred within a week of the action, such as through students' writing Learning Papers and the staff's responses. Sometimes the feedback cycle occurred over the course of months, such as in the student evaluations of their learning in the course after its first ten weeks.

Chapter 10

Endnote 14

The *Peer Culture* at SMU was in its earliest days of forming when the *Superior Culture* attacked it. Neither Canavan nor Torbert were in a position to lead the response – Canavan because he was the one attacked, Torbert because he was literally flat on his back, and both because they were such new and junior members of the organization and of their profession.

Members of both the *Subordinate* and the *Superior Cultures* are most likely guided by the Opportunist, Diplomat, Expert, or Achiever action-logics, all of which understand power as unilateral in different ways. Then, if and when persons enter the Redefining, Transforming, and Alchemical action-logics, they gradually develop the capacity for exercising mutual inquiry, mutual power, and mutual love, and become members of *Peer Cultures*. The *Superior Culture* often actively combats *Peer Cultures* because they threaten its assumptions about reality and its hegemony over the institutions it controls.

It is worth noting that, while the simplicity of this tri-partite Superior/ Subordinate/Peer distinction in social status is attractive, the distinctions themselves are complexly phenomenological, not simply empirical. For example, the Supreme Court justices probably view themselves as a *Peer Culture*, but are probably viewed as part of a *Superior Culture* by most others. Also, people at any level in a superior/ subordinate organizational hierarchy may be seeking to create a *Peer Culture*, or may experience themselves primarily as members of the *Subordinate Culture*. Even a CEO at an early action-logic may act and feel more like a Subordinate than like a Peer or Superior: performing as if without choice at the whim of the Board, the market, and other social forces.

Chapter 11

Endnote 15

We have already noted two of Torbert's early, triple-loop Alchemical moments. One occurred when, after a night of arguing with his wife, he roared angrily at her, doing the last thing he could imagine would help. Another occurred when he smoked marijuana for the first time on the Vermont hilltop with his two women friends and experienced his thinking as occurring within a more encompassing body-and-feeling-based ontological awareness.

We can see that such moments – when a lot feels at stake and you know only that your habitual thoughts and actions won't be timely – began to occur more frequently to Torbert at SMU, beginning with his fight with Pat Canavan on the second morning of planning the new course. Two months later, his Blocks to Creativity experience with the **I Ching**, was an Alchemical, triple-loop learning experience in which his habitual, rational, indecisive self-talk yielded to a deeper listening into his feelings and desires. This deeper listening into the dark overcame his Expert-ish 'reluctance to let go,' and yielded a clear, firm, intuitive decision, transforming marriage into divorce. Then, in spite of Torbert's willingness to experiment with a sexual foursome at Princeton and, later, a sexual threesome (in Dallas), he actually ended up playing a leading role in the decisions not to consummate either of those two possibilities — not because he didn't want to, but rather because he found that neither felt mutual to one of the other members and because of his commitment to exercise mutual inquiry, mutual power, and mutual love that inspires the Alchemical action-logic.

It is interesting to note how quickly Torbert's triumphalist tone in his essay about 'making love as a life act' is chastened.

Chapter 12

Endnote 16

In a continuation of his occasional Alchemist moments, in this chapter Torbert experienced the breakdown of the AS1 peer evaluation process. In his small office, he entered into the Eternal Present, and envisioned different Future Possibilities. Returning to Durational time, he and the staff created a design-change for the class/ organization. They exercised *coercive* power by disqualifying the initial student evaluations. They exercised *charming* power by penalizing no students in particular; *logistical* power via the essay critiquing groups' performance; *productive* power by all working together to vastly improve the self-evaluations; *re-visioning* power by the staff in reorganizing the last two weeks of the semester; and *praxis* power demonstrated by the actual confrontations within student groups to correct the initial incongruities in the peer assessment results. This event illustrates how and why *Liberating Disciplines* require leadership capable of double – and triple-loop learning and design change in the immediacy of action, if the organizing process is to remain effectual and trustworthy among its participants.

Overall, Torbert's principal new learning at SMU seems to have been how to create and implement Liberating Disciplines in the micro-organizational environments of the large AS1 classes. In fact, he came to see that what had been his greatest weakness as a leader when he founded Yale Upward Bound four years earlier– namely, his difficulties with engaging conflict constructively – was the key dynamic of successful Liberating Disciplines.

By the time he got to SMU, he was personally more capable of engaging in direct conflict, as evidenced by his fight with his "ally," Pat Canavan, on the second day of creating AS1, and again when at a school faculty meeting he confronted a senior faculty member and earned the label "blindly antagonistic."

In conclusion to this section of the book, we think readers may find it instructive to compare Katz and Kahn's 1978 conventional definition of an organizational context in **The Social Psychology of Organizations** with Fisher and Torbert's mirror-image post-conventional definition of Liberating Disciplines in their 1995 **Personal and Organizational Transformations**.

> Katz and Kahn wrote: *The organizational context is by definition a set of restrictions for focusing attention upon certain content areas and for narrowing the cognitive style to certain types of procedures. This is the inherent constraint. To call a social structure organized means that the degrees of freedom have been limited. Hence organizations often suffer from the failure to recognize the dilemma character of a situation and from blind persistence in sticking to terms of reference on the basis of which the problem is insoluble.* (p.277)

> Fisher and Torbert wrote: *A Liberating Discipline is by experience a set of challenges for questioning (the quality of one's) attention and widening it and one's cognitive-emotional tracking to include the enacted task, process*

and mission. This is the enacted dynamism. To call a social psychological process liberating means that the degrees of freedom and discipline in the situation are expanding. Hence organizations that cultivate transforming inquiry rarely suffer from the failure to recognize the dilemma character of a situation and from blind persistence in sticking to terms of reference on the basis of which the problem is insoluble. (p.259)

Chapter 13

Endnote 17

As Torbert moves from SMU to Harvard and the Channing Place Commune, we feel a background/ foreground shift in his approach to his life and work. His primary emphasis seems to shift somewhat from the more structured sphere of work, organizational change, and institutional ethics and politics to the less boundaried sphere of leisure, intimacy, aesthetics, and the spiritual.

He becomes more engaged in first- and second-person Alchemical research-in-action, and in seeking to create Foundational Communities of Inquiry at the Channing Place Commune, as well as among his Yale friends. For example, the sequence of events and escalating confrontations between Bill and Morris about the latter's alcoholism can be viewed as a process of 2nd-person research involving increasingly 'hot' double-loop feedback from Bill to Morris, until a transformation from Morris' addiction to alcoholism occurred.

Torbert's LSD experience in Austria, when he throws the ***I Ching***'s Wanderer archetype...and then envisions painting his communal room as a kind of portrait of his soul...appear to be instances of triple-loop learning that feel to him, not like mere happenstance fantasies, but rather as resonant with the 'ultrastability' of a larger universe beyond his ego.

Torbert was finishing his book on Upward Bound (*Creating a Community of Inquiry*) and writing his book about SMU (*The Power*

Of Balance) during his Harvard years. The latter included his first attempt to envisage a future social science that would encompass a far wider and deeper existential, ontological, and epistemological field than Empirical Positivism, while still employing empirical measures as a subset of his research strategies.

Eventually, Torbert theorized an entire developmental scale of social scientific action-logics analogous to the individual and organizational action-logics. These can be found in Appendix A. Here, we simply name them, to give the reader an impression of the range of possibilities:

> Behaviorism (analogous to Opportunist action-logic);
> Gestalt Psychology, Sociology and Anthropology (Diplomat);
> Empirical Positivism (Expert);
> Multi-Method Eclecticism (Achiever);
> Postmodern Critical Interpretivism (Redefining);
> Action Science Praxis (Transforming);
> Cooperative, Ecological Inquiry (Alchemical); and
> Collaborative Developmental Action Inquiry (Ironic).

Chapter 14

Endnote 18

1. Of the three 'Harvard' stories retold in this chapter, the story about the 'sufi jester' is one of the few cases up to this point in these memoirs when we hear another participant in Torbert's activities report his 2nd-person experience of Torbert. Taking a Postmodern Critical Interpretivist perspective on the data from his story, we can tell from the outset – just by the titling of 'sufi jester' – that the writer is a rather histrionic, exaggerating, myth-making kind of observer. In contrast, Torbert claims he's never been a feather taller than 6'-even and that he has no memory of stripping to a superman suit on that occasion

(or ever, for that matter); simple black tights are his preferred under-costuming. However, he admits that the description of the suit and tie evoke his outer-costuming well enough.

2. The second, deeply-layered story, about Argyris and how trust is and is not generated, includes the mythic act of Oedipus killing his father, which became Freud's killing of the father by the son, and now Torbert's 'killing' of Argyris – except that, whereas Oedipus was unaware he was killing this father, Torbert was *very* aware of the symbolism of his request to the Committee on Degrees to appoint a new member to the three-person Qualifying Paper Committee in place of his long-time mentor and hero, Argyris.

   In their subsequent conversations, Torbert felt that he could, for the first time, see all way round Argyris' worldview and action-logic, see its assumptions, see its limitations, see beyond Argyris' cognitive, conversational brilliance to a disinclination toward ontological self-probing.

   Nevertheless, Argyris' continued influence on Torbert is testified to by many of us action inquiry community members who are aware of his efforts to continue engaging with Argyris until his death – always with rueful, yet deep, appreciation for his inspiration and long mentorship. Yet another testament to Torbert's generations'-long relationship to the Argyris family was his participation on Chris' daughter Dianne's Ed School Dissertation Committee, along with Carol Gilligan and Larry Kohlberg.

3. As for the third story, the most pessimistic inference one might draw from the Standing-Philosophy-on-its-Head Colloquium is that the erudition of leading philosophers doesn't protect them much from regressing to their unilateral, Opportunistic self-interest as soon as they imagine their grant money is threatened.

   Another rather pessimistic conclusion one can induce from the episode is that Torbert had not yet learned much about how to act in a timely manner that could invite the Expertish, Philosophy-Guild, Superior Culture participants sitting around the Colloquium table, to test their assumptions about the purpose and practice of philosophizing. Indeed, one of our community of inquiry members offered the following comment about Bill's action upon reading the story:

> *I've been struggling with my mixed feelings about your literal standing on your head as a way of standing philosophy on its head at Harvard. In our discussion of your chapter, another of our friends said he was "annoyed" by that act. The first time I heard about it through your retelling, I enjoyed the story and empathized with your counter-cultural stance. This time around I found myself judging it more critically. Your default action logic may well be Diplomat. But I think you have a counter-dependent (Diplomat/Expert) strand that leads you to thumb your nose at authority structures/superior cultures. You are wonderfully self-reflective about your behavior, typically adopting multiple perspectives. In this instance I don't think you fully explore or acknowledge the pattern that may have driven that particular act.*

Chapter 15

Endnote 19

This chapter about some of Torbert's Gurdjieff Work experiences seems to highlight first-person voice, second-person practice, and triple-loop, four-territory learning experiences in the present.

These experiences included the intense listening toward the source as he sat in front of meetings, an intensity of listening so difficult to cultivate in other circumstances. They also included the 'Nun, N\n, None' mantra – a kind of first-person, triple-loop feedback that he first had 'dreamed' for himself and then returned to many times.

As with the Numbskull name, the Nun name contains a hint of ironic humor characteristic of the Alchemical perspective The strange reading Torbert listened to, about the Devil archetype, invoked a third-person cosmology that a participatory action inquiry ontology requires if thoughtless desire is to be transformed into mutual awakening. His final, unique and highly ironic experience of triple-loop learning during that Work week had his heart melting and glowing as his teacher sliced his personality away, a form of intimacy he has told us he has never otherwise experienced.

Chapter 16

Endnote 20

The Longstaffs and Torbert formed an intimate learning trio, among the most powerful possible of 2nd-person developmental practices, and therefore also among the most risky and relationally dangerous of 2nd-person action inquiry experiments.

Torbert evidently had some unconscious proclivity for playing "second man" in two-man-one-woman trios. This pattern occurs not only with regard to the Longstaffs, but remember also his ill-fated relationship with the married couple at Yale and his brief attempt at generating a trio at SMU with Jill and her other boyfriend. And remember too his great love for his mother, where he was second man to his father.

Torbert's more general reason for advocating Learning Trios for developmental exercises through his teaching and workshop career is that a trio includes four different relationships to be observed and intervened in – the three pairs, each of whom can be counseled by a third member, and the dynamics of the trio as a whole. A trio is, thus, less likely to get polarized or paralyzed than a duo. The deep spiritual work of trio learning can include the burning away, through voluntary suffering, of possessiveness, jealousy, and envy. A trio's danger, especially if it enters the sexual territory, is that it will develop more quickly than the participants can consciously follow.

Then the unconscious, shadow archetypes take over and cause especially painful misjudgments, such as Jason's when he violated Lee's private diary.

Interlude

Endnote 21

What do third-person organizing processes that approach the 'Foundational Communities of Inquiry' action-logic look like? One likely time when temporary 'Communities of Inquiry' may come together is around the death of a beloved elder who has displayed uniquely fine human qualities of spirit, like Torbert's friend Minor White,. Those of us close to such a one wish both to honor and to imbibe that spirit-in-the-flesh one final time, and do whatever we can to create an atmosphere in which that spark of spirit both rises at death and more deeply infuses each of us.

Can our own developmental 'deaths' and 'rebirths' during our lives serve as analogical preparation for our ultimate death and possible rebirth?

Chapter 17

Endnote 22

As Torbert dies to his communal home and his academic career in the summer of 1976, he launches into what eventually become a series of three round trips to California's Bay Area and his brother's goat ranch in Mendocino, circling back to Boston each time, wandering and homecoming, wandering and homecoming, dying and birthing, dying and birthing, exploring the relationship between intimacy and aloneness. He appears to be trying to birth something new in himself, in his work, and in his relationships, particularly to Lee. To do so, he takes a kind of meandering, inconclusive, circling route in the outside world, while resorting to his Black Journal to record a few of his moments of circling within his inner world.

These inner/ outer four-territories-of-experience moments — starting with his very first journal entry on his first flight to California — are filled with paradoxes about acting to awaken to the relationships among the ordinarily subconscious (e.g. Bill's early memory of being buried in sand), one's ordinary mental awareness (his on the airplane, enclosed in his own thoughts), and four-territory super-vision (his 'awakening' to his physical state, the roar of the engines, and the analogy between his childhood dissociation between body and feeling and his current [occasional] efforts to reawaken into all four territories of experience at once.

After returning to Boston and re-uning with Lee, he again sets out toward California, this time in a venerable VW camper. His uncomfortable conversation with Mrs. Dooling while visiting her illustrates an ongoing incongruity between his cognitive, Diplomatic self-consciousness and his efforts at dispassionate self-observation. This state contrasts, in turn, with his fluid timing and passionate action in joining his brother Jim and Theta in the dark outside their kitchen, having allowed them just enough time to reconnect beforehand.

All of these incidents display qualities of triple-loop learning at particular moments, aligning with Ian Mitroff's *Methodological Approaches of the Social Sciences* that later assigned Bill as an early and paradigmatic practitioner of present-moment, 'Sensing-Feeling' science (see end of Endnote 12 and end of Appendix A for more detail on triple-loop moments). The fact that Torbert's journal entries tend to record memorable moments rather than a calendar of daily events seems further evidence of his 'sensing-feeling' approach to social science.

Chapter 18

Endnote 23

Torbert's inconclusive circling between Boston and California continues — except this time his prolonged, intentionally indecisive inaction reaches a climactic, kairotic moment of action ('kairos': the fulness of time for creative action; commitment to a future-altering possibility): Bill suddenly returns to Boston to plight his troth to Lee, only to learn of the action-commitment she has made, by plotting her pregnancy, to having his child. The mysterious synchronicity of their separate decisions leads to further synchronicities – first, Lee's morning sickness in front of the Tiburon real estate office where they finally find not only a place to live, but also a small source of income; next, the Mendocino Christmas with the newly-enlarged Torbert family together for the first time ever; and then 'the baby' becoming twins on April Fools Day, 1977. Such was the mythical, mutually-transforming alchemy of that time, transforming two lone individuals into the intimacy of a family of four.

The above is, of course, a highly romantic perspective on this course of events. An alternative interpretation might be that Bill made his commitment to Lee because he was feeling lonely and directionless, while she had acted manipulatively in secretly conceiving their child without consulting him.

Chapter 19

Endnote 24

After years of cultivating good friends and good questions, rather than narrower, more immediately self-interested goals, Torbert asks his friends to invest in the Theatre of Inquiry, with no suggestion that their contributions will lead to any monetary gain for them. He receives gifts from fully 40% of the people to whom he writes, ranging from cash, to performance spaces for the theatre's activities, to negative feedback. This result seems to illustrate the discussion in Appendix A about how treating good questions and good friends as the two primary goods of the good life can generate the next two foremost goods — good work and good money.

The case of Torbert's staying out of his own (and out of the group's) way — actively inactive — at the moment of the Conception of the Stirring Occasions party consulting business by the Business/School's members illustrates two qualities of CDAI: first, how cultivating four-territory awareness (being actively inactive) permits him to hold, rather than to mechanically express his own emotional reactivity; and second, how his developmental theory can be applied at different, but analogical scales of personal or organizational activity — to octaves within octaves of development. In later writings he applied the theory to the hundred year history of IBM, to a single meeting of a team, and to a sixty second radio ad, as well as to numerous organizations (Torbert, 1987, 1989, Fisher & Torbert, 1995).

Chapter 20

Endnote 25

A number of us former students and ongoing friends of Bill's — who are contributing to these endnotes and who have felt new worlds open through our contact with his theories and his practices — find this 'climactic' chapter disappointing. It may be that the Theatre of Inquiry Song generates some intrigue, that Teiresias' chant conveys some mytho-poetic resonance, or that the societal visions of theatrical Adulthood Initiation Rites and Sex Education Trios prompt other future visioning. Perhaps treating oneself as in The Theatre of Inquiry at any moment of one's life can serve for some as a liberating metaphor.

But, in general, the chapter seems to be about Torbert's failed efforts to adapt his relatively successful personal and organizational practices (witnessed as recently as the previous chapter) to a public, societal scale. It seems that he *was* capable of conceptualizing the two interwoven questions he raised in his public letter — what kind of attention is necessary to see and influence social sculptures, and what kind of public institution encourages members to play a role in sculpting the definition of the situations in which they participate? — but that he *was not* capable of addressing these questions with inspiring and inclusive performance artistry that drew strangers to the dance in The Theatre of Inquiry.

Was he, perhaps, too flagrantly Alchemical in this period, as gay persons sometimes seem when they first come out as gay? Was his action during this period overbalanced toward the transformational and relatively inattentive to the human yearning for stability — a dialectic he more satisfactorily resolved during his subsequent thirty years at Boston College (see Chapter 21)?

Was his spiritual teacher perhaps right that there can never be a 'market' for such work and play, such conscious labor and intentional suffering? Certainly, Torbert's work has never succeeded in engaging a wide market during his long lifetime until now (he is 76 as this, his final book, goes to press).

One dilemma the reader faces in assessing the success of The Theatre of Inquiry is the relative lack of data about how the participants experienced it. We have recently discovered that Torbert actually commissioned an interview study of twelve participants' perspectives on their experiences. The interviewer — Bill Joiner, Torbert's former student at SMU, and current (1978) doctoral advisee of Chris Argyris — estimated, after doing and writing up the interviews, that about a third of the interviewees were primarily disappointed, about a third felt the process had promise and they had learned something, and about a third believed deeply in Torbert's competence, in what he was doing, and even more in the necessarily paradoxical nature of what he was trying to do. We have excerpted a series of representative quotations from the interviews:

> *The Theatre of Inquiry is like August. It's a very difficult time, hot and sticky and uncomfortable. Yet there's the occasional flash — the classical summer day. And for anyone who's gone to school for a number of years, August is a preliminary period before school starts. The Theatre of Inquiry is a preliminary thing. It doesn't feel at all like a finished thing.*

■ ■ ■

> *I see an adolescent eagle who is no longer in the nest, no longer in relationship with the older eagles. I see this*

eagle looking for other eagles like itself. So far it hasn't found too many. This eagle really likes to fly around. The other eagles are sitting on rocks. So there's some sort of call to action, but the bird issuing the call doesn't yet have the authority to evoke the other birds' responses. But he's definitely flying and some of the other birds are starting to fly too.

■ ■ ■

I didn't learn anything about business period. I'm disappointed I didn't learn anything about business. I did learn about a role I tend to play. Bill had structured the course so we each could take over a session. I initiated a deference to him when it came my turn. That made it plain to me that I was refusing the opportunity to be a leader. I decided the next opportunity I had outside the group I would deliberately volunteer for leadership. The opportunity came and I took it.

■ ■ ■

Where I've learned from him is how he doesn't rise to the bait, to being superchief, as many of us do. As soon as assumptions start to liquidate, he likes it. This is a special quality he has. It's hard to find.

■ ■ ■

I've been using everyday situations as material for inner work. When I feel resistance to something, I go toward it. The Public Performances provided a tremendous inner conflict for me. At that juncture in emotional time, you can either leave or shut off your feelings and feel bored. Or you can open up further and experience a new reality that moment. This is the point at which it's possible to 'respond' instead of simply 'reacting' to something.

I learned a lot about theater from Bill's struggles with finding a form for what he wishes to express. It's a very interesting idea that we are acting roles all the time. If we can really choose to do it, it's different from just doing it unconsciously.

▪ ▪ ▪

I don't want to change people or change the world. I'm in recoil when Bill talks about the transformation of society. I think that's really my failing.

I'm more Machiavellian and sneaky. I'm always avoiding rather than confronting problems. Even if I were going to change the world, I wouldn't do it like Bill's trying to do it.

▪ ▪ ▪

The things I learned most from him had a physical aspect. One event was when I was wrestling with a woman. It started out face to face. I was caught between feeling guilty about controlling her and not wanting to give up and just let her win. Bill suggested we wrestle back to back by interlocking our arms behind ourselves. In that position I couldn't control it all myself. That experience had implications for me on how I deal with issues of control. I experienced the freedom I feel when I allow others to be empowered.

▪ ▪ ▪

I've learned something about not letting my self-consciousness get in my way, which has to do with courage. It's like being loosened up to some extent. It doesn't bother me to do things that would have made me nervous and scared to do before. I'm more comfortable to do things others might notice and might disapprove of. But now I'll do it anyway.

■ ■ ■

His weaknesses include that he still hasn't explained clearly what The Theatre of Inquiry is. Maybe he can't do it any more than he has, but there must be some way to describe it so it can be understood.

■ ■ ■

Bill has a tremendous charisma and he knows it and that it can become his greatest weakness. He initiates a force and then makes a demand for the other person to continue. What he's doing is trying to awaken something in the other people, not give them his answers, which may not apply to them.

■ ■ ■

A major problem for The Theatre of Inquiry is making itself understood and relevant to larger and larger numbers of people. Its biggest problem is between its creative undertaking and marketing itself, making a living. Great ideas have economic significance, are politically effective, and become part of the culture.

■ ■ ■

As far as Bill's leadership, he has an incredible amount of integrity, and I think people listen to him intellectually because they sense something emotional from him: his integrity, his vision of what he wants to see happen in the world. This perception of him keeps people close, although Bill doesn't give people too many handholds. This approach leads to confusion because he's throwing off their holds and expecting them to learn from that.

■ ■ ■

I don't know if the things people comment about are necessarily Bill's weaknesses. I think he's at an early stage in his development. He's still in search for a place to do inquiry on this. He has a vision beyond that of existing organizations. He postulates humans beyond those who are around. It's remarkable. People aren't used to being given that much credit from those who lead them. There's a lot of generosity and a lot of stumbling.

Chapter 21

Endnote 26

Although Torbert speaks in the first-person voice in this chapter, as he has in earlier ones, readers will no doubt have noticed that he contributes mostly research about third-person practice in a third-person voice. Unlike the rest of the book, we are offered virtually no insight into his first-person experience. We have confirmed with him that this choice is intentional on his part (based on the ***Ironic*** action-logic?).

Nevertheless, we Endnote authors believe it to be fitting to end with a more intimate portrait of him from later in his life. We are therefore exercising our editorial privilege to conclude with the impressions of him offered in his early sixties by his masseuse of fifteen years. In his search for feedback from all sides, he asked if she would be willing to share her impressions of him in writing in return for the usual price per hour that he paid her. She agreed to give it a try and handed him the following letter the following week.

Bill,

How to put down on paper what I see? It has been a pleasure for me that you've been willing to explore who you are and willing to risk going into some uncomfortable corners in the course of that exploration. Like most of the human race, you have the contradiction of being so sure of how important you are, while simultaneously having that tiny voice in the background that whispers 'maybe you're not', so you need to keep righting it, coming back to center and trusting.

I enjoy your bright, inquisitive mind; the richness of what you take from your interchange with others; the way you've chosen not to make your wife the 'bad gal'. I really believe you want to understand what it is that makes you tick! And her. It has been a challenge to not throw in the towel; to continue to see and appreciate her gifts.

When I watch your face, I see such a rich mixture – the vulnerable boy; the strong, sexually alive man; the assertive professor; the uncertain knower of life; the one whose conviction of the essence of Spirit is alive and well. You've done a lot of soul and spiritual searching. It makes you much more accessible to me. I think it makes you much more accessible to life, actually, because it lets you be the observer and the participant at the same time.

Your connection with your parents has been touching. They gave you many gifts, especially the opportunity to make use of your bright mind. But I sometimes wonder if your earlier experience set it up for you to find intimacy very difficult. Much as you have sought, and consciously invited, intimacy, I see it often elude you.

Part of the rhythm of life — open/close? Perhaps. Part of the internal self-protector? I'm sure.

When push comes to shove, you retreat to that place so familiar in boyhood when you lived in other countries and, so many times, were the outsider – your own inner landscape. It was, when it came down to it, the only constant. Your parents had their own challenges – the adjustments to and familiarization with their new environments – Spain, Austria, Italy, Hungary, Somalia, Bulgaria. But they were adults, choosing to be in those other lands. You were a child, going through the painful evolution of growing, without the anchor of the constantly familiar environment, or friends who'd always been there. No wonder you had to strengthen that presence that could emit a certain confidence and assurance. I suspect you even had your parents fooled ... not to mention yourself. Still, you really do have that wonderful confidence that makes you bigger than life and able to be seen in the world.

There have been many moments in our time over the years when I wished I could take the young Bill in my arms and make him totally safe, give him that haven which would permit him to relinquish a few moments of his vigilance, let him just relax. That doesn't mean you don't relax; I know that not to be true. However, there is for me a sense of the sweetness a moment of total, safe surrender would have for you. Now that I've said that, there are actually times when I feel I provide that. The unique nature of our relationship – intimate but non-sexual; one where you are able to attend to your own exploration and release without needing to attend to mine – has been valuable from my vantage point. There's a wonderful relaxation that gets to take place when sex is out of the way. (Not that that has totally been the case. There were moments when the temptation to seduce was palpable. It was alive and well, and mercifully able to be observed without the need of action. One of the gifts of maturity! The hormones didn't have to take over and direct the show in the same way they would have when younger.)

I have often felt your joy when you've talked about your male friends. It is such a rich part of your life. You've been blessed with being able to attract a number of men into your life who are fine reflections of yourself – bright, articulate, exploratory human beings. Their inquisitive minds and passionate natures help keep these parts of you alive in the best way, and fill your heart with richness. I've seen plenty of women have these kinds of friendships, but I've found it much more rare for men, and admire it when I encounter it. I like the way these friendships help sustain you, adding dimension to your passion.

Your professional life is impressive. There are those odd moments when I see a crack in your certainty that it has worth– rare, but there. However, you have such a strong intellect, and it would have been a terrible loss to the academic community if you hadn't been part of it. You've inspired many. That's a gift.

For me, though, the biggest gift is your humanness. You have such a strong ego – a reflection of the persona you had to develop as a child and the vulnerable man you are as an adult, who still, in subtle ways, needs reassurance of his worth. You also have a beautiful compassionate self, who knows what it feels like to seek that haven, whether it be person or place. You have a sweetness that reflects the innocence of a child; a savvy that shows the strongly seductive man. You have a great sense of humor and enthusiasm that are infectious – valuable gifts. And you have a great lust for life.

In the last couple of years, I've seen a slight lessening of your drive. Male menopause? Wanting to relax a bit? Probably. Giving up and becoming depressed? No doubt a fear.

Postscript, I

Endnote 26

The young woman's story begins with a discussion of differences in 'class rank' (both in the sense of social status and in the sense of school grade ranking) in her early elementary school years. Higher social status and higher school grades are, in general, 'better,' more desirable, more charming than lower social status or school grades. All of these calculations derive from the Diplomatic action-logic and the Charming power exerted by what's already authoritatively defined as 'good' and has to be imitated if possible.

At the same time, getting good grades, while clearly meant in significant part to please her teacher and increase her own status by becoming the 'teacher's pet,' also exemplifies the early stirrings of the Expert action-logic, which the teacher enacts to a high degree (supplemented by the occasional Opportunistic threat of physical punishment).

The climax of the story, however, involves the writer's 'cousin' suddenly exercising a kind of power that had been unimaginable before that. With the teacher about to strike the 'lazy' student with the ruler, our narrator retreats to a sort of Opportunistic self-protective action-logic, in which she takes for granted that non-action and silent support of the teacher/authority is her only alternative.

But her 'cousin' begs the teacher to relent, offering an alternative, potentially-shared vision of what may occur next (Redefining action-logic, Visioning power). To the emotionally painful incongruity of the other girl not being able to get the right answer, the cousin achieves a result that doesn't involve corporal punishment (Coercive power) <u>and</u> that increases the likelihood of the 'lazy' girl actually learning (Transforming action-logic, Praxis power).

Her 'cousin' has offered the teacher double-loop feedback – a whole new structure for accomplishing the teacher's goal – which the teacher accepts (for reasons we don't know). The narrator recognizes that, counterintuitively (from the Diplomat point of view), her 'cousin's opposition to the immediate goal of the higher authority has raised her status both with the teacher and her classmates. The narrator interprets her cousin's action as a kind of double-loop feedback to herself about her false assumption of what was possible in this situation. Indeed, all four protagonists – the cousin, the 'lazy' girl, the writer, and the teacher – may have experienced a Transforming moment of mutually-transforming power at the climax of the story.

Thus, in this culture dominated by the Diplomat action-logic among students and the Expert action-logic among teachers and institutional standards, we see evidence in this particular scenario of the Opportunist, Diplomat, Expert, Redefining, and Transforming action-logics at work. How could the author, a young, elementary school girl, have so convincingly adopted the Redefining action-logic and the Postmodern Critical Interpretivist position with regard to her own role in the situation? Is this just a case of post-hoc revisionism and rationalization on her part?

Postscript, II

Endnote 27

At the outset of this story, our narrator offers several reasons rooted in the Diplomat action-logic for her anorexia, showing both its sway over her and her concurrent rebellion against it. She admits to terrible loneliness and loss of social role. She's proud of wearing a size 2 and not seeming fat to others, but being popular was not her aim.

Really, she says, she was trying to exert control over some area of her life, and she found that, although (or because) it involved real discipline, she could control her eating, deny herself dinner. So, the non-eating was in some ways a (warped?) spiritual discipline to help her grow from the Diplomat to the Expert action-logic and into Logistical power –the power of mind over matter, the power of technology, often accompanied by denial of the body's own intrinsic wisdom.

Toward the end of her freshman year, she describes how she generalizes from not needing food to not needing social or professional status, nor middle class economic achievement, not even marriage. (To this day, she and her life partner, father of her children, describe themselves as 'happily unmarried.')

In these imaginative moves, we see her beginning to disentangle herself from all conventional identity categories and open herself to fresh visions of herself and the Redefining action-logic. This redefining process may well go on occasionally for many years before it becomes her center-of-gravity action-logic...

Postscript, III

Endnote 28

From the very first page of our narrator's third story, we see signs of a late-action-logic, mutuality-seeking leadership approach: she prefers to create a peer-like atmosphere by being called by her first name, rather than hierarchically distinguished as "Dr."; she also has a set of what can be called "transformational allies" on campus, of whom Alden is one.

As soon as she realizes the explosive issue she is being asked to assume responsibility for, she has a paradoxical, 'simultaneously bi-polar' experience of being excited by the opportunity and wondering what excitement at participating in such a painful situation means about her. Experiencing a conjunction of opposites and standing in the tension of opposites are attractive at the Alchemical action-logic. She recalls a similarly-difficult recent facilitation role she has played on behalf of a queer rights organization, realizing that there was not only a positive immediate outcome, but that the process seems to have strengthened the whole system in the longer run (late-action-logic leadership seeks to create positive outcomes across multiple time horizons). She again demonstrates her propensity for highlighting opposites and proceeding ironically, by first proposing a design for the Israeli-Palestinian evening directly opposite that proposed by her (prospective) client and then arguing why she is wrong for the job. She is offered the job on the spot!

In the following pages, she describes the kinds of procedures she develops for leading potentially explosive and potentially transformational events (exercising the power of liberating disciplines). One step is to develop agreements and ground rules with the entire group at the outset of the evening (excercising shared visioning power).

Once the substantive discussion begins, her attention is meant to be focused entirely on creating a container for the entire group, which faces participants with constant choices about where to move (closer to or further from what somebody else says) and what to say. Meanwhile, she seeks to gain everyone's trust by empathically and accurately reflecting and amplifying what each says (exercising praxis power). She is working at the meta-level, focusing on the shape and quality of the overall conversation, its inclusiveness of multiple perspectives

She speaks of this as exercising "neutrality," and we can see how this is true, but one could also argue that, whereas everyone else is almost entirely identified with one position or another, she and her procedures are advocating for a community inquiry that embraces all present. She abjures her own first-person voice, as well as her second-person relational voice, in favor of her third-person voice. (Late in the evening, she is, in effect, joined by the Palestinian and Israeli student who commit to standing by the other side if anyone tries to harm them after the referendum.)

Before she describes the "liberating disciplines" she creates for the collective evening, our narrator has described the liberating and transforming disciplines of emotional and embodied contemplation she herself engages in during the prior week and during that particular day. At the Alchemical and Ironic action-logics, one fully recognizes the need for self-transformation before (and possibly during) any event that is intended to serve as a crucible for others' transformation.

It seems likely most readers will agree that this woman has, in effect, organized and conducted a Theatre of Inquiry Public Performance with greater transformational resonance for the participants than any that Torbert conducted forty years previously in 1978.

Appendix A

Torbert's Theories of Learning from Experiencing in Brief Summary

The Phenomenological/Ontological/Ethical Theory of Four Territories of Experience

The Epistemological Theory of the Developmental Action-Logics for Persons

A Theory of Interpersonal Effectiveness

The Cybernetic Theory of Single-, Double-, and Triple-Loop Feedback

A Political Theory of Justice Consistent with the Above, and

The Developmental Theory of Social Science

Torbert originally proposed the ontological, phenomenological, and cybernetic theory of learning from past experience, from present experiencing, and from future possibilities that underlies all his later work in his doctoral dissertation. Influenced primarily by the work of Chris Argyris, Karl Deutsch, Maurice Merleau-Ponty, P.D. Ouspensky, and E.F. Schumacher, it was published as *Learning from Experience: Toward Consciousness* by Columbia University Press in 1973. The foundational notion (open to continual inquiry) is that there are four ontological 'layers of reality,' or 'territories of experience,' with which our attention can make contact. These territories of experience, from outside in, can be named:

1) the outside world;
2) one's own current behavior as sensed from within oneself;
3) one's internal cognitive-emotional-sensory structure; and
4) consciousness.

Ordinarily, we are aware of just one of the four territories at a time when we are awake. As I write and you read these words, we are probably both primarily aware of the meaning of these words within the 'cognitive' territory. But if I notice I've made a typo, my awareness has shifted momentarily to this page in the 'outside world' territory, and then shifts again to my 'own behavior' territory as I deliberately delete and retype. Perhaps for a moment or two, my attention (your attention?) has included two or even three of these territories. The more one can move one's attention among all four territories in an agile way, the more one can learn from single-, double-, and triple-loop feedback (to be defined below). The more one can contact all four territories simultaneously, the more one experiences how each successive territory interpenetrates all the earlier ones in a non-dual dynamic reality. But most of us most of the time live in non-conscious, single-territory awareness.

By contrast to this fourfold set of primordial territories of which we can become aware, modern philosophy and science posit but two such territories – mind and matter, or map and territory, or consciousness and brain – with various attempts to reduce the one to the other. Approaching the world in the 'two territory' manner introduces three so-called 'hard' problems. The first is why and how we experience anything (pain, pattern, or confusion) *subjectively* from the inside. The second is how we can 'know' a second-person *intersubjectively*, beyond the projections and interpretations we make (the so-called 'theory of mind' problem). And the third problem is how we can translate an inner quality (an aesthetically-felt purpose or vision) into an *objective* 'outer' quality (a profit or a house).

These three problems are to be answered, according to Torbert's four-territory paradigm – not by an intellectual formulation that is logically and empirically proven to be universally true in the 'objective' terms of two-territory science – but rather by a gradual life-long process of learning through first-person, second-person, and third-person experiencing and deliberate inquiry-in-action. We test whether we find the four territories when we seek them and explore both moments of harmony and moments of incongruity among them in our subjective, intersubjective, and objective inquiry. Whereas two-territory, modern science seeks truth through the triangulation of three third-person measures, action inquirers are seeking to triangulate among first-, second-, and third-person inquiry to produce uniquely timely actions alone and with others. This inquiry never ends in absolute, eternal truths because each emergent situation demands renewed inquiry into what constitutes timely (inter)action(s) *now*.

This ontological theory of four territories of experience is closely interwoven with Torbert's epistemological theory of successive, developmental action-logics. Movement through the action-logics is theorized as gradually increasing awareness of how the four territories of experience interweave. This developmental journey also involves progressively dis-identifying with the most concrete and small-self-ish aspects of one's identity in favor of a transforming and relating self, more concerned with the common goods we can create (personal integrity, loving mutuality, and sustainable justice) than with narrow personal interests or tribal customs.

The Theory of Developmental Action-Logics

In dialogue with Susanne Cook-Greuter, Erik Erikson, Carol Gilligan, Bob Kegan, Larry Kohlberg, Jane Loevinger, and Ken Wilber (and surprisingly resonant with journalist David Brooks' recent book, *The Second Mountain*), Torbert's theory of developmental action-logics is also distinct in its emphasis on the primacy of embodied practice and of post-cognitive consciousness among the four territories of experience. It describes a very general path that persons, communities, and scientific inquiry itself can follow to generate increasing awareness of the four territories of experience and of the extent to which our practices and institutional procedures translate congruently or incongruently from intent to effect.

One can summarize Torbert's developmental theory as portraying the earliest years of a person's life as manifesting an *Impulsive* action-logic, whereby the child is led to act primarily by whim, by fantasy, and by imitativeness. Then, between (approximately) five and ten, most children become primarily engaged in the *Opportunist* action-logic, attempting to master (or protect themselves from) the outside-world territory of experience, learning the myriad skills involved in physical game-playing, bike riding, etc.

Between twelve and seventeen (again approximately), most boys and girls are exploring the *Diplomat* action-logic, seeking to act in ways that 'fit in,' learning emotional game-playing, mastering elements of *the second territory of experience – ongoing control of one's own behavior from within.*

After that, especially if they attend college and if they transform further at all, young men and women enter into the *Expert* action-logic, which is intent on mastering some sub-field of *the thinking territory of experience*.

At the *Achiever* action-logic, persons deliberately try to *coordinate the three territories* they have (partially) mastered – from plan to action to outcome – willingly receiving *single-loop feedback* and adjusting their behavior to improve the likelihood of success.

As they mature, some adults begin to question the very goals and norms that their cultural, familial, and organizational milieu have set for them, recognizing that these goals and norms they've personally inherited are themselves socially constructed and are, therefore, potentially reconstructable through *double-loop learning*. At this *Redefining* action-logic, they begin to realize that different people are interpreting and enacting their own lives through different meaning-making systems (different action-logics, different epistemologies), each of which privileges different aspects of outer, empirical reality and inner, psycho-somatic reality. They also begin to value creative moments of insight, of artistic practice, or of intimate engagement in a relationship, moments when a special sense of presence in the present occurs as one makes occasional contact with *the post-cognitive* consciousness territory of experience.

As one gives more attention, thought, and practice to such creative experiences and contributions, one may begin to sense that reality is more dynamic than static and that there is a developmental process of successive transformations in the evolution of the universe, in the evolution of life forms on earth, in the evolution of consciousness in members of humankind, and in the evolution of our specific projects and organizations. As one evolves toward the *Transforming* action-logic, one becomes increasingly aware that, while external factors felt like the prime movers in one's early development, one is becoming increasingly capable of identifying and influencing moments of potentially transformational action in one's own, others', organizations', and societal trajectories as one intentionally cultivates a more continual presence to, and co-ordination of, all four territories of experience.

Eventually, however, the heroic (and tragic) confidence of this *Transforming* action-logic may founder upon the humbling (and comic) trans-egoic *Alchemical* action-logic. This is no longer a stable action-logic at all, but rather a conscious listening into the dark, in the spirit of inquiry, to all one's feelings and action-logics as they express themselves in our daily actions.

A Theory of Interpersonal Effectiveness

Torbert's fourfold ontological theory of experience is reflected in all human domains — not just at the individual scale, but also at the interpersonal, conversational scale, the organizational scale, and the political scale, as well as different domains such as science, ethics, and the good life, as will be suggested in the following sections.

Chris Argyris first articulated some patterns of speech that generate greater or lesser interpersonal efficacy. He noted that many senior management business conversations were dominated by dueling abstract "advocacies" about what to do. He found that such conversations were more likely to yield decisions to which the group was genuinely committed if advocacies were balanced by more concrete "illustrations" of how to enact a given advocacy and by "inquiries" which brought out more detail about what another meant or tested whether others agreed or disagreed with one's own proposal.

Looking at these three types of speech through the four territories of experience lease, Torbert saw that "inquiries" sought information from the "outside world" territory; "illustrations" described specific "behaviors as sensed by oneself"; and "advocacies" represented the "thinking" territory of experience. Missing from this model was a type of speech representing the fourth territory of experience — "post-cognitive consciousness." This was not surprising considering that post-cognitive consciousness is a rare phenomenon. Thus, we would expect the corresponding type of speech to be rare. Torbert named this type of speech "framing." A framing statement is one that attempts to describe a definition of the current situation that all participants share, or the game they all agree to play. As a conversation goes on and possibly loses its way, one can intervene to re-frame it.

Advocacy and illustration reveal one's own view of the world. Framing and inquiry attempt to transcend one's own ego view and establish a joint view or hear someone else's view.

Argyris and his MIT colleague Don Schon later published ***Theory in Practice: Increasing Professional Effectiveness***, in which they proposed two more general models of how professionals behaved, based on data generated by the professionals themselves as they described their strategies and actions in real cases they experienced. They called these two models Model I and Model II. Model I was far more prevalent, accounting for about 95% of all the cases. Argyris and Schon induced four "governing variables" of Model I:

1) Maximize winning and minimize losing;
2) Minimize generating or expressing negative feelings;
3) Be rational; and
4) Define (your own) goals and try to achieve them.

Torbert later recognized a remarkable aspect of these four governing variables: that they perfectly mimicked the four early (and most prevalent) developmental action-logics among professionals: 1) Opportunist; 2) Diplomat; 3) Expert; and 4) Achiever. He called this the Mystery-Mastery model of interpersonal relations: you unilaterally maintain a mystery about your feelings and strategies and seek unilateral control of outcomes.

Argyris and Schon's developed their Model II by a combination of deduction and induction. Model II was partially deduced from the *espoused theories* of professionals about how they behaved; and it was partially induced from efforts by Argyris and Schon to teach professionals how to act in ways that increased group learning, trust, and efficacy. They came up with three governing variables for Model II: 1) valid information; 2) free and informed choice; and 3) internal commitment to the choice and constant monitoring of its implementation. We can see right away that these governing variables are more abstract than those of Model I and that, although they imply a process of collaborative inquiry like Torbert's later action-logics, they do not directly mimic the later action-logics, nor do they indicate how to act in a timely way in a complex real-world setting of many pressures. This sense of the incompleteness of Argyris and Schon's Model II led Torbert to generate his own version, which he calls the Collaborative Inquiry model:

1. Optimize internal commitment of partners to shared vision (Redefining – visioning power)
2. Optimize inquiry and valid information about actual performance vs espoused values (Transforming – praxis power)
3. Maximize mutual influence and positive freedom of choice (Alchemical – mutually-transforming power)
4. Enact timely action (according to multiple criteria including intergenerational sustainability) (Ironical – the power of liberating disciplines)

Just as attention to all four territories of experience at once requires a special inner effort, so does ongoing attention to balancing the four parts of speech and enacting the four governing variables of Collaborative Inquiry in conversation.

The Cybernetic Theory of Single-, Double-, and Triple-Loop Feedback and Learning

Torbert's fourfold ontological model of experience also suggests that three quite different and increasingly subtle and challenging types of learning from (past) experience, from (present) experiencing, and from (future) possibilities are possible for a person, an organization, or a science (Erfan & Torbert, 2015; Torbert & Erfan, 2020).

The first type – **single-loop learning** – occurs when feedback from the outside world (natural and/or social) leads one to change one's behavior in order to reach a goal. In this type of learning one is weaving together a pattern in *durational time*, from the moment the goal is set, through the various efforts to achieve the goal and the feedback that reorients one's striving, until the time when the goal is achieved (or abandoned). In two-territory, modern science this process is thought of as hypothesis testing. One conducts a tightly controlled experiment that generates feedback from the outside world that either confirms or disconfirms the hypothesis.

The second type of learning from experience – **double-loop learning** – occurs when feedback leads one to change one's cognitive-emotional-sensory structure (i.e. action-logic) in order to enact a higher vision and a more embodied, more timely practice. This can occur, for example, when a leader says, "I insist that from now on we make our decisions as a team, collaboratively!" Here, the leader espouses a double-loop, transformational change in how the team should work ("collaboratively"). But in practice the leader continues to use power unilaterally ("I insist…").

Obviously, double-loop feedback is much harder than single-loop feedback to offer artistically, to receive without defensiveness, and to correct for. This is because receiving double-loop feedback involves transforming one's cognitive-emotional-sensory structure or strategy (one's ego), at least temporarily. To make the matter even trickier, double-loop feedback can easily boomerang on the person offering it. The boss may think they are offering double-loop feedback to the team in the example above, but successful double-loop change for the team as a whole will occur only if a subordinate has the courage and perspicacity to offer the leader double-loop feedback on their present incongruity. Only if the leader in turn has the courage and vulnerability to accept and learn from the episode will double-loop learning and collaboration, for the boss and the team, actually have occurred. This type of learning requires access to a different dimension of time – to *presence in the present* or the *eternal now* – that allows one to see and compare two (or more) territories of experience at once. Although many persons have occasional unanticipated experiences of *presence in the present*, few intentionally cultivate this quality of conscious experiencing.

The third type of learning from experience – **triple-loop learning** – occurs when feedback shakes the very foundations of one's cognitive-emotional-sensory structure so thoroughly as to reveal a spiritual quality, a post-cognitive, post-egoic, presencing consciousness as its own distinctive territory of experience. In his recent book, **How to Change Your Mind**, Michael Pollan offers an example of the difference between ego-centered thought (the third territory of experience) and presencing consciousness (the fourth territory of experience):

> During a psilocybin trip … I experienced the complete dissolution of my ego. All at once I had burst into a sheaf of paper slips, no bigger than Post-its, that were being scattered to the wind. Yet there was still an "I" observing this seeming catastrophe, a paradox I couldn't explain but needed to address.
>
> So who was this other I? "Good question," I wrote, turning once again to the reader. "It wasn't *me*, exactly. Here, the

> limits of language become a problem: In order to completely make sense of the divide that had opened up in my perspective, I would need a whole new first-person pronoun." And then, having acknowledged the squishy new terrain of identity onto which we had stepped, I went on to characterize this "bare disembodied awareness," which gazed upon the scene of the self's dissolution with benign indifference. I was present to reality but as something other than my self.... There was life after the death of the ego. This was big news.

Through practices of psychedelic experimentation, meditation-in-action, presencing-speech, and the occasion-design that Torbert calls *Liberating Disciplines*, this trans-egoic consciousness is potentially capable of including the three other territories within its purview simultaneously and increasingly continually. The Gurdjieff Work and Argyrisian practices were Torbert's primary introductions to the consciousness territory and its ability to 'hold' the other three territories. Hindu philosophy also aims for such conscious seeing, listening, or intuiting ('darsana'), although, unlike Torbert's action inquiry, it often opts for detachment from thought, sensation, and the outer world. The Japanese philosopher Nishida's 'action intuition' comes closer to the 'this-worldly' quality of action inquiry and its aesthetic search for timely grace-in-practice. Or, as poet/philosopher Charles Olson put it: "If there is any absolute, it is never more than this one — you, this instant, in action."

This type of 'four-territory,' 'triple-loop' learning generates access to a third dimension of time that includes *duration* and *presence in the present*. This third dimension of time can be named *the volume of all possibilities* and is the erotic source water within which creative inaction and timely, kairotic action are spawned. As the Japanese Zen philosopher and practitioner Suzuki writes, "reality goes beyond definability and cannot be qualified as this or that. It is beyond categories of universal and particular... It is the fullness of things, containing all possibilities."

The ultimate aim of action inquiry – timely action – requires a sense of one's own developmental timing, that of others with whom one interacts directly, and that of larger organizational and historical institutions within which the action occurs. Because the contexts in which we are acting are constantly changing (a grocery store, a sporting game, an office, your family, etc.), and because our actions may have different effects when considered across different time horizons, we repeat that there can be no finally and universally true answer about what constitutes effective, ethical, and timely transforming action.

Moreover, insofar as timely action is estimated by comparison to past events, to future intents, or by determining whether one's conscious purpose, one's cognitive-emotional strategy, and one's performance are congruent in the present, it requires a high capacity to analogize among outer events and among the territories of experience… and no analogy is ever perfect. Hence, the primacy of inquiry, mutuality, and presence in the inclusive present across a lifetime.

Whereas technological AI (artificial intelligence) operates via disembodied logical algorithms, based on binary 0/1 distinctions, and cultivates false pride; human AI (action inquiry) operates primarily via embodied, attention-widening analogical rhythms and cultivates humility.

A Theory of Justice Compatible With the Foregoing Theories of Learning

Next, we explore how the ontological theory of four territories of experience and the epistemological theory of developmental action-logics relate to the perennial and slippery human project of creating increasingly just societies.

Harvard professor John Rawls' magisterial book on political philosophy, ***A Theory of Justice*** (1971) appeared as Torbert himself moved from SMU to Harvard in 1972. Torbert taught the book in a seminar the following spring, and then wrote an essay review entitled "Doing Rawls Justice" for the *Harvard Educational Review* (1974). He argued that Rawls provided the building blocks for a "paradigm of just action," without having made that paradigm fully explicit.

Rawls wrote that, to raise children who will preserve a just society, parents must formulate rules comprehensible to their children, enact a consistent morality themselves, and gradually make the underlying principles explicit. Note the immense demand placed on parents in this single sentence. This is an educational paradigm which depends for its felicitous effects on a parental awareness that embraces the "four territories of experience" –

1) the "outside world" territory of our effects on our children, intended to be congruent with the other three territories of experience;
2) the world of our own actions experienced from within, intended to be congruent with the rules and principles we hold;
3) the realm of rational, comprehensible rules, intended to be congruent with our principles;
4) the realm of intuitive principles, alert attention, active intention.

Since no parents can be expected to get this all right to begin with, or once and for all time, they must cultivate a quality of attention in the fourth 'consciousness' territory of experience *that observes and corrects errors and incongruities in translations from one realm to another* as they interact with their children. This last aspect of just parental action is italicized because it is this dynamic feedback and learning process – this *vulnerably loving educational action* – that must be present if incongruities are to be corrected within the family, and it is to become increasingly just. Those words are also italicized because it is that process that Rawls misses even though he so clearly implies it.

How can we go beyond parental practices to generalize this approach to creating more just lives for ourselves and within other social institutions? Rawls continues to help us by enunciating an analogous four-territory practice for each individual person who tries to determine what his or her primary goods are. He suggests that there are four primary goods that all rational persons will want, whatever other idiosyncratic goods one or another of us may want. He names the four primary goods in ways that align them with the four territories of experience. In this enumeration of the four territories, we name them from the inside out rather than the outside in:

(4) *intuitive self-respect or self-esteem*: "Without it nothing may seem worth doing, or if some things have value for us, we lack the will to strive for them" (p. 400);
(3) *a "rational long-term plan of life* given reasonably favorable circumstances... [for] the good is the satisfaction of rational desire" (pp. 92-93);
(2) the liberty and opportunity to develop and exercise the *action competencies* necessary to realize a rational life plan; and finally,
(1) the *income* and wealth that results from such competent work and permits one increasingly to realize all four primary goods.

Again, we see the need to cultivate an awareness that embraces the realms of the intuitive whole, rational strategy, action, and outcomes (in this case, income)... *and that observes and corrects errors and incongruities in translations from one realm to another.*

Torbert has since written that these four primary goods of the good life can more colloquially be named (from the outside in):

1) good money (in the 'outcomes' territory);
2) good work (socially valuable and personally self-fulfilling 'action');
3) good friends (intimates with whom to explore how to 'structure' one's own good life); and
4) good questions (such as how to balance these four and other goods).

Of these four goods, money is the only one that is purely extrinsic and instrumental. The other three primary goods have intrinsic qualities and are ends in themselves. Good money is, thus, the least amount of wealth necessary to cultivate the other three goods, and is best gained through good work. Good work that makes a net positive social contribution based on the exercise of one's best crafts earns money and generates self-esteem. Good friends engage the conversations whereby we each determine what good work and a rational long-term plan of life is for us and how to become capable of love in the spirit of inquiry. Only the truest and trustiest of friends challenge and support us in the full depth of our inquiry. Good questions live at the core of the good life because the most profound questions we can ask (such as "what is the most loving action I can take now?") can never be rightly answered once and for all.

From an ethical point of view, the four major contesting ethical systems in Western philosophy – utilitarian ethics, virtue ethics, the ethics of principle, and the existential, situational ethics of responsibility – each refer primarily to one of the four territories of experience and can often complement one another rather than contest absolute priority. Utilitarian ethics attempts to calculate the amount of pain or pleasure produced by outcomes in the outside world territory. Virtue ethics apply predominantly to personal choices of behavior in the self-sensing territory and the degree to which they contribute to personal integrity and a wider good. The ethics of principle are discovered and applied predominantly through the thinking territory. And the existential, situational ethics of responsibility (which includes intuitive alignment with all three other types of ethics) depends upon one's capacity to engage the consciousness territory while in action.

Of these four ethical approaches, Rawls' theory of justice is good at interrelating the utilitarian and principled ethical concerns. In his two principles of justice, he calls for: 1) social and economic inequalities arranged for the greatest benefit of the least advantaged (combining utilitarian and principled ethics); and 2) a system of liberty for all (principled ethics). But he is less cognizant of issues of virtuous action and moment-to-moment responsibility.

In political life, the paradigm of just action that Torbert finds hidden in Rawls theory is again analogous. Those actions are relatively more just which (from the inside out):

(4) gradually explicate the underlying, intuitive principles of justice;
(3) elaborate laws and policies consistent with those principles, as well as internally consistent with one another;
(2) duly administer this conceptual system of justice in a way that is both substantively and procedurally congruent;
(1) gain increasing voluntary compliance by the citizenry;

and *observe and correct incongruities among principles, laws, administration, and effects on the citizenry.*

For business enterprises and other organizations to transform toward economic and environmental sustainability, yet another analogous, dynamic process is necessary: of cultivating an embracing awareness of

4) mission;
3) strategy;
2) operations;
1) the bottom line;

and *of observing and correcting incongruities among them.*

Yet another analogous dynamic process is necessary to generate a truly informative, liberating, and responsible social science. Such a social science will cultivate an awareness of the interplay among

4) paradigm;
3) theory;
2) research methods;
1) data;

and *will correct incongruities among them* – at the first-person, the second-person, and the third-person scales of research, through single-, double-, and triple-loop learning.

Here, it is worth recognizing that incongruities among the four territories of experience are difficult to "see," require interpretation, and are rarely easily amenable to correction. The simplest incongruities to observe and correct are the "single-loop" incongruities between an action and an effect. Both actions and effects (say swinging a hammer and hitting the nail effectively [or not]) are generally visible. Also, the visible way in which the first try may have been ineffective (the hammer lands beyond the nail) suggests the behavioral correction necessary to have the effect one intends (shorten the swing).

If, however, repeated single-loop changes of behavior don't work; if, no matter how true the hammer blow, the nail yet bends; it becomes likely that a "double-loop" (strategic) or a "triple-loop" (true vision not-yet-awakened) incongruity exists. But these are literally invisible, can be hard to imagine, and acknowledging them can make one feel vulnerable. To return to our example, the wood may be too hard for nailing and may require a double-loop, strategic change to using a drill, a screw, and a screwdriver. Or, perhaps you come to realize that building a porch is merely a diversion from 'awakening' to the risky realization that you would rather move to a different part of the country with a new home (triple-loop learning).

In any event, as structurally coherent as Torbert found Rawls' argument, he also found it missing the dynamic action elements of how to generate developmentally-transforming Liberating Disciplines and "loving educational action" via a "paradigm of just action." Such actions are necessary if we are, first in act and then in fact, to create increasingly just societies in the 21st-century.

In his 2010 book, ***The Idea of Justice***, Nobel laureate Amartya Sen agrees with Torbert in his response to Rawls, arguing for the importance of seeking, not only more just first principles and institutional arrangements for the political economy in general, but also more just outcomes on an action-by-action, situation-by-situation basis.

The Theory of Social Scientific Development

Beyond the theories of personal and social development that Torbert generated during his career and illustrates in this book, he also generated another analogous developmental theory — this one of social scientific paradigms. Table 1, below, names seven social science paradigms and offers a paragraph of description of each. As in the case of individual development, the later scientific action-logics continue to include the capacities of the earlier ones. Thus, as was demonstrated in Chapter 21 and will again be demonstrated in Appendix E, the Collaborative Developmental Action Inquiry paradigm includes the capacity to do Empirical Positivist and other earlier action-logic studies.

Table 1: Brief Descriptions of Seven Social Scientific Paradigms

Behaviorism: Assertive, physical quest for reliable, unilateral control through 'operant conditioning' of an unapologetically objectified and atomized external world. Preferred method: laboratory experiments (maximizing the scientist's unilateral control over variation). Nominalist presumption of isolatable "stimuli" and "responses." B.F. Skinner – an archetypal Behaviorist.

Gestalt Psychology/Sociology/Anthropology: Appreciative, emotional quest for understanding of the overall pattern of subjective beliefs, values, and rituals of a given "Other," whether person or culture. Preferred method: case studies based on non-interventionist, ethnographic field observation. Essentialist presumption of integrative ideas, norms, and selves. Physician/ neurologist/ author Oliver Sacks – an archetypal Gestalt Psychologist.

Empirical Positivism: Critical (but not hermeneutically self-critical), intellectual quest for predictive certainty about deductively logical, universally generalizable, empirical propositions. Privileges randomized sample, experimental, statistically-analyzed hypothesis testing studies, along with computer modeling of intelligence, because of the crisply clear quantitative, binary certainty about distinctions between 0 and 1, between confirmation and disconfirmation. Herbert Simon's theoretical and empirical demonstrations of the concept of bounded rationality exemplify Empirical Positivism.

Multi-Method Eclecticism: Practical quest to increase validity, understanding, applicability, and percentage of the variance explained. Recommends triangulation among quantitative and qualitative methods, as well as evidence-based practice in management, education, medicine, etc. (Rousseau, 2020). Management researcher Jean Bartunek – an archetypal practitioner of Multi-Method Eclecticism.

Postmodern Critical Interpretivism: Self-conscious accounting for the radical subjectivity and fragmentariness of perspective that embraces every languaged perception and conception. Preferred method: to deconstruct the implicit, taken-for-granted background (1) of the objects foregrounded in single-frame, early-paradigm studies; (2) of the researcher's praxis during the research; and (3) of the writing of the author of the critique. The Pfeffer-Van Maanen debate in 1990s management scholarship between an early single-frame 'Pfeffer-digm' and Van Maanen's rhetorical interpretivism offered an exemplar of Postmodern Critical Interpretivism.

Action Science Praxis: Scientist becomes actor/ interventionist as well as researcher, studies self and others in interaction with one another, seeking to generate greater interpersonal and organizational capacity for building trust, confronting theory/ practice incongruities, and accomplishing desired outcomes. Practiced most intensively in Organization Development interventions, T-groups, Tavistock conferences, Power & Systems workshops, and group psychotherapy by scholar-practitioners like Clay Alderfer, Chris Argyris and Irvin Yalom.

Cooperative Ecological Inquiry: Commitment to creating real-time communities of inquiry (i.e. communities that bridge subjectivities and differences of perspective, that confront incongruities among vision, strategy, action, and outcomes, and that support voluntary, mutual personal and social transformation). Yale Upward Bound an example of a temporary experiment toward a community of inquiry. The careers of Hilary Bradbury and Peter Reason, editors of the *Handbook of Action Research*, and of Otto Scharmer and his Presenting Institute — early exemplars of Cooperative Ecological Inquiry as well.

Collaborative Developmental Action Inquiry: Recognizes that different moments, persons, organizations, sciences, and cultures are complex, chaotic interweavings of the six prior paradigms. Highlights the contrapuntal rhythms, interruptions, and interventions in developmental movement from one paradigm to another and across the individual-societal scales, whether in single conversations or in whole lives. Seeks interweaving of past-, present-, and future-oriented, 1st-, 2nd-, and 3rd-person research/practice (action inquiry), with single-, double-, and triple-loop feedback that can sustain inter-paradigmatic conversation, work, meditation, and play in a quest for timely action with mutually-transforming power and love.

Table 2 gives a flavor for the analogies among the personal, organizational, and scientific action-logics. The two tables are followed by a discussion of how this memoir and its surrounding essays illustrate some of the many types of data that characterize studies conducted according to the late action-logic Collaborative Developmental Action Inquiry paradigm, in contrast to the much more limited types of data studied by the Empirical Positivist paradigm.

Table 2: Outline of Analogies Among Personal, Organizational and Scientific Action-Logics *

Personal Development	Organizational Development	Social Scientific Development
I. Birth-Impulsive	**I. Conception**	**I. Anarchism** (Feyerabend)
(Multiple, distinctive impulses gradually resolve into characteristic approach [e.g., many fantasies into a particular dream for a new organization])		
II. Opportunist	**II. Investments**	**II. Behaviorism**
(Dominant task: gain power [e.g., bike riding skill] to have desired effect on outside world.)		
III. Diplomat	**III. Incorporation**	**III. Gestalt Psych & Soc**
(Looking-glass self: understanding others' culture/ expectations and molding own actions to succeed in their [e.g., market] terms.)		
IV. Expert	**IV. Experiments**	**IV. Empirical Positivism**
(Intellectual mastery of outside-self systems such that actions = experiments that confirm or disconfirm hypotheses and lead toward valid certainty.)		
V. Achiever	**V. Systematic Productivity**	**V. Multi-Method Eclecticism**
(Pragmatic triangulation among plan/ theory, operation/ implementation, and outcome/ assessment in incompletely predefined environment. Reliably uses single-loop feedback to improve real-time performance.)		

VI. Redefining	**VI. Social Network**	**VI. Postmodern Critical Interpretivism**

(Critique of conventional assumptions and goals, development of shared vision, creative experiential learning, inventive qualitative methods, 'loose coupling' of initiatives.)

VII. Transforming	**VII. Collaborative Inquiry**	**VII. Action Science Praxis**

(Self-conscious mission/ philosophy, sense of timing/historicity, invitation to conversation among multiple voices and to reframing of boundaries. Occasionally uses double-loop feedback to transform performance.)

VIII. Alchemical	**VIII. Foundational Community**	**VIII. Cooperative Ecological Inquiry**

(Life/science = a mind/ matter, love/ death/transformation praxis among others; cultivation of triple-loop feedback among four territories of experience and reattunements among inquiry, friendship, work, and earthly/ material goods)

IX. Ironic	**IX. Liberating Disciplines**	**IX. Collaborative Developmental Action Inquiry**

(Full acceptance of multi-paradigmatic nature of human consciousness/reality, including distances/ alienations among paradigms, resulting in interruptions of, and failures to listen into, single-, double-, and triple-loop feedback, across the first-, second-, and third-person scales. Inherently developmental tasks designed and undertaken)

* There are, of course, also many ways in which personal, organizational, and scientific development are *not* analogous. For example, personal development is in general either static or progressive throughout one's lifetime (with temporary periods of fallback), permanently regressing only in cases of significant disease, trauma, injury, or losses of old age. An organization, however, may regress anytime its executive function changes (e.g. the CEO is replaced, the Board is significantly shuffled, or the organization is acquired). And, with regard to the scientific action-logics, individual scientists often take on a single one of the scientific paradigms as graduate students and remain committed to it throughout their career, or they may tend to adopt the scientific paradigm most compatible with their personal action-logic.

In general, the philosophy of social science recognizes two fundamentally different approaches to social science — naturalism and interpretivism (Rosenberg, 2012). Naturalism, like natural science, approaches reality as that which is externally observable and objectively measurable, wherein certain things 'cause' other things. The paradigms of Behaviorism and Empirical Positivism in Table 1 exemplify naturalism. By contrast, interpretivism approaches social reality as that which is subjectively and intersubjectively known or assumed by a given person or culture. Subjective intentions and intersubjective norms guide behavior. The paradigms of Gestalt Pychology, Sociology and Anthropology and of Postmodern Critical Interpretivism in Table 1 exemplify interpretivism.

What new paradigms may emerge in the 21st-century? Beyond the "language-turn" of Postmodern Interpretivism lies the "action turn" in social science (Reason and Torbert, 2001), still not generally recognized to this day, but exemplified by the paradigms of Action Science Praxis, Co-operative Ecological Inquiry, and Collaborative Developmental Action Inquiry. Beyond the action turn, social science includes both naturalism and interpretivism, but now studies the action, as well as the inquiry, of the social scientists themselves, with a normative aim of creating real-time communities of inquiry within existing institutions and friendship circles.

Habermas (1981, 1984) distinguishes among three 'knowledge interests' — a technological interest served by empirical/analytic social science (Rosenberg's naturalism); a practical interest in mutual and self understanding served by hermeneutic social science (Rosenberg's interpretivism); and an emancipatory interest aimed at overcoming dogma, compulsion, and domination and served by Torbert's three latest, after-the-action-turn paradigms. Habermas' tripartite distinction corresponds best from within the philosophy of science to the developmental meta-paradigm of social scientific paradigms presented here.

To gesture in the direction of the wide inclusiveness of types of data sought in Collaborative Developmental Action Inquiry

(CDAI) — Torbert uses four dimensions – **voice**, **practice**, **feedback**, and **time** – each of which can vary in three ways. Together, these four dimensions can construct a 3x3x3x3 figure of 81 different types of action inquiry methodologies. In short, the research **voice**(s) may be *1st-, 2nd-, or 3rd-person*. The focus of the research may be *1st-, 2nd-, and/or 3rd-person* **practice**. The study may generate *single-, double-, and/or triple-loop* **feedback**. And the data may come from the *past*, the *present*, and/or the *future*, which are understood as three different dimensions of **time**, as described earlier in this appendix (see Ramos, 2017, for a review of other approaches to futures research).

To get a very approximate first taste of the relative breadth of CDAI methods, it can be helpful to indicate how few of the 81 methods Empirically Positivistic (EP) scientific method uses. Empirical Positivism is a form of science that strives always to achieve a truly neutral, generalizable **third-person voice** (the first – and second-person pronouns and voices are rigorously abjured [except when properly framed and introduced as additional data]). In addition, Empirical Positivist methods are almost exclusively used to study **third-person practices** and social processes in which the researcher is not a direct participant (rarely, one hears of an Empirical Positivist who does [some of] their research on themselves). EP also researches **events that occurred in the past**. The events may already have occurred in the past when the data is collected, but they are definitely in the past once the data has been analyzed, validity-tested through statistical and peer review procedures, and publicly reported. Finally, hypothesis-testing in Empirical Positivism results in **single-loop feedback**: the results either support or disconfirm a hypothesis.

So, EP generally studies just one of the 81 domains of human inquiry – using 3rd-person voice to study 3rd-person practice in the past, seeking single-loop feedback. EP can be used to study 2nd – or 1st-person practice as well, but it virtually never studies the practices of the researchers conducting the research. Thus, at best, EP studies parts of three of the 81 domains – those of 1st-, 2nd-, and 3rd-person practice (in 3rd-person voice, in the past, with single-loop feedback).

Considering the very small proportion of the potential domains of social inquiry that EP engages in (at most 1/27th or just under 4%), it hardly seems surprising that its studies rarely account for more than 5-20% of the variance in the variables studied (and even less, on average, if one takes into account all those unpublished studies that show no significant results).

Of course, the kinds of data and feedback that the different CDAI methods generate are not all of the same quality and cannot all be quantified. Nevertheless, they all may achieve some form of validity (or not). For example, Torbert's first-person, future, dream of how to paint his Channing Place room achieved a kind of motivational and practical validity when he actually did (his best to) paint it that way. Likewise, when four members of a six member team give the assistant director feedback that he seems incapable of disagreeing with the director, it will likely do his future credibility on the team good if he does some exploring and experimenting vis a vis his relationship with the director, rather than treating the feedback as insignificant because based on the small n of 4. As the 10-organization study in Appendix E shows, greater frequencies and degrees of first- and second-person forms of feedback seem to add up to the greater likelihood of quantitatively-confirmed, third-person organizational transformations. A great deal more work lies ahead to illustrate and more rigorously define the many CDAI methods. The following section merely begins that work by pointing to specific instances in these memoirs when some nineteen distinct CDAI methods are illustrated. The reader is invited to consider to what degree the interweaving of the research methods enhances the validity and meaningfulness of the story.

These Memoirs as Example of Collaborative Developmental Action Inquiry

These memoirs consist primarily of qualitative stories that gain their credibility as representationally valid and as analogically meaningful from their intrinsic richness, from their gradual accumulation and mutual intertwining, from their influence on readers' future actions, and from their apparent sequencing in a way generally congruent with the theories of individual and organizational development outlined in the Endnotes. In addition, Chapter 21 and Appendix E offer examples of quantitative studies based on reliability-tested measures of development (the Global Leadership Profile in particular) that show how CDAI can "beat Empirical Positivism at its own game" of attempting to confirm (or disconfirm) hypotheses by accounting for large percentages of the variance beyond the .01 level of likelihood of error.

The following paragraphs point to nineteen types of action inquiry illustrated in this memoir.

Voice. This book represents, as a whole, primarily Torbert's *1st-person, subjective voice* on his *1st-person practice* in the *past*. The fact that he tells rather detailed stories of his own practice is itself one qualitative validity check on his overall perspective. More importantly, the different types of data that the book also includes each contributes, additively or critically, to the overall validity of the theories presented.

When Torbert quotes from diaries and letters he wrote at the time of the events, we hear his *1st-person, subjective voice* on his *1st-person practice* in the *present* (at that time). Such data lend credibility because they bypass the potential distortions of memory.

Torbert is writing about the *Future*, the *Volume of All Possibilities*, in his *1st-person voice*, when he tells us of his dreams about painting his room at the Channing Place commune; about how the name N-n appeared to him and how he subsequently used it in his first-person action inquiry; about how to lead the Tol Business School meeting to choose the *Stirring Occasions* business to start together; or about a novel societal future in the last Tol *Mass-Age Mess-Age* Public Performance. The fact that he went on to enact most of these dreams is one testament to their having actually occurred.

On a number of occasions, we have *2nd-person, intersubjective voices* on Torbert's *1st-person practice* in the *present* (at that time). Examples include his brother's early story about him in Madrid; the Harvard teaching fellow's story (Sufi Jester) about how Torbert confronted him when he misled his section; his spiritual teacher's letter to him at the outset of The Theatre of Inquiry; the participants' assessments of The Theatre of Inquiry found in the Endnote to Chapter 20; and the reflections of Torbert's masseuse in the Endnote of Chapter 21.

On still other occasions, we have an element of *3rd-person, objective voice* on Torbert's *2nd-person practice*. For example, the Upward Bound staff meeting that was tape recorded, transcribed, and fed back to the staff and advisers, via Torbert's 'minutes' of the meeting. Also, in the Introduction, in the Endnotes to the text, and here in Appendix A, action inquiry community members take on the 3rd-person voice to present Torbert's theories and how they relate to particular experiences in his own life.

Practice. Similarly, although Torbert's primary focus in this book is on his own *1st-person practices*, the prior chapters quite often describe his and others' *2nd-person practice* in meetings (e.g. with the Somali tribe; with his family discussing the Vietnam War; with the ASI staff at SMU; and at the Theatre of Inquiry Action Workshop).

His references to *3rd-person research on 3rd-person practice* (such as the national study of married couples in which he and his first wife participated; such as the outcome data on Upward Bound students' improvement in grades and decline in dropout rates; and such as the reports with quantitative data about how students responded to the large ASI course at SMU) are briefer and rarer, except in the very last chapter about his later research at Boston College. Obviously, though, it is the third-person action inquiry outcomes that will influence social scientists to pay attention to the significance of first – and second-person action inquiry that generates the third-person results.

Single-, Double-, and Triple-loop Feedback. In addition to three types of voice and three types of practice, this book and the CDAI paradigm can also be said to consist of three different types of stories about feedback and learning – stories of adventures toward goals reached through *single-loop feedback and incremental learning*; stories of adventures that lead to *double-loop feedback and* *transformational learning*; and stories about *triple-loop feedback and openings into trans-cognitive consciousness*. For example, the story about how, when Torbert moved from SMU to Harvard, a group of six acquired 6 Channing Place as a communal home is basically a story of *single-loop feedback and learning*. They achieved their goal of finding a place to live and people to live with, but none of them were transformed in any basic way in the process.

In contrast, some stories can be interpreted as stories of *double-loop feedback and transformation*: 1) when Torbert realized there had been a unilateral quality to his attempt as a Yale undergraduate to bring Argyris to Elihu; 2) the story about his fight with Chris Argyris in regard to the "Learning to Trust" paper; and 3) the story about his struggle with his friend Morris over the latter's near-death-Bloody-Mary. Another example of *double-loop learning and transformation* occurring successfully is the one when Lee Longstaff heard Chuang-Tsu's story about the chef and the ever-sharp knife and reclaimed her ability to drive first her car and then her career. Also, the story about "standing philosophy on its head" at a Harvard colloquium can be interpreted as a case of Torbert offering *double-loop feedback,* but not succeeding in catalyzing any *transformational learning* among the academic philosophers at the colloquium (or himself).

That someone has experienced double-loop, transformational learning is hard to prove in third-person empirical terms because it happens relatively rarely, because it often occurs over long periods of time, and because there are few well-regarded psychometric measures of double-loop change. That is why the Global Leadership Profile — which Torbert improved over forty years, starting with Jane Loevinger's Washington University Sentence Completion Test and modifying it with the support of Susanne Cook-Greuter and Elaine Herdman-Barker — is so important... because it is such a measure of transformational change on an individual scale.

Triple-loop feedback and openings to transcognitive consciousness are even more difficult to illustrate and to prove empirically than *double-loop, transformational feedback*. These 'consciousness-events' are often only momentary and very interiorized, though they may repeatedly 'ring' at unexpected moments in one's life thereafter. Possible examples from Torbert's time at Harvard, from his time circling back and forth from Boston to San Francisco and Mendocino, and from the birth of the twins and The Theatre of Inquiry include:

- His LSD trip at the Wolfgangsee when the I Ching named him as The Wanderer for the second of four times ... and when he had a dream about how to paint his room at Channing Place (and later made the dream come true);
- Becoming aware of himself in the airplane as he wrote in the Black Journal for the first time ("My vision does not yet put everything in question");
- The night at the goat ranch when his brother disappeared into the dark outside his kitchen, and Torbert stumbled into him and his wife hugging one another and weeping ... and joined them;
- His glowing and melting heart under the loving assault of his spiritual teacher at a Gurdjieffian Week of Work;
- His stuttering state of witnessed incongruity in conversation with Mrs. Dooling at her home;
- The 'miraculous' timing of his commitment at Thanksgiving, 1976, to Lee; and her declaration of her pregnancy to him;
- The quality of consciousness which The Theatre of Inquiry song "You are an actor" attempts to evoke;
- The paradoxical action/inquiry quality of consciousness he attempted to foster at the Action Inquiry Workshop when he stated, "If **I** give **you** your money's worth, I will not be giving you The Theatre of Inquiry."

Despite the difficulty in authenticating particular examples of triple-loop learning with empirical certainty, wouldn't you prefer to work and play within a paradigm of social science that included the possibility of, and the search for such experiences rather than a kind of science, like Empirical Positivism, that admits as knowledge only those phenomena about which we can be certain? Readers can pursue this question in Appendix C.

Studying the Past, the Present, and the Future. Finally, although this book is primarily about Torbert's *past* life, from 1944 to 1978, it also concerns and illustrates types of action inquiry that generate *presence in the present* and/ or contact with *the volume of future possibilities*. Quite a few of the stories, especially in the second half of the memoir, are about attempts to interweave inquiry and action (or deliberate pauses and inaction) in the *present* – about how to become more *present* in the *present* and tell a *present* truth.

Fewer stories concern the more mysterious idea and practice of research on *the volume of future possibilities*. The first explicit example of this occurred when Torbert consulted the ***I Ching*** about whether to divorce his first wife. A second occurred when he learned at SMU about the undermining of the student evaluation procedure and first became more fully present and then began to reconstruct the course design for the final weeks. A third occurred when the four friends naked on a bed at Princeton decided not to make love together.

The story told about his planning for the Theatre of Inquiry Business/School meeting – when he exercised a for-him extraordinary effort of attention in the hope of helping the group invent/discover/generate their new business – is perhaps the most detailed example of such theoretically and intuitively guided future visioning. Finally, the Theatre of Inquiry Public Performance about the future is an attempt to envision a possible future for global society, which will depend for its (approximate) realization on extraordinary efforts of conscious inquiry, love, and just action, as well as inner struggle and voluntary suffering by millions of people.

■ ■ ■

In that possible future, increasing numbers of us will strive to enact inquiry-in-action in a self-chosen, leisurely way, at work and at home, with friends and with strangers. We will directly address the perennial issue of constructing true intimacy and mutuality among beloveds. And we will all have to be born again at least once or twice after our 21st birthday, if we are to find the capacity for collaborative action that generates true intimacy through mutual self-disclosure, challenge, and support.

This theme of mutuality and mutually-transforming power will be equally relevant to the global issues we face:

- deconstructing sexual violence and constructing full mutuality in post-binary gender relations;
- dismantling the war culture prevalent amidst humankind til now;
- achieving mutuality with our planet before climate change and Covid-19-like pandemics kill increasing proportions of us;
- rehabilitating ourselves by attention-widening action inquiry from the global addiction to the manipulative, unilateral, attention-narrowing social media, cell phones, drugs, and alcohol that retard our human development beyond the earliest action-logics; and
- learning for ourselves and teaching our artificially intelligent machines to act with mutual power before they (the AI machines) incorporate us within their diminished reality and we lose our souls.

The AI we've practiced so far (Artificial Intelligence) will kill us in the name of setting us free, unless we properly subordinate it to our practice of AI of the Action Inquiry variety.

To learn mutuality will require many more of us globally to take on the challenge of transforming toward later action-logics beyond Achiever. Only thus do we come to act with increasing integrity, increasing mutuality, increasing economic and social egalitarianism, and increasing environmental sustainability.

The time for each of us to begin entering the inclusive present more fully and creating this developmental search into the future for ourselves and with others is never not now. Good wishes...

Appendix B

Excerpts from *Humanitas* article, "On the possibility of revolution within the boundaries of propriety" [12(1), 111-146, 1976].

Ordinarily we think of originality and conformity as "deadly enemies" of one another. We assume that to be original requires non-conformity, and that in conforming one forswears originality. Then we take sides, some bemoaning the prevalence of conformity and the rarity of originality, others defending conformity as the necessary glue of social cohesion and arguing that originality has no special intrinsic merit. This essay, by contrast, will search to see whether originality and conformity may not, actually, inform one another—indeed require one another—whether, that is, "revolution within the boundaries of propriety" may be less ridiculous than it initially sounds and turn out instead, upon examination, to be the only genuinely revolutionary movement and the only truly conservative form...

(this was the first paragraph of the article; we next skip ten pages)

...Let us try to imagine further what the world would look like if we reversed the metaphor of originality and conformity and took the attitude that originality is the central social phenomenon and conformity more peripheral.

One aspect of this new point of view that immediately seems appropriate is the notion of conformity as peripheral. After all, the form to which behaviors conform is a boundary—is the periphery— within which behavior is free to vary without violating uniformity. But this suggests a surprising perspective on originality: if originality is central, is it to be found *within* the boundaries of propriety rather than outside the boundaries? Wittgenstein seems to suggest as much when he draws our attention to the fact that no game is "everywhere circumscribed by rules." For example, he says, there are no rules for how high one throws the ball in tennis when serving.

Since I am attempting to conform to the metaphor of center and periphery in this article, I would change Wittgenstein's observation to: "no game is everywhere *inscribed* with rules." Does not the whole interest and excitement in games lie in the possibility of doing something original *within* the rules? Is it not precisely the combination of absolute originality and absolute conformity that makes Willie Mays' over-the-shoulder catch in the 1951 World Series, or Shakespeare's sonnets, so memorable?

From this point of view, the greater the skill of the game-player in conforming to the rules of the game, the greater the leeway he or she has to act originally. For under such conditions the player need not be distracted by the rules and will not have his or her efforts suddenly entangled in and frustrated by the rules ... (pp120-121)

... The recent history of philosophy can serve as an example of revolution from within and of the subtlety of what "within" means. Looking back now over the past century and a half, we can see a number of revolts within philosophy against Hegel's thought. We might name Marx, Kierkegaard, Nietzsche, Wittgenstein, Husserl, and Heidegger as the foremost proponents of a return from abstract generalizations to the material, to the personal, to the sensuous, to the particular, to the actual working of intuitive consciousness, to an existential openness to mystery. Or we might name these men as proponents of philosophy as a lifetime task for each human being rather than as an academic task for certain professionals. Their own philosophical positions, which they argued against Hegel in their writings and which in turn now form part of our philosophical tradition, led the first four of these men to choose lives different from that of the conventional academic, so that in their own time they appeared as non-confomists in various ways. Was theirs a revolution from within or from without?

A closer examination of Wittgenstein's life and work can aid us here, not so much to clarify the confusion as to encourage us in it – perhaps we might say, to clarify the necessity for, and the revolutionary potential of, the confusion. Wittgenstein's most famous work (*Tractatus Logico Philosophicus*) was written as his doctoral thesis under Bertrand Russell at Oxford, with an introduction by Russell when it was published. Wittgenstein's argument (if it is fair to summarize his aphoristic style as argument) was that the nature of language is such that clear and meaningful propositions can be framed only about empirical matters, not about the metaphysical and ethical issues with which philosophers through the ages (including Marx, Kierkegaard, and Nietzsche) had grappled. His attack against Hegelian metaphysical generalizations could, thus, be said to be more radical even than the attacks of Marx, Kierkegaard, and Nietzsche. Rather than arguing against the generalizations directly (and thereby to a certain degree validating them), Wittgenstein denied them the very ground in which they flourished— language itself—the medium which previous philosophical speculation had taken for granted.

His work, obviously produced "within" the established conventions of education and publication in philosophy, was quickly greeted as revolutionarily original and led to the founding of a new school of philosophy—logical positivism. Wittgenstein himself, however, regarded his own conclusions as both finishing and leading away from the professional practice of philosophy, so he became an elementary school teacher and an architect. Moreover, he regarded Russell's introduction to, and the logical positivists' appropriation of, his work as involving serious misunderstandings and misrepresentations. Whereas they interpreted him as holding that ethical and aesthetic issues were not worthy of discussion because not possible to discuss rationally, because not reducible to unambiguous propositions, he in fact regarded such issues as the ones *most* worthy of solitary and mutual contemplation for those very reasons. He would not meet with his purported followers and, on the one occasion when he was prevailed upon, insisted on reading Tagore's poetry to them.

Gradually, Wittgenstein became famous despite himself for a position he did not hold. In the meantime, his thought was itself undergoing a revolution from within. Thirty years later he had returned to writing and teaching philosophy, producing a new book *(Philosophical Investigations)* with very different arguments from his first book. Although he still concentrated on the medium of language itself, his later thought was as though permeated by a continuous consciousness that he himself was using language in a very particular and original way as he wrote, in order to obtain certain effects. That is, he experienced and attempted to exemplify how language is not merely a passive, representative medium but rather an active, performative medium that takes part in and gains meaning from the particular contexts in which it is used. The aphoristic style was even more pronounced and less sequential, congruent with his insistence that he was not arguing a simple, general point. In this way, he carried his critique of generalization still further, against his own previous view that it was possible to make valid generalizations about empirical scientific matters.

Now he saw that scientific work was itself one particular context within which given words could mean different things than they might in other contexts. Because the same words are used differently (not just in the sense of representing different things but also in the sense of affecting the action differently) in different contexts, there can be no valid, general definitions of them. Indeed, the danger of empirical social science, as of metaphysics before it, is that it claims to discover generally valid truths and thus distracts individuals from awareness of, appreciation of, and responsibility for the actual judgments they make about and the actual effects they have on the social contexts in which they participate whenever they speak (or remain silent)...

Wittgenstein now described the contexts within which one speaks or writes as language-games within which specific words and sentences gained their meaning, as "moves" do in a game, by their relation to the "rules" of the "game." The metaphor of "moves" and "rules" is useful because it reminds one of the active, judgmental qualities of language—the way in which language creates reality as well as represents it —but this metaphor has shortcomings as well. One shortcoming is that it may mislead us into thinking of social contexts as operating according to shared, explicit, unambiguous rules, which would make it fairly easy for us to distinguish conformity from non-conformity. But social life is far more ambiguous than pre-defined games. Laws are shared and explicit, though hardly unambiguous, as judicial systems testify. Norms are assumed to be shared, although how generally is in question if they are implicit rather than explicit. Since norms are usually implicit, they are also likely to be ambiguous. Thus, unlike the moves in a game, social actions do not necessarily have clearly defined meanings even within specific contexts.... Indeed, Wittgenstein shows that the most general concepts, such as those we might choose to distinguish among contexts, are those least susceptible to a single, unambiguous definition. For example, he demonstrates that we cannot give a single, unambiguous definition to the word "game," covering all the different kinds of games we play...

Here, then, lies immense potential for revolution from within toward a more just society. The "System" is not so all-embracing and all-controlling as it appears. Creative action can often make ambiguities and alternatives evident and develop new and more just rules *without even needing to oppose existing boundaries.* Opposition to existing boundaries, when it *is* useful, can be carried on in the attractive spirit of clarifying alternatives rather than in the repulsive spirit of unilaterally destroying the existing "way." But conventional thinking cannot appreciate the vast potential for revolution from within because it "sees" only boundaries. Hence, the appearance of the "System" as all-embracing and all-controlling.

Revolution from within does not depend on apparent ambiguities of situations, but rather on the inevitability that the situation contains implications to which any given explicit definition, however clear, does not do full justice. Thus, even when the context seems clear and the norms firmly established, perspicacious action can change the whole definition of the situation.

A prisoner-of-war or concentration camp is certainly one of the most extreme examples of an institution in which those in power bend every effort to completely pre-structure the situation, both definitionally and physically, so as to make it impossible for a revolution from within to occur. Yet even here there is enough freedom within the boundaries of propriety for the prisoners to invent alternative realities. These alternative realities may consist of ethical structures developed by individuals, such as those practiced by Bettelheim, Bonhoeffer, Frankl, and Ettie van Helsing in Nazi concentration camps, which give different weights and meanings to events than the captors intend. Or they may consist of plans and activities developed in secret among a number of prisoners which lead to actual escape from the camp.

The prisoner-of-war setting emphasizes the risk, excitement, and esprit-de-corps that accompanies the sense of developing a shared, initially hidden, new definition of reality and deciding upon the appropriate timing for explicating it. Such risk and excitement always accompanies the search for more appropriate definitions of reality because there is always initially an element of hiddenness about the search, even if it is hidden only within the intimacy of a family's living room, and there is always an issue about the appropriate timing for sharing new realities more widely. (The widespread penchant for leading or at least reading about double lives—whether in terms of business crime, marital infidelity, or international espionage— may be a diminished and distorted reflection of an aspiration to participate in hidden conceptions, in nurturing the implicit, and in communicating back and forth between implication and explication.)

As a more personal and microscopic example of redefining an apparently pre-defined and coercive situation, I offer the story of a woman friend describing how she was held up at gun point in a deserted New York church by a thin, strung-out man who snatched her purse and ran. The purse held all the money she had. A person who believed passively that "power comes from the barrel of a gun" would have assumed the event was completed and thanked her stars that she had not been hurt, or rushed to the police. But this woman immediately called out in a commanding tone, "Just a minute! Are you a junkie?" As he hesitated and said "Yes," apparently still in control of the situation since he now held both gun and purse, she continued with genuine sympathy but lying, "I was a junkie too, and I guess it was pure luck that they got me to a hospital and I was able to get off it before it killed me." By this time, she was his confrere and in temporary emotional control as well. He was rooted to his spot, trembling. She continued without a pause, acknowledging his control of the situation but in fact controlling him: "Look, take the money, but leave me the purse because it's a complete pain to replace all the cards. And would you leave me a couple of dollars carfare? You should really get yourself to a hospital right away. Don't wait till tomorrow: do it right now while you're being reasonable. Here, give me the purse and I'll give you the money." He handed her the purse; she handed him some of the money; and she wondered afterwards whether she might not have saved it all and gotten him to a hospital as well if she had been a bit more self-confident and thus risked even more inventiveness.

We can note that the woman's concern was for the whole situation, for the junkie as well as for herself, that her redefinition of the situation derived from an appreciation of his inner reality, and that it was, potentially, to the benefit of both parties. Although her initiative was behaviorally as unilateral as the junkie's, its structure (mutual concern) and its effect (sharing the money) were less exploitative and thereby opened toward the possibility of shared control of the definition of the situation.

Another notable aspect of this situation is the risk the woman took. All attempts to explicate the implicit involve the risk of incongruity and failure, but the danger becomes most palpable when the initial definition of the situation is unilateral and exploitative. For her initiative to succeed, her tone, her demeanor, and her timing—all had to be impeccably precise and integrated. She had to be at once perfectly controlled and perfectly sincere, utterly self-possessed in her purpose and at the same time fully attuned to the implications of each tone and gesture of the man. We can note that the woman's risks were subtle, experimental, and progressive. That is, the junkie could simply not have heeded her initial call without much additional danger to her. The fact that he stopped indicated a certain ambiguity in his sense of purpose, which made the second comment worth risking. Then the fact that he "stood for" her second comment suggested an even stronger susceptibility to her influence, which made her reaching for her purse far less risky than it would originally have been.

Unlike original contributions in philosophy, science, or the arts which can germinate in privacy and favorable circumstances, which can undergo many revisions before they are made public, which need not be immediately accepted once they are made public in order ultimately to succeed, and which do not require originality and precision of the originators in their everyday behavior: original social action requires instantaneous communication between the implicit and the explicit in unfavorable as well as favorable circumstances, experimentation and revision *in vivo,* and a fluidity of behavior based on an integration of the intuitive, the conventional, and the somatic that makes for "perfect" timing. Thus, original social action in politics or everyday life is a far more demanding art than any particular discipline or profession.

But, if Wittgenstein is right, all disciplines and professions are merely particular contexts for the practice of particular types of original social action. Writing philosophy in solitude is itself a certain form of social action. Perhaps Wittgenstein's own early and unintended social influence, through (mis)interpretations of the *Tractatus,* impressed this truth upon him more strongly than on most philosophers.

The course of Wittgenstein's life exemplifies the personal changes of direction that gradual existential clarification and restructuring involves, while the content of his later thought battles against false clarity in order to clarify the scale of the unknown and, thereby, the scale of our potential freedom of action and originality (132-139).

Appendix C:

Review of *A Guide for the Perplexed* By E. F. Schumacher in ***Parabola***, Vol II, No. 4, 1977, p.104-107

All people throughout history have shared certain dilemmas. One such dilemma permeates everyone's life at every moment. Yet this dilemma is rarely felt directly, even by geniuses. Even more rarely does someone *address* this dilemma directly, thereby cultivating ongoing awareness of it.

The dilemma is simply that our knowledge of what is occurring at any given moment in our lives, conditioned as it is by cultural habits of attention and modes of thought, *must* be inadequate to what is actually occurring. The inadequacy of our knowledge has two faces, one empirical, one significational. We are, on the one hand, simply not aware of much that is occurring: we are rarely aware of what is occurring in our bodies, for example, even our breathing which is perfectly accessible if we turn our attention toward it. We are, on the other hand, not aware of the significance of what is occurring: we may assign an event a certain significance as it occurs, only to realize later that it takes a very different place in the overall pattern of our activities.

When we recognize the inadequacy of our knowledge in a given instance, we generally either excuse it and forget it or try to repair it. Much less known is the movement whereby we actively enter into, feel and address this inadequacy.

Felt directly, the dilemma of necessarily inadequate knowledge would, at each moment, throw our knowledge of a given situation into relief against the vast and obscure background of our ignorance, teaching us a deeper humility. Addressed directly, this dilemma would inspire a new kind of initiative, a new kind of reaching out toward all that is somehow Other, a new kind of awareness.

A deep and abiding irony attends the process of becoming aware of the necessary inadequacy of our knowledge. Initially, it seems reasonable to presume that some kinds of knowledge could help us to become aware and remain aware of this inadequacy. Indeed, one can even imagine a knowledgeable argument demonstrating that knowledge-tinged-by-awareness-of-its-own-inadequacy is qualitatively more adequate to our true state than knowledge-which-claims-adequacy.

Here is where Schumacher's new book enters the picture. With quick, deft strokes he outlines the argument that the modern scientific worldview is inadequate as a map of reality precisely because it will admit as knowledge only that about which we can be certain. Although such scientific knowledge deserves a *place* on an adequate map of reality, to make it the *whole* map "maximizes the risk of missing out on what may be the subtlest, most important, and most rewarding things in life."

Schumacher reminds us at the outset that a map does not solve problems or explain mysteries, but rather helps to identify them. Then he sets out to provide a more adequate map of (1) the world, (2) humankind, (3) how humankind learns about the world, and (4) what it means to live in this world. First, he returns to traditional wisdom to assert that the world consists of four qualitatively different "levels of being" – mineral, plant, animal and human. Only the mineral level is fully externalized, fully visible, and thus fully knowable by modern science. Each of the other three levels include progressively more internalized, invisible qualities as well as their external appearances, and these invisible qualities are not fully accessible to scientific observation through our five senses. Humanity must develop the illumination implicit in our potential for self-awareness if we are to know these higher qualities, for the "instrument" of knowledge must mirror the complexity of the quality to be known if that quality is to be known adequately. One who is not self-aware cannot "see" self-awareness.

From these initial considerations about the world and humanity, Schumacher derives four qualitatively different fields of knowledge which respond to the questions: (1) What is really going on in my own inner world? (2) What is going on in the inner world of other beings? (3) What do I look like in the eyes of other beings? (4) What do I actually observe in the world around me? Again, he argues that modern science is an adequate instrument for knowing only the fourth kind of question. Moreover, he goes on to distinguish between the *convergent* problems in life, which can in principle be fully known and solved in a hypothetico-deductive-technological sense, and the *divergent* problems, such as education and politics, where opposite solutions, freedom v. discipline, individuality v. equality, seem to vie with one another circularly and eternally "*unless something intervenes from a higher level*" (emphasis in the original). These divergent problems "are refractory to mere logic and discursive reason and constitute, so to speak, a strain-and-stretch apparatus to develop the Whole Man."

The foregoing summary fails to convey the force, the clarity and the elegance of Schumacher's presentation. But it does outline a structure of knowledge which, instead of proclaiming primarily its own final adequacy, intends to remind us of the possibility and importance of developing toward higher levels of being and self-awareness, if our knowledge is even to approach the complexity of what is actually occurring.

The irony is that the very accessibility, attractiveness and adequacy of Schumacher's line of thought may substitute itself for, and divert us from, the work toward self-awareness to which he intends to call us. One can easily imagine that the many people already inspired by his earlier writings will make of this book a kind of Bible. By contrast, Maimonedes' book of the same title, which Schumacher nowhere acknowledges, is much less accessible on first reading. To interpret Maimonedes seems to require the exercise of the very qualities of attention and self-awareness of which Schumacher merely speaks.

The writings that Schumacher cites most often when he seeks to give the reader an impression of what he means by self-awareness are Maurice Nicoll's *Psychological Commentaries on the Teaching of G. I. Gurdjieff and P. D. Ouspensky*. Nicoll's many-volumed and eminently understandable fragments are based on his long association with Ouspensky who was his teacher. Ouspensky, in turn, wrote a much more systematic book subtitled *Fragments of an Unknown Teaching* based on his years as a student with Gurdjieff. So cosmos-encompassing is the theory presented in Ouspensky's book that when this reader first encountered it he repeatedly felt the inadequacy of his knowledge by contrast. Gurdjieff also wrote a book, a remarkably *inaccessible* book entitled *All and Everything: Beelzebub's Tales to His Grandson*, which altogether defies the casual reader and the dogged reader alike and seems to require an interest qualitatively different from that which we ordinarily bring to reading.

It is likely that many more people will read Schumacher's book than either Nicoll's or Ouspensky's. And many more people will read Nicoll's or Ouspensky's books than Gurdjieff's.

Questions remain. What kind of writing would guide us toward a direct feeling of the inadequacy of our knowledge and toward a new kind of awareness? Do contemporary interpreters of ancient traditions really do us a service when they make their formulations accessible to ordinary thought?

Appendix D:

Description of First- and Second-Person Action Inquiry by a Consultant to a Small Computer Software Company

A small software company has burned through its initial round of venture financing, with net revenues for its products not yet foreseeable on the horizon. The partners are seeking a second round of venture capital, and everybody at the company knows they must achieve a breakthrough in marketing and sales. Yet, this "bottom-line" negative feedback alone, as stark as it is, is not propelling the company into a new operating pattern.

An organizational consultant who takes a **CDAI** approach is invited to help the company over a two-day period. He approaches the assignment with the sense that he must discover what disharmonies among the corporate dream, the leadership's strategies, and the day-to-day operations account for the company's continuing losses. But more than this, he must discover a positive way to reframe or restructure the situation with the leadership and company members, so that they become motivated to correct those disharmonies.

The consultant interviews the top management (the president and the three vice presidents for production, marketing, and sales) of the computer software company, which numbers 35 employees in all. The president is a generation older than the three vice presidents, and the company is a partnership between the president and one of the vice presidents. Together, the two of them developed the initial product.

In the following three years, the company has produced a large number of high-quality products, but they are not selling well. The consultant discovers numerous problems that have remained unresolved for a long time. Neither mission nor market is well defined. Pricing is a subject of acrimonious controversy. Employee morale is fragile because it is unclear whether competence or cronyism is the basis for rewards. Decisions are not driven by any internal sense of mission; they are made only when situations deteriorate into external emergencies.

The bottleneck in decision making appears to be the relationship between the two partners. They respect one another and attempt to share responsibility as though equals. But they repeatedly fall prey to differences in age, formal role, and managerial style. The president plays the role of optimistic, benign, absent-minded father. The vice president plays the role of pessimistic, sharp, rebellious son.

Having interviewed the senior managers individually during the first six hours of his two-day visit, the consultant is next slated to meet with the two partners to set the agenda for the next day's senior management retreat. But based on what he has heard, the consultant fears that the agenda-setting session may itself fall prey to the partners' well-intentioned wrangling.

In his 10-minute walk around the outside of the building prior to the session, the consultant engages in a first-person research/practice of intentionally bringing his attention first to his breathing and then, following that, to the vividness of the outside world, then to his feelings, and, only when he has established an ongoing circulation of attention, to what he now knows about the company. First, he becomes clear that the partners' pattern of behavior must change before any other productive decisions are likely. Next, he applies developmental theory to the individual partners, to his two-day intervention itself, and to the company as a whole, to help him generate design ideas for his meeting with the partners ... only moments away.

Applying the developmental theory to each of the partners as individuals, the consultant estimates that the vice president is in transition from **Expert** to **Achiever**, both itching for and resisting the true executive responsibility that a person at the **Achiever** action-logic relishes. The consultant estimates that the president is in transition from **Achiever** to **Redefining**, ready to give up day-to-day executive responsibility in favor of an elder statesman role of mentoring his junior partner and godfathering the company's research and development function (indeed, the president has spoken wistfully of his preference for the VP R&D position).

Applying the developmental theory to the company as a whole, the consultant sees the organization as spread-eagled across the fluid, decentralized **Investments** and **Experiments** action-logics, still living off venture capital on the one hand, while on the other hand experimenting with a whole line of products. At the same time, the company is failing to "bite the bullet" and meet the limiting, centralizing, differentiating demands of the **Incorporation** action-logic – the demand, in short, for net revenues.

Applying the developmental theory to his own two-day visit, the consultant interprets the initial interviews as the **Conception** action-logic of the intervention. In this light, the agenda-setting session with the two partners may represent **Investments** – in particular, how much investment each of the three leaders in this meeting is willing to make in truly experimenting with new ways of working together. If so, the question is how open is the consultant himself to restructure his consulting style at this point from a more passive, receptive interviewing process to a more active, intervening process that highlights both the consultant's own investment in the process and the new investment the partners must be willing to make in decisiveness, if they are to achieve the major changes necessary in the organization as a whole. Looking ahead to the following day, the consultant also feels that binding decisions need to be made there and then in the spirit of the **Incorporation** action-logic, which the company has been shying away from. The consultant must help the two partners, the company as a whole, and the senior managers to act conclusively in the next day.

In this **Incorporation** action-logic spirit, the consultant first decides to recommend at the upcoming agenda-setting session that only the partners and the consultant participate in the next day's retreat and that whatever decisions the partners reach the next day be put in writing with definite implementation dates. As for the agenda-setting session itself, the consultant's reasoning leads him to ask how he can reframe the partners' expectations and pattern of behavior from the very outset of the agenda-setting session. In their initial interviews earlier in the day, both partners have used the image of ballots to describe their relative power within the company. The president, referring to their equal salaries and to his style of consulting his partner on all significant decisions, speaks of the partners as holding "ballots of the same size" in company decisions. The vice president, however, spoke of the president as having the larger vote. The consultant now reasons that if the two switch their formal roles, at least for this one day, the (erstwhile) president should still see their votes as equal, while the (erstwhile) vice president should see his vote as having become larger. Thus, the twosome should be more powerful, especially since the junior partner will now be in a proposing role rather than an opposing role. Moreover, the new roles should be more appropriate to each partner in terms of helping each to move to a wider action-logic. More immediately, the mere fact of having the two officers reverse roles for the agenda-setting meeting and the day-long retreat should alter their usual dynamics and put them into the serious-role-playing posture of simultaneous rehearsal and performance conducive to action inquiry. (All these images occur in much less time than it takes to read about them in this paragraph.)

Of course, the consultant himself will be in a similar posture as he makes this unexpected suggestion (and of course the partners won't necessarily agree!). He arrives two or three minutes early, viewing himself as the host of this meeting, just as the partners are his hosts at the company. It can be a meeting of three peers. He arranges the three chairs in a triangle, without a table between them, and sits, facing the door through which the partners will enter. Leaning forward in a relaxed position, with his hands on his thighs, he exhales thoroughly, then draws in his hara three or four times before his next longer and deeper and quieter inhaling, followed by an equally long exhale, and now perhaps 7 or 8 clenchings-in-of-his-hara, and a third turn. His challenge in this meeting, he realizes, is to "bite through" and invite the partners to *collaboratively* "bite through" the norms that paralyze their action-taking capacities.

The consultant begins his feedback/agenda-setting session with the two partners by proposing that the vice president either resign or become president. This puts the vice-president in the action role right away, rather than his usual role of reacting to the president. Although quiet, the president seems to smile slightly, ready to play whatever this game may be. On the other hand, true to his customary "opposing" role, the vice president objects to "rehearsing" as president. "It's fake." "Oh, you don't believe you could be or ought to be president?" asks the consultant. After considerable further probing by the vice president, the two senior officers agree to play this serious game.

Now the vice president (in the role of the president) acts decisively rather than reacting combatively. He and the consultant propose various changes, with the president (in the subordinate role) making constructive suggestions and raising questions. The two partners reach written agreement on six major organizational changes the next day. The first of these is implemented at lunch that day. The vice president for sales is invited to join them. The partners discuss the major changes they are considering, and ask him to accept a demotion. He agrees, expressing both his disappointment that he has let the company down and his relief that his duties will be more circumscribed.

A month later, all the changes have been implemented. Two months later, the company completes, six months ahead of schedule, a first-of-its-kind product for a definite and large market. The company fails to get a second round of venture financing, but sales revenues begin to exceed costs for the first time in the company's history due to the new product.

In the meantime, the vice president decides *not* to become president. The president stipulates that henceforward he will draw a higher salary and exercise the managerial authority of CEO on a day-to-day basis.

Another three months later, the vice presidential partner decides he wishes to become president after all and negotiates the change with the other partner.

Appendix E:

Excerpt from "Listening into the dark: An essay testing the validity and efficacy of Collaborative Developmental Action Inquiry for describing and encouraging the transformation of self, society, and scientific inquiry. ***Integral Review***. 2013, 9(2), 264-299. (This excerpt pp. 282-292.)

A Quantitative, Third-Person Study of Organizational Transformation in Ten Cases

Four consultants each engaged for many years in various forms of First- and second-person research/practice prior to taking organizational consulting roles with the ten organizations included in the third-person study presented next...

Here, we offer a brief overview of the quantitative study in particular, first as an exemplar of how first-, second-, and third-person research/practices can mutually interweave, and second in order to help explain why triangulating in this way is likely to explain more of the empirical variance than third-person-research-only studies. This study tests the empirically confirmable or disconfirmable proposition, derived from developmental theory (Torbert, 1987, 1991), that only CEOs and consultants who transform to the Transforming action-logic or beyond reach the capacity to reliably support organizational transformation. This is so because only at these late action-logics do people regularly (and more and more intensively) inquire about and transform their own action for greater efficacy, and also because only at late action-logics do people seek to exercise shared-commitment-enhancing, mutually-transforming powers, not just unilaterally-forcing types of power that gradually erode others' trust and commitment.

To determine the center-of-gravity action-logics of the key individual players, the 10-organization study uses one of several measures derived from Jane Loevinger's Washington University Sentence Completion Test and adapted to work settings and leadership issues by Cook-Greuter, Herdman-Barker, and Torbert. These three closely related measures are Cook-Greuter's (1999) Mature Adult Profile, Harthill's Leadership Development Profile, and Herdman-Barker and Torbert's Global Leadership Profile (see Herdman & Torbert, 2010, and Torbert & Livne-Tarandach, 2009 for reliability and validity studies of the measure).

In the 10-organization study, five of the ten organizations' CEOs are measured as performing at relatively early action-logics (1 Diplomat, 2 Experts and 2 Achievers). It measures the other five CEOs and three of the four consultants as performing at the Transforming action-logic, and the fourth consultant as enacting the Early Alchemical action-logic. Table 3, below, summarizes the data from the study.

The four consultants worked in different combinations with the ten organizations for unusually long periods – an average of 4.2 years. Using various additional data sources, including organizational growth and profitability, customer and employee satisfaction, reputational measures, archival data, and "thick descriptions" (Geertz, 1983) of longitudinal cases, as well as a measure of organizational transformation to be described, the study calls itself a "retrospective field quasi-experiment" (Rooke & Torbert, 1998: 16).

Business and reputational measures showed that seven of the ten organizations improved dramatically during the intervention/ studies, while the other three declined either mildly or dramatically. Based on the thick descriptions of the individual cases, three raters achieved perfect reliability (1.0) in scoring whether each organization transformed, remained at the same organizational action-logic, or regressed (they also achieved .90 reliability in agreeing how many transformations occurred in each organization). During the ten consulting interventions, the seven economically-and-reputationally-successful organizations all transformed (sometimes more than once) to later organizational action-logics. The three remaining organizations either remained at the same action-logic or, in one case, regressed. The initial main findings were that: 1) The five CEOs at the Transforming action-logic or beyond all supported positive organizational transformations and increased business success; and 2) by contrast, three of the five CEOs at earlier action-logics were associated with lack of transformations and even organizational regression and business failure.

The CEOs' action-logic accounted for a statistically significant 42% of the variance in whether the organization positively transformed (Spearman's rank order coefficient rho=.651, one-tailed p<.05). Cohen (1983) classifies a "large effect size" as one that accounts for 25% of the variance in a correlational test (that is, r=.50). Thus, a test that accounts for 42% of the variance, as this one did, represents an unusually robust empirical finding. Moreover, if one adds together the action-logic scores for the CEO and the lead consultant in each effort at organizational change the resulting correlation accounts for 59% of the variance at the .01 level of significance (Torbert & Associates, 2004). The increase in percentage-of-the-variance – explained in the later analysis is due to the fact that the one Early Alchemical action-logic consultant led the only two engagements when pre-Strategist CEOs were associated with positive organizational transformation. In short, in these ten cases the developmental action-logic of the CEOs and their lead consultants emerged as the single largest cause in whether or not the organization transformed.

The foregoing study appears to offer powerful, quantitative confirmation for CDAI theory, practice, and method. But no critical reader will want to accept such results at face value. The critical reader will wish to inquire in greater detail how this "small-n" study coped with various potential threats to the Empirical Positivist, third-person, quantitative conception of validity-testing, and how it holds up against additional and different standards of validity associated with first-, and second-person research/practices, that we will presently adduce from the varied and dispersed social science literature on validity (Scheurich, 1997).

Table 3

Ten Organization Study
Size & Type of Organization, Length of Consultant Relationship, Lead Consultant & CEO Action-Logics, and Number of Organizational Transformations or Regressions

Type of **Org'n**	**Size** (# of employees)	**Length** of cons.	**Consultant** action-logic	**CEO** action-logic	**Organizational Transformations**
1. Not-for-profit	325	5 yrs	Alchemical	Transforming	+5 (Concep to Collab Inq)
2. For-profit	43	6 yrs	Alchemical	Transforming	+3 (Incorp-Collab Inq)
3. For-profit	10	7 yrs	Transforming	Transforming	+3 (Concep-Exps)
4. For-profit	732	15 mos	Transforming	Transforming	+1 (SystProd-Collab Inq)
5. Not-f-profit	627	6 yrs	Alchemical	Transforming	+2 (Exps-Collab Inq)
6. Not-f-profit	847	5 yrs	Alchemical	Expert	+2 (Exps-Collab Inq)
7. For-profit	183	2 yrs	Alchemical	Achiever	+1 (Exps-Syst Prod)
8. For-profit	1019	2 yrs	Transforming	Achiever	0 (Syst Prod)
9. Not-for-profit	584	4 yrs	Transforming	Achiever	0 (Syst Prod)
10. Not-f-profit	481	4 yrs	Alchemical	Diplomat	-3 (Collab Inq-Incorp)

Testing the Third-Person, Internal and External Validity of the 10 – Organization Study

Validity criteria that test the third-person generalizability of empirical findings "after-the-fact" are enumerated and described relatively exhaustively by Cook and Campbell (1979). Their conceptualization of validity has two general components, internal validity and external validity, defined as follows:

Internal validity refers to the approximate validity with which we infer that a relationship between two variables is causal or that the absence of a relationship implies the absence of cause.

External validity refers to the approximate validity with which we can infer that the presumed causal relationship can be generalized to and across alternate measures of the cause and effect and across different types of persons, settings, and times. (Cook & Campbell, 1979: 37)

Cook and Campbell (1979) list 19 different potential threats to internal validity and 13 different threats to external validity. They suggest that researchers focus on the threats most likely to have a significant effect on the validity of their work. We will, therefore, here address only the most salient threats to the validity of the Rooke and Torbert (1998) study. (In Cook and Campbell's terms, the study is best described as a nonequivalent control group quasi – experimental design, whose "treatment" is the presence and action of a CEO and lead consultant at the Transforming action-logic or later and whose "effect" is organizational transformation.)

The most significant threats to internal validity in such a study are the interaction of selection and maturation, instrumentation, local history, and threats to statistical conclusion validity. And the most significant threat to external validity comes in the form of insufficient construct validity (Cook & Campbell, 1979). Another important threat to the external validity of the study would appear to come from the small sample size.

Let us start at the beginning. The internal validity threat of selection-maturation would arise in the Rooke and Torbert (1998) study... if

Transforming action-logic CEOs happened to be associated with types of organizations that had growth patterns systematically not encountered by the types of organizations headed by CEOs at earlier action-logics. In such a case, it could well be that extraneous causes, not CEOs' and consultants' action-logics, would account for the organizations' transformation. In the Rooke and Torbert study, however, there was considerable variety: 1) in the size (10-1,019 employees, average=485); 2) in type (5 for-profit / 5 not-for-profit); and 3) in line of business (investing, automobiles, energy, consulting, education, health care). Moreover, the successes and failures in organizational transformation are not associated with any of these variables (e.g. two of the three organizations that failed to transform were not-for-profits, but three of the five not-for-profits succeeded in transforming).

The threat of instrumentation arises when there are scaling problems with the measurement of the dependent variable (organizational transformation, in this case)... such that changes are more likely to be measured in one group than the other. Looking, we find differences in the baseline action-logics of organizational development of the different organizations, and we find that the three organizations unsuccessful in transforming were among the four organizations in the study that began at the Systematic Productivity action-logic (see Table II). At first, this seems to suggest that the coding scheme the raters employed may not be sensitive to transformations above the Systematic Productivity action-logic, or that such late-action-logic transformation is much less likely to occur than transformations through the earlier action-logics (and all this could be explained as statistical regression toward the mean). However, a closer look reveals that six of the seven organizations that were coded as having transformed actually progressed to the Collaborative Inquiry organizational action-logic (beyond Systematic Productivity), thus showing that the dependent variable was in fact sensitive to such transformations and that they do occur with some frequency.

Another credible threat to internal validity, local history, is troublesome if there are events that only affect the experimental group and not the control group. Here, there were ten experimental groups of somewhat varying developmental configuration and no control groups, one might say. Or, one might say, there were five experimental groups (the five organizations with Transforming CEOs) and five non-Transforming-led control-group organizations. As far as we can tell, this threat of local history is substantially eliminated by the variety in geography (multi-national), industry (six industries), and market niche of the ten organizations in the Rooke and Torbert (1998) paper.

Lastly, threats to statistical conclusion validity also endanger the internal validity of studies in the Empirical Positivist tradition. Statistical conclusion validity concerns our ability to determine statistically significant (within a specified α level) co-variation between our independent and dependent variables (Cook & Campbell, 1979). In the focal study, the threats to statistical conclusion validity were minimized since the authors used the Spearman rank order test, which is the appropriate nonparametric statistical test, and found results that were statistically significant at the .01 level. (Note that nonparametric tests make fewer assumptions about normality of the distribution and interval distances between numbers, and that they are therefore less likely to make false assumptions.)

With regard to external validity of the measure of a person's leadership action-logic, Rooke and Torbert's (1998) detailed discussion of the history of reliability and validity studies of the sentence completion measure at that time minimize many of the threats to construct—and also, by definition, external—validity. A decade later, additional reliability and validity studies of the measure have further demonstrated its reliability and validity (McCauley et al, 2006; Torbert & Livne-Tarandach, 2009; Torbert et al, 2010).

The construct validity of the organizational action-logics can be claimed, less voluminously and less conclusively, on three grounds:

1) by the theoretical analogy between personal and organizational development;

2) by the clinical usefulness of the developmental theory for organizations to the consultants themselves and their clients during their interventions (e.g. the consulting case offered earlier in this article; see also Fisher, Rooke, and Torbert, 2000, chs.8-10, for thick qualitative descriptions of numerous organizational interventions using CDAI); and
3) by the high inter-rater reliability achieved by the three coders in this study (again, 1.0 on whether and if so, which way, an organization transformed; and .90 on the exact number of transformations in each case).

But what about the small sample size in the 10-organization study? Isn't that a huge barrier to claiming that the results are in any way externally generalizable to other organizations? *(It's always been amazing to me how it's the quant jocks that jump in with these objections first, even though they're the ones who ought to know better.)*

In fact, the answer is "No." The small sample size did introduce a slightly higher risk of a Type II error (falsely rejecting a valid finding), since the statistical power is slightly less than the conventional .80. But this small-sample-size effect would have affected the interpretation of the results only if a significant correlation had *not* been found. What a small sample that explains a high percentage of the variance indicates is how powerful a causal factor the independent variable is, for almost every recorded case must align with the hypothesis. Put differently, what an n of 10, accounting for 59% of the variance at the .01 level of statistical significance means is just the same as an n of 1,000 at the .01 level of statistical significance – namely, that the hypothesis is confirmed, with less than one in a hundred chance that the inference is in fact false. Put yet again differently, if the n had been 1,000 and the result had achieved the .01 level of statistical significance, then although the hypothesis would still be confirmed, the independent variable (CEOs' & consultants' action-logic, as measured by the LDP) might have accounted for a much lower percentage of the variance in the dependent variable and would therefore not have been demonstrated to be as powerful a causal factor as it has been demonstrated to be in this study.

At the same time, however, it is important to remain cautious about the generalizability of the findings in two regards. Since the largest business unit in the study had 1,019 employees, we cannot know whether the findings will hold for Fortune 500 size. Also, the organizations in this study, whether for-profit or not-for-profit, are all productive, economically-oriented, work organizations; hence, the findings may not be representative of all types of organizations (e.g. spiritual organizations, temporary political campaign organizations, families, or government agencies). On the other hand, the results should be generalizable to the more than 95% of business and competitive not-for-profit organizations that have 1,000 employees or less.

Other Third-Person Validity-Enhancing Criteria

Cook and Campbell (1979) are not the only authors who have addressed the validity of third – person research. For instance, Lincoln and Guba (1985) have advocated for methods that are likely to positively increase the validity and trustworthiness of objective social science, rather than explicating lists of threats to be minimized. The qualitative validity-enhancing methods that Lincoln and Guba recommend include: 1) conducting prolonged engagements; 2) engaging in persistent up-close observation; and 3) triangulating sources, methods, and investigators.

Let us review briefly how the Rooke and Torbert (1998) CDAI action/research in the 10-organization study fares in these terms: 1) the engagements were certainly prolonged (4.2yr.s on average),with 2) persistent observation (the four participant/ consultant/ researchers intensively engaged at least the CEOs and the top management levels, attending and intervening in meetings, as well as coaching); 3) the researchers triangulated methods (by using an extensively validated psychometric measure to test the developmental stage of the CEO and many members of the top management teams and the consultants as well as using wide-ranging business indicators, interview data, and meeting-behavior data to make assessments about organizational development and success. The use of multiple coders who displayed a high level of inter-rater reliability also increased the credibility of the assessments. In terms of the 27 'flavors' of action research [Chandler & Torbert, 2003], the organizations that successfully transformed engaged in as many as 15 different kinds of action research, whereas those that did not engaged in no more than 9.

These validity-enhancing Postmodern Interpretivist features of the study suggest that it produced credible findings and predictions (reinforcing the Empirical Positivist validity test findings described in the previous pages). Note that the researchers' intimacy with the data is supported by the fact that they included themselves within the experiment and collected data on themselves as well as the other subjects.

First- and Second-Person Validity Testing and Enhancing Methods Applied to the 10-Organization Study

While Lincoln and Guba (1985) do address the objective, third-person aspects of qualitative validity, they also emphasize the techniques used to increase the trustworthiness of research by attending to the second-person aspects of research. Two additional, key techniques that they propose are 1) peer debriefing among researchers as a qualitative external check on the inquiry process; and 2) member checking, or direct testing of findings and interpretations with the human sources from which they have come. In Rooke and Torbert's (1998; Torbert & Associates, 2004) 10-organization study, we find a high degree of both peer debriefing and member checking. By engaging each other as mutual co-researchers, the four consultants would repeatedly (at every possible break when directly engaged with clients) seek each other's (dis)confirmation of the validity of their actions. Moreover, member checking is a vital, ongoing feature of research in the CDAI paradigm. All senior management members in the ten organizations who agreed to take the developmental psychometric measure were offered feedback about the results, along with careful inquiry about the participant's sense of the validity of the result (further member checking). Seven of the ten CEOs had estimated themselves at the same action-logic as the LDP found; the rest agreed after discussion and further clinical debriefings of later action episodes. In a later study, we offer an example of a case when member checking about the LDP rating led to a change in both the member's estimate and in the researcher's view (McGuire, Palus & Torbert, 2007).

More generally, theories related to first- and second-person research encourage on-the-spot and at-the-moment validity tests. Thus, the first-person theory of "four territories of experience" (Torbert 1973; Torbert & Associates, 2004) permits any of us to test how many territories of experience our awareness is embracing ('the outside world,' 'our own sensations as we know them from within,' 'our own thoughts and feelings,' and 'the dynamics of the attention itself') anytime we choose to investigate. Likewise, the second-person theory of four distinct, but interweavable speech acts that generate increasing efficacy as they are interwoven permits any of us in conversation the potential to test which we are missing as we are speaking (the four speech acts are named 'framing,' 'advocating,' 'illustrating,' and inquiring' [Torbert, 2000b; Torbert & Associates, 2004, ch. 2]). (Argyris' version of action science [Argyris, 1993; Argyris, Putnam, & Smith, 1985] offers a challenging discipline for going beyond mere member checking to testing whether the entire quality of interpersonal dialogues is such as to increase or decrease the likelihood that one is learning the most significant valid information available. Currently, increasing attention is being paid to the validity of intersubjective, second-person, "during-the-act" research [Bradbury & Lichtenstein, 2000; Heron, 1996; Reason & Bradbury, 2001; Torbert, 2000b].

Let us explore further, into the realm of second-and-first-person criteria of validity. In her article "Validity after Poststructuralism," Lather (1993) introduces four additional types of validity that have implications for first-, second-, and third-person research/practice. Lather calls these qualitative, Postmodern Interpretivist ways of enhancing validity: paralogical validity, ironic validity, rhizomatic validity, and voluptuous validity.

> **Paralogical validity**, according to Lather, requires the researcher to develop methods that help her "unlearn her own privilege" (Lather, 1993, p680) and be open to multiple interpretations from the audience. Here, Lather uses the Lincoln & Guba categories of "peer debriefing" and "member checking" that we have already discussed above; so we will take this criterion as having been met by the ten-organization study, without further discussion.
>
> **Ironic validity**, according to Lather, problematizes the existence of "truth." It invites the researcher, writer, and readers to question the foundations of their epistemologies (their assumptions about what knowledge is and how to tell the difference between truth and error). Developmental theory itself, properly understood, should problematize each person's sense of truth. For, in studying the theory, we come to recognize that, no matter what our action-logic, all our perceptions and conceptions are framed by assumptions that only a minority of other people share. How come any of us is so sure?
>
> A third example of ironic validity is found in the hypothesis of the Rooke and Torbert (1998) study:
>
>> *CEOs whose cognitive-emotional-sensory structure recognizes that there are multiple ways of framing reality and that personal and organizational transformations of structure require mutual, voluntary initiatives—not just single-framed hierarchical guidance—are more likely to succeed in leading organizational transformation.*

In other words, the ironic proposition of the ten-organization study is: leadership that relies primarily on unilateral causal power based on the leaders' 'truth' is less likely to cause organizational transformation than leadership that 'listens into the dark' beyond its current version of truth (because that leadership, based more on inquiry-in-the-present and mutually-transforming power than on unilateral power, is attuned to generating mutual causality and outcomes better than anyone's unilateral truth would have predicted at the outset).

Rhizomatic validity, Lather's third type of validity (in analogy with the underground stems and aerial roots of rhizomes), fits jigsaw-puzzle-like with the mutual-power idea just mentioned. Rhizomatic validity requires the maintenance of contradiction by a listening and a reportage that both reflects, and is itself an instantiation of, the unexpected emerging present in all of its multi-voiced contradictoriness. In the ten-organization study this form of validity was enhanced by interviewing all members of the senior management teams early in the consulting processes before the consultants developed other preconceptions, with feedback to each member shortly afterwards of the verbatim (anonymous) comments of his or her peers, so that each "heard" the raw, possibly discordant voices of all one's significant others. The teams were then offered a non-compulsory opportunity to reflect on that feedback with those same peers. Usually, the first to volunteer was the person who had received the most unexpected negative feedback. Thus, that person, usually the most discordant and disliked before, suddenly became the most transparent and vulnerable, therefore playing a big role in setting a new norm of testing differences of perspective early and often in the subsequent organizational transformation effort.

Yet another example of rhizomatic validity (and, more generally, of 1st – and 2nd-person research/practice written up for a 3rd-person audience) is the book Action Inquiry (Torbert & Associates, 2004). It is full of vignettes, analyses, and action experiments described in the voices of many different protagonists holding many different interpretive frameworks (different action-logics). Lastly, to pick an example closer to your (the reader's) current experience: we expect that different readers may be touched by different "moments" of this writing, while feeling indifferent to, or alienated from, other sections... member check invited!

Voluptuous validity. Lather's fourth and final type of validity-enhancing method, voluptuous validity, increases when the researcher is both engaged and self-reflexive in the study, not distanced and detached. Indeed, Lather "goes wild" here, espousing such engaged and self-reflexive practice "to the point of leaky, runaway, risky practice" (Lather, 1993, p. 686). A neophyte musician is encouraged "to play the difficult passages and mistakes loudly," in order to hear the mistakes better and to learn faster. Based on the earlier examples in this writing, would you call those practices "runaway, risky practices"? (I might call them more self-reflexive, disciplined dances.) In any event, the landscape and the writing style provided through first- and second-person verbal and written action research descriptions surely promise to be slightly livelier, or at least less dessicated, than the traditional third-person peer-reviewed academic-research-journal article.

The notion of voluptuous validity offers a final opportunity to state why the GLP, based on CDAI theory, is so successful at pinpointing which CEOs and consultants successfully support organizational transformation in the ten-company study: each later action-logic is increasingly open and committed to integrating action and single-, double-, and triple-loop inquiry ("listening into the dark" "engaged and self-reflexive at each moment of practice"). This increasing frequency of listening into the dark is likely to increase the frequency of timely, transforming actions and organizational results. Because the CDAI paradigm at its core understands and enacts power as primarily mutual, and only secondarily and usually less effectively as unilateral... And because the vast majority of organizational members in all contract-organizations today operate at action-logics that treat unilateral power as real-er than mutual power... Organization-members' behavior will initially tend to be heavily influenced by whom they regard as having the most conventionally-framed unilateral power (e.g. a CEO or a lead consultant to an organization-wide strategic-action). Such CEOs must be able, by example, not just rhetoric, and through the liberating disciplines of timely action-projects, to lead mutually and thereby teach others to lead mutually as well. Exercising vulnerable, mutually-transforming power and inquiry in spontaneously timely action amidst others may constitute the essence of voluptuous validity.

Validity-threats that apply to positivist research more than to CDAI research

Once one commits in practice to first- and second-person action inquiry, some of Cook and Campbell's (1979) specific threats to internal and external validity are much less likely ever to become an issue in research theoretically and practically informed by CDAI. For example, Cook and Campbell (1979) address the threat of hypothesis-guessing by subjects, which is best avoided by making hypotheses hard to guess or deliberately giving subjects false hypotheses. These "remedies" (utilizing uninformed researchers and lying to subjects) are neither attractive, nor regarded as ethical in paradigms after the action turn, like Cooperative Ecological Inquiry and Collaborative Developmental Action Inquiry. Paradigms after the action turn invite researchers to test the efficacy of their own actions and assumptions with peers (Kahane, 2010; Senge, 1990; Scharmer, 2007; Torbert, 2000b), and invite all involved in the research to become "observant participants" (Torbert, 1991) who seek mutuality and trust through their actions and inquiries as one condition for the inquiry element of each timely action, as well as for the full mutuality necessary for successful relational and organizational transformations.

Another threat to the Empirical Positivist version of validity that applies much more lightly to CDAI is the threat of experimenter expectations. This threat describes any situation in which the researcher taints the subjects with his or her experimental goals. To reduce the effects of this threat, Cook and Campbell suggest employing experimenters with no expectations or false expectations (Cook & Campbell, 1979: 67). Since the 'experimenters' in paradigms after the action turn are sometimes also key actors in the experiment, and since the experiments themselves are practical in nature rather than artificial contexts devised by the researchers, providing them with false expectations would be stupid and unethical. Efficacy and validity would more likely be attained by:

1) empowering all research/participants to aim high for themselves and the community of inquiry as a whole in terms of new 'actionable' learning;
2) creating exercises for all research/participants to master performances synchronous with their own aims;
3) creating measures by which research/participants may estimate their own and the community's performance on issues that matter to them;
4) assuring the primary experimenter(s) operate(s) at a late action-logic (since action inquirers at late action-logics are the least likely to rely on expectations to begin with and the most likely to recover from false expectations the fastest by testing the validity and efficacy of their own and others' actions, theories, and assumptions in the course of the study); and
5) creating a context where the experimenter is motivated to help all research/participants equally (a condition the ten organization study meets because each organization was

an independent, paying client and the division between experimental and control groups was made only analytically and only after all the consulting assignments were complete).

A second way that social scientific research after the action turn combats the threat of experimenter expectations is by studying topics, such as adult development and organizational transformation in real time, as the 10-organization study does, where positive results are very desirable, but also very difficult to achieve. (Jane Loevinger, a self-confessed Expert and Empirical Positivist, once advised against using her original developmental psychometric in studies seeking to generate transformation... because, she said, she knew of no studies that showed anything other than "no change," like most educational-intervention research. [And at that time, given the pre-action-turn-methods used both in research and in intervention practice, she was right (Torbert, 1981)].)

A third way that social scientific research after the action turn guards against the distorting effect of experimenter expectations is by using measures that are difficult to cheat on, no matter what experimenter or participants expectations may be. For example, there is specific research to show that even when research subjects are invited to "cheat up" on the measure, they almost never succeed (Redmore, 1976).

Fourth, experiments after the action turn concern real-time events of vital concern to the research participants (e.g. the future of their careers and their organizations), so they are much less likely to abdicate power to researcher/ consultant/ interventionists who are not acting credibly or effectively.

Fifth, the primary researcher/activists themselves (if they have developed to the Transforming action-logic or later and are attuned to the action-turn-spirit of acknowledging incongruities as a precondition for transformation) want to learn the truth about how and when their theories work or do not work in practice, since they want to increase their effectiveness in real-time in the future more than they want to fake results for the purpose of academic success.

For example, in the Rooke and Torbert (1998) study the primary purpose of the third-person research project, undertaken after the first-and-second-person research-and-consulting processes had been completed, was not to prove the success of the approach in general, but rather to learn more about why we clearly failed in certain cases. One way of generalizing what we learned is that, as consultants with the mission of helping small and mid-sized organizations transform constructively, when we encounter an organization whose CEO does not measure at Transforming or later, we ought to direct as much attention to testing the validity of that finding and to helping the CEO transform (or find a different role) as we direct toward helping the organization more broadly to transform.

Appendix F

William Rockwell Torbert: Walk the Talk

by Steven S. Taylor, Professor of Leadership and Creativity
Foisie School of Business, Worcester Polytechnic Institute

Condensed and Adapted from chapter for Szabla, D., Pasmore, B., & Barnes, M., Palgrave Great Thinkers of Change Handbook, 2017

Bill Torbert's career has combined being a leader, teaching leadership, consulting to leaders, and researching leadership. Above all else he has been intent on embodying and explicating what he eventually came to call his "collaborative developmental action inquiry" (CDAI) approach to life, social science, and leadership (moving from the general case to the specific). I say embody and explicate because Bill has always tried to walk his talk. His published works are efforts to talk his walk, to explain in text what Bill was trying to live, often drawing upon his own adventures (and misadventures) as illustrations of his ideas. And, unlike many action researchers, Bill has not rebelled against quantitative research. In fact, he is the first to have introduced the notion of integrating "first-, second-, and third-person" research (Torbert, 1997) on the past, present, and future (Chandler & Torbert, 2003), interweaving quantitative measures, qualitative data, and action interventions (Torbert, 2000b, 2013).

Bill was one of my professors when I did my PhD at Boston College. I was never his research assistant, nor was he my advisor (although he was on my PhD committee). After I finished my PhD and left Boston College, he and I were part of a small group that met regularly to inquire into our own practice for over a decade. Bill and I eventually wrote one chapter together (Torbert & Taylor, 2008), and even though I have read most (but certainly not all) of his work, I primarily know Bill and his work from our efforts to walk our talk together, which in some ways continues to this day. The lessons I learned about living, social science, and leadership were profound and in this chapter I hope to offer some small sense of that.

PEACE, YALE AND ACTION RESEARCH (INFLUENCES AND MOTIVATIONS)

Bill went to Yale as an undergraduate in the early 1960s and as a graduate student in the late 1960s. With the civil rights movement domestically and the Vietnam war abroad, it was a time of unrest when it seemed possible to question everything and Bill was well situated to do so. His father worked for the State Department and Bill spent time in a several countries growing up, which may be where he first learned that there are many different ways of being and that our deepest cultural assumptions and rules about how to be in the world are not simply taken for granted facts of nature, but rather social constructions of a particular human culture.

His first great influence at Yale was the pastor and civil rights and peace activist William Sloane Coffin (Coffin, 2004). Through Coffin's influence, Bill played a leadership role, first in Yale-in-Mississippi, which led (along with many other initiatives) to the 1964 and 1965 civil rights acts; and then as Director of Yale Upward Bound, an innovative War on Poverty high school program, which cut New Haven's dropout rate in half through the practice of "collaborative inquiry."

Bill's second great influence at Yale was Chris Argyris, whom Bill first met and studied with as an undergraduate, and who chaired Bill's dissertation committee in graduate school. Like Coffin, Argyris' influence was not only intellectual, but also behavioral and emotional. Argyris raised questions about whether one's actions were in fact consistent with one's values, and introduced Bill to experiential learning in groups (Bethel t-groups, Tavistock group relations, Esalen encounter groups).

The third great influence Bill encountered while he was at Yale was the Gurdjieff Work (Ouspensky, 1949), based in New York and Paris, which Bill attended for 25 years. The central inquiry of this spiritual work is how one can develop an impartial, post-cognitive consciousness amidst the stresses of everyday action. In addition, while at Yale, Bill met, read the work of, and was significantly influenced by political theorists Hannah Arendt, Paul D'Entreves, Karl Deutsch, and Herbert Marcuse, psychologists Erik Erikson and Abraham Maslow, political economist Charles Lindblom, philosopher Don Schön, and theologian Paul Tillich.

After Yale, Torbert taught at Southern Methodist University (SMU) in Dallas for two years and at the Harvard Graduate School of Education for four years. He chose to go to Harvard in part to learn more about developmental theory from Lawrence Kohlberg and Bill Perry, and in the end learned even more from Carol Gilligan and Bob Kegan (who was then a grad student), as well as from the writings of John Rawls and Amartya Sen. After his time at Harvard, he was influenced primarily by several of his peers in our field – Ian Mitroff, Lou Pondy, Bob Quinn, Peter Senge, and Karl Weick – but most of all by his British action research colleague and coauthor Peter Reason.

After he resigned from Harvard, Torbert directed The Theatre of Inquiry for two years, and then joined the faculty at Boston College, initially as Graduate Dean of the Management School. There he remained for thirty years until his retirement in 2008. At The Theatre of Inquiry, Bill led weekly hour and a half "Action Workshops," a thirteen week "Business/School" whose members first created a business together, then went on to start their own businesses, and a monthly Public Performance which began as a theatrical play for an audience and gradually invited the audience into a profound action inquiry by the end of the evening. All of these exercises became fodder for the Action-Effectiveness MBA program that he later co-created with faculty at Boston College. This unique approach transformed the BC MBA program from a rank below the top 100 to #25 nationally.

Later, in the late 1980s and until his retirement in 2008, Bill served as Director of BC's PhD program in Organizational Transformation, consulted to more than two dozen organizations, served on the Board of Directors of unusual companies (e.g. Trillum Asset Management, the original socially responsible investing company, and Harvard Pilgrim Health Care, which became #1 HMO nationally at that time), and won local and national teaching prizes, as well as national research awards. His most well-known books during this period were *Managing the Corporate Dream*; *The Power of Balance: Transforming Self, Society and Scientific Inquiry*; and *Action Inquiry: The Secret of Timely and Transforming Leadership*."

Since 2008, he has functioned as principal of Action Inquiry Associates, continuing to sponsor and do research on and with the Global Leadership Profile (GLP). The GLP is the psychometric measure that, since 1980, has evolved from Loevinger's Washington University Sentence Completion Test (WUSCT), and served as the quantitative anchor for his and a number of his colleagues' and students' third-person action research. Since 2008, Torbert has also changed his focus from organizations to friendships; has co-created the Action Inquiry Fellowship, wherein three dozen highly diverse international scholar/practitioners sharpen their first- and second-person action inquiry capacity with one another; and in 2016, he co-authored with Hilary Bradbury, *Eros/Power: Love in the Spirit of Inquiry*.

COLLABORATIVE DEVELOPMENTAL ACTION INQUIRY (KEY CONTRIBUTIONS)

Returning to the beginning of his career, Bill's senior undergraduate thesis *Being for the Most Part Puppets: Interactions Among Men's Labor, Leisure, and Politics* (1972), written in collaboration with his classmate Malcolm Rogers, became his first published book. This sociological field survey of 209 blue collar workers in three industries showed that the relative amount of discretion a man had in his job directly predicted the degree of his creative leisure engagement and political action. These findings, along with Bill's direct experience of the poverty and mechanicity of assembly-line workers' jobs, motivated him to try to learn how organizations could be re-organized to encourage creativity and responsibility at all levels, and how he himself could play a leadership role in such processes.

As his dissertation chair, Argyris had agreed that Bill could do an action research dissertation on a) his founding and leadership of Yale Upward Bound; and b) the school's evolution toward becoming a truly collaborative venture between faculty and students (as documented primarily by innumerable tape recordings of meetings and interviews of all participants). This eventually led to the explication of an eight-stage theory of organizational development at the end of Bill's third book, *Creating a Community of Inquiry: Conflict, Collaboration, Transformation* (1976), written largely in the first person. This book documented both how the author himself learned and changed as a collaborative leader, and how each of six different sub-cycles of the program followed the same developmental sequence (the six distinct cycles were the two spring staff-selection and curriculum planning periods, the two distinct 7-week residential summer programs, the 5-person core staff, and the overall two-year endeavor). This theory of eight organizational development stages has proven to be the most differentiated in the field of organization development. By showing what stage of development an organization was currently at, the theory also became key to Torbert's later, quantitatively-verified successes (Torbert, 2013) in generating organizational transformations in his action research/ consulting interventions with colleagues and clients who measured at the 'Transforming' action-logic on the GLP.

But, why, you may be asking, was this Bill's third book and not his second? Because, after he had completed his two-year study of Upward Bound during graduate school, just as he was about to write it up, the department's faculty concluded that it could not possibly be objective and scientific if the researcher was also an actor in the field experiment. Unfortunately for Bill, he had not yet generated the concept of how first-, second-, and third-person research can complement and strengthen one another. Faced with a choice between discontinuing the doctoral program and designing and executing a completely different study in nine months, Bill chose the latter, doing a laboratory experiment on learning from experience, asking why it is so difficult to learn from experience in a way that transforms one's initial assumptions. Thus, this dissertation, *Learning from Experience: Toward Consciousness* (1973) became Bill's second book.

Learning from Experience first introduces the notion that, contrary to the general modern view that the outside world is the "territory" that we attempt to "map" via social science: there are actually four distinct "territories of experience" – the outside world, our inner sense of our own embodiment and action, our thinking and feeling, and a post-cognitive attention that any of us can cultivate, but few do.

This laboratory study produced a reliable verbal behavior scoring system that was shown to be able to distinguish which of two educational processes generated the most moments in action when participants were conscious of all four territories at once. This quality of first-person awareness-in-action was shown to be necessary, in turn, for a person to learn whether his or her assumptions at the outset of an "action inquiry" process deserved to be transformed. In his later work, to which we now turn, Bill showed how second-person conversations, third-person organizations, and social science itself can gradually cultivate a conversational and organizational awareness-in-action that spans all four territories of experience, by evolving through analogous personal, organizational, and paradigmatic developmental trajectories.

We can date the second half of Torbert's career from his acceptance of the position of Graduate Dean at the Boston College School of Management in 1978 to his retirement from Boston College in 2008. His scholarly work has been the development of "collaborative developmental action inquiry" (CDAI), which although not often recognized as such, is a fundamentally new and different paradigm for social science research. That is to say, Bill takes seriously the idea that we are co-constructing our social world as we act and interact. Bill's first articulation of this approach was to suggest that we need an "action science" (Torbert, 1976, pp 167-177). The term *Action Science* was picked up by Chris Argyris and eventually became the title of the book (Argyris, Putnam & Smith, 1985) that lays out the philosophic and academic foundations for Argyris' approach. Meanwhile, Bill came to the conclusion that "science" was too cognitive a word and instead adopted the term "action-inquiry" (Torbert & Associates, 2004) to better convey the more holistic and embodied work he was trying to describe.

Argyris conceived of Action Science as a way of extending the naturalistic science tradition. Torbert conceived of Action Inquiry as a new paradigm that includes third-person, generalizable theory, data, and quantitative testing of hypotheses; but that also breaks away from many of the assumptions and methods that constitute empirically positivist scientific inquiry, in order to include first- and second-person inquiry into the very action settings in which we researchers are ourselves also participants. One of the most important ideas in Argyris' Action Science is the Popperian notion of disconfirmability – Action Science argues strongly for treating all of our mental models (Senge, 1990) about the world as hypotheses that we should actively be trying to disconfirm, especially when those mental models lead us to act in ways that prove to be problematic in some way. This is the essence of Argyris and Schön (1974) Model II double loop feedback as I understand it. Torbert is all for holding our mental models loosely and inquiring into them, but Action Inquiry does not rest on the same belief that we can apply the processes of naturalistic scientific inquiry to our actions in the social world (indeed, action inquiry comes closer to a quantum understanding of physical science, and Torbert believes CDAI represents a paradigm change relevant to both the social and natural sciences).

The Popperian idea of disconfirmability implies both a certain stability and a certain distance. That is, you need a phenomenon that is stable enough to be testing the same phenomena that you formulated the hypothesis about. And you need to be able to observe the phenomenon from enough distance that you can see what it is. Often neither of these conditions are met in the case of social action (Lehrer, 2010). Instead, Action Inquiry sees every action as an inquiry and every inquiry as an action. That is to say we are constantly inquiring into the social world and also acting to change (or not) that social world. When I see my colleague first thing in the morning and ask her or him how they are doing, it is an inquiry, a probe into the system (even when I intend it as a simple social ritual that doesn't require an answer). When my colleague responds with "same old, same old" I learn that the social world is much as it usually is. But when my colleague responds, "my dog died last night," I have learned something else and our relationship has changed in some – perhaps small – way. Action Inquiry is based in this understanding of the social world as something that is constantly shifting and in which we are embedded, often unable to assume either stability or distance.

Torbert's response to this is to suggest a social science that is based in multiplicity. Rather than a single set of practices, he suggests that social science research can have a first, second, or third person research voice; have first, second, or third person practice as its subject; be about the past, present, or future; with single, double, or triple loop feedback (Chandler & Torbert, 2003). This results in 81 different research types – Torbert's argument is that modern social science includes a woefully small subset of these research types and that the more types we include, the more powerful the research will be. I say powerful, because another way in which Action Inquiry represents a new and different paradigm is that Torbert holds that the primary aim of social science research is – not only to gain greater and greater certainty about a conceptual map of the world, supported by various sets of empirical facts, as is the aim of most modern social science – but also to generate more and more instances and patterns of timely action in our practice, based on our active inquiries into the present and the future.

In order to "do" action inquiry, Torbert has created various ideas and tools for practice. The idea of first, second, and third person research/practice (Torbert, 1997) has been perhaps the most popular, at least in terms of being adopted by the academic community (e.g. Reason & Bradbury, 2001; Shear & Varela, 1999; Velmans, 2009). For first and second person practice of Action Inquiry, Torbert has developed two powerful tools, the four territories of experience, shown in table 1 (Torbert, 1973) and the four types of speech (Fisher & Torbert, 1995). The four territories of experience are 1) *the outside world*, 2) *one's own sensed behavior and feeling*, 3) *the realm of thought*, and 4) *the realm of vision/attention/intention;* and one of the practices of Action Inquiry is to pay attention and recognize feelings of fit and/or incongruity across the four territories. Is a given outcome congruent or incongruent with an organizations' vision?

It is probably not possible to always be paying attention to all four territories of experience at the same time – I know I have trouble being aware of more than one at a time; and in most of my life, I'm not consciously aware of any of them. However, the feelings in each of these territories are useful data that can help guide action. Here we can plainly see a difference between paying attention to a feeling of incongruity and seeking disconfirming data – a strict action *science* can't accept feelings of incongruity as legitimate data to disconfirm a mental model. Action *inquiry* requires paying attention to those feelings and inquiring further, that is acting to further explore those feelings. (Eugene Gendlin's *Focusing* (1982) and his subsequent work on exploring 'felt sense' is another body of first-person research in the same spirit.)

the outside world	objectified, discrete, interval units, of which 'I' am actively aware when 'I' notice the color and manyness of what 'I' see or the support the outside world is giving me through the soles of my feet (focused attention)
one's own sensed behav-ior and feeling	processual, ordinal rhythms in passing time, of which 'I' an sensually aware when I listen to the in-and-out of my breathing or the rhythms and tones of my own speaking (subsidiary, sensual awareness)
the realm of thought	eternal nominal distinctions and interrelations, of which I can be actively aware if my attention 'follows' my thought, if I am not just thinking, but 'mindful' that I am thinking (witnessing awareness)
vision / attention / intention	noumenal vision/attention/intention that can simulta-neously inter-penetrate the other three territories of experience and note incongruities or harmonies among them

Table 1. Four territories of experience of an individual person (Torbert & Taylor, 2008)

Torbert's four types of speech takes the idea that speech is action (Austin, 1962), or rather conversational inter-action across the four territories of experience, which at its best includes 1) *framing* a joint intent, 2) *advocating* one or more strategies, 3) *illustrating* how specific behavioral tactics and contextual conditions favor a strategy, and 4) *inquiring* how one's conversational partners respond. Here the contention is that a balance of the four types of speech will be more effective in generating timely action and receptivity to feedback on the part of all participants (Steckler & Torbert, 2010; Torbert, 2000a). Of course, in day-to-day life it is not always easy to distinguish advocacy from framing and it is not unusual for people to mask an advocacy as an inquiry (e.g. "why are you being such a jerk?" is usually not an honest inquiry, but really advocating that the other is being a jerk). The more authentic the inquiry, the more likely it is to yield a valid response. The point is less to provide a precise analytic tool with which to map out interactions, and more to provide a guide for the messy practice of interacting with other human beings in real time.

Torbert is best known (McCauley et al, 2006) in academia for his use of the third person idea of developmental theory (Loevinger, 1998). The theory suggests, and is supported by increasing empirical evidence based on studies using many different methods (Torbert, 1994, 2013), that, not just as children, but also as adults, we may develop through various stages that are defined by having different governing action-logics and that gradually lead toward a greater and greater capacity for continual four-territory awareness, for timely action, for receptivity to pertinent feedback, and for the development of organizations that support such personal development.

Each action-logic determines how we make sense of and act in the world. The stages are described in Table 2. Torbert adopted and adapted Loevinger's sentence completion test instrument for determining developmental level for business use (now referred to as the *Global Leadership Profile*). He is not the only scholar to study and elaborate adult developmental theory (Kegan, 1982, 1994; Kegan & Leahy, 2009). However, he led the use of developmental theory in organization change and extended the theory to create stage-like models of organizational development (Fisher & Torbert, 1995; Torbert, 1976, 1987) and of social scientific development (Torbert, 2000b, 2013).

Opportunistic	Short time horizon, flouts power and sexuality, rejects feedback, hostile humor, deceptive, manipulative, externalizes blame, punishes, views luck as central, punishment rules, views rules as loss of freedom, eye for an eye ethic.

Diplomatic	Observes rules, avoids inner and outer conflicts, conforms, suppresses own desires, loyalty to group, seeks membership, right versus wrong attitude, appearance and status conscious, tends towards cliches, works to group standard.
Expert	Interested in problem solving via data, critical of others and self, chooses efficiency over effectiveness, perfectionist, values decisions based on merit, wants own performance to stand out, aware of alternative constructions in problem resolution but can be dogmatic, accepts feedback only from objective craft masters.
Achiever	Results and effectiveness oriented, long term goals, concerned with issues of ethics and justice, deliberately prioritizes work tasks, future inspires, drawn to learning, seeks mutuality in relations, aware of personal patterns of behavior, feels guilty if does not meet own standards, blind to own shadow, chases time.
Redefining	Collaborative, tolerant of individual difference, aware of context and contingency, may challenge group norms, aware of owning a perspective, inquiring and open to feedback, seeks independent, creative work, attracted by difference and change, may become something of a maverick, focuses on present and historical context.
Transforming	Process and goal oriented, strategic time horizons, systems conscious, enjoys a variety of roles, recognizes importance of principle and judgment, engaged in complex interweave of relationships, aware of own personal traits and shadow, high value on individuality, growth, self-fulfillment, unique market niches, particular historical moments.

Alchemical	Alert to the theatre of action, embraces common humanity, disturbs paradigms of thought and action, dispels notions of heroic action, deeply internalized sense of self-knowledge held with empty mind, sees light and dark, order and mess, treats time and events as symbolic, analogical, metaphorical (not merely linear, digital, literal).

Table 2: Action Logics (Adopted from the Action Inquiry Associates' *Global Leadership Development Profile Report* created by Bill Torbert and Elaine Herdman-Barker in 2012)

Torbert's empirical work linking leadership development to organizational transformation includes one of the most stunning findings in the literature. Change leaders (CEOs and lead consultants) measured at the Transforming and Alchemical action-logics predicted 59% of the variance of the success in organizational transformation (Torbert, 2013). In short, according to that study, the change leaders' personal developmental action-logic is the single most important factor in whether an organization transforms, and it is more important than all the other sources of variance taken together. In modern social science where seemingly no variable ever explains more than a few percent of the variance, this is a truly noteworthy result. Couple it with Torbert's other empirical work which finds that only about 5% of managers in organizations are at the Transforming or Alchemical action-logics (Fisher & Torbert, 1995) and his work offers both a compelling explanation for the relative lack of success of organizational change efforts and a clear prescription for how organizations can more successfully manage change.

WHAT I'VE LEARNED FROM BILL (NEW INSIGHTS)

I have tried to take seriously Bill's ontological idea that every action is an inquiry and every inquiry an action. The idea of speech as action comes easily to me because it was also part of my theater training

(Stanislavski, 1936a, 1936b, 1961) and I have brought that into my own academic work(e.g. Taylor & Carboni, 2008). Perhaps because of my theater training, I have been much more attracted to the first and second person practice of Action Inquiry and the tools, such as the four types of speech. I have worked on articulating how to teach Action Inquiry approaches (Taylor, Rudolph & Foldy, 2008) and my latest book (Taylor, 2015) is a how-to guide that brings together Bill's approach with other tools within the reflective practice tradition for leader development.

It has felt like a natural fit to take Bill's work and mix it with artistic methods. This is in part because there is a history of action research methods that use artistic forms and in part because of the way Bill has always welcomed art into his own practice (e.g. The Theatre of Inquiry) and in part because Bill's Action Inquiry paradigm for social science might more appropriately be called a paradigm for social art. One of the great lessons for me is that Action Inquiry is a craft for living – with the hope that if you master the craft you might live artfully. Charlie "Bird" Parker said, "You've got to learn your instrument. Then you practice, practice, practice. And then when you finally get up there on the bandstand, forget all that and just wail" (Pugatch, 2006, 73). Action Inquiry provides tools and methods for practicing how we interact with each other. It offers developmental theory as an overarching pathway. But it is really about getting up there and just wailing in a way that produces more and more patterns of timely action in the service of social justice and human flourishing.

What does it look like to just wail when we interact with others? Isn't that what we do most of the time and often with disastrous results? The wailing that Bird speaks of isn't just doing whatever pops into your head and body. It is acting from a deeply embodied skill set and awareness of the context and situation. Below is a small example from a group of academics that had been meeting regularly for years to work on their Action Inquiry skills.

On this cold November day, the members of the group had arrived and were exchanging greetings and catching up with each other. Faustina entered the kitchen where Paula was standing.

"How are you doing, the super commuter?" said Paula.

"I'm cranky," responded Faustina.

"Oh what else is new, you are always cranky when you come to these meetings," answered Paula. And like after most "little things", they didn't engage with it further. However, a few minutes later when the group started to discuss their agenda for the meeting, Faustina suggested that they explore the interaction she had with Paula rather than working on the case that had previously been planned. Paula advocated that the group work on the originally planned case.

"Why do you want to do it?" asks Faustina.

"Because we said we were going to do it," replied Paula.

"So what?" responded Faustina.

Those two simple words, which we can imagine being said a hundred different ways, jolted the room. Robert had been feeling tired and frustrated with the way the group was being so nice to each other and not deciding which case to analyze and Faustina's "so what" brought him back to earth, back to feeling grounded. Robert thought, "ah, this is real and suddenly we're back to what matters." It was like a splash of cold water on his face.

Meanwhile, Robin was excited by Faustina's "so what." She believed that Faustina had the self awareness and skill to say something very diplomatic and analytical, but had chosen to bluntly, emotionally, and somewhat confrontationally express what is going on for her with her "so what." Robin found her choice to be provocative, exciting and beautiful. It was not provocative enough to make Robin afraid – Faustina knew the group and had a sense of how much the group could take.

It was also an effective action as it moved the group out of their wandering discussion of what they should do in their meeting to focusing on the sort of work that they all have previously agreed that they should be doing (Taylor, 2013, 75-76).

This interaction is not earth shaking and it might not even be noteworthy for most people. But for this group, it was an example of mastery of the craft skill of interacting with others, an example of Action Inquiry performed at a high level – a purposive and strategically-distinctive exemplar of double-loop feedback (see Figure 1) to both Paula and the group as a whole that changed the group's planned activity for the session. My great takeaway from working with Torbert's ideas and practices is that leadership is largely about the day-to-day interactions, these small moments and the immense craft skill that can be needed to navigate them well and in congruity with one's vision and values. This is more than leadership: it is an art of life.

CONTINUING BILL'S WORK (LEGACIES AND UNFINISHED BUSINESS)

It is perhaps not surprising that, other than doctoral students writing their dissertations based on CDAI theory and practice, often using the GLP instrument, having become Certified GLP Coaches through workshops with the Global Leadership Associates, the academic community as a whole has not (yet?) embraced Torbert's new paradigm for social science research. No existing paradigm ever yields easily

(Kuhn, 1962). However there are areas where his work is influential, notably in non-traditional educational programs that emphasize practice – such as in-company leadership development workshops globally, such as Center for Creative Leadership programs and research, the Fielding Graduate University, the California Institute of Integral Studies, Naropa University in Boulder, or in the UK the Ashridge Business School.

It is also not surprising that the business world has not wholeheartedly embraced his work, even though his international-award-winning 2005 *Harvard Business Review* article "Seven Transformations of Leadership" continues to be widely studied as one of *HBR*'s top ten leadership articles ever. Beyond the underlying aims of promoting social justice and human flourishing (both of which much of the business world has trouble serving). Torbert's approach is hard. It is not a quick fix, it cannot be applied en masse, and he asks people and organizations to walk the talk. It takes years to develop your own craft and practice of Action Inquiry. This art is worthy of a lifetime, of many persons' lifetimes.

The empirical findings from Torbert's developmental theory work also suggest that the challenges for businesses, universities, churches, or governments are large and cannot be easily addressed. Generally, it takes from 2 to 4 years to fully transition from one individual or organizational stage to the next. Moreover, as already pointed out, consistently successful change leadership requires post-conventional development, but to date only small percentage of managers have reached this level of development. This implies that organizations need to spend decades to develop managers who will be able to consistently lead significant change efforts. Very few institutions work with those sorts of time frames.

Torbert calls for development into the post-conventional stages, the move from exercising Mystery/ Mastery unilateral power to increasingly exercising Collaborative-Inquiry mutual power in all one's professional and personal affairs. It is a similar, but more radical, movement as Argyris and Schön's (1974) move from Model I to

Model II governing values, or as Stone, Patton & Heen's (2000) move in *Difficult Conversations* from "A Battle of Messages" to "A Learning Conversation." In all cases the movement involves becoming curious about how you and the other are understanding the situation, why that is different from one another, and how that leads you to act differently and in ways that are problematic for each other.

At the very center of CDAI, in between research on the past or the future and in between first-person or third-person voice or practice lies present-centered, second-person action inquiry that makes the most difficult topics discussable (e.g. how included one feels, what kinds of power different members exercise, how intimate one wishes to be). In short, personal, organizational, and scientific transformation require openness and deep curiosity towards ourselves and the friends, colleagues, or strangers with whom we are engaged.

References

Argyris, C., Putnam, R., & Smith, D. (1985). *Action science: Concepts, methods, and skills for research and intervention*. San Francisco: Jossey-Bass.

Argyris, C., & Schön, D. (1974). *Theory in Practice – Increasing Professional Effectiveness (First ed.).* San Francisco: Jossey-Bass Publishers.

Austin, J. L. (1962). *How to do things with words.* Oxford: Clarendon Press.

Bradbury, H., & Torbert, W. (2016). *Eros/Power: Love in the Spirit of Inquiry.* Tucson, AZ: Integral Publishers.

Chandler, D., & Torbert, W. R. (2003). Transforming inquiry and action. *Action Research, 1*(2), 133-152.

Coffin, W. S. (2004). *Credo.* Westminster, John Knox Press.

Fisher, D., & Torbert, W. R. (1995). *Personal and organizational transformations: The true challenge of continual quality improvement.* New York: McGraw-Hill.

Gendlin, E. T. (1982). *Focusing.* New York: Bantam.

Kegan, R. (1982). *The evolving self.* Cambridge MA: Harvard University Press.

Kegan, R. (1994). *In over our heads: The mental demands of modern life.* Cambridge, MA: Harvard University Press.

Kegan, R., & Lahey, L. (2009). *Immunity to change: How to overcome it and unlock the potential in yourself and your organization.* Boston: Harvard Business Press.

Kuhn, T. (1962). *The structure of scientific revolutions.* Chicago: The University of Chicago Press.

Lehrer, J. (2010). The Truth Wears Off: Is There Something Wrong with the Scientific Method. *The New Yorker*, 52-57.

Loevinger, J. (1998). *Technical foundations for measuring ego development: The Washington University sentence completion test.* Psychology Press.

McCauley, C. D., Drath, W. H., Palus, C. J., O'Connor, P. M., & Baker, B. A. (2006). The use of constructive-developmental theory to advance the understanding of leadership. *The Leadership Quarterly, 17*(6), 634-653.

Ouspensky, P. D. (1949). *In search of the miraculous: Fragments of an unknown teaching.* New York: Harcourt and Brace.

Pugatch, J. (2006). *Acting Is a Job: Real-life Lessons About the Acting Business* New York: Allworth Press.

Reason, P., & Bradbury, H. (2001). *Handbook of Action Research – Participative, inquiry & practice.* London: SAGE.

Senge, P. M. (1990). *The fifth discipline: The art and practice of the learning organization.* New York: Currency Doubleday.

Shear, J., & Varela, F. J. (1999). *The view from within: First-person approaches to the study of consciousness.* Imprint Academic.

Stanislavski, C. (1936a). *An actor prepares* (E. R. Hapgood, Trans.). New York: Routledge.

Stanislavski, C. (1936b). *Building a character* (E. R. Hapgood, Trans.). New York: Routledge.

Stanislavski, C. (1961). *Creating a role* (E. R. Hapgood, Trans.). New York: Routledge.

Steckler, E., & Torbert, W. R. (2010). Developing the 'Developmental Action Inquiry' approach to teaching and action researching: Through integral first-, second-, and third – person methods in education. In S. Esbjorn-Hargens, J. Reams, & O. Gunnlaugson (Eds.), *Integral Education: New Directions in Higher Education.* Albany, NY: SUNY Press.

Stone, D., Patton, B., & Heen, S. (2000). *Difficult Conversations: How to Discuss What Matters Most.* New York: Penguin Books.

Taylor, S. S. (2013). Little beauties: Aesthetics, craft skill, and the experience of beautiful action. *Journal of Management Inquiry, 22*(1), 69-81.

Taylor, S. S. (2015). *You're a genius: Using reflective practice to master the craft of leadership*: Business Expert Press.

Taylor, S. S., & Carboni, I. (2008). Technique & Practices from the Arts: Expressive Verbs, Feelings, and Action. In D. Barry & H. Hansen (Eds.), *The SAGE Handbook of New Approaches in Management and Organization* (pp. 220-228). London: Sage.

Taylor, S. S., Rudolph, J. W., & Foldy, E. G. (2008). Teaching reflective practice: Key stages, concepts and practices. In P. Reason & H. Bradbury (Eds.), *Handbook of Action Research* (2nd ed., pp. 656-668). London: Sage.

Torbert, W. R. (1973). *Learning from Experience: Toward Consciousness*. New York: Columbia University Press.

Torbert, W. R. (1976). *Creating a Community of Inquiry: Conflict, Collaboration, Transformation*. London: Wiley.

Torbert, W. R. (1987). *Managing the corporate dream: Restructuring for long-term success*. Homewood, IL: Dow Jones-Irwin.

Torbert, W. R. (1991). *The power of balance: Transforming self, society, and scientific inquiry*. Newbury Park, CA: Sage.

Torbert, W. R. (1994). Cultivating postformal adult development: Higher stages and contrasting interventions. In M. Miller & S. Cook-Greuter (Ed.s) *Transcendence and mature thought in adulthood: The further reaches of adult development,* 181-203.

Torbert, W. (1997). Developing courage and wisdom in organizing and in sciencing. S. Shrivastva & D. Cooperrider (Ed.s) *Organizational wisdom and executive courage,* 222-253.

Torbert, W. R. (2000a). The Challenge of Creating a Community of Inquiry. In F. Sherman & W. Torbert (Eds.), *Transforming social inquiry, transforming social action* (pp. 161-188). Norwell MA: Kluwer Academic Publishers.

Torbert, W. R. (2000b). Transforming social science: Integrating quantitative, qualitative, and action research. In F. Sherman & W. Torbert (Eds.), *Transforming Social Inquiry, Transforming Social Action: New Paradigms for Crossing the Theory/Practice Divide* (pp. 67-91). Norwell, MA: Kluwer Academic Publishers.

Torbert, W. R. (2013). Listening into the Dark: An Essay Testing the Validity and Efficacy of Collaborative Developmental Action Inquiry for Describing and Encouraging Transformations of Self, Society, and Scientific Inquiry. *Integral Review: A Transdisciplinary & Transcultural Journal for New Thought, Research, & Praxis,* 9(2), 264-299.

Torbert, W. R., & Rogers, M. P. (1972). *Being for the most part puppets: Interactions among men's labor, leisure, and politics.* Cambridge MA: Schenkman Publishing.

Torbert, W. R., & Associates. (2004). *Action Inquiry: The secret of timely and transforming leadership.* San Francisco: Berrett-Koehler.

Torbert, W. R., & Taylor, S. S. (2008). Action inquiry: Interweaving multiple qualities of attention for timely action. In P. Reason & H. Bradbury (Eds.), *Handbook of Action Re – search (2nd ed.)* pp. 239-251). London: Sage.

Velmans, M. (2009). *Understanding consciousness.* London: Routledge.

Bibliography of Scholarly Action Inquiry & GLP Studies Other than Torbert's publications noted in above references (most of Torbert's books, articles and chapters can be found in the cyber-library at www.actioninquiryleadership.com **)**

Alderfer, C., (2011). *The Practice of Organizational Diagnosis: Theory and Methods.* Oxford University Press: Oxford UK.

Allen, J. & Gutekunst, H. (2018). *Street Smart Awareness and Inquiry-in-Action.* Amara Collaboration, Helsinki, Finland.

Banerjee, A. (2013). *Leadership development among scientists: Learning through adaptive challenges* (Unpublished doctoral dissertation). University of Georgia, Athens, Georgia.

Beatty, J. & Torbert, W. (2003) The false duality of work and leisure. *Journal of Management Inquiry.* 12(3), 239-252.

Bradbury, H. (Ed.)(2015). *Handbook of Action Research, Vol III.* Sage: Thousand Oaks, CA.

Chapters on Action Inquiry by Practicing Action Inquiry Fellows:

Nancy Wallis, "Unlocking the Secrets of Personal and Systemic Power: The Power Lab and action inquiry in the classroom"
Steve Taylor, Jenny Rudolph, and Erica Foldy, "Teaching and Learning Reflective Practice in the Action Science/ Action Inquiry Tradition"
Grady McGonagill and Dana Carman, "Holding Theory Skillfully in Consulting Inter ventions"
David McCallum and Aliki Nicolaides, "Cultivating Intention (as we enter the fray): The skillful practice of embodying presence, awareness, and purpose as action researchers" Elaine Herdman-Barker and Aftab Erfan, "Clearing Obstacles: An exercise to expand a person's repertoire of action"
Hilary Bradbury, "The Integrating (Feminine) Reach of Action Research: A nonet for epistemological voice"
Erica Foldy, "The Location of Race in Action Research"
Lisa Stefanac and Michael Krot, "Using T-Groups to Develop Action Research Skills in Volatile, Uncertain, Complex, and Ambiguous Environments"
Yumi Sera, "Practice of Mindful Intuition: Bi-directional Awareness: The Skill of Expressing and Sensing Leadership"
Aftab Erfan and Bill Torbert, "Collaborative Developmental Action Inquiry"

Bradbury, H. & Torbert, W. (2016). *Eros/Power: Love in the Spirit of Inquiry*. Integral Publishers, Tucson AZ.

Chandler, D. & Torbert, W. (2003). Transforming inquiry and action: 27 flavors of action research. *Action Inquiry*. 1(2), 133-152.

Cheng, A., Morse, K., Rudolph, J., Arab, A., Runnacles, J. & Eppich, W. (2016). Learner-centered debriefing for health care simulation debriefing: Lessons for faculty development. *Simulation in Healthcare*. 11:32-40.

Coghlan, D. & Shani, A. (2020). Abductive reasoning as the integrative mechanism between first – second – and third-person practice in action research. *Systemic Practice and Action Research.* Online 9/16/20

Cook-Greuter, S. (1999). *Postautonomous ego development: A study of its nature and measurement,* Unpublished Harvard University doctoral dissertation, Cambridge MA.

Cook-Greuter, S. (2011). A report from the scoring trenches. A. Pfaffenberg, P. Marko & A. Combs (Ed.s), *The postconventional personality*. SUNY Press, Albany NY. 57-74.

Drath, W. H., Palus, C. J., & McGuire, J. B. (2010). Developing an interdependent leadership culture. In C. D. McCauley & E. Van Velsor (Eds.), *The Center for Creative Leadership Handbook of Leadership Development, 3rd Ed.* San Francisco: Jossey-Bass.

Drath, W. H., McCauley, C.D., Palus, C. J., Van Velsor, E., O'Connor, P. M. G., & McGuire, J. B. (2008). Direction, alignment, commitment: Toward a more integrative ontology of leadership. *Leadership Quarterly*, *19*, 635–653.

Dunbar, R., Dutton, J. & Torbert, W. (1982). Crossing mother: ideological constraints on organizational improvements. *Journal of Management Studies*. 19(1) 91-108.

Erfan, A. & Torbert, W. (2015). Collaborative Developmental Action Inquiry. In Bradbury, H. (Ed.) *Handbook of Action Research (3rd Ed.).* London: Sage, 2015. 64-75.

Fisher, D. & Torbert, W. (1991). Transforming managerial practice: beyond the Achiever stage. In Woodman, R. & Pasmore, W. (ed.s) *Research in Organizational Change and Development* (vol. 5). JAI Press, Greenwich CT. 143-174.

Fisher, D. & Torbert, W. (1992). Autobiographical awareness as a catalyst for managerial and organizational development. *Management Education and Development Journal.* 23(3), 184-198.

Fisher, D. & Torbert, W. (1995). *Personal and organizational transformations*. London: McGraw-Hill. Foster, P. (2014). Collaborative developmental action inquiry. In Coghlan, D., & Brydon-Miller, M. (Eds.), *SAGE Encyclopedia of Action Research*. Thousand Oaks, CA.: Sage Publications.

Foster, P. & Torbert, W. (2005). Leading through positive deviance: A developmental action learning perspective on institutional change. In R. Giacalone, C. Dunn & C. Jurkiewicz (Ed.s) *Positive Psychology in Business Ethics and Corporate Responsibility.* Greenwich CT: Information Age Publishing. 123-142.

Habermas, J. 1981, 1984. The Theory of Communicative Action, Vol 1 & 2. T. McCarthy (trans.). Boston: Beacon

Hartwell, J. & Torbert, W. (1999a). A group interview with Andy Wilson, Founder and CEO of Boston Duck Tours, and Massachusetts Entrepreneur of the Year. *Journal of Management Inquiry.* 8(2), 183-190.

Hartwell, J. & Torbert, W. (1999b). Analysis of the group interview with Andy Wilson: An illustration of interweaving first-, second-, and third-person research/ practice. *Journal of Management Inquiry.* 8(2) 191-204.

Herdman-Barker, E. & Torbert, W. (2012). The Global Leadership Profile Report. Accessible via www.gla.global

Herdman-Barker, E. and Wallis, N. (2016). Imperfect beauty: Hierarchy and fluidity in leadership development. *Challenging Organisations and Society Journal*, 5(1) 866-885.

Kelly, E. (2013a). Transformation in leadership, part 1: A developmental study of Warren Buffet. *Integral Leadership Review*. Integralleadershipreview.com. March.

Kelly, E. (2013b). Warren Buffett's transformation in leadership, part 2. *Integral Leadership Review*. Integralleadershipreview.com. June.

Kwon, C. & Nicolaides, A. (2017). Managing diversity through triple-loop learning: A call for paradigm shift. *Human Resource Development Review*. 16(1), 85-99.

Lichtenstein, B., Smith, B. & Torbert, W. (1995). Leadership and ethical development: a balance of light and shadow. *Business Ethics Quarterly.* 5(1) 97-116.

Livesay, T. V. (2013). *Exploring the paradoxical role and experience of fallback in developmental theory* (Unpublished doctoral dissertation). University of San Diego. San Diego CA.

Livne-Tarandach, R. & Torbert, W. (2009). Reliability and validity tests of the Harthill Leadership Development Profile in the context of Developmental Action Inquiry theory, practice and method. *Integral Review.* 5 (2) 133-151.

McCallum, D. C. (2008). *Exploring the implications of a hidden diversity in group relations conference learning: A developmental perspective* (Unpublished doctoral dissertation). Teachers College, Columbia University, NY.

McCauley, C. Drath, W., Palus, C., O'Connor, P. & Baker, B. (2006). The use of constructive-developmental theory to advance the understanding of leadership. *The Leadership Quarterly*, 17, 634-653.

McCauley, C. D., Palus, C. J., W, D., Hughes, R. L., McGuire, J., O'Connor, P. M. G., & Van Velsor, E. (2008). Interdependent leadership in organizations: Evidence from six case studies. *CCL Research Report No. 190.* Greensboro NC, USA: Center for Creative Leadership.

McGuire, J., Palus, C. & Torbert, W. (2008). Toward interdependent organizing and researching. In A. Shani et al. (Eds.), *Handbook of collaborative management research*, Sage, Thousand Oaks CA. 123-142.

McGuire, J.B., Rhodes, GB. (2009). *Transforming Your Leadership Culture.* San Francisco: Jossey-Bass.

McGuire, J.B., Frankovelgia, C. (January 2015), Transforming Organizations : Coaching and Guiding Senior Teams. In the Center for Creative Leadership's *Handbook of Coaching in Organizations.* San Francisco: Jossey-Bass.

McGuire, J.B., Palus, C.P., (2015), Toward interdependent leadership culture: A transformation case study of KONE Americas. In D. D. Warrick & J. Mueller (eds.) *Learning from Real World Cases : Lessons in Changing Culture*, Warwickshire : RossiSmith.

McGuire, J. M., & C.J. Palus (2018). Vertical development of leadership culture. *Integral Review.*

Marshall, J. (2016). *First-person action research: Living life as inquiry.* London, Sage.

Merron, K., Fisher, D. & Torbert, W. (1987). Meaning making and managerial action. *Journal of Group and Organizational Studies.* 12 (3), 274-286.

Miller, C. (2012). *The undergraduate classroom as a community of inquiry* (Unpublished doctoral dissertation). University of San Diego, San Diego, CA.

Montuori, A. & Donnelly, G. (2017). Transformative leadership. In J. Neal, *Handbook of Personal and Organizational Transformation.* Springer International Publishing. 1-33.

Nicolaides, A. (2008). *Learning their way through ambiguity: Exploration of how nine developmentally mature adults make sense of ambiguity in times of uncertainty.* (Doctoral Dissertation). Teachers College, Columbia University, NY.

Nicolaides, A & McCallum, D. (2013). Inquiry in action for leadership in turbulent times: Exploring the connections between transformative learning and adaptive leadership. *Journal of Transformative Education.* 11(4), 246-260.

Palus, C. J., Harrison, S., & Prasad, J. (2016). Developing relational leadership in Africa. In K. G. Schuyler (Ed.), *Leadership for a Healthy World: Creative Social Change.* International Leadership Association.

Palus, C. J., & McGuire, J.B. (2015). Mediated dialogue in action research. In H. Bradbury (Ed.) *SAGE handbook of action research, 3rd Edition.* Thousand Oaks, California: SAGE Publications. 691-699.

Palus, C.J. McGuire, J.B., & Ernst, C. (2012). Developing interdependent leadership. In *The Handbook for Teaching Leadership: Knowing, Doing, and Being.* Snook, S., Nohria, N. & Khurana, R. (Eds.). Sage Publications with the Harvard Business School. Chapter 28, 467-492.

Palus, C. J., McGuire, J. B., & Rhodes, G. (2010). Evolving your leadership culture. In D. L. Dotlich, P. C. Cairo, & S. H. Rhinesmith (Eds.), *2010 Pfeiffer Annual: Leadership Development*. San Francisco: Pfeiffer.

Palus, C. J., & Horth, D. M. (2002). *The leader's edge: Six creative competencies for navigating complex challenges*. San Francisco: Jossey-Bass.

Palus, C. J., & Drath, W. H. (1995). *Evolving leaders: A model for promoting leadership development in programs*. Greensboro, NC, USA: Center for Creative Leadership.

Palus, C., McGuire, J., Stawiski, J. & Torbert, W. The art and science of vertical development. In J. Reams (Ed.), *Maturing Leadership: How Adult Development Impacts Leadership*. Emerald Publishing Ltd. UK, 2020.

Presley, S. (2013). A constructive-developmental view of complexity leadership (Unpublished doctoral dissertation). Fielding Graduate University, Santa Barbara, CA.

Ramos, J. (2017). Linking Foresight and Action: Toward a Futures Action Research. InThe Palgrave International Handbook of Action Research(pp. 823-842). Palgrave Macmillan, NewYork.

Reason, P. (Ed.). (1994). *Participation in Human Inquiry*. London : Sage Publications.

Reason, P. (Ed.). (1988). *Human Inquiry in Action: Developments in new paradigm research*. London : Sage Publications.

Reason, P. (1994). Three approaches to action research. In N. Denzin & Y. Lincoln (Eds.), *Handbook of Qualitative Research*. Thousand Oaks: Sage. 324-339.

Reason, P. & Torbert, W. (2001). The action turn: Toward a transformational social science. *Concepts and Transformation*. 6(1), 1-37.

Reason, P. & Torbert, W. (2002). Toward a participatory worldview: In physics, biology, economics, ecology, medicine, organizations, spirituality, and everyday living. Co-Editors and contributors to two Special Issues of *ReVision.* 23(3-4), 2001.

Rooke, D. & Torbert, W. (1998). Organizational transformation as a function of CEO's developmental stage, *Organization Development Journal*, 16, 11-28.

Rooke, D. & Torbert, W. (2005). Seven transformations of leadership. *Harvard Business Review.* 66-76, April.

Rosenberg, A. (2012). *Philosophy of Social Science.* Boulder CO: Westview Press.

Rousseau, D. 2020. The realist rationality of evidence-based management. *Academy of Management Learning and Education.* 19, 1, 415-424.

Rudolph, J. Taylor, S. & Foldy, E. (2001). Collaborative off-line reflection: A way to develop skill in action science and action inquiry. In Reason, P. and Bradbury, H. (Eds.), *Handbook of action research*, Sage Publications, London. 405-412.

Rudolph, J., Morrison, J., & Carroll, J. (2009). The dynamics of action-oriented problem solving: Linking interpretation and choice. *Academy of Management Review.* 34(4), 733-758.

Sherman, F. & Torbert, W. (Ed.s). (2000). *Transforming social inquiry, transforming social action: New paradigms for crossing the theory/practice divide.* Norwell MA: Kluwer Academic Publishers.

Smith, S. (2016). *Growing together: The evolution of consciousness using collaborative developmental action inquiry* (Unpublished doctoral dissertation). University of Georgia, Athens, Georgia.

Smith, S. & Wilkins, N. (2018). Mind the gap: Approaches to addressing the research-to-practice, practice-to-research chasm. *Journal of Public Health Management Practice.* 24(1), 6-11.

Starr, A. & Torbert, W. (2005). Timely and transforming leadership inquiry and practice: Toward triple-loop awareness. *Integral Review* 1(1) 85-97.

Taylor, S. S. 2015. *You're a genius: Using reflective practice to master the craft of leadership.* Business Expert Press.

Taylor, S. (2017). William Rockwell Torbert: Walking the talk. Szabla et al. (ed.s) *The Palgrave Handbook of Organization Change Thinkers*. Macmillan, NY.

Torbert, W. (1973). An experimental selection process. *Journal of Applied Behavioral Science*. 9(2) 331-350.

Torbert, W. (1974). Pre-bureaucratic and post-bureaucratic stages of organizational development. *Interpersonal Development*. 1(5) 1-25.

Torbert, W. (1978). Educating toward shared purpose, self-direction and quality work: the theory and practice of liberating structure. *Journal of Higher Education*. 49(2) 109-135.

Torbert, W. (1981). Interpersonal competence. In Chickering, A. (ed.) *The Modern American College*. Jossey-Bass: San Francisco CA.

Torbert, W. (1981). Three chapters in Reason, P. & Rowan, J. (ed.s) *Human Inquiry: A Sourcebook of New Paradigm Research*. Wiley: London, 1981:

Why educational research has been so uneducational: the case for a new model of social science based on collaborative inquiry.

A collaborative inquiry into voluntary metropolitan desegregation.

Empirical, behavioral, theoretical, and attentional research skills necessary for collaborative inquiry.

Torbert, W. (1981). The role of self-study in improving managerial and institutional effectiveness. *Human Systems Management*. 2(2) 72-82.

Torbert, W. (1983). Research cultivating Executive Mind, timely action. *ReVision*. 4(1) 1-23.

Torbert, W. (1983). Initiating collaborative inquiry. In Morgan, G (ed.) *Beyond Method*. Sage Publications: Newbury Park CA, 1983.

Torbert, W. (1987). Management education for the 21st century. *Selections*. 3(3) 31-36.

Torbert, W. (1987). Education for organizational and community self-management. In Bruyn, S. & Mehan, J. (ed.s) *Beyond Market and State*. Temple University Press: Philadelphia PA. 171-184.

Torbert, W., (1989). Leading organizational transformation. In Woodman, R. & Pasmore, W. (ed.s) *Research in Organizational Change and Development* (vol. 3). JAI Press, Greenwich CT, 1989. 83-116.

Torbert, W. Reform from the center. In Mitchell, B. & Cunningham, L. (ed.s) *Educational Leadership and Changing Contexts of Families, Communities, and Schools*. National Society for the Study of Education Yearbook, University of Chicago Press, Chicago IL, 1990.

Torbert, W. (1994). The good life: good money, good work, good friends, good questions. *Journal of Management Inquiry*. 3(1) 58-66.

Torbert, W. (1996). The 'chaotic' action awareness of tranformational leaders. *International Journal of Public Administration* 19 (6), 911-939.

Torbert, W. (1999). The distinctive questions Developmental Action Inquiry asks. *Journal of Management Learning*. 30(2), 189-206.

Torbert, W. (2000a). A developmental approach to social science: Integrating first-, second-, and third-person research/ practice through single-, double-, and triple-loop feedback. *Journal of Adult Development*. 7 (4) 255-268.

Torbert, W. and Fisher, D. (1992). Autobiography as a catalyst for managerial and organizational development", *Management Education and Development Journal*, 23, 184-198.

Torbert, W., Herdman-Barker, E., Livne-Tarandach, R., McCallum, D. & Nicolaides, A. (2010). Developmental Action Inquiry: A distinct integral approach that integrates theory, practice, and research in action. In S. Esbjorn-Hargens et al (Ed.s) *Integral Theory in Action*. Albany NY: SUNY Press.

Torbert, W. (2014). Six-Dimensional Space/Time: Mathematical intuitions underlying the integral meta-paradigm of science named 'Collaborative Developmental Action Inquiry. *Integral World* (integralworld.net) Reading Room, November.

Torbert, W. (2017). Brief Comparison of Five Developmental Measures: the GLP, the LDP, the MAP, the SOI, and the WUSCT. www.actioninquiryleadership.com .

Torbert, W. (2017). The pragmatic impact on leaders & organizations of interventions based in the Collaborative Developmental Action Inquiry approach. *Integral Leadership Review*. August-November.

Torbert, W., Miller, C., Wallis, N., and Yeyinmen, K. (2019). Team coaching through CDAI and the GLP. In D. Clutterbuck et al Ed.s *The Practitioner's Handbook of Team Coaching.* London: Routledge, 2019.

Torbert, W. & Erfan, E. (2020). Learning for timely action: An introduction to the Cybernetics of Collaborative Developmental Action Inquiry (CDAI). Presented at the American Cybernetics Society Annual Meeting, Vancouver BC, 2019. Published in *Computing and Human Knowing.* 27(2), 81-90.

Torbert, W. & Erfan, A. (2020). Possible mistakes of late action-logic actors in a polarized world. Presented at the Growth Edge Network Meeting, Bon Secours MD, 2019. Published in *Integral Review.* 16(2), 148-156.

Torbert, W. (2020). Warren Buffett's and your own seven transformations of leadership. *Global Leadership Associates Press*. www.gla.global. 1-14, September.

Wallis, N. (2014). Insights from intersections: Using the Leadership Development Framework to explore emergent knowledge domains shared by individual and collective leader development. In Scala, K., Grossman, R., Lenglachner, M., and Mayer, K. (Eds.), *Leadership learning for the future – A volume in Research in Management Education and Development.* Information Age Publishing, New York. 185-201.

Yeyinmen, C. (2016). *Uses of complex thinking in higher education adaptive leadership practice: A multiple-case study.* (Doctoral Dissertation) Harvard University: Cambridge MA.

Acknowledgments

I am so grateful to my colleagues and friends in our action inquiry communities over the past decade and more who have explored the heights and depths of inquiry, power, and love together. Most of them have read and critiqued earlier drafts of this book, have offered invaluable suggestions, and have contributed to the crafting of the Introduction, the Endnotes, and the Postscript. They include Jane Allen, Jennifer Garvey Berger, Hilary Bradbury, Dana Carman, Anne Donald, Halim Dunsky, Aftab Erfan, Erica Foldy, Julie Freyberg, Mina Gibb, Elaine Herdman-Barker, Heidi Gutekunst, Richard Izard, Ed Kelly, Michael Krot, Valerie Livesay, David McCallum, Grady McGonagill, Jesse McKay, Veronica Menduina, Cara Miller, Aliki Nicolaides, Nick Owen, Chuck Palus, Robin Postel, Irena Pranskeviciute, John and Sophie Sabbage, Tom Schmid, Yumi Sera, Shakiyla Smith, Lisa Stefanac, Steve Taylor, Nancy Wallis, Gayle Young White, and Karen Yeyinmen. Longtime colleagues Bob Kegan, Roger Lipsey, Peter Reason, and Ed Schein have also kindly (and severely!) critiqued an earlier version of the manuscript. Sarah Audsley of Global Leadership Associates has played a critical and indispensable virtuoso role in bringing the book to publication.

In addition to my gratitude for direct help on this book, I also happily owe an immense debt of gratitude to the teachers, colleagues, and friends who influenced my development of Collaborative Developmental Action Inquiry. Starting in my decade at Yale in the 1960s, these teachers included Chris Argyris, Rev. William Sloane Coffin, Paul D'Entreves, Karl Deutsch, Erik Erikson, Peter Frost, J. Richard Hackman, Roger Harrison, Daniel Levinson, Charles

Lindblom, John Sinclair, Herb Shepard, Fritz Steele, and Mary Watt. My closest colleagues and friends from that time – many of them participating on the Yale Upward Bound staff – include Clay Alderfer, Lee Bolman, Mark Foster, Joanna Hiss, Dennis Holahan, Morris Kaplan, Roger Putzel, Mac Rogers, Tom Schmid, Rick and Mary Sharpe, and Jim Walsh.

At SMU, Pat Canavan, Roger Dunbar, Paul Heyne, Craig Lundberg, and Mick McGill became close collaborators. Annette Allen, Gene and T Byrne, and Julie Heyne became lasting friends, and Bill Joiner became the first student to dedicate himself closely to my first-, second-, and third-person developmental action inquiry.

At Harvard, Adam Curle, Sergio Foguel, Carol Gilligan, Bob Kegan, Suzanne Prysor-Jones, Bill Trueheart, and Blenda Wilson became valued colleagues and friends, as did Donald Schon and Minor White at MIT. Students with whom I worked closely and who went on to careers of action inquiry and publication included Esther Hamilton, Rita Weathersbee, Margaret Wheatley, and Shoshona Zuboff. During my post-Harvard, Theatre-of-Inquiry years, Ian Mitroff, Lou Pondy, Peter Vaill, and Karl Weick became important academic colleagues. Mary Jane Garand, Peter Haines, Jimmy Metzner, Pam Renna, Barry Svigals, and Joe Wheelwright were key participants in the Theatre of Inquiry.

During my thirty years at Boston College, I learned most about friendly collaboration from Sev and Louise Bruyn, Phyllis Cheng, Judy Clair, Marcy Crary, Erica Foldy, Pacey Foster, Jim Gips, Paul Gray, Bob Krim, Barbara Morrill, Jack Neuhauser, Peter Olivieri, Jenny Rudolph, Otto Scharmer, Peter Senge, Eve Spangler, Steve Taylor, Joan Thompson, Steve Waddell, and Sandra Waddock. In my research, my closest partners were Susanne Cook-Greuter and Dal Fisher; and Dal was my most frequent co-author as well. Outside Boston College, Joan Bavaria, CEO of Trillium Asset Management, the original 'socially responsible investing' company, was my greatest inspiration about how to blend action and inquiry in timely and transforming ways, as I interacted with her in my roles as consultant and board member for twenty years.

Finally, I meditate upon my gratitude for my family's primordial role in providing me with the security, trust, and love to risk living my life in The Theatre of Inquiry. Thank you Mom, Dad, and Dee. Thank you my stalwart, family-and-community-loving brother, Jim. Thank you, dear sons, Michael, Patrick, and Benjamin, for becoming so fully your own idiosyncratic selves. And thank you, thank you, my dear wife Reichi, for staying in the struggle of our love with me.

Index

B

C

D

E

F

G

H

I

J

K

L

O

P

U

V

W

Y

Z

Made in the USA
Middletown, DE
05 April 2021